Kraken Latin 2
Student Edition

More Latin from Canon Press

Latin Primer: Book 1, Martha Wilson
Latin Primer 1: Student Edition
Latin Primer 1: Teacher's Edition
Latin Primer 1: Flashcard Set
Latin Primer 1: Audiō Guide CD

Latin Primer: Book 2, Martha Wilson
Latin Primer 2: Student Edition
Latin Primer 2: Teacher's Edition
Latin Primer 2: Flashcard Set
Latin Primer 2: Audiō Guide CD

Latin Primer: Book 3, Martha Wilson
Latin Primer 3: Student Edition
Latin Primer 3: Teacher's Edition
Latin Primer 3: Flashcard Set
Latin Primer 3: Audiō Guide CD

KRAKEN LATIN for the Logic Years: Book 1, Natali H. Monnette
KRAKEN LATIN 1: Student Edition
KRAKEN LATIN 1: Teacher Edition

KRAKEN LATIN for the Logic Years, Book 2, Natali H. Monnette
KRAKEN LATIN 2: Student Edition
KRAKEN LATIN 2: Teacher Edition

KRAKEN LATIN for the Logic Years, Book 3, Natali H. Monnette
KRAKEN LATIN 3: Student Edition (forthcoming)
KRAKEN LATIN 3: Teacher Edition (forthcoming)

Orbis Pictus 1: The Natural World, Timothy Griffith

Published by Canon Press
P.O. Box 8729, Moscow, Idaho 83843
800.488.2034 | www.canonpress.com

Natali H. Monnette, *Kraken Latin for the Logic Years 2: Teacher Edition*
Second edition. Copyright © 2015, 2019 by Natali H. Monnette. First edition 2015.

Cover design by Rachel Rosales (orangepealdesign.com). Cover illustration by Forrest Dickison. Interior design by Phaedrus Media and Valerie Anne Bost. Typesetting by Laura Storm and Valerie Anne Bost.

Printed in the United States of America.

All rights reserved. No part of this publication may be reproduced, stored in a retrieval system, or transmitted in any form by any means, electronic, mechanical, photocopy, recording, or otherwise, without prior permission of the author, except as provided by USA copyright law.

Library of Congress Cataloging-in-Publication Data:

Kraken Latin 2 Student:
Monnette, Natali, author.
Kraken Latin 2 : student edition / by Natali Monnette.
Kraken Latin two
Student Edition. | Moscow, Idaho : CanonPress, 2019. | Series:
  Kraken Latin | Includes bibliographical references and index.
LCCN 2019033814 | ISBN 9781947644359 (Paperback)
LCSH: Latin language—Textbooks. | Latin language—Grammar.
Classification: LCC PA2080.2 .M67 2019 | DDC 475—dc23
LC record available at https://lccn.loc.gov/2019033814

19 20 21 22 23 24 25 26 27 28 29   10 9 8 7 6 5 4 3 2 1

BOOK 2

Kraken Latin
for the
Logic Years

by NATALI H. MONNETTE

Contents

Introduction vi
Pronunciation Guide vii

Unit 1: Lessons 1–8　　　　　　　　　　　　　　　　　　　　　1

Lesson 1: Review of Verbs 3
Lesson 2: Review of Nouns, Pronouns, Adjectives, and Demonstratives. 12
Lesson 3: Pronouns: Relative Pronoun and Intensive Pronoun *ipse* 22
Lesson 4: Adjectives: Comparison of Adjectives; Additional *-ius* Adjectives 36
Lesson 5: Adjectives: Irregular Comparison; Nouns: Dative of Possession 49
Lesson 6: Verbs: Present Passive Infinitive, Present Passive Imperative, Deponents 60
Lesson 7: Adverbs: Formation and Comparison; Questions (*-ne, nōnne, num*) 77
Lesson 8: Review and Test 90

Unit 2: Lessons 9–16　　　　　　　　　　　　　　　　　　　103

Lesson 9: Interrogative Pronoun and Adjective 105
Lesson 10: Participles 115
Lesson 11: Ablative Absolute / Irregular Verb *Ferō* 131
Lesson 12: Indefinite Pronouns and Adjectives / Review of Participles 145
Lesson 13: Passive Periphrastic with Dative of Agent 158
Lesson 14: Nouns: Locative Case and Other Place Constructions /
　　　　　Verbs: *Volō, Nōlō, Mālō* 170
Lesson 15: Gerund vs. Gerundive 185
Lesson 16: Review and Test 199

Appendices　　　　　　　　　　　　　　　　　　　　　　　　219

Chant Charts 221
Latin to English Glossary 249
English to Latin Glossary 280
Sources and Helps 303
Verb Formation Chart 305

INTRODUCTION

Discipulī Discipulaeque,

If you are reading this, you have successfully completed your first year of *Kraken Latin* and are poised to begin another. At this point I really should give you some inspiring Latin quotes such as *ad astra per aspera*, "to the stars through difficulties"; *citius, altius, fortius*, "faster, higher, stronger" (the motto of the Olympics, incidentally), or perhaps simply *excelsior!*, "[ever] higher!" You have, after all, competently navigated the shallows of Latin grammar, mastering the entire indicative verb system and all declensions of nouns, not to mention adjectives and other little words along the way. So perhaps your battle cry should be *ālea iacta est*, "the die has been cast"—for now, after last year's taste of Latin, you must inevitably progress to the delightful grammatical banquet before you. However, I've always had a sneaking fondness for old Lucius Accius' phrase *ōderint dum metuant*, "let them hate, provided they fear." (It became a favorite saying of the Emperor Caligula, an unpleasant and insane man by most accounts, but let us disregard that for the moment.) Now of course I do not wish for any of you to hate Latin, but realistically I know that not all of you approach your Latin lessons with dances of joy. So for those of you who find Latin a struggle, a challenge, even a battle with a thrashing sea monster—you are hereby permitted not to love Latin if you must, provided that you respect and appreciate her beauty and utility.

And for those of you who are quivering with anticipation about this next voyage, it promises to be a wild ride. You will learn more complex grammatical concepts, particularly delving deeper into verbs and coming to grips with the remaining moods (infinitive, participle, and subjunctive). You will also add to your knowledge of pronouns, adjectives, and nouns. But most importantly, you will begin to translate increasingly unadapted Latin texts as you transition out of this last year of logic-stage Latin. Memorizing a few Latin words to improve your English vocabulary was never the goal (although it is a side benefit). Reading, savoring, and feasting upon Latin history, poetry, speeches, and theology can all be yours. It's just a few battles away.

Ex animō,
Natali H. Monnette,
Magistra Discipulaque

Pronunciation Guide

By now you have settled in to your own Latin pronunciation. The following is meant to serve as a reminder of the classical pronunciation, although keep in mind that there are other schools of thought. The main thing is to ensure the Latin sounds beautiful as you say or read it.

Vowels

Vowels in Latin have only two pronunciations, long and short. When speaking, long vowels are held twice as long as short vowels. Long vowels are marked with a "macron" or line over the vowel (e.g., ā). Vowels without a macron are short vowels.

When spelling a word, including the macron is important, as it can clarify the meaning of the word (e.g., *liber* is a noun meaning "book," and *līber* is an adjective meaning "free").

	LONG VOWELS		SHORT VOWELS
ā	like a in father: *frāter, suprā*	a	like a in idea: *canis, mare*
ē	like e in obey: *trēs, rēgīna*	e	like e in bet: *et, terra*
ī	like i in machine: *mīles, vīta*	i	like i in this: *hic, silva*
ō	like o in holy: *sōl, glōria*	o	like o in domain: *bonus, scopulus*
ū	like oo in rude: *flūmen, lūdus*	u	like u in put: *sum, sub*
ȳ	like i in chip: *grȳps, cȳgnus*		

Diphthongs

A combination of two vowel sounds collapsed together into one syllable is a diphthong:

	DIPHTHONGS
ae	like ai in aisle: *caelum, saepe*
au	like ou in house: *laudō, nauta*
ei	like ei in reign: *deinde*
eu	like eu in eulogy: *Deus*
oe	like oi in oil: *moenia, poena*
ui	like ew in chewy: *huius, huic*

Consonants

Latin consonants are pronounced like English consonants, with the following exceptions:

		CONSONANTS
c	like c in come	never soft like city, cinema, or peace
g	like g in go	never soft like gem, geology, or gentle
v	like w in wow	never like Vikings, victor, or vacation
s	like s in sissy	never like easel, weasel, or peas
ch	like ch in chorus	never like church, chapel, or children
r	is trilled	like a dog snarling or a machine gun
i	like y in yes	when used before a vowel at the beginning of a word or between two vowels within a word (otherwise it's usually a vowel)

Unit One

UNIT 1: GOALS

Lessons 1–8

By the end of Unit 1, students should be able to . . .

- Decline the relative pronoun and translate it in a relative clause
- Decline and translate the intensive pronoun
- Understand, form, and translate comparative adjectives and adverbs, both regular and irregular
- Identify and translate the dative of possession
- Form and translate the present passive infinitive
- Recognize, form, and translate deponent verbs
- Recognize, form, and translate Latin questions

Lesson 1

Review of Verbs

Word List

No new words this lesson. It's time to review all your verbs, adverbs, prepositions, and conjunctions from last year.

Chant

No new chants this lesson. You will be reviewing all of your verb knowledge from last year.

Memorization

Ego sum Dominus Deus tuus qui eduxi te de terra Aegypti de domo servitutis.

I am the Lord your God who led you out of the land of Egypt, out of the house of slavery.

1. Non habebis deos alienos coram me.

    You shall have no foreign gods before me.

Worksheet 1

The worksheet will focus primarily on verbs—the entire indicative system in all tenses and moods, as well as the five verb conjugations. As you go through the worksheet, pay close attention to which verb tenses or conjugations are causing you trouble. In particular, make sure you get third and fourth conjugation verbs right, as well as passives.

A. Vocabulary Review

1. ac: _____
2. āiō: _____
3. agō: _____
4. appellō: _____
5. ardeō: _____
6. audiō: _____
7. bene: _____
8. cantō: _____
9. captō: _____
10. cēdō: _____
11. certātim: _____
12. clam: _____
13. cōgitō: _____
14. cōgō: _____
15. crēdō: _____
16. creō: _____
17. cupiō: _____
18. cūrō: _____
19. dēclārō: _____
20. deinde: _____
21. dēfendō: _____
22. dēligō: _____
23. dīcō: _____
24. diū: _____
25. doceō: _____
26. dormiō: _____
27. ecce: _____
28. ergo: _____
29. etiam: _____
30. exspectō: _____
31. festīnō: _____
32. fleō: _____
33. fortasse: _____
34. fugiō: _____
35. gerō: _____
36. habeō: _____
37. herī: _____
38. iaceō: _____
39. iam: _____
40. ibī: _____
41. interim: _____
42. inveniō: _____
43. itaque: _____
44. iterum: _____

45. iungō: _____
46. līberō: _____
47. lūdō: _____
48. magnoperē: _____
49. male: _____
50. māneō: _____
51. minūtātim: _____
52. modo: _____
53. mordeō: _____
54. mox: _____
55. narrō: _____
56. nec (neque): _____
57. nesciō: _____
58. nō: _____
59. numquam: _____
60. nuntiō: _____
61. occupō: _____
62. oppugnō: _____
63. paene: _____
64. pōnō: _____
65. possum: _____
66. postea: _____
67. quam: _____
68. quando: _____
_____
69. -que: _____
70. quia: _____
71. quod: _____
72. quōmodo: _____

73. quoniam: _____
74. rēgō: _____
75. removeō: _____
_____
76. reptō: _____
77. resurgō: _____
78. rīdeō: _____
79. saepe: _____
80. satis: _____
81. sed: _____
82. semper: _____
83. sēū/sīve: _____
84. sī: _____
85. sīcut: _____
86. spectō: _____
87. stō: _____
88. superō: _____
89. surgō: _____
90. tangō: _____
91. terreō: _____
92. torreō: _____
93. ubi: _____
94. undique: _____
95. valeō: _____
96. vertō: _____
97. videō: _____
98. vincō: _____
99. vīvō: _____
100. volō: _____

B. Grammar

1. Verb Endings: Write out all of the verb endings you learned last year. Try to do it from memory first and only then look up any you can't remember in the back of the book.

PRESENT ACTIVE	SINGULAR	PLURAL
1ST		
2ND		
3RD		

PRESENT PASSIVE	SINGULAR	PLURAL
1ST		
2ND		
3RD		

IMPERFECT ACTIVE	SINGULAR	PLURAL
1ST		
2ND		
3RD		

IMPERFECT PASSIVE	SINGULAR	PLURAL
1ST		
2ND		
3RD		

FUTURE ACTIVE	SINGULAR	PLURAL
1ST		
2ND		
3RD		

FUTURE PASSIVE	SINGULAR	PLURAL
1ST		
2ND		
3RD		

PERFECT ACTIVE	SINGULAR	PLURAL
1ST		
2ND		
3RD		

PERFECT PASSIVE	SINGULAR	PLURAL
1ST		
2ND		
3RD		

PLUPERFECT ACTIVE	SINGULAR	PLURAL
1ST		
2ND		
3RD		

PLUPERFECT PASSIVE	SINGULAR	PLURAL
1ST		
2ND		
3RD		

	FUTURE PERF. ACTIVE	
	SINGULAR	PLURAL
1ST		
2ND		
3RD		

	FUTURE PERFECT PASSIVE	
	SINGULAR	PLURAL
1ST		
2ND		
3RD		

2. Do a synopsis (remember those?) of *amō* in the 2nd person plural, then give the imperatives.

	INDICATIVE			
	ACTIVE		PASSIVE	
	LATIN	ENGLISH	LATIN	ENGLISH
PRESENT				
IMPERF.				
FUTURE				
PERFECT				
PLUPRF.				
FUT. PRF.				
IMP. SG.				
IMP. PL.				

3. Now that you're warmed up, do another synopsis of *capiō* in the 3rd person singular and give imperatives.

	INDICATIVE			
	ACTIVE		PASSIVE	
	LATIN	ENGLISH	LATIN	ENGLISH
PRESENT				
IMPERF.				
FUTURE				
PERFECT				
PLUPRF.				
FUT. PRF.				
IMP. SG.				
IMP. PL.				

4. Preposition Review: Translate the following prepositions, putting the meaning in the appropriate column(s). (That is, if the preposition takes accusative, write down the preposition's meaning in the accusative column and not the ablative.)

PREPOSITION	WITH ACCUSATIVE	WITH ABLATIVE
1. ā		
2. ante		
3. contrā		
4. cōram		
5. cum		
6. dē		
7. ex		
8. in		

9. inter		
10. iūxtā		
11. per		
12. post		
13. prō		
14. prope		
15. propter		
16. secundum		
17. sine		
18. sub		
19. super		
20. suprā		
21. trāns		

C. Memorization: Fill in the blanks

Fill in the blanks to complete the Prologue and the First of the Ten Commandments.

Ego _____ tuus qui _____ te dē terra _____ domo _____.

1. Non _____ deos _____ me.

D. English to Latin Translation

1. At that time the women had worshipped many evil gods and were destroyed.

2. I do not eat dogs; I will choose the bread.

3. The poet is beginning to love the queen but she will never love him.

4. Tomorrow you (pl.) will have finally forgiven the boys' words.

5. We were daring to hide the pirates' money and it was never found.

6. O beautiful girl, you say "goodbye" but I say "hello."

7. Together the brothers were tying [up] the wild pig and were being wounded by it.

8. Why do you run and hurry away from me, handsome sailor?

9. Moreover, I have come with love in my heart and I will sing many songs of love.

10. God made the heavens and the earth and said, "It is good."

E. Latin to English Translation

1   Ōlim malus dracō omnem terram cremābat et castellum etiam vastāverat. Rēx rēgīnaque ululāvērunt et dīxērunt: "Heu! Nōs pulchram terram ōlim gubernāvimus et pācem habuimus; hōdie caelum ātrum est. Quid nōs et terram nostram servāre potest?" Rēx vetus erat et nōn iam pugnāre poterat. Ergo omnēs virōs rogāvit, "Vōs hunc dracōnem necābitis?" sed nihil rēspondērunt. Sed ūnus fortis, Oswaldus,
5   rēspondit: "Crās hunc dracōnem domābō et necābō aut necābor!" Rēx dīxit: "Quid tibi dabimus sī eum necābis?" Oswaldus, "Nihil," ait, "rogō. Servāre terram meam et populum meum et rēgem meum modo cupiō." Ad villam ambulāvit et eius cor et mentem et gladium parāvit. Māter eius eī vīnum forte

dedit sed malum erat et id nōn potāre potuit. *Proximō* diē Oswaldus gladium cēpit et malum vīnum et ad spēluncam dracōnis appropinquāvit. Dracō ignem ad eum iaciēbat, sed Oswaldus dīxit: "Ō magne dracō, tibi dōnum ferō—hoc vīnum mīrum!" Dracō avārus omne vīnum potāvit, statim dormīvit, et gladiō Oswaldī necātus est. Deinde rēx dīxit: "Veterēs sumus et līberōs nōn habēmus. Itaque Oswaldus proximus rēx erit!" Omnēs gaudēbant quod servātī erant.

Glossary:
proximus, -a, -um: next

Lesson 2

Review of Nouns, Pronouns, Adjectives, and Demonstratives

The worksheet will focus primarily on nouns. As you go through the worksheet, pay close attention to the noun declensions that give you the most trouble. The third declension is difficult, but also make sure you get the fourth and fifth declensions right as well.

Word List

No new word list this lesson. Review all nouns, pronouns, and adjectives from last year.

Memorization

Ego sum Dominus Deus tuus qui eduxi te de terra Aegypti de domo servitutis.

1. Non habebis deos alienos coram me.
2. Non facies tibi sculptile neque omnem similitudinem quae est in caelo desuper et quae in terra deorsum nec eorum quae sunt in aquis sub terra.

   You shall not make for yourself an engraved [image] nor any likeness which is in heaven above nor which [is] on the earth below nor of those things which are in the waters under the earth.

Grammar

No new chants this lesson; spend the time going over all noun, pronoun, and adjective declensions.

Worksheet 2

The worksheet will focus primarily on nouns. As you go through the worksheet, pay close attention to the noun declensions that give you the most trouble. The third declension is difficult, but also make sure you get the fourth and fifth declensions right as well.

A. Vocabulary

1. Give the meaning of these Latin words. First go through all of them without looking any up and see how many you remember from last year; then go back through and correct yourself using the glossary in the back of the book.

    1. ācer: _____
    2. ager: _____
    3. āla: _____
    4. albus: _____
    5. amita: _____
    6. animus: _____
    7. aqua: _____
    8. argenteus: _____
    9. asinus: _____
    10. aurum: _____
    11. avia: _____
    12. avus: _____
    13. bellum: _____
    14. bonus: _____
    15. caecus: _____
    16. calidus: _____
    17. canis: _____
    18. cantus: _____
    19. caput: _____
    20. cārus: _____
    21. cāsus: _____
    22. centaurus: _____
    23. cibus: _____
    24. cōnsilium: _____
    25. cor: _____
    26. corpus: _____
    27. diēs: _____
    28. dīvitiae: _____
    29. domus: _____
    30. dulcis: _____
    31. ēgregius: _____
    32. eques: _____
    33. exercitus: _____
    34. faciēs: _____
    35. facilis: _____
    36. fātum: _____
    37. fenestra: _____
    38. fidēs: _____
    39. fīdus: _____
    40. flōs: _____

41. fortis: _____
42. frūmentum: _____
43. gelidus: _____
44. geminus: _____
45. soror: _____
46. gladius: _____
47. grātia: _____
48. harēna: _____
49. homo: _____
50. hostis: _____
51. Iēsus: _____
52. improbus: _____
53. inimīcus: _____
54. īrātus: _____
55. iter: _____
56. lac: _____
57. lātus: _____
58. liber: _____
59. littera: _____
60. lītus: _____
61. lūx: _____
62. malus: _____
63. māter: _____
64. mensa: _____
65. meus: _____
66. miser: _____
67. mors: _____
68. mundus: _____
69. niger: _____
70. novus: _____

71. ōceanus: _____
72. onus: _____
73. orbus: _____
74. pastor: _____
75. patruēlis: _____
76. paucī: _____
77. pāx: _____
78. piscis: _____
79. porcus: _____
80. proelium: _____
81. rēgia: _____
82. rēs: _____
83. saeculum: _____
84. sanctus: _____
85. sīca: _____
86. sōl: _____
87. spīritus: _____
88. tempestās: _____
89. tigris: _____
90. tristis: _____
91. unda: _____
92. valles: _____
93. vēritās: _____
94. vesper: _____
95. vetus: _____
96. vidua: _____
97. virgō: _____
98. vīta: _____
99. vōx: _____
100. vultus: _____

2. Numerals: Fill in the chart below with the appropriate Latin and English numbers.

ROMAN NUMERAL	LATIN ORDINAL	ENGLISH ORDINAL	LATIN CARDINAL	ENGLISH CARDINAL
		one	prīmus	
	duo			second
	trēs			third
		four		
		five	quīntus	
	sex	six		
	septem			seventh
	octō			
		nine		ninth
	decem	ten		
			ūndecimus	eleventh
				twelfth
		thirteen	tertius decimus	
	quattuordecim			fourteenth
	quīndecim	fifteen		
			sextus decimus	sixteenth
	septendecim	seventeen		
			duodēvīcēsimus	eighteenth
		nineteen	ūndēvīcēsimus	nineteenth
	vīgintī ūnus	twenty-one		twenty-first
			quīnquāgēsimus	fiftieth
			centēsimus	
	quīngentī			
			mīllēsimus	

B. Grammar

1. Write out all the endings for all the declensions (from memory if you can).

	1ST DECL.	
NOM.		
GEN.		
DAT.		
ACC.		
ABL.		
VOC.		

	2ND DECL. M.	
NOM.		
GEN.		
DAT.		
ACC.		
ABL.		
VOC.		

	2ND DECL. N.	
NOM.		
GEN.		
DAT.		
ACC.		
ABL.		
VOC.		

	3RD DECL. M./F.	
NOM.		
GEN.		
DAT.		
ACC.		
ABL.		
VOC.		

	3RD DECL. N.	
NOM.		
GEN.		
DAT.		
ACC.		
ABL.		
VOC.		

	3RD DECL. I-STEM M./F.	
NOM.		
GEN.		
DAT.		
ACC.		
ABL.		
VOC.		

	3RD DECL. I-STEM N.	
NOM.		
GEN.		
DAT.		
ACC.		
ABL.		
VOC.		

	4TH DECL. M./F.	
NOM.		
GEN.		
DAT.		
ACC.		
ABL.		
VOC.		

	4TH DECL. N.	
NOM.		
GEN.		
DAT.		
ACC.		
ABL.		
VOC.		

	5TH DECL.	
NOM.		
GEN.		
DAT.		
ACC.		
ABL.		
VOC.		

2. Decline the following phrases. (And remember, demonstratives do not have a vocative form.)

   a. That big mouth, *istud ōs magnum*

	LATIN SINGULAR	LATIN PLURAL
NOM.		
GEN.		
DAT.		
ACC.		
ABL.		
VOC.		

   b. This unlucky sailor, *hic īnfēlix nauta*

	LATIN SINGULAR	LATIN PLURAL
NOM.		
GEN.		
DAT.		
ACC.		
ABL.		
VOC.		

   c. That tired bird, *illa avis fessa*

	LATIN SINGULAR	LATIN PLURAL
NOM.		
GEN.		
DAT.		
ACC.		
ABL.		
VOC.		

d. This small fear, *is parvus metus*

	LATIN SINGULAR	LATIN PLURAL
NOM.		
GEN.		
DAT.		
ACC.		
ABL.		
VOC.		

3. Pronoun Review: Give the correct Latin form.

   a. 1st person singular, nominative: _____

   b. 3rd person singular, feminine, accusative: _____

   c. 3rd person plural, masculine, genitive: _____

   d. 2nd person plural, ablative: _____

   e. 1st person plural, dative: _____

   f. 3rd person singular, neuter, accusative: _____

   g. 3rd person plural, neuter, nominative: _____

   h. 1st person plural, nominative: _____

   i. 2nd person singular, genitive: _____

   j. 3rd person singular, masculine, dative: _____

   k. 2nd person plural, accusative: _____

   l. 3rd person singular, feminine, genitive: _____

   m. 1st person singular, ablative: _____

   n. 2nd person singular, dative: _____

   o. 3rd person plural, masculine, ablative: _____

C. Memorization

Fill in the blanks for the Prologue through the Second of the Ten Commandments.

_____

_____

_____ _____ _____ _____ me.

2. Non _____ tibi _____ _____ omnem similitudinem _____ _____

in _____ desuper _____ _____ in terra _____ nec _____ _____

sunt in _____ sub _____.

D. English to Latin Translation

1. Why are you pirates always hungry and greedy?
   _____

2. After nine days the wild cows were not tamed and with white horns attacked the farmer's knees.
   _____
   _____

3. My sister is afraid of all animals and will always run away from them.
   _____

4. Write me a long letter, my son, and tell me stories about your new life.
   _____
   _____

5. Our castle has been besieged for many years, but we will never be conquered!
   _____
   _____

6. The black ships sailed into your harbor and were dragged to the beach by your enemies.
   _____
   _____

7. God put the rainbow in the sky and it tells us, "I will never destroy all the earth with water again."
   _____
   _____

8. What will the pirate do on account of the beloved queen?

9. I love her but she loves him and he doesn't love anyone.

10. Her brother saw the strange birds and knew a dreadful fear.

E. Latin to English Translation

1 **Trēs Voluntātēs**

Ōlim erant trēs frātrēs, Iulius, Fabius, et Oswaldus. Unō diē in agrīs labōrābant et *serpentem magicum* invēnērunt. *Serpēns* dīxit, "Mē invēnistis. Nunc rogāte et *cuique* vestrum voluntātem dabō." Iulius, frāter *māximus*, statim dīxit: "Cupiō magnās dīvitiās quod amō fīliam rēgis et *pauperem* nōn *nūbet*.
5 Frāter medius, Fabius, dīxit: "Cupiō *citaram* auream quod ego quoque fīliam rēgis amō et cor eius cantibus pulchrīs vincam." Oswaldus *iuvenissimus* diū cōgitābat, et deinde: "Bonum gladium," inquit, "cupiō." Duō frātrēs eius rogāvērunt, "Cūr gladium cupis? Nihil eris, sed ūnus nostrum fīliam rēgis in matrimōniō dūcet et rēx erit!" Respondet Oswaldus: "Vidēbimus." Proximō diē Iulius cum vestibus novīs ad castellum in equō novō vēnit, et pecūniam omnibus hominibus iēcit. Fabius etiam cum novā
10 citarā aureā vēnit et sub turrem fīliae rēgis stetit et multa carmina amōris cantāvit. Sed fīlia rēgis eōs vidēre nōn cupīvit, quod malus dracō terram vastāverat et eius patrem rēgem etiam necāverat. Interim Oswaldus ad montem *igneum* dracōnis ambulāvit et eum novō gladiō necāvit. Fīlia rēgis grāta *perpetuō* erat, itaque eum *nupsit* et feliciter in *aeternum* vixērunt. (Iulius eīs dōnum *pretiōsum nūptiāle* dedit et Fabius pulchrum cantum *nūptiālem* cantāvit.)

Glossary:
citara, -ae, (f): harp
cuique: dat. sg. of *quisque*, each (one)
feliciter in aeternum: happily ever after
igneus, -a, -um: fiery, burning
iuvenissimus: superlative from *iuvenis, -e* young
magicus, -a, -um: magic, magical
māximus, -a, -um: biggest, greatest; here, oldest
nūbō, -ere, nūpsī, nūptum: I marry, am married to (of a bride)

nūptiālis, -e: of a wedding, wedding (adj.), nuptial
pauper, -eris: poor
perpetuō: forever
pretiōsus, -a, -um: expensive
serpēns, -entis (m): serpent, snake
voluntās, -tātis (f): wish, desire

Lesson 3

Relative Pronoun and Intensive Pronoun *Ipse*

Word List

Nouns

1. arma, -ōrum (n, pl) *arms, weapons*
2. oculus, -ī (m) *eye*
3. opus, operis (n) *work, deed*
4. ovis, ovis (f) *sheep*
5. pars, partis (f) *part; side, direction*
6. prīnceps, -cipis (m) *leader, chief, prince*
7. sacerdōs, -dōtis (m) *priest*
8. sanguis, -guinis (m) *blood*

Pronouns

9. ipse, ipsa, ipsum *himself, herself, itself; the very*
10. quī, quae, quod *who, what, which, that*

Adjectives

11. mortuus, -a, -um *dead*
12. sacer, -cra, -crum *holy, sacred*
13. tōtus, -a, -um *all, every, whole*
14. trīstis, -e *sad, gloomy, grim*

Verbs

15. ēripiō, -ere, -ripuī, -reptum *I snatch away/from, rescue*
16. percutiō, -ere, -cussī, -cussum *I strike (through), beat, pierce*
17. quaerō, -ere, quaesīvī, quaesītum (-situm) *I ask, seek, inquire*

Prepositions/Adverbs/Conjunctions

18. forte *by chance, perhaps, perchance*
19. ob (+acc.) *on account of, for; in front of*
20. quidem *indeed, certainly, even*

Memorization

Ego sum Dominus Deus tuus qui eduxi te de terra Aegypti de domo servitutis.

1. Non habebis deos alienos coram me.
2. Non facies tibi sculptile neque omnem similitudinem quae est in caelo desuper et quae in terra deorsum nec eorum quae sunt in aquis sub terra.
3. Non adsumes nomen Domini Dei tui in vanum.

    You shall not take the name of your Lord God in vain.
4. Memento ut diem sabbati sanctifices.

    Remember to sanctify the Sabbath day.

Grammar

Relative Pronoun

After two lessons of review, it is time to take the plunge back into new grammatical concepts. The relative pronoun is a very important one to nail down, so let's begin with what we know: a pronoun is a word that takes the place of a noun. A *relative* pronoun, then, will take the place of a noun and relate or connect a phrase with that noun. The noun which the pronoun refers to is called its *antecedent*. English relative pronouns are *who, whom, whose, what, which,* and *that*. In English, *who, whose,* and *whom* refer to people; *which* and *that* to things. Surprisingly, relative pronouns are some of those few words in English that have cases! *Who* is the subject case, *whose* is possessive, and *whom* is used for objects. Some examples:

Only a sword **that** is enchanted will be able to kill this dragon.

This sword, **which** I pulled from the stone, will kill the dragon.

Subject: The princess, **who** is beautiful, loves Oswald.
Possessive: Oswald, **whose** sword is bright, will slay the dragon.
Object: Oswald will marry the princess, to **whom** he has given his heart.

The woman **whom** Oswald loves is a princess.

Hopefully you see how each clause is related to the main clause by the pronoun. We could make complete sentences simply substituting the relative pronoun with the noun.

A sword is enchanted.	Oswald's sword is bright.
I pulled this sword from the stone.	He has given his heart to the princess.
The princess is beautiful.	Oswald loves the woman.

These are all complete sentences. We call the more important part of the sentence the main clause, while we call the part of the sentence joined by the relative pronoun the relative clause.

In English, we often omit the relative pronoun. We can also say, "The woman Oswald loves is a princess." However, in Latin you will always need to include that relative pronoun.

The chant for the relative pronoun (below) will of course need to be memorized. Although some of the forms are a little strange, some will have familiar-looking endings (bold):

	SINGULAR			PLURAL		
	MASC.	FEM.	NEUT.	MASC.	FEM.	NEUT.
NOM.	quī	quae	quod	quī	quae	quae
GEN.	cuius	cuius	cuius	quōrum	quārum	quōrum
DAT.	cui	cui	cui	quibus	quibus	quibus
ACC.	quem	quam	quod	quōs	quās	quae
ABL.	quō	quā	quō	quibus	quibus	quibus

Just like the *hic, haec, hoc* chant (and other demonstratives), this one flows much better if you chant horizontally: all nominative singulars, then genitive singulars, down through all the singulars, then up to all the nominative plurals in a row, etc. Thus you would chant out loud *quī, quae, quod! cuius, cuius, cuius! cui, cui, cui!* and so on.

Since the relative pronoun is referring back to a noun, **it must match its antecedent in gender and number. However, its case depends on its function in the relative clause.** A few examples should help clarify this principle.

Example 1: The princess, who is beautiful, loves Oswald.
*Fīlia rēgis **quae** pulchra est Oswaldum amat.*

Example 2: The princess loves Oswald, whose sword is sharp.
*Fīlia rēgis **Oswaldum cuius** gladius ācer est amat.*

Example 3: The princess, to whom Oswald gives a gift, also loves him.
*Fīlia rēgis **cui** Oswaldus dōnum dat etiam eum amat.*

Example 4: The princess, whom Oswald rescued, will love him always.
*Fīlia rēgis **quam** Oswaldus ēripuit eum semper amābit.*

Example 5: The princess loves Oswald, by whom she was rescued from the dragon.
*Fīlia rēgis **Oswaldum** ab **quō** ex dracōne ērepta est amat.*

Because there will be more verbs going on with relative clauses, you may get confused. Therefore, I recommend using the "bracket approach." Whenever you read a whole sentence and you hit a relative pronoun, place a bracket before it. You should continue reading and place the closing bracket usually after the first verb, which will be the verb of the relative clause. Bracketing off the clause helps us see what the main sentence is all about, and then you can fit the clause into that. Let's go through all the examples again, bracketing the relative clauses.

Example 1: *Fīlia rēgis [quae pulchra est] Oswaldum amat.* Once the relative clause is set off, it's easy to see that the main sentence is the very simple: "The princess loves Oswald." Then we can decipher the clause *quae pulchra est*. *Quae* is either feminine singular nominative or neuter plural nominative/accusative, but since it immediately follows *fīlia*, it makes most sense to go with the first option: "who is beautiful." Thus the *quae* matches its antecedent *fīlia* in gender (feminine) and (number); they both happen to be nominative here, since *fīlia* is the subject of the main verb *amat* and *quae* is the subject of the subordinate verb *est*.

Example 2: *Fīlia rēgis Oswaldum [cuius gladius ācer est] amat.* The main sentence in this example also translates into "The princess loves Oswald." In the relative clause, the subject of *est* is *gladius*, and *ācer* is the predicate adjective. So what do we do with the *cuius*? It is genitive, and so we treat it just like the genitive of any other old noun or pronoun—it possesses *gladius*. Although initially we may not be sure whether *cuius* is masculine, feminine, or neuter, because all of those forms are identical, it makes the most sense for it to be masculine singular and refer to *Oswaldum*. Notice that they match in gender and number, but *cuius* is genitive and *Oswaldum* is accusative. Thus our clause means "whose sword is sharp."

Example 3: *Fīlia rēgis [cui Oswaldus dōnum dat] etiam eum amat.* In our third example the main sentence is along similar lines to our previous sentences: "The princess also loves him." Now we can dissect the relative clause, first finding our nominative subject (*Oswaldus*) and our verb (*dat*). So we have "Oswald gives"—what does he give? The accusative *dōnum*, of course, and then we have our indirect object *cui*—"to whom." Although in isolation *cui* could be either masculine, feminine, or neuter singular; in this particular sentence it makes the most sense for it to be feminine singular to match the antecedent *fīlia*. Putting things all together, our clause then reads "to whom Oswald gives a gift." (*Cui* could potentially be modifying *rēgis*, but that doesn't make sense once you read the sentence out. Be careful not to understand all the grammar before you rush to conclusions, but always try to figure out what makes the most sense.)

Example 4: *Fīlia rēgis [quam Oswaldus ēripuit] eum semper amābit.* After the relative clause is bracketed, the quite simple main sentence stands out: "The princess will always love him." In our relative clause, Oswald is again the subject, this time of the verb *ēripuit*—"Oswald rescued." Since *quam* is the feminine singular accusative form of the relative pronoun, we know that, in addition to referring to the feminine singular *fīlia*, it must be the object of *ēripuit*, and so our clause means "whom Oswald rescued."

Example 5: *Fīlia rēgis Oswaldum [ab quō ex dracōne ērepta est] amat.* In our final example, the main clause is again simply "The princess loves Oswald." Then we have the slightly complicated-looking relative clause to deal with. Last year, you learned to look for verbs and nouns first and foremost. Let's look for them here. There are no nominatives in this relative clause, but there is a verb *est* and it seems to go with *erepta*. Together *erepta est* is 3rd person singular, perfect passive indicative of *ēripiō*. We can also see from the *-a* ending that the subject of this verb is feminine. Thus it means: "she was rescued." The *ex dracōne* means "from the dragon," and notice how Latin loves repetition here. Even though the verb *ēripiō* already has an *ex-* prefix, that preposition is repeated in the phrase *ex dracōne*.

So now what do we do with the *ab quō*? Remember that with passive verbs, the ablative of agent (the person performing the action of that passive verb) uses the preposition *ab*. The phrase *ab quō* can then be translated "by whom," and fits into the rest of the clause like this: "by whom she was rescued from the dragon." The relative pronoun *quō* matches its antecedent *Oswaldum* in gender (masculine) and number (singular), but its case is ablative because it is the object of the preposition *ab* while *Oswaldum* is accusative since he is the object of the verb *amat*. Make sure that you understand what is going on in sentences like this, or you will be destroyed by relative pronouns.

Intensive Pronoun

Fear not, the intensive pronoun is much less complicated than the relative pronoun. As its name suggests, the intensive pronoun intensifies or emphasizes someone or something. It can appear right alongside any form of the 1st person personal pronoun (*ego, nōs*) or the 2nd (*tū, vōs*), as well as with any 3rd person pronoun (e.g., *is, ea, id*) or noun. And like any good pronoun, it can stand alone as a substantive. In English, we can add emphasis with an intensive pronoun as well (by adding "-self" to the personal pronoun in question), but we can also add emphasis with other words (thus the other meaning for *ipse*, "the very"), or with voice intonation (reflected in print by italics, capital letters, bold, etc.). Here are some examples, just to show you how unafraid you should be.

> Ego ipse dracōnem necāvī. *I myself killed the dragon.*
>
> Oswaldus vōs ipsōs ē dracōne ēripuit. *Oswald rescued you yourselves from the dragon.*
>
> Vidimus ipsum quī dracōnem necāvit. *We saw the very man [or, the man himself] who killed the dragon.*

Note: Sometimes you will encounter a super-awkward translation that will need to be smoothed out in English. Take, for example, this sentence: *Ipse hoc dōnum mihi ipsī, nōn tibi ipsī dedit*, "He himself gave this gift to me myself, not to you yourself." Now this sounds just plain silly in English. So, use your creativity to show the emphasis in other ways, as in "HE gave this gift to ME, not to YOU."

As to the declension of the intensive pronoun, it will be similar to the other demonstrative pronouns you've already learned, such as *ille* or *iste* (KL2, Lesson 14). Here is its full declension for your reference:

	SINGULAR		
	MASC.	FEM.	NEUT.
NOM.	ipse	ipsa	ipsum
GEN.	ipsīus	ipsīus	ipsīus
DAT.	ipsī	ipsī	ipsī
ACC.	ipsum	ipsam	ipsum
ABL.	ipsō	ipsā	ipsō

	PLURAL		
	MASC.	FEM.	NEUT.
NOM.	ipsī	ipsae	ipsa
GEN.	ipsōrum	ipsārum	ipsōrum
DAT.	ipsīs	ipsīs	ipsīs
ACC.	ipsōs	ipsās	ipsa
ABL.	ipsīs	ipsīs	Ipsīs

Review

As we begin the new year, be sure to take time to review anything you are rusty on. In particular, make sure you review demonstratives (*hic, haec, hoc/ille, illa, illud/iste, ista, istud*) and pronouns (*is, ea, id*).

Worksheet 3

A. Vocabulary

1. sacerdōs: _____
2. who: _____
3. perchance: _____
4. sanguis: _____
5. carō: _____
6. prīnceps: _____
7. opus: _____
8. holy: _____
9. sheep: _____
10. ob (+_____): _____
    _____
11. black (give both options): _____
12. I strike: _____
13. ipse: _____
14. iste: _____
15. I respond: _____
16. tōta: _____
17. quidem: _____
18. pars: _____
19. I rescue: _____
20. autem: _____
21. oculus: _____
22. weapons: _____
23. trīstis: _____
24. quaerō: _____
25. dead: _____

B. Grammar

1. Fill in the blanks for the relative pronoun chant.

	SINGULAR			PLURAL		
	MASC.	FEM.	NEUT.	MASC.	FEM.	NEUT.
NOM.	quī				quae	
GEN.		cuius				quōrum
DAT.					quibus	
ACC.		quam		quōs		
ABL.	quō		quō			

2. Synopsis: Do a synopsis of *ēripiō* in the 1st person plural. First write out all the principal parts, and then complete the synopsis, including the imperatives.

Principal Parts: ēripiō, _____

	ACTIVE		PASSIVE	
	LATIN	ENGLISH	LATIN	ENGLISH
PRES.				
IMPF.				
FUT.				
PERF.				
PLUPF.				
FT.PF.				
IMP. SG.				
IMP. PL.				

3. Noun/Adjective Review: Decline *every holy work*. The first one is done for you.

	LATIN SINGULAR	LATIN PLURAL
NOM.		
GEN.		
DAT.		
ACC.		
ABL.		
VOC.		

Kraken Latin 2 // Student Edition

C. Memorization

Fill in the blanks to complete the Prologue through Fourth Commandment. (Try to do it without peeking.)

_____

_____

_____

_____

_____

_____

_____

3. Non _____ nomen Domini _____ vanum.

4. Memento _____ diem _____ sanctifices.

D. English to Latin Translation

1. I sing about arms and the man who came from the great city.

   _____

   _____

2. You used to know the man whose wife will perhaps be queen.

   _____

   _____

3. That lucky farmer's son wrote joyful songs for the very sheep that had been rescued from the grim dragon yesterday.

   _____

   _____

   _____

4. The old priests, about whom our mother warned us, were giving the blood of sheep and goats to wicked gods.

   _____

   _____

   _____

5. He who kills the giant with one eye will become the leader of the men with whom he himself is sailing.

6. You speak what you yourselves do not know; indeed, this holy man speaks the truth and does powerful deeds.

7. Your son was struck by the angry farmer on account of the dead horse, which he himself did not kill.

8. My tired daughter, to whom bread and wine were finally given, was then able to walk through all the fields to the castle.

9. Part of the soldiers never believed the things that had been spoken about the sad king.

10. Blessed are those who seek the kingdom of God, for all these things will be given to them.

E. Latin to English Translation

John 3*—*Nicodemus*

1 Erat autem homo ex *Pharisaeis*, *Nicodemus* nomine, princeps *Iudaeorum*. Hic venit ad Iesum nocte et dixit ei: "Rabbi, *nemo* potest haec *signa* facere quae tu facis sine Deo." Respondit Iesus et dixit ei: "*Amen, amen* dico tibi: debes nasci* iterum." Dicit ad eum* Nicodemus: "Quomodo potest homo senex nasci?" Respondit Iesus: "*Amen, amen* dico tibi: homo debet nasci ex aqua et Spiritu aut non potest intrare in
5 regnum Dei. Quod natum est* ex carne caro est et quod natum est ex Spiritu spiritus est. Spiritus ubi vult* *spirat* et vocem eius audis; sic est omnis qui natus est ex Spiritu." Respondit Nicodemus et dixit

ei: "Quomodo possunt haec fieri*?" Respondit Iesus et dixit ei: "Tu es magister *Israhel* et haec non scis? *Amen, amen* dico tibi quia* quod scimus dicimus et quod vidimus declaramus et verba nostra non accipitis. Et *nemo ascendit* in caelum *nisi* qui *descendit* de caelo, Filius hominis qui est in caelo.
10   Enim amavit Deus mundum et Filium suum *unigenitum* dedit; omnis qui credit in eum non delebitur sed habebit vitam aeternam. Qui credit in eum non *iudicatur*; qui autem non credit iam *iudicatus est*, quia non credidit in nomine unigeniti Filii Dei. Hoc est autem *iudicium* quia lux venit in mundum et amaverunt homines tenebras et non lucem; erant enim eorum mala opera. Omnis enim qui mala agit odit* lucem et non venit ad lucem, qui autem facit veritatem venit ad lucem."

Notes:
* John 3 is adapted from the Vulgate, which does not include macrons or punctuation. I've added punctuation, but I left out macrons so that you can accustom yourself to that.
* *nāscī*: infinitive of *nāscor* (a deponent); translate as "to be born"
* *ad eum*: Note the "ungrammatical" use of *ad* + accusative rather than the simple dative, which is used with *dicit* elsewhere in this passage.
* *nātus/a/um est*: 3rd person singluar perfect passive deponent indicative of *nāscor*; translate as "he/she/it is born, has been born"
* *vult*: irregular 3rd person singular present active indicative of *volō*, "I wish."
* *fieri*: *to become*, infinitive of the semi-deponent *fiō*
* *quia*: remember, it can also mean "that"
* *ōdit*: 3rd person singular perfect active from the defective verb *ōdī*, "I hate" (although perfect, it is translated as a present—see Lesson 22)

Glossary:
āmēn (indecl.): You should probably be able to guess what this one means. (Ok, it can also means truly.)
ascendō, -ere, -dī, -censum: I ascend, go up
dēscendō, -ere, -dī, -censum: I descend, go down
Isrāhel, -ēlis (or indecl., m): Israel
Iūdaeus, -a, -um: Jewish; as noun, *Iūdaeus, -i (m)* or *Iūdaea, -ae (f)*: a Jew
iūdicium, -iī (n): judgment
iūdicō (1): I judge
nēmō, nēminis (m/f): no one, nobody
Nicodemus, -i (m): Nicodemus
nisi if not, unless, except
Pharisaeus, -i (m): Pharisee
sīgnum, -i (n): sign
spīrō (1): I breathe, blow
ūnigenitus, -a, -um: only-begotten

E. For Fun: Word Search Puzzle

Solve the clues and then find those answers in the letters below. Latin words may be forwards, backwards, vertical, or diagonal. (Note: Macrons have been omitted in the puzzle.)

1. *opus* in the Sing. Acc.: _____
2. Sing. Nom. of *oculus*: _____
3. *sacerdōs* in the Plur. Acc.: _____
4. Plur. Gen. of *ovis*: _____
5. "she defended": _____
6. Sing. Dat. of *princeps*: _____
7. 3rd Plur. Fut. Perf. Act. Indic. of *quaerō*: _____
8. "burdens" as a direct object: _____
9. 4th principal part of *ēripiō*: _____
10. Fem. Sing. Abl. of *trīstis, -e*: _____
11. Means "indeed, certainly, even": _____
12. "I will rescue": _____
13. Fem. Plur. Dat. of *ipse, -sa, -sum*: _____
14. "we have struck": _____
15. "you (pl.) are seeking": _____
16. *mortuus, -a, -um* in the Fem. Plur. Dat.: _____
17. Neut. Plur. Nom. of *sacer, -cra, -crum*: _____
18. *tōtus, -a, -um* in the Masc. Sing. Dat.: _____
19. 2nd Pers. Sing. Pres. Act. Indic. of *spectō*: _____
20. *ager* in the Abl. Plur.: _____
21. "to/for the ocean": _____
22. 1st Pers. Plur. Fut. Act. Indic. of *surgō*: _____
23. "I touch": _____
24. "they had been able": _____
25. Four words meaning "because": _____
26. Neut. Plur. Gen. of *tōtus, -a, -um*: _____
27. "they are warned": _____
28. Neut. Pl. Abl. of *quī, quae, quod*: _____
29. "gradually": _____
30. *arma* in the Plur. Gen.: _____
31. "we will have touched": _____
32. 1st Sing. Pres. Act. Indic. of *superō*: _____
33. "never": _____
34. 3rd Pers. Plur. Pres. Act. Indic. of *oppugnō*: _____
35. Masc. Sing. Abl. of *spīritus*: _____
36. Means "perchance": _____
37. 3rd Pers. Plur. Pres. Pass. Indic. of *terreō*: _____
38. "of the window": _____
39. 3rd Pers. Plur. Imperf. Pass. Indic. of *percutiō*: _____
40. "tiger" as the subject of the sentence: _____
41. *inimicus* in the Gen. Plur.: _____
42. Masc. Abl. Sing. of *sanctus, -a, -um*: _____

43. "of the ocean": _____
44. the word for "truth" in the Dat. Sing.: _____
45. Neut. Plur. Acc. of *saeculum*: _____
46. "to touch": _____

47. Neut. Sing. Abl. of *iter*: _____
48. "you (sg.) join": _____
49. Masc. Sing. Dat. of *eques*: _____
50. "pigs" in the Nominative: _____

```
I N I M I C O R U M A O R E P U S B A R I U
F S U M I S S U C R E P A R E N O C E A N I
D P A M V M E D I U Q U A E S I V E R I N T
T E X O Q E O C U L U S I P I M I N T F A O
A C F N V U R Q U P I A M P O C U B A R P T
O T D E M S A I X O B I S C I L M T I P D O
V A P N N A X M T E U I P A X C T U U O L R
S S E T O D R E C A S O M R T A N G E R E U
U P U U M O I M A N T U A C O G N I E C O M
M O B R F U N T O P B I M A I A P N R I S A
I T E C G Q U A E R I T I S N O G R I P I I
R U M P U E F M I N U T A T I M O R P T I N
E E P I T O M A N O C M O R T U I S I L V O
G R A P O N E U P S U N S F O Q E U A S C U
I A U T I R I P S T O I M U T U Q I M F U Q
T N O U F R A C P E R C U T I E B A N T U R
E T A N G O P E N G U I F X A L U C E A S I
T U I F R P R X I B O M S A N C T O N U C P
V A R M I E N T E R R E N T U R O D A M O T
F E N E S T R A E R E N I T I M O C E A N O
```

Lesson 4

Adjectives: Comparison of Adjectives; Additional *-ius* Adjectives

Word List

Nouns

1. anima, -ae (f) *soul, spirit, life; wind, breath*
2. nēmō, nēminis (m/f) *no one, nobody*
3. ōstium, -iī (n) *door, gate, entrance*
4. sacrificium, -iī (n) *sacrifice, offering*

Adjectives

5. alius, -ia, -iud *other, another*
6. alter, -era, -erum *the other (of two), second*
7. excelsus, -a, -um *high, lofty, noble*
8. fidēlis, -e *faithful*
9. nūllus, -a, -um *no, none, not any*
10. plēnus, -a, -um *full, plump, abundant*
11. sapiēns, -entis *wise*
12. sōlus, -a, -um *only, alone*
13. superbus, -a, -um *proud, haughty*
14. ūllus, -a, -um *any*

Verbs

15. aedificō (1) *I build, make*
16. tendō, -ere, tetendī, tentum *I stretch; hasten, strive; aim*
17. trādō, -ere, -didī, -ditum *I hand/give over, surrender; hand down, teach*

Adverbs/Prepositions

18. sīc *so, thus*

19. tunc *then, thereupon, at that time*

20. apud (+acc.) *among, at the house of*

Memorization

Ego sum Dominus Deus tuus qui eduxi te de terra Aegypti de domo servitutis.

1. Non habebis deos alienos coram me.
2. Non facies tibi sculptile neque omnem similitudinem quae est in caelo desuper et quae in terra deorsum nec eorum quae sunt in aquis sub terra.
3. Non adsumes nomen Domini Dei tui in vanum.
4. Memento ut diem sabbati sanctifices.
5. Honora patrem tuum et matrem tuam ut sis longevus super terram quam Dominus Deus tuus dabit tibi.

   Honor your father and your mother that you may be long-lived upon the land which the Lord your God will give to you.

Grammar

Comparison of Adjectives

Knowing how to use Latin adjectives has certainly brightened the place up. But sometimes it's not enough to simply describe something; we often desire to compare or contrast that thing with something else: *Wow, this cake is* **good**. *This is the* **best** *peanut butter chocolate cake I have ever eaten! It's so much* **better** *than the cake I made last year!* When we compare two or more items in English with regular adjectives, we use *-er* or *-est*: *Oswald is* **braver** *than this man. Oswald is the* **bravest** *knight of the realm.* (Note that when comparing only two things, you must use *-er*; *-est* is reserved for more than two.)

There are three degrees of comparison in both English and Latin. The positive degree is when you simply state the adjective: *big*. The comparative is used when comparing two things: *bigger*. The superlative comes into play when you have more than two things: *biggest*. All the adjectives you have learned so far have been listed in the positive degree, and indeed, that is the way they will be found in Latin dictionaries.

As in English, where you must add *-er* or *-est* to the positive form of the adjective, so also in Latin you must add a new ending to the base of the positive. So how do we "add" an ending to an adjective. For a three-termination adjective (*-us, -a, -um* or *-x, -is, -e*), go to the second form (the feminine) and remove the ending (*-a* or *-is*, respectively). Thus the stem of *superbus, -a, -um* is *superb-*, and the stem of *acer, -acris, -acre* is *acr-*. For a two-termination adjective (such as *fortis, forte*) or single-termination (such as *sapiēns, -ntis*), go to the genitive and remove the genitive ending.

FINDING AN ADJECTIVE'S STEM		
ADJECTIVE TYPE	DICTIONARY ENTRY	STEM
three-termination	*superbus, -a, -um* *acer, acris, acre*	superb- acr-
three-termination	*fortis, -e*	fort-
three-termination	*sapiēns, -ntis*	sapient-

An important thing to keep in mind with all of this is that no matter what declension the adjective is born into in the positive degree, it will become a third declension adjective in the comparative degree and a 1st/2nd declension adjective in the superlative degree.

Let's decline some of these to make this clear: *superbus, -a, -um* is a 1st/2nd declension adjective (three-termination), meaning "proud." If we want to say, "The king is proud," all we have to do is *Rēx superbus est*. But what if we want to say "The king is prouder than the knight"? Then we must move on to the comparative. We find the stem of *superbus* by taking off the *-a* of the feminine nominative (second form) = *superb-*. Then we add our *-ior* (for masculine or feminine) and *-ius* (for neuter). Now we have *superbior, superbius*, "prouder." The comparative is a 3rd declension adjective—but here's where it gets a tad tricky. The comparative usually declines like a regular old 3rd declension noun, not an i-stem like other 3rd declension adjectives. Thus in the genitive plural the ending is *-um* rather than *-ium*, and in the ablative plural it is an *-e* (although sometimes you will see *-ī*, as in the phrase *a fortiōrī*).

	SINGULAR		PLURAL	
	MASC./FEM.	NEUT.	MASC./FEM.	NEUT.
NOM.	superbior	superbius	superbiōrēs	superbiōra
GEN.	superbiōris	superbiōris	superbiōrum	superbiōrum
DAT.	superbiōrī	superbiōrī	superbiōribus	superbiōribus
ACC.	superbiōrem	superbius	superbiōrēs	superbiōra
ABL.	superbiōre (-ī)	superbiōre (-ī)	superbiōribus	superbiōribus
VOC.	superbior	superbius	superbiōrēs	superbiōra

Now we are able to say "The king is prouder," *Rēx superbior est*. But that isn't enough. We need to compare this king to someone else—he is prouder *than* somebody. There are two ways to express "than" in Latin. The first is to use *quam* (*KL1*, Lesson 12), which means "as, than, how." Since it is linking two nouns together, the second noun will match the case of the first one:

The king is prouder than the knight. *Rēx* [nominative] *est superbior quam eques* [nominative].

I saw the king, prouder than all the men of the land. *Vīdī rēgem* [accusative] *superbiōrem quam omnēs virōs* [accusative] *terrae*.

We can also compare by using our multi-talented old friend the ablative. The ablative of comparison is often used (rather than *quam*) when the first noun to be compared is in the nominative or accusative. When that first noun is in genitive, dative, or ablative, it's better to use *quam*.

The king is prouder than the knight. *Rēx* [nominative] *est superbior equite* [ablative of comparison].

I saw the king, prouder than all the men of the land. *Vīdī rēgem* [accusative] *superbiōrem omnibus virīs* [ablative of comparison] *terrae*.

Sometimes in Latin, a word in the comparative degree is not necessarily being compared to something else; in such a case the comparative can be translated as "rather" or "too."

Iste rēx superbior est. That king is rather proud. That king is too proud.

So much for the comparative degree; now on to the superlative! When comparing more than two things, the superlative is used: "The king is the *proudest* man in the land." Forming the regular Latin superlative is as simple as adding the *-est* in English. Simply add *-issimus, -a, -um* to the stem of the adjective, and that superlative adjective will decline just like other *-us, -a, -um* adjectives. When added to our stem *superb-* we get *superbissimus, -a, -um*. In case you are not convinced that this is a very easy process, here is the superlative declined (oh so normally!).

	SINGULAR			PLURAL		
	MASC.	FEM.	NEUT.	MASC.	FEM.	NEUT.
NOM.	superbissimus	superbissima	superbissimum	superbissimī	superbissimae	superbissima
GEN.	superbissimī	superbissimae	superbissimī	superbissimōrum	superbissimārum	superbissimōrum
DAT.	superbissimō	superbissimae	superbissimō	superbissimīs	superbissimīs	superbissimīs
ACC.	superbissimum	superbissimam	superbissimum	superbissimōs	superbissimās	superbissima
ABL.	superbissimō	superbissimā	superbissimō	superbissimīs	superbissimīs	superbissimīs
VOC.	superbissime	superbissima	superbissimum	superbissimī	superbissimae	superbissima

Now we can translate our example sentence, "The king is the proudest man in the land," as *Rēx superbissimus vir in terrā est*. I told you it was easy. Sometimes it will be awkward to translate a Latin superlative with "-est," and so you can also translate it simply with a "very"—"very proud." We often use superlatives in English to exaggerate, as in "I just had the best cookie ever!" We don't (usually) mean that the cookie was in fact the best cookie in the world, past, present, and future; we just mean that it was very, very good. This usage of the superlative in Latin has been handed down into Italian, when Italians will describe things as "bellissima!" or "bellissimo!" They usually just mean to describe something as "very beautiful." Another example is in music, with the dynamic markings (Italian, of course) *pianissimo* or *fortissimo*—they mean "very soft" and "very loud," respectively, not "most soft" and "most loud."

There is one more little fun thing we can do with the superlative—if you want to have a super-superlative, simply put *quam* before the superlative adjective, and it will mean "the _____ est possible" or "as _____ as possible": *Rēx est vir quam superbissimus in terrā*, "The king is the proudest possible man in the land" or "The king is a man as proud as possible."

Additional *-ius* Adjectives

In this lesson you will learn several new adjectives that share a slightly irregular declension: *alius, alter, nūllus, sōlus,* and *ūllus*. In the genitive and dative singular, they will imitate several words we have already learned (*is, iste, ille;* and *ipse* and *totus* from the last lesson). The only trick is remembering that these adjectives have an *-īus* ending in the genitive singular, and an *-ī* in the dative singular; otherwise they are the same as regular *-us, -a, -um* adjectives. Here is one of them, *sōlus*, declined in full with the unusual forms in bold.

	SINGULAR			PLURAL		
	MASC.	FEM.	NEUT.	MASC.	FEM.	NEUT.
NOM.	sōlus	sōla	sōlum	sōlī	sōlae	sōla
GEN.	**sōlīus**	**sōlīus**	**sōlīus**	sōlōrum	sōlārum	sōlōrum
DAT.	**sōlī**	**sōlī**	**sōlī**	sōlīs	sōlīs	sōlīs
ACC.	sōlum	sōlam	sōlum	sōlōs	sōlās	sōla
ABL.	sōlō	sōlā	sōlō	sōlīs	sōlīs	sōlīs

There are a total of nine of these special *-īus* adjectives; you are learning five in this lesson, and you have already learned *ūnus* back in *KL1*, Lesson 5, and then *tōtus* in the last lesson. In Lesson 15 you will learn the final two, *neuter* and *uter*.

Finally, you need to know a few more quirks about two of your new adjectives. Sometimes *alius, alia, aliud* will have as its genitive singular *alīus, alīus, alīus*; but sometimes it borrows the genitive of *alter: alterīus, alterīus, alterīus*. And, sometimes the genitive and ablative singular of *nūllus* will appear instead of the genitive and ablative singular of our new noun *nēmō*:

NOM.	nēmō
GEN.	nēminis [*or* nūllīus]
DAT.	nēminī
ACC.	nēminem
ABL.	nēmine [*or* nūllō]

(And this does make a little sense, for as a substantive adjective, *nūllus* would mean "no one.")

Review

Make sure you review anything you're fuzzy on (passive forms, fourth or fifth declensions, regular pronouns), and be sure to review relative and intensive pronouns in this lesson. Relative pronouns massively expand everything you can do in Latin, so whatever else you do, review them!

Worksheet 4

A. Vocabulary

Give Latin word or English meaning as appropriate. Also fill in principal parts for verbs and case(s) for prepositions.

1. trādō, _____
2. ōstium: _____
3. the other (of two): _____
4. other: _____
5. tunc: _____
6. whole: _____
7. sapiēns: _____
8. sīc: _____
9. pōtēns: _____
10. I build: _____
11. superbus: _____
12. laetus: _____
13. faithful: _____
14. anima: _____
15. nūllus: _____
16. ūllus: _____
17. at the house of: _____
18. sanguis: _____
19. plēnus: _____
20. nobody: _____
21. sōlus: _____
22. iūstus: _____
23. tendō, _____
24. sacrificium: _____
25. noble: _____

B. Grammar

1. Decline *other saddest sheep*.

	LATIN SINGULAR	LATIN PLURAL
NOM.		
GEN.		
DAT.		
ACC.		
ABL.		
VOC.		

2. Decline *no holier eye*.

	LATIN SINGULAR	LATIN PLURAL
NOM.		
GEN.		
DAT.		
ACC.		
ABL.		
VOC.		

3. Do a synopsis of *tradō* in the 3rd person plural. Give principal parts first and imperatives afterward.

Principal Parts: tradō, _____

		ACTIVE		PASSIVE	
		LATIN	ENGLISH	LATIN	ENGLISH
INDICATIVE	PRES.				
	IMPF.				
	FUT.				
	PERF.				
	PLUPF.				
	FT.PF.				
IMP.	SG.				
	PL.				

C. Memorization

Fill in the blanks for the Ten Commandments, Prologue through Fifth Commandment.

_____

_____

_____

_____

_____

_____

3. Non _____ nomen _____ tui in _____.

4. _____ ut diem _____.

5. Honora _____ tuum et _____ ut _____ longevus _____ terram _____ _____ Deus tuus _____.

D. English to Latin Translation

1. I used to know a priest who was nobler than all the leaders of the town.

2. Our camel, to whom no one had given any food, was the saddest possible animal in the whole world.

3. Thus the plumpest farmer was not the wisest, because he had eaten all the sacrifices of the proud gods.

4. "Is that cow blacker than night itself? And are the very stars more distant than the moon?" asked the children.

5. That unlucky nation, whose city was besieged for a long time, was nobler than its enemies but finally surrendered to them.

6. Either I will have the spirit of a lion and kill the other giant, or I will flee from this most dreadful danger.

7. For ten years the very faithful dog waited for [his] master, finally saw him, and then suddenly became very dead [use the superlative to translate "very dead"].

8. The king himself came to the door of the cave, and gave to the Beast of Green Poison many sacrifices that were holier than those of the priest.

9. We had found hope at the home of other women, who were the happiest mothers possible.

10. I was very tired but hurled rocks at the sinister sea serpent; he however aimed angry fire at me.

E. Latin to English Translation

1 **Nēmō Cӯclopsque**

Ego ipse cum meīs virīs ab *Troiā* ad patriam nostram nāvigābam. Dēnique ad īnsulam unius ex *Cyclōpibus* cui nōmen *Polyphēmus* est* vēnimus. Per hanc terram ambulāre et gigantem quī solus ibī habitābat—amīcus aut inimīcus erat?—vidēre cupīvī. Mēcum vīnum potentissimum quod sacerdōs
5 mihi dedit portāvī. Nōs ipsam spēluncam eius, in quā ovēs eius dormiēbant et quam cum *cāseīs* multīs *implēverat* invēnimus. Virī meī *cāseōs* manducāvērunt et plēnī erant. Deinde Polyphēmus, excelsior omnibus nobīs, in spēluncam vēnit, et nōs occultāvimus. Saxum quam ingentissimum in ōstiō posuit et nōs vīdit. "Cur," nobīs rogāvit, "ibī estis? *Quis* estis?" Ego rēspondī: "Nōmen mihi Nēmō est*." Iste autem duō ex virīs meīs ad tellūrem percussit et carnem sanguinemque eōrum manducāvit, sed nōs flēvimus.

10 *Māne* Cӯclops ovēs ex spēluncā dūxit sed nōs saxō in spēluncā *incarcerāvit*. Illō diē ego sīcā meā *baculum* Polyphēmī acriorem fēcī, et eum tum exspectāvimus. Polyphēmus dēnique *revertit* et aliōs duōs manducāvit. Timeō, sed eī vīnum potentissimum dedī. Potāvit, et potāvit, et iterum potāvit. Dēnique *ēbriissimus* factus est et dormīvit. Novam hastam nostram in igne posuimus, et eō Polyphēmum in ūnō oculō eius tunc percussimus. Clāmāvit et ululāvit; itaque aliī Cyclōpēs ad spēluncam eius cucurrērunt.
15 "*Quis* tibi vulnerāvit?" rogāvērunt. Rēspondit: "Nēmō!" Sīc *abiērunt* et Polyphēmus īrātissimus erat. Saxum mōvit et ovēs *abīre incēpērunt*. *Quemque* tetigit quod nōs capere et interficere cupīvit. Ego autem ūnum virum sub ove *quōque* vīnxeram, et sīc nōs omnēs ad nāvem nostram fūgimus.

Notes:
* *cui nōmen est*: dative of possession, lit., "to whom was the name" but can be translated "whose name was"
* *nōmen mihi...est*: see above; translate as "My name is..."

Glossary:
abeō, -īre, -iī, -itum: I go away, depart
baculum, -ī (n): staff, (walking) stick
cāseus, -ī (m): cheese
Cӯclops, Cӯclōpis (m): Cyclops, pl. Cyclopes
ēbrius, -a, -um: drunk
impleō, -ēre, -plēvī, -plētum: I fill up, satisfy, complete
incarcerō (1): I imprison, incarcerate
incipiō, -ere, -cēpī, -ceptum: I begin
māne: in the morning, early
Polyphēmus, -ī (m): Polyphemus, a Cyclops
quis: who? (interrogative pronoun)
quisque, quidque: each (except for the nominative, declines a lot like *quī, quae, quod*)
revertō, -ere, -vertī, —: I return
Troia, -ae (f): Troy

Lesson 5

Adjectives: Irregular Comparison; Nouns: Dative of Possession

Word List

Adjectives (The numbered words are your new vocabulary words for this lesson.)

	POSITIVE	COMPARATIVE	SUPERLATIVE
ENDING IN -ER	miser, -era, -erum *wretched*	miserior, -ius *more wretched*	miserrimus, -a, -um *most wretched*
	pulcher, -chra, -chrum *beautiful*	pulchrior, -ius *more beautiful*	pulcherrimus, -a, -um *most beautiful*
	celer, -eris, -e *swift*	celerior, -ius *swifter*	celerrimus, -a, -um *swiftest*
6 ENDING IN -LIS	1. similis, -e *similar, like*	similior, -ius *more similar*	simillimus, -a, -um *most similar*
	2. dissimilis, -e *dissimilar, unlike, different*	dissimilior, -ius *more dissimilar*	dissimillimus, -a, -um *most dissimilar*
	3. facilis, -e *easy*	facilior, -ius *easier*	facillimus, -a, -um *easiest*
	4. difficilis *difficult*	difficilior, -ius *more difficult*	difficillimus, -a, -um *most difficult*
	5. gracilis, -e *slender, thin*	gracilior, -ius *thinner*	gracillimus, -a, -um *thinnest*
	6. humilis, -e *humble, low(ly)*	humilior, -ius *more humble*	humillimus, -a, -um *most humble*
JUST PLAIN IRREGULAR	magnus, -a, -um *big, great*	7. māior, māius *bigger, greater*	8. māximus, -a, -um *biggest, greatest*
	parvus, -a, -um *small*	9. minor, minus *smaller*	10. minimus, -a, -um *smallest*
	bonus, -a, -um *good*	11. melior, melius *better*	12. optimus, -a, -um *best*
	malus, -a, -um *bad, evil*	13. pēior, pēius *worse, more evil*	14. pessimus, -a, -um *worst, most evil*
	15. īnferus, -a, -um *below*	16. inferior, -ius *lower*	17. infimus, -a, -um *or* 18. īmus, -a, -um* *lowest, deepest*
	19. superus, -a, -um *above, high*	20. superior, -ius *higher*	21. suprēmus, -a, -um *or* 22. summus, -a, -um* *highest, greatest*
	multus, -a, -um *much*	23. ——, plūs *more*	24. plūrimus, -a, -um *most*
	—— [prō *or* 25. prae (adv. & prep. + abl.), *below*]	26. prior, prius *former*	prīmus, -a, -um *first*
	—— [prope (adv.) *near*]	27. propior, -ius *nearer*	28. proximus, -a, -um *next, nearest*
	—— [29. ultrā (adv.) *beyond*]	30. ulterior, -ius *farther*	31. ultimus, -a, -um *farthest*

*īmus and summus are often regarded as alternate superlatives of inferus and superus, respectively, even though they are technically not from these positive forms.

Memorization

Ego sum Dominus Deus tuus qui eduxi te de terra Aegypti de domo servitutis.

1. Non habebis deos alienos coram me.
2. Non facies tibi sculptile neque omnem similitudinem quae est in caelo desuper et quae in terra deorsum nec eorum quae sunt in aquis sub terra.3. Non adsumes nomen Domini Dei tui in vanum.
4. Memento ut diem sabbati sanctifices.
5. Honora patrem tuum et matrem tuam ut sis longevus super terram quam Dominus Deus tuus dabit tibi
6. Non occides.

    You shall not kill.

7. Non moechaberis.

    You shall not commit adultery.

8. Non furtum facies.

    You shall not commit theft.

Grammar

Irregular Comparatives

Since comparing adjectives was so easy last lesson, it's time to mix things up for this lesson. Of course there are irregular comparatives, just like in English! Have you ever wondered why we say "good, better, best" or "bad, worse, worst"? Or "much, more, most?" Similarly, in Latin some of the most common adjectives will compare irregularly, and their forms will have to be memorized. Fortunately, English derivatives will help the memory considerably!

First, however, let us discuss some slightly irregular but still predictable variations in the superlative. Any adjective ending in *-er* in the masculine nominative singular, regardless of declension, will end in *-rimus, -a, -um* in the superlative rather than *-issimus, -a, -um*.

	POSITIVE	COMPARATIVE	SUPERLATIVE
ENDING IN -ER	miser, -era, -erum *wretched*	miserior, -ius *more wretched*	miserrimus, -a, -um *most wretched*
	pulcher, -chra, -chrum *beautiful*	pulchrior, -ius *more beautiful*	pulcherrimus, -a, -um *most beautiful*
	celer, -eris, -e *swift*	celerior, -ius *swifter*	celerrimus, -a, -um *swiftest*

A few things of note: The comparative of *-er* adjectives is perfectly regular; the endings *-ior, -ius* are added to the stem. The superlative endings *-rimus, -a, -um* are added to that masculine nominative singular, not to the stem—thus it is *pulcherrimus* not *pulchrrimus* (which would be awfully hard to say!).

There are six adjectives ending in *-lis* which add *-limus, -a, -um* to the stem in the superlative rather than *-issimus, -a, -um*. Again, the comparative of these six is completely normal.

	POSITIVE	COMPARATIVE	SUPERLATIVE
6 ENDING IN -LIS	similis, -e *similar, like*	similior, -ius *more similar*	simillimus, -a, -um *most similar*
	dissimilis, -e *dissimilar, unlike, different*	dissimilior, -ius *more dissimilar*	dissimillimus, -a, -um *most dissimilar*
	facilis, -e *easy*	facilior, -ius *easier*	facillimus, -a, -um *easiest*
	difficilis *difficult*	difficilior, -ius *more difficult*	difficillimus, -a, -um *most difficult*
	gracilis, -e *slender, thin*	gracilior, -ius *thinner*	gracillimus, -a, -um *thinnest*
	humilis, -e *humble, low(ly)*	humilior, -ius *more humble*	humillimus, -a, -um *most humble*

Not all adjectives ending in *-lis* have *-limus* in the superlative; only these six. In the last lesson your learned *fidelis, -e*, which has the perfectly normal superlative form of *fidelissimus, -a, -um*.

Finally, there are some adjectives that are just plain irregular (just like English). These comparisons will need to be memorized—I have counted each word separately as its own vocabulary entry, and thus there are 31 words in this lesson's word list.

	POSITIVE	COMPARATIVE	SUPERLATIVE
JUST PLAIN IRREGULAR	magnus, -a, -um *big, great*	māior, māius *bigger, greater*	māximus, -a, -um *biggest, greatest*
	parvus, -a, -um *small*	minor, minus *smaller*	minimus, -a, -um *smallest*
	bonus, -a, -um *good*	melior, melius *better*	optimus, -a, -um *best*
	malus, -a, -um *bad, evil*	pēior, pēius *worse, more evil*	pessimus, -a, -um *worst, most evil*
	inferus, -a, -um *below*	inferior, -ius *lower*	infimus, -a, -um *or* īmus, -a, -um* *lowest, deepest*
	superus, -a, -um *above, high*	superior, -ius *higher*	suprēmus, -a, -um *or* summus, -a, -um* *highest, greatest*
	multus, -a, -um *much*	——, plūs *more*	plūrimus, -a, -um *most*
	——[prō or prae (adv. & prep. + abl.), *below*]	prior, prius *former*	prīmus, -a, -um *first*
	——[prope (adv.) *near*]	propior, -ius *nearer*	proximus, -a, -um *next, nearest*
	——[ultrā (adv.) *beyond*]	ulterior, -ius *farther*	ultimus, -a, -um *farthest*

Declension of *plūs*

As if it weren't weird enough that the comparative of *multus* is *plūs*, this little guy has some interesting variations of his own. For one thing, there is no masculine or feminine singular for this adjective, and the neuter singular almost always appears as a noun. And for some reason, the dative singular never appears in classical Latin so we just pass over that form! In the plural, *plūs* (stem *plūr-*) does decline in all genders as an adjective, but declines partially as a 3rd declension i-stem (genitive plural ending *-ium*), but not quite (neuter nominative and accusative plural ending is *-a*, not *-ia*).

Oh, and one more thing—remember how I said that *plūs* is most often a noun in the neuter singular? Well, like *satis* (*KL2*, Lesson 14), *plūs* is therefore usually followed by a partitive genitive. You have seen a phrase such as *Satis pānis manducāvit*, "He ate enough bread" (literally, "enough of bread," but we omit that "of" in English). You will also see phrases such as *Plūs pānis quam gigās manducāvit*, "He ate more bread than the giant" (again, literally, "more of bread," but you should translate it in English as "more bread.")

This partitive genitive phenomenon occurs with the neuter singular only; in the plural of all genders *plūs* will function like a normal adjective (finally!) and modify nouns in gender, number, and case: *Plūrēs dracōnēs in montibus quam in agrīs vīdit*, "He saw more dragons in the mountains than in the fields."

	MASC./FEM. SG.	NEUT. SG.	MASC./FEM. PL.	NEUT. PL.
NOM.	———	plūs	plūrēs	plūra
GEN.	———	plūris	plūrium	plūrium
DAT.	———	———	plūribus	plūribus
ACC.	———	plūs	plūrēs	plūra
ABL.	———	plūre	plūribus	plūribus
VOC.	———	plūs	plūrēs	plūra

Dative of Possession

We are of course by now well used to using the genitive to show possession; we translate "Oswald's sword" as *gladius Oswaldī* without batting an eye. Now sometimes the dative grows jealous of the genitive possessing everything all the time, and so it occasionally gets in on the action. The dative joins up with *sum* (or a similar linking verb) to possess something like this:

> *Est Oswaldō hic gladius.* This sword is Oswald's (lit., "This sword is to Oswald," which isn't good English).
>
> *Nōmen mihi Oswaldus est.* My name is Oswald (lit., "The name to me is Oswald"; again, not the best English).

Make sure you translate the dative possession into *good* English. We don't go about saying, "The name to me is . . . ", so why should your translations? You can even translate it sometimes using a verb like "has" or "owns"—The first example, for instance, could be translated as "Oswald owns this sword" as well as "This sword is Oswald's."

If you really really want to know how the dative of possession is different from the genitive, and when you would want to use one over the other, the genitive places emphasize on the possessor. *Hic gladius Oswaldī est*—This sword belongs to Oswald and Oswald alone; don't you dare touch it! The dative, however, emphasizes the possession; *Est Oswaldō hic gladius*—Oswald owns this sword.

That may seem like a lot: all these exceptions and a whole new use of the dative. Don't worry. The big words like *plus* are pretty easy to learn, since they're built on a bunch of other nouns. But remember, practice makes perfect.

Review

Make sure you review demonstratives (*hic/haec/hoc, ille/illa/illud, iste/ista/istud*), relative pronouns (*quis, quae, quod*), and intensive pronouns (*ipse, ipsa, ipsum*).

Worksheet 5

A. Vocabulary and Grammar

Use your logic skills to determine all possible gender/number/case combinations of each noun-adjective phrase given below. Then translate these possibilities. The first one is done for you.

LATIN PHRASE	ALL POSSIBLE GENDER, NUMBER, & CASE COMBINATIONS	ALL POSSIBLE TRANSLATIONS
1. miserrimīs ovibus	fem. pl. dat., fem. pl. abl.	to/for the most/very wretched sheep, by/with/from the most wretched sheep
2. ōstium māius		
3. pessimī oculī		
4. animae graciliōris		
5. summum nēminem		
6. dissimillimōrum armōrum		
7. solī sacrificiō		
8. optimō sanguine		
9. silvae ultimae		
10. minimī sacerdōtis		

11. plurēs cervī		
12. deābus superīs		
13. humilia opera		
14. parte difficilī		
15. princeps melior		

B. Plain Ol' Grammar

Do a synopsis of *tendō* in the 1st person plural. Give principal parts first and imperatives afterward.

Principal Parts: tendō, _____

	INDICATIVE			
	ACTIVE		PASSIVE	
	LATIN	ENGLISH	LATIN	ENGLISH
PRES.				
IMPF.				
FUT.				
PERF.				
PLUPF.				
FT.PF.				

IMPERATIVE			
LAT. SG.	ENG. SG.	LAT. PL.	ENG. PL.

C. Memorization

Fill in the blanks for the Prologue through the Eighth Commandment.

_____
_____
_____
_____
_____
_____
_____
_____
_____
_____

5. Honora _____ _____ et _____ tuam ut _____ longevus _____ _____ quam _____ Deus _____ _____ tibi.

6. Non _____.

7. Non _____.

8. Non _____ facies.

D. English to Latin Translation

1. The leader who had more money was not more humble than the farmer whose children were hungry.

_____
_____
_____

2. The deepest parts of the sea will surrender all its dead on that day.

_____
_____

3. "Bread is good, but cookies are better!" said the smaller brother to the very ugly pirate.

_____
_____

4. The boys to whom I had given the easiest work did not walk into the fields that were farther than the farmhouse.

5. The holiest priest had handed the biggest cow over to the gods above as a sacrifice.

6. The black goat is worse than all other animals in the world because he is the enemy that we have feared for all time.

7. The evil young man desired to be nearer to the queen, but her heart was nearest to Oswald, whom she loved greatly.

8. I found a most grim beast in the lower caves of the earth, in which no one had been for very many years.

9. The spirits below, who do not have bodies, are always hastening toward the great river, the small boat, and beyond.

10. You were reading about the former king, who was the greatest leader of our land.

E. Latin to English Translation Translation

1 *Trōiānī Cȳclōpsque*

Ad *Ītaliam* et nostrum rēgnum novum nāvigāmus et ad īnsulam *Siciliam* appropinquāmus. *Clāmōsissimum* mare audīmus et ingentissima saxa vidēmus, et meus pater *Anchīsēs* "Cavēte!" inquit, "hic est *gurges Charybdis*!" *Rēmīs* tendimus sed *ter* portāmur in caelum gurgite; *ter* prae *descendimus*
5 ad īmās partēs. Dēnique, fessissimī et *ignārī* viae, ad lītora *Cȳclōpum* venimus. Est portus bonus, sed mōns ingentissimus, *Aetna*, sub quō gigās *Enceladus sepultus est*. Cum aliīs gigantibus deōs superōs pugnāverat, sed victus est et cum vulneribus sub hōc monte nunc dormit. Vertit et corpus eius terram *quatit*; spīritūs eius ignis sunt et saxa quae dē monte cadunt cremant.

Māne repentē *Graecus* quī immundus famēlicusque est ē silvīs ad lītora tendit. "Ego contrā vōs
10 in bellō Troiānō pugnāvī, sed mē ēripite!" clamat. "Aut mē nunc necāte! *Hīc* sunt gigantēs cum ūnō oculō!" Nōmen eī *Achaemenidēs* erat, et erat ūnus ex militibus *Ulixis* quī cum eō nāvigāvit. Nōbīs dē *caecitāte Polyphēmī* dīxit; sed ipse ab aliīs Graecīs quī sub ovibus fūgērunt relictus est. "Mē in diū silvīs occultāvī, sed nunc nāvigāte, aut vōs Polyphēmus inveniet et interficiet!"

Subitō ipse *Polyphēmus* ex silvīs vēnit, māior horrendiorque quam gigās dē quō cogitāverāmus.*
15 Et ambulat arbore quam *baculō* ad mare, in quō faciem ubī unus oculus ōlim fuerat lavat. Magnoperē terrēmur et ad nostrās nāvēs tendimus. *Polyphēmus* nostrōs rēmōs in marī audit, et īrātus ululat et aad nōs venit, sed salvī nāvigāmus. Sīc nōs et miserrimum *Graecum* ex īnsulā *Cyclōpum* ēripuimus.

Notes:
* *cogitāverāmus*: here, translate as "we imagined"

Glossary:
Achaemenidēs, -ae (m): Achaemenides, a Greek under Ulysses
Aetna, -ae (f): Etna, volcano on Sicily
Anchīsēs, -ae (m): Anchises, father of Aeneas
baculum, -ī (n): staff
caecitas, -tātis (f): blindness; here, "blinding"
Charybdis, -is (f): Charybdis: a whirlpool in the Straits of Messina between Italy and Sicily
clāmōsus, -a, -um: loud
Cȳclops, -ōpis (m): Cyclops, pl. *Cyclopes*
dēscendō, -ere, -scendī, -scensum: I descend, go down
Enceladus, -ī (m): Enceladus, a fire-breathing giant
Graecus, -a, -um: Greek, of Greece
gurges, -gitis (m): whirlpool
hīc: here, in this place
ignārus, -a, -um: ignorant
immundus, -a, -um: dirty, filthy
māne: in the morning, early
Ītalia, -ae (f): Italy
Polyphēmus, -ī (m): Polyphemus
quatiō, -ere, ——, quassus: I shake
rēmus, -ī (m): oar
sepeliō, -īre, -īvī, sepultus: I bury
Sicilia, -ae (f): Sicily
subitō: suddenly
ter: three times, thrice
Trōiānus, -a, -um: Trojan, of Troy
Ulixēs, -is (m): Ulysses (Odysseus)

Lesson 6

Verbs: Present Passive Infinitive, Present Passive Imperative, Deponents

Word List

Verbs

1. cōnfiteor, -ērī, -fessus sum *I confess*
2. cōnor, -ārī, cōnātus sum *I try, attempt*
3. ēgredior, -gredī, -gressus sum *I go out, march out*
4. ingredior, -gredī, -gressus sum *I go in, advance, undertake*
5. lābor, -ī, lapsus sum *I slip, fall, glide*
6. loquor, -quī, locūtus sum *I say, speak*
7. mīror, -ārī, mīrātus sum *I marvel at, am amazed at, admire*
8. misereor, -ērī, misertus sum (+gen. or + dat.) *I pity, have mercy on*
9. mōlior, -īrī, mōlītus sum *I labor, build, undertake*
10. morior, morī, mortuus sum *I die*
11. operor, -ārī, operātus sum *I work, labor, am busy*
12. orior, -īrī, oritus sum *I (a)rise, am born/created*
13. patior, -ī, passus sum *I suffer, endure*
14. revertor, -vertī, reversus sum *I turn back, return, go back*
15. sequor, -quī, secūtus sum *I follow*
16. vereor, -ērī, veritus sum *I respect, reverence, fear*

Adjectives

17. reliquus, -a, -um *remaining, rest (of)*
18. vastus, -a, -um *vast, enormous, desolate*

Adverbs

19. ita *so, thus, therefore*
20. māne *in the morning, early*

Memorization

Ego sum Dominus Deus tuus qui eduxi te de terra Aegypti de domo servitutis.

1. Non habebis deos alienos coram me.
2. Non facies tibi sculptile neque omnem similitudinem quae est in caelo desuper et quae in terra deorsum nec eorum quae sunt in aquis sub terra.
3. Non adsumes nomen Domini Dei tui in vanum.
4. Memento ut diem sabbati sanctifices.
5. Honora patrem tuum et matrem tuam ut sis longevus super terram quam Dominus Deus tuus dabit tibi
6. Non occides.
7. Non moechaberis.
8. Non furtum facies.
9. Non loqueris contra proximum tuum falsum testimonium.

   You shall not speak false testimony against your neighbor.

Grammar

Present Passive Infinitive

The present active infinitive has been known to us for quite some time now as the second principal part of the verb. We freely use it to form present, imperfect, and future actives and passives. We see the sentence *Dracōnem necāre debet* and without blinking (or even wincing) translate it as "He ought to kill the dragon." At other times, however, we may wish (for stylistic or deep personal reasons) to say "The dragon ought *to be killed*." This will require using a present *passive* infinitive.

The present passive infinitive ending is a simple -ī. For all the conjugations except the third (and third -iō), remove the -*e* off of the -*re* infinitive ending and add the ī:

1st Conjugation: *necāre*, to kill > *necār-* + *-ī* = *necārī*, to be killed

2nd Conjugation: *vidēre*, to see > *vidēr-* + *-ī* = *vidērī*, to be seen, to seem*

4th Conjugation: *audīre*, to hear > *audīr-* + *-ī* = *audīrī*, to be heard

The third conjugation likes to be different, so it and its -*iō* cousin drop their entire -*ere* ending and then take the -ī.

3rd Conjugation: *dūcere*, to lead > *dūc-* + *-ī* = *dūcī*, to be led

3rd -*iō* Conjugation: *capere*, to capture > *cap-* + *-ī* = *capī*, to be captured

Just to make sure you get this new infinitive form firmly entrenched in your mind, since it will be added to synopses from now on.

---

* Note: The special meaning of *videō* in the passive—if someone *is seen* to be kind, then he *seems* kind.

Present Passive Imperative

While we're on the subject of new passive forms, we may as well take a gander at the present passive imperative. Long ago (*KL1*, Ls. 11), you learned about the present active imperative: *Necā dracōnem! Necāte dracōnem!* Forming a singular imperative is quite easy; you merely drop the *-re* off of the 2nd principal part (a.k.a. present active infinitive), and there you are. The plural is formed simply by adding *-te* to that stem. The passive imperative will use the very same stem, and add *-re* for the singular and *-minī* for the plural.

Now this is where I must make a confession—I've been hiding something from you. Remember back in the day when we went over the present passive indicative (*KL2*, Lesson 4), I gave you the endings *-r, -ris, -tur, -mur, -minī, -ntur*. Here's where the little secret comes in—that second person singular actually has two possible forms, the *-ris* we are familiar with and also *-re*. (And this holds true for the imperfect, *-bāris* or *-bāre*, and the future, *-beris* or *-bere*). Thus both *necāris* and *necāre* mean "you are (being) killed." Note that the present passive imperative forms are identical to the 2nd person present passive indicatives: *necāre!* "be killed," using our alternate form, and the plural *necāminī!* "be killed." Moreover, as you may have also noticed (and see the chart below), that alternate ending *-re* gives us a form that looks exactly like the infinitive! Context will help decipher which form is being used, and this possible confusion is one reason I have kept this from you until now. Here is a chart listing the present imperative in both active and passive for all conjugations.

	SINGULAR	PLURAL
PRESENT ACTIVE IMPERATIVE	*present active stem* *necā!* kill! *vidē!* see! *duc!* [irreg.] lead! *cape!* capture! *audī!* hear!	*present active stem + -te* *necāte!* kill! (pl.) *vidēte!* see! (pl.) *ducite!* lead! (pl.) *capite!* capture! (pl.) *audīte!* hear! (pl.)
PRESENT PASSIVE IMPERATIVE	*present active stem + -re* *necāre!* be killed! *vidēre!* be seen! seem! *ducere!* be led! *capere!* be captured! *audīre!* be heard!	*present active stem + -minī* *necāminī!* be killed! (pl.) *vidēminī!* be seen! seem! (pl.) *duciminī!* be led! (pl.) *capiminī!* be captured! (pl.) *audīminī!* be heard! (pl.)

You may already have guessed that passive imperatives do not appear as frequently as active ones, and you are correct. However, learning the forms is helpful for when you do run across them, and, as you will soon learn, it will assist you with deponent verbs. Present passive imperatives will also appear on synopses from henceforth.

Deponents

Deponent verbs were briefly introduced in the grammatical introduction of *Kraken Latin 1*. Put most simply, a deponent verb is *passive in form, active in meaning*. Think of the deponent as a spy—an active fellow swathed in a mysterious passive cloak. A lot of Latin deponent verbs are intransitive (they don't take a direct object) or are reflexive in some way (the action affects the subject).

Deponents can be difficult to grasp. First off, let's go over a deponent verb's principal parts. There are usually three, the passive versions of a normal verb's principal parts: *cōnor, cōnārī, cōnātus sum*, meaning "I try, attempt." *Cōnor* is the first person singular present passive indicative form of the verb, and means "I try." Notice that although the *form* is passive, the *meaning* is active. The second principal part *cōnārī* is the present passive infinitive, "to try." The third principal part *cōnātus sum* is first person singular perfect passive indicative, "I tried, have tried."

To determine which conjugation a deponent verb belongs to, go to the second principal part (just like with normal verbs). Now you have to get a little creative. When you see that present passive infinitive ending, you have to think "Now what would the active counterpart be if it existed?" Then you will be able to identify the conjugation with confidence. Here are some examples, one from each conjugation.

- *cōnor, cōnārī, cōnātus sum*: Go to the second principal part and find the present passive infinitive ending, *-ārī*. This is the passive version of *-āre*, and thus *cōnor* is a first conjugation verb.
- *cōnfiteor, -ērī, -fessus sum*: The second principal part is *cōnfitērī*, and by looking back at the first principal part we can see that the stem is *confit-*. The active equivalent of *-ērī* is *-ēre*, so hello second conjugation!
- *loquor, -quī, locūtus sum*: This is where it gets a little more interesting. You may freeze up when you see *loquī* since it's so short. Just remember that *-ī* is the passive infinitive ending that replaces the entire *-ere* for the third conjugation. When you take that *-ī* off, you are left with the stem *loqu-*. Look at the first principal part. Since there is no *-i-* between the *loqu-* and the *-or*, then this is a simple third conjugation verb and not a third *-iō*.
- *ēgredior, -gredī, -gressus sum*: Analyzing this verb begins in a similar fashion to that of *loquor*. The present passive infinitive ending is a simple *-ī*, and so then we check the first principal part. The stem *ēgred-* is followed by an extra *-i-* and then there is the *-or* ending. Thus, this is a third *-iō* verb.
- *orior, -īrī, ortus sum*: The infinitive of this verb is *orīrī*, and has the full *-īrī* ending. This is the passive equivalent of *-īre*, which is of course the infinitive of a fourth conjugation verb.

Go through each of the deponent verbs in this lesson's word list and practice identifying the conjugation. Here are the answers for you for this lesson!

1. cōnfiteor, -ērī, -fessus sum: *2nd conjugation*
2. cōnor, -ārī, cōnātus sum: *1st conjugation*
3. ēgredior, -gredī, -gressus sum: *3rd -iō conjugation*
4. ingredior, -gredī, -gressus sum: *3rd -iō conjugation*
5. lābor, -ī, lapsus sum: *3rd conjugation*
6. loquor, -quī, locūtus sum: *3rd conjugation*

7. mīror, -ārī, mīrātus sum: *1st conjugation*
8. misereor, -ērī, misertus sum (+gen.): *2nd conjugation*
9. mōlior, -īrī, mōlītus sum: *4th conjugation*
10. morior, morī, mortuus sum: *3rd -iō conjugation*
11. operor, -ārī, operātus sum: *1st conjugation*
12. orior, -īrī, ortus sum: *4th conjugation*
13. patior, -ī, passus sum: *3rd -iō conjugation*
14. revertor, -vertī, reversus sum: *3rd conjugation*
15. sequor, -quī, secūtus sum: *3rd conjugation*
16. vereor, -ērī, veritus sum: *2nd conjugation*

Now it is high time that we actually conjugate one of these verbs. Since a deponent verb is generally passive in form, active in meaning, we will only need to conjugate it in the passive. In other words, it will have about half the forms of a normal verb!

Let us start with our old friend, the first conjugation, and go over how a deponent verb will look and be translated.

Full Indicative Conjugation of *cōnor, -ārī, cōnātus sum*: I try, attempt

		SINGULAR		PLURAL	
		LATIN	ENGLISH	LATIN	ENGLISH
INDICATIVE	PRES.	cōnor	I try	cōnāmur	we try
		cōnāris	you try	cōnāminī	you (pl.) try
		cōnātur	he tries	cōnantur	they try
	IMPF.	cōnābar	I was trying	cōnābāmur	we were trying
		cōnābāris	you were trying	cōnābāminī	you (pl.) were trying
		cōnābātur	he was trying	cōnābantur	they were trying
	FUT.	cōnābor	I will try	cōnābimur	we will try
		cōnāberis	you will try	cōnābiminī	you (pl.) will try
		cōnābitur	he will try	cōnābuntur	they will try
	PERF.	cōnātus/a/um sum	I (have) tried	cōnātī/ae/a sumus	we (have) tried
		cōnātus/a/um es	you (have) tried	cōnātī/ae/a estis	you (pl.) (have) tried
		cōnātus/a/um est	he (has) tried	cōnātī/ae/a sunt	they (have) tried
	PLUPF.	cōnātus/a/um eram	I had tried	cōnātī/ae/a erāmus	we had tried
		cōnātus/a/um erās	you had tried	cōnātī/ae/a erātis	you (pl.) had tried
		cōnātus/a/um erat	he had tried	cōnātī/ae/a erant	they had tried
	FT.PF.	cōnātus/a/um erō	I will have tried	cōnātī/ae/a erimus	we will have tried
		cōnātus/a/um eris	you will have tried	cōnātī/ae/a eritis	you (pl.) will have tried
		cōnātus/a/um erit	he will have tried	cōnātī/ae/a erunt	they will have tried

There are no new endings to be learned here! Once you grasp the concept of the deponent and are able to translate those passive forms actively, you will have no trouble with them. How will you know when a verb is deponent? You must memorize which ones are born deponent. If a verb is listed in the dictionary and has that passive *-r* ending on the first principal part rather than *-ō*, then it's a deponent. This is yet another reason to not go easy on memorizing vocabulary.

And so now we can discuss deponent imperatives. As with regular verbs (see above), the present imperative for deponents is the same as the present indicative 2nd person singular (alternative ending) and 2nd person plural. Recall that the subject of an imperative is an implied 2nd person: "Kill the dragon!" is aimed at you—"(You) Kill the dragon!" So if the king wanted to tell Oswald, "Try to kill the dragon!" then he would take the 2nd person singular present passive deponent form, but rather than using *cōnāris* would use that alternative ending, *cōnāre*: "*Cōnāre dracōnem necāre!*" (Looks fun with that other infinitive, doesn't it?) The plural imperative is identical to the 2nd person plural present passive deponent indicative, and so the king can tell all of his knights, "*Cōnāminī dracōnem necāre!*" "Try to kill the dragon!"

Deponent Imperative

LAT. SG.	ENG. SG.	LAT. PL.	ENG. PL.
cōnāre!	try!	cōnāminī!	try! (pl.)

Whew. And that is how a deponent is conjugated. Examples of deponents from the other conjugations appear in the appendix. I will mention a few forms of interest here, but for other questions refer to the appendix. First, I suppose I should give an imperative example from each conjugation just to make sure things are clear.

CONJ.	PRES. INFINITIVE	LAT. SG.	ENG. SG.	LAT. PL.	ENG. PL.
1ST	cōnārī	cōnāre!	try!	cōnāminī!	try! (pl.)
2ND	cōnfitērī	cōnfitēre!	confess!	cōnfitēminī!	confess! (pl.)
3RD	loquī	loquere!	speak!	loquiminī!	speak! (pl.)
3RD -IŌ	ēgredī	ēgredere!	go out!	ēgrediminī!	go out! (pl.)
4TH	orīrī	orīre!	rise!	orīminī!	rise! (pl.)

Be careful to the vowel changes in the 3rd, 3rd *-iō*, and 4th conjugations, particularly in the present and future tenses. Present vowels are *o, i, i, i, i, u* (or *iu*), while the future vowels are *a, e, e, e, e, e*. Here are side by side comparisons of these tenses using an example verb from each conjugation:

Present Indicative of *loquor*

	LATIN SINGULAR	LATIN PLURAL
1ST	loquor	loquimur
2ND	loqueris	loquiminī
3RD	loquitur	loquuntur

Future Indicative of *loquor*

	LATIN SINGULAR	LATIN PLURAL
1ST	loquar	loquēmur
2ND	loquēris	loquēminī
3RD	loquētur	loquentur

Present Indicative of *orior*

	LATIN SINGULAR	LATIN PLURAL
1ST	orior	orīmur
2ND	orīris	orīminī
3RD	orītur	oriuntur

Future Indicative of *orior*

	LATIN SINGULAR	LATIN PLURAL
1ST	oriar	oriēmur
2ND	oriēris	oriēminī
3RD	oriētur	orientur

The trickiest forms above are the 2nd person singulars. Remember that the Romans did not like the grating sound of a short *i* next to that *r*, so rather than *-iris*, the ending is *-eris*. You should pay attention to the macrons here, since *loqueris* means "you speak" and *loquēris* is "you will speak." The Romans did not mind using a long *ī* with the *r*, and so had no problem saying *orīris*. Make sure that, when you are reviewing forms, you are still paying attention to those pesky macrons. It really can help you figure things out.

The Deponent Synopsis

In this book I will be using only one template for a verb synopsis, whether that verb is normal or a deponent, so you need to know how to fill in this chart correctly. If you are faced with a deponent verb, then you simply need to cross out or fill in the boxes you won't need (see below). Since deponent verbs generally have passive forms in the indicative, they don't need the active boxes. You can fill in the "active" English translation in the passive boxes to keep things simple. Here is an example synopsis of *cōnfiteor* in the 3rd person singular:

		ACTIVE		PASSIVE	
		LATIN	ENGLISH	LATIN	ENGLISH
INDICATIVE	PRES.			cōnfitētur	he confesses
	IMPF.			cōnfitēbatur	he was confessing
	FUT.			cōnfitēbitur	he will confess
	PERF.			confessus/a/um est	he (has) confessed
	PLUPF.			confessus/a/um erat	he had confessed
	FT.PF.			confessus/a/um erit	he will have confessed
INF.	PRES.			cōnfitērī	to confess
IMP.	SG.			cōnfitēre!	confess!
	PL.			cōnfitēminī!	confess! (pl.)

Parsing a Deponent

I like to tweak parsing just a little bit for deponents. Parsing a normal verb entails, of course, listing off that verb's Person/Number/Tense/Voice/Mood (the five attributes). *Necatus est* is parsed 3rd person singular, perfect passive indicative of *necō*. Now let's parse the corresponding form in a deponent verb, *confessus est*: 3rd person singular, perfect passive deponent indicative of *cōnfiteor*. Just a tiny difference between the two—I like including that "deponent" in there, because that way you know that this is a deponent verb, not just the passive of a normal verb.

Semi-Deponents

As the name suggests, some verbs are normal in certain forms and deponent in others. You have already learned two fairly common semi-deponents: *audeō, -ēre, ausus sum* (KL1, Ls. 11) and *gaudeō, -ēre, gavisus sum* (KL2, Ls. 6). By looking at the principal parts you can see that the present systems of both of these verbs (present, imperfect, and future) are normal, but their perfect systems (perfect, pluperfect, and future perfect) are deponent.

Although you may be skeptical at this point, seriously, deponents are not as difficult as they may seem at first. As long as you learn which verbs are deponent, you will not have trouble translating them! You know all the passive forms already, so this should be a cinch.

Review

Be sure to review some of the weird adjectives. In particular, look at *solus, miser, pulcher, celer, similis, dissimilis, difficilis, facilis, gracilis, humilis,* and *plus*.

Worksheet 6

A. Vocabulary

1. morior: _____
2. who: _____
3. vereor: _____
4. I slip: _____
5. vast: _____
6. mōlior: _____
7. sīc: _____
8. ingredior: _____
9. early: _____
10. sequor: _____
11. cōnfiteor: _____
12. mīror: _____
13. loquor: _____
14. beyond: _____
15. I work: _____
16. I go out: _____
17. reliquus: _____
18. ita: _____
19. I suffer: _____
20. perchance: _____
21. misereor (+gen.): _____
22. I return: _____
23. orior: _____
24. I attempt: _____
25. quidem: _____

B. Grammar

1. Conjugate and translate *patior* fully in the present system (present, imperfect, future).

	SINGULAR		PLURAL	
	LATIN	ENGLISH	LATIN	ENGLISH
PRES.				
IMPF.				
FUT.				

2. Conjugate and translate *vereor* fully in the perfect system (perfect, pluperfect, future perfect).

	SINGULAR		PLURAL	
	LATIN	ENGLISH	LATIN	ENGLISH
PERF.				
PLUPERF.				
FUT. PF.				

3. Do a synopsis of *morior* in the 2nd person singular. First give principal parts and identify conjugation, and include the imperatives.

Principal Parts: _____

		ACTIVE		PASSIVE	
		LATIN	ENGLISH	LATIN	ENGLISH
INDICATIVE	PRES.				
	IMPF.				
	FUT.				
	PERF.				
	PLUPF.				
	FT.PF.				
INF.	PRES.				
IMP.	SING.				
	PL.				

4. Decline *any vast gate*.

	LATIN SINGULAR	LATIN PLURAL
NOM.		
GEN.		
DAT.		
ACC.		
ABL.		
VOC.		

C. Memorization

Fill in the blanks for the Prologue through the Ninth Commandment.

_____

_____

6. Non _____.

7. Non _____.

8. Non _____ facies.

9. Non _____ contra _____ tuum _____ testimonium.

D. English to Latin Translation

Translate these sentences into Latin. If an English verb has a few Latin options, make sure you pick the deponent one for practice!

1. The young man tried to follow the very beautiful woman with flowers, but she did not pity him.

   _____

   _____

2. The first priest reverenced the ancient gods with more sacrifices than the other priest, but nevertheless a sheep sat on him and he died.

   _____

   _____

   _____

3. Perchance the soldiers will march out to the nearest town and then will dare to remain at my aunt's house and eat all her food.

   _____

   _____

   _____

4. The giant who was running over the highest mountain slipped and the whole earth moved.

5. The noble queen had once built very many farmhouses for the most wretched citizens, who marveled at her good heart.

6. In the morning some sheep were going into the field, but the rest (who were worse animals) attacked the farmer and his sons.

7. Therefore the angry mothers spoke: "Children, always follow us in the vast woods!"

8. Your leader, to whom I did not confess my very bad deed, is plumper and the proudest

9. Will the sun rise early on this day, and at night will it return to those mountains beyond?

10. O Lord, have mercy on us, because we have not followed Your law.

E. Latin to English Translation

1 **Perseus et Gorgō**

Perseus erat fīlius fēminae *mortālis*, *Danaē*, et rēgis *immortālis* deōrum, *Iuppiter*. *Ōrāculum Danaēs* patrī, cui nōmen erat *Ācrisius*, locūtum erat: "Fīlius tuae fīliae tē ūnō diē interficiet." Īta *Ācrisius Danaem* et īnfantem *Persēum* in *arcā līgneā* posuit et eam in marī vastissimō mīsit. *Arca* ex marī ab *piscātōre* in īnsulā
5 longinquā erepta est. Post multōs annōs, *Perseus* adulescēns erat, et *piscātōris* frāter, quī rēx īnsulae erat, *Danaem* in matrimōniō magnoperē dūcere* cupīvit. *Perseus* rēgī nōn *confīsus est*, hoc matrimōnium itaque nōn cupīvit. Ergō rēx *Persēum āmittere* cōnābātur. Epulās māximās dedit et omnibus *hospitibus* locūtus est: "Portāte mihi dōnum ad epulās!" Reliquī *hospitēs* equōs dedērunt, sed *Perseus* dīxit: "Quod rogābis, tibi dabō." Rēx eī locūtus est: "Mihi caput *Medūsae* portā!" *Medūsa*, fēmina horrendissima cum
10 serpentibus quam *capillīs*, ūna ex tribus *Gorgonibus* erat. Oculī eius hominēs in lapidem mūtāre poterat.

Perseus auxilium ab *Minervā* quaesīvit, quae eī locūta est: "Invenī *Hesperidēs* et eīs optima arma rogā." *Prīmum* vēnit ad *Graeās*, trēs sorōrēs *Gorgonum*, quae sōlum ūnum oculum quem inter eās *commūnicābant* habēbant. Perseus oculum eārum ēripuit, itaque auxiliō eārum *Hesperidēs* invēnit. Eae *nymphae* quae in pulcherrimō *hortō* in vespere* habitābant erant. *Perseō saccum* in quō caput *Medūsae tūtē* portāre poterit
15 dedērunt. Gladium ab Iove, *galeam* tenebrārum ab *Plūtōne*, *soleās pennātās* ab *Mercuriō*, et scūtum *aēneum* ab *Minervā* quoque accēpit. Hīs armīs fortissimīs ad spēluncam *Gorgonum* volāvit. *Leviter* ingressus est, sed *Medūsam* dormiēbat—Perseus eam in scūtō spectāvit! Ad eam *levissimē* appropinquāvit, et caput eius *praecīdit*! Aliae duae *Gorgonēs* eum *persecūtae sunt*, sed *galeā* tenebrārum *soleīsque pennātīs ēlapsus est*.

Perseus domum* volāvit, ubī rēx pessimus mātrem Perseī *persecūtus est*. Perseus eī caput Medūsae
20 ostendit et in lapidem ille mūtātus est. Deinde Perseus deīs arma trādidit, et Athēnae caput Medūsae dedit. Ea id in scūtō, quod *aegis* saepe appellātum est, posuit. *Trīste* ōrāculum dē *Ācrisiō* tunc *complētum est* quōd Perseus *discum* iaciēbat et forte *Ācrisium* percussit et eum interfēcit.

Notes:
* *in matrimōniō ... dūcere:* Remember that *dūcere in matrimōniō* is an idiom for "to marry"; lit., "to lead in marriage."
* *vespere: vesper* can also mean "west"
* *domum:* With certain common nouns (such as *domus*) and the names of cities, a preposition showing motion toward (such as *ad*) was omitted. Similarly, in English we say "Perseus flew home"; we don't say "Perseus flew to home."

Glossary:
Ācrisius, -ī (m): Acrisius, king of Argos and father of Danaë
aegis, -gidis (f): an aegis (a shield often indicating a god's protection; Athena's aegis is perhaps the most well-known)
aēneus, -a, -um: (made of) bronze or copper
āmittō, -ere, -mīsī, -missum: I send away
arca, -ae (f): box, chest
capillus, -ī (m): hair
commūnicō (1): I share
compleō, -ēre, -plēvī, -plētum: I fulfill, fill up
confīdō, -ere, confīsus sum (+dat.) (semi-deponent): I trust, have confidence in

Danaē, -ēs [3rd decl.] (f): Danaë, the mother of Perseus
discus, -ī (m): discus
ēlābor, -lābī, -lapsus sum: I slip away, escape
galea, -ae (f): helmet
Gorgō, -onis (f): a Gorgon; the three Gorgons were daughters of Phorcus—Medusa was mortal but Stheno and Euryale immortal
Graeae, -ārum (f, pl): the Graeae (lit., "old women" or "gray ones") in Greek mythology shared one eye between them and were sisters of the Gorgons
Hesperidēs, -um (f, pl.): the Hesperides, nymphs who lived in a garden in the west guarding golden apples
hortus, -ī (m): garden
hospes, -pitis (m): guest
immortālis, -e: immortal
Iuppiter, Iovis (dat. Iovī, acc. Iovem, abl. Iove) (m): Jupiter, Jove, Roman equivalent of Zeus
leviter: softly, lightly; superlative *levissimē*
līgneus, -a, -um: wooden
Medūsa, -ae (f): Medusa, once a beautiful woman but now a Gorgon with snake hair

Mercurius, -ī (m): Mercury, messenger god (Roman equivalent of Hermes)
Minerva, -ae (f): Minerva, goddess of wisdom (Roman equivalent of Athena)
mortālis, -e: mortal
nympha, -ae (f): nymph
ōrāculum, -ī (n): oracle
ostendō, -ere, -dī, -sum/tum: I show, point out, declare
pennātus, -a, -ūm: winged
persequor, -quī, -secūtus sum: I pursue, chase
Perseus, -ī (m): Perseus
piscātor, -ōris (m): fisherman
Plūto, -tōnis (m): Pluto, god of the underworld (Roman equivalent of Hades)
praecīdō, -ere, -cīdī, -cīsum: I cut off, lop
prīmum (adv. from prīmus): first, at first
saccus, -ī (m): sack, bag
solea, -ae (f): sandal
trīste (adv. from trīstis): sadly
tūtē (adv. from tūtus): safely

F. For Fun

Match each mythological hero to his own great deed, quest, or the monster he slew. Some heroes have more than one answer!

HERO	GREAT DEED, QUEST, OR MONSTER SLAIN
1. Achilles	a. Captured the Erymanthian Boar
	b. Thought of the Trojan Horse plan
	c. Stole the belt of Hippolyta, Queen of the Amazons
	d. Slew the Chimaera, a fire-breathing monster with a lion's head, goat's body, and serpent's tail
2. Amphitryon	e. Slew the Lernean Hydra
	f. Tamed Pegasus
	g. Captured the Cretan Bull
3. Bellerophon	h. Defeated the Teumessian Fox, a huge vixen destined never to be caught
	i. Obtained the Golden Fleece
4. Diomedes	j. Greatest Greek hero in the Trojan War who killed Hector
	k. Slew the Caledonian Boar
	l. Stole the apples of the Hesperides
5. Hercules	m. Slew Medusa
	n. Spent 10 years sailing home after the Trojan War and had many adventures
6. Jason	o. Slew the sea monster Cetus to save Andromeda
	p. Cleaned the Augean stables in one day
7. Meleagar	q. Mighty Greek warrior who went on night missions with Ulysses and even fought with the gods
	r. Slew the Stymphalian Birds
8. Ulysses	s. Stole the Mares of Diomedes
	t. Slew the Minotaur
9. Perseus	u. Slew the Nemean Lion
	v. Stole the cattle of Geryon
10. Theseus	w. Slew Procrustes, a bandit who forced travelers to fit into his iron bed by stretching them or cutting off their legs
	x. Captured Diana's Golden Deer
	y. Captured Cerberus, three-headed guard dog of Hades, and brought him back

Lesson 7

Adverbs: Formation and Comparison; Questions (-ne, nōnne, num)

Word List

Nouns

1. annus, -ī (m) *year*
2. arx, arcis (f) *citadel, fort; hill*
3. cīvis, -is (m/f) *citizen*
4. cīvitās, -tātis (f) *city, state, citizenship*
5. locus, -ī (m) *place*; loca, -ōrum (n, pl) *places [geographic]*; locī, -ōrum (m, pl) *places, passages, topics [in a book]*
6. nūmen, -minis (n) *divinity, god, divine will*

Verbs

7. impleō, -ēre, -plēvī, -plētum *I fill up, satisfy, complete*
8. oblīvīscor, -vīscī, oblītus sum (+gen.) *I forget*
9. proficīscor, -ficīscī, -fectus sum *I start, set out*

Adverbs

10. facile *easily*
11. magis *more, rather*
12. māximē *most, especially, very*
13. parum *(too) little, not enough*
14. minus *less*
15. minimē *least, not at all*
16. melius *better*
17. optimē *best*
18. pēius *worse*
19. pessimē *worst*

20. multum *much*

21. plūrimum *most*

22. prīmum/prīmō *(at) first*

Interrogative Adverbs/Enclitics

23. -ne *interrogative enclitic indicating a simple yes/no question*

24. nōnne *interrogative adverb expecting a yes answer*

25. num *interrogative adverb expecting a no answer*

Memorization

Ego sum Dominus Deus tuus qui eduxi te de terra Aegypti de domo servitutis.

1. Non habebis deos alienos coram me.
2. Non facies tibi sculptile neque omnem similitudinem quae est in caelo desuper et quae in terra deorsum nec eorum quae sunt in aquis sub terra.
3. Non adsumes nomen Domini Dei tui in vanum.
4. Memento ut diem sabbati sanctifices.
5. Honora patrem tuum et matrem tuam ut sis longevus super terram quam Dominus Deus tuus dabit tibi
6. Non occides.
7. Non moechaberis.
8. Non furtum facies.
9. Non loqueris contra proximum tuum falsum testimonium.
10. Non concupisces domum proximi tui nec desiderabis uxorem eius non servum non ancillam non bovem non asinum nec omnia quae illius sunt.

    You shall not covet your neighbor's house nor desire his wife nor [his] servant nor [his] maidservant nor [his] cow nor [his] donkey nor any of the things which are his.

Grammar

Formation of Adverbs

Although you have been learning lots of adverbs in your vocabulary lists, we have not yet discussed how to form an adverb. An adverb, as you may have learned from studying English grammar, is a word that modifies a verb, adjective, or another adverb. How do we form adverbs in English? The most obvious way is simply to add an *-ly* to an adjective: The fox is *quick* → The fox runs *quickly*; That man is *grim* → That man smiled *grimly*. A fun tidbit is that *friendlily* is actually a word, as in "She is *friendly*" vs. "She looked at me *friendlily*."

Granted, it is a bit difficult to say (especially three times fast), so usually we use "friendly" as the adverb or rephrase it "in a friendly manner." Some English adverbs are not formed from adjectives, however, and are called "independent adverbs" (e.g., Look over *there*!). And, still other adverbs are identical to their related adjectives: The fox is *fast*. The fox runs *fast*. That rock is *hard*. He hit me *hard* with that rock.

In Latin, there are also adverbs formed from adjectives, independent adverbs, and adverbs that are identical to some adjective forms. From the beginning you have been learning independent adverbs (*sīc, īta, māne,* etc.), and now you only need to learn a few simple principles on the formation of regular adverbs.

To form an adverb from many of the 1st/2nd declension adjectives, simply add *-ē* to the stem. You have already learned *male* from *malus*—granted, *male* ends with a short *-e*, but it still illustrates the principle. Adding this *-ē* is like adding *-ly* in English. Some examples:

ADJECTIVE	POSITIVE ADVERB
superbus, -a, -um *proud*	superbē *proudly*
miser, -era, -erum *wretched*	miserē *wretchedly*
pulcher, -chra, -chrum *beautiful*	pulchrē *beautifully*

To form an adverb from most 3rd declension adjectives, add *-ter* or *-iter* to stem (avoid a double *-tt-*): *fortis, -e* → *fortiter*; *prudēns, -ntis* → *prudenter* (not *prudentter*). [Note: When a stem ends in *-nt-*, you are actually only adding an *-er*, but I find it easier to remember *-iter/-ter* rather than *-iter/-er*.

ADJECTIVE	POSITIVE ADVERB
celer, -eris, -ere *swift*	celeriter *swiftly*
potēns, -entis *powerful*	potenter *powerfully*

Of course, some 1st/2nd declension adjectives will have an adverb formed both with the *-ē* and with a *-ter*—*miserē* and *miseriter* from *miser*, for example. However, you should be able to recognize and translate these words as adverbs from *miser*.

Some adverbs are taken from a particular form of the adjective, the neuter accusative singular, to be precise. Two examples from this lesson's vocabulary are as follows:

ADJECTIVE	POSITIVE ADVERB
facilis, -e *easy*	10. facile *easily*
multus, -a, -um *much*	20. multum *much*

Sometimes the neuter ablative singular is also used adverbially. You have already learned *forte* (*KL2*, Lesson 3), which is the ablative of the noun *fors, fortis* (f), "chance, fortune, luck."

If you are starting to panic a bit about the vagueness of all of this adverb formation, rest easy. I will not be asking you to form adverbs on any quizzes or tests, even though you might in a few exercises. These trends and patterns are useful to learn, however, because they can help you recognize an unfamiliar adverb for what it is and translate it without having to look it up.

Comparison of Adverbs

Forming positive adverbs is difficult, but the comparative and superlative are fairly easy to form. **The comparative adverb** (as in the English "more quickly") **is the same as the neuter singular accusative form of the comparative adjective.** This is true even of irregular adjectives. **The superlative adverb is formed by adding -ē to the stem of the superlative adjective form.** Here are some examples:

ADJECTIVE	ADVERB
The king is proud. *Rēx **superbus** est.*	The king walks proudly. *Rēx **superbē** ambulat.*
The king is rather proud. *Rēx **superbior** est.*	The king walks rather proudly. *Rēx **superbius** ambulat.*
The king is very proud. *Rēx **superbissimus** est.*	The king walks very proudly. *Rēx **superbissimē** ambulat.*
This is a good song. *Hoc carmen **bonum** est.*	He sings well. ***Bene*** *cantat.*
This is a better song. *Hoc carmen **melius** est.*	He sings better. ***Melius*** *cantat.*
This is the best song. *Hoc carmen **optimum** est.*	He sings the best. ***Optimē*** *cantat.*

If you are worried about how they will be able to distinguish between the comparative adverb and the neuter singular accusative comparative adjective, I'm sure you know what the answer is—context! If there is not another neuter singular accusative for the word in question to modify (such as *melius* in the examples above), then it is an adverb rather than an adjective.

Translational Note

Observe in the examples above that comparative and superlative adverbs can be translated similarly to their corresponding adverbs. In other words, *superbius* does not always mean "more proudly," but can also mean "rather proudly" or "too proudly." *Superbissimē* can mean "very proudly" as well as "most proudly."

And of course there will always be irregular adverbs. Some of the more common irregular adverbs are included in this lesson's word list; others happening to occur in this text will be noted as they appear. Notice that in the chart below, some are quite irregular (*magnoperē* and *magis*, for example), but others are formed predictably even though they are derived from an irregular adjective. Thus *bene*, *melius*, and *optimē* are listed as "irregular," even though you can form them easily (well, except perhaps for *bene*, but you've known that word from forever ago) if you know the irregular comparison of *bonus* → *melior* → *optimus*.

	ORIGINAL ADJECTIVE	POSITIVE ADVERB	COMPARATIVE ADVERB	SUPERLATIVE ADVERB
	facilis, -e *easy*	10. facile *easily*	facilius *more easily*	facillimē *most easily*
	magnus, -a, -um *large, great*	magnoperē *greatly*	11. magis *more, rather*	12. māximē *most, especially, very*
	parvus, -a, -um *small, little*	13. parum *(too) little, not enough*	14. minus *less*	15. minimē *least, not at all*
IRREGULAR	bonus, -a, -um *good*	bene *well*	16. melius *better*	17. optimē *best*
	malus, -a, -um *bad*	male *badly*	18. pēius *worst*	19. pessimē *worst*
	multus, -a, -um *much*	20. multum *much*	plūs *more*	21. plūrimum *most*
	——	[prō]	prius *before, earlier*	22. prīmō/prīmum *(at) first*
	——	diū *for a long time*	diūtius *longer*	diūtissimē *very long*

Questions (*-ne, nōnne, num*)

You have already been translating some simple questions, and have seen that in Latin, direct questions use the indicative mood. In English, we often rearrange the word order to indicate a question:

(Statement) Oswald killed the dragon.

(Question) Did Oswald kill the dragon?

Notice that we also use the helping verb "did" and put it at the beginning of the sentence to indicate that we are asking a question. Of course we can also use tone of voice and our handy question mark: *Oswald killed the dragon?* (However, notice the slight change of meaning here—without that helping verb at the beginning, this question expresses surprise or even skepticism.)

Usually in Latin there will be some kind of interrogative word showing us that we do indeed have a question. Rearranging the word order (as in English) is not required, although it can be done for emphasis. One common way to ask a question is to attach the enclitic *-ne* (see definition of "enclitic" above under the word list teaching notes) to the emphatic word in the sentence, and put that word at the beginning of the question:

Necāvitne Oswaldus dracōnem? Did Oswald *kill* the dragon? (Could be a simple question asking whether the dragon-slaying happened or not, or perhaps could be asking did he *kill* it as opposed to merely wounding it.)

Oswaldusne dracōnem necāvit? Did *Oswald* kill the dragon? (Implied: Did Oswald do this, as opposed to someone else?)

Dracōnemne Oswaldus necāvit? Did Oswald kill the *dragon*? (Implied: Did he kill the dragon, or some other creature?)

As seen in these examples, the interrogative enclitic *-ne* not only asks a question, but it is asking a so-called "simple" question—it merely expects a yes or no answer. The word *nōnne* (or *-ne* added to another negative word; *nōnne = nōn + -ne*), however, expects a "yes" answer.

Nōnne Oswaldus dracōnem necāvit? Didn't Oswald kill the dragon? Oswald killed the dragon, didn't he?

Notice that in English we have a couple of ways to translate this question—basically, any way that shows you are expecting a "yes" will work (and sometimes this seems easier when using one's tone of voice to help out!). If you want to ask a question expecting a "no" answer, then you will use the word *num*:

Num Oswald dracōnem necāvit? Oswald didn't kill the dragon, did he?

Sometimes students have a hard time distinguishing these two types of questions in English as well as in Latin. Here's a few more scenarios in case the difference isn't clear:

Did you clean your room? (Simple question; use *-ne*)

You cleaned your room, didn't you? (Expects "yes"; use *nōnne*)

Didn't you clean your room? (or the more archaic *Did you not clean your room?*) (Expects "yes"; use *nōnne*)

You didn't clean your room, did you? (Expects "no"; use *num*).

Review

Be sure to review your relative pronoun (*Quis, quae, quod*), intensives (*ipse, ipsa, ipsum*), and demonstratives (*hic, ille, iste*).

Worksheet 7

A. Vocabulary

1. places (in a book): _____
2. places (in the world): _____
3. impleō, -ēre, -plēvī, -plētum: _____
4. nūmen: _____
5. oblīvīscor, -vīscī, oblītus sum (+___.): _____
6. year: _____
7. arx: _____
8. proficīscor, -ficīscī, -fectus sum: _____
9. citizenship: _____
10. citizen: _____

Write a little story in English in which you use at least seven of your new Latin adverbs—simply use the Latin adverb in the midst of the English. (Choose from *facile, magis, māximē, parum, minus, minimē, melius, optimē, pēius, pessimē, multum, plūrimum,* and *prīmum* or *prīmō.*)

Example macaronic sentence: I am such an amazing student I can read 500 pages in one night *facile*.

B. Grammar

1. Decline "that worst place" (use *iste*), but remember that our word for "place" has two plural options, so go ahead and decline both. For fun.

	LATIN SINGULAR	LATIN MASCULINE PLURAL	LATIN NEUTER PLURAL
N			
G			
D			
AC			
AB			
V			

2. Verb Synopsis:

   Do a synopsis of *impleō* in the 1st person plural, first writing out the principal parts:

   impleō, _____

		ACTIVE		PASSIVE	
		LATIN	ENGLISH	LATIN	ENGLISH
INDICATIVE	PRES.				
	IMPF.				
	FUT.				
	PERF.				
	PLUPF.				
	FT.PF.				
INF.	PRES.				
IMP.	SING.				
	PL.				

Do a synopsis of *oblīvīscor* in the 1st person singular, first writing out the principal parts: *oblīvīscor*, _____

		ACTIVE		PASSIVE	
		LATIN	ENGLISH	LATIN	ENGLISH
INDICATIVE	PRES.				
	IMPF.				
	FUT.				
	PERF.				
	PLUPF.				
	FT.PF.				
INF.	PRES.				
IMP.	SING.				
	PL.				

C. Memorization

Fill in the blanks for the Prologue through Tenth Commandment.

_____
_____
_____
_____
_____
_____
_____
_____
_____
_____
_____
_____
_____
_____

9. Non _____ contra _____ tuum _____.

10. Non _____ domum _____ tui nec _____ _____ eius non _____ non _____ non _____ non asinum ___ _____ quae _____ sunt.

D. English to Latin Translation

1. Over the desolate mountains the dragon glided more easily than a bird.

2. In other places people like to eat sheep more than cows.

3. Most lowly citizens haven't forgotten the divine will already, have they?

4. The priests had set off to the highest citadel with as many sacrifices as possible.

5. The man in black clothes was grimmer than my brother and laughed less too.

6. At first the camel did not eat enough, but then he attempted to eat the smaller elephant.

7. That wretched woman will believe the passages in the Bible and confess God's name, won't she?

8. Did the ancient poet have many friends, or was he only reverencing the moon and sad songs?

9. Didn't that most wicked queen pity the maiden more beautiful than all?

10. I am a very angry little boy, and a new dog will not satisfy me, a new sheep will satisfy me less, and a new horse least.

E. Latin to English Translation

1 **Perseus et Andromeda**

Ōlim Rēx *Cēpheus* et Rēgīna *Cassiopēa Aethiopiae* fīliam pulchram, *Andromedam*, habēbant. Cassiopēa superbissima erat et rogāvit: "Nōnne est mea fīlia Andromeda pulcherrima omnium? Etiam est pulchrior quam *nymphae* maris!" Īrātissimus erat deus maris *Neptūnus* propter eius verba, et *bēluam*
5 feram, *Cētum*, quae litora Aethiopiae perdere incēpit statim mīsit. Frumenta, bōvēs, etiam canēs parvī omnia dēlēta sunt. Rēx ad *ōrāculum Apollōnis* dēnique profectus est, et rogāvit: "Possumusne vincere hanc bēluam celeriter? celerius, amābō tē*?? quam celerrimē, tē ōrō???" Ōrāculum prīmō *tacēbat*. "Num moriēmur?" Dēnique locūtum est ōrāculum: "Nōn moriēminī sī vōs *bēluae* vestram fīliam Andromedam *sacrificābitis*. Vincīte eam ad saxum iūxtā mare et relinquite."
10 Itaque virgō miserrima ad saxum vincta est et Cētum exspectāvit. Forte *Perseus* simul iūxtā volābat. *Medūsam* modo necāverat et eius caput in *saccō* portābat. Andromedam in saxō vīdit et eius prīmum misertus est, tum eam amāvit. Eam rogāvit, "Cur hīc es?" Ea eī dē mātre superbā, *bēluā*, et *ōrāculō* narrāvit. Stātim Perseus ad patrem et mātrem eius volāvit et dīxit: "Dabitisne mihi vestram fīliam in matrimōniō sī eam servābō?" Celerrimē rogāvērunt, "Eam servā! Tua uxor erit et tū nostrum rēgnum etiam habēbis!"
15 Ecce! *Bēlua* per aquās maris tendit! Caldīs oculīs et ōre ingentī miseram petit. Sed Perseus celerius volāre potest, et gladiō bēluam in collō percutit! Bēlua ululat et māximē *convolutat*, et *soleae pennātae* Perseī *gravissimae* aquā fiunt. Perseus in saxō magnō *exponit*, et deinde *bēluam* iterum et iterum oppugnat. Dēnique mortuus est *Cētus*, et Andromeda servātur!

Notes:
* *amābō tē*: please (idiom)

Glossary:
Aethiopia, -ae (f): Ethiopia, a name used by ancient authors to describe pretty much all of inland central Africa or, specifically, south of Egypt, corresponding more often to modern Sudan than modern Ethiopia. However, Pausanius, Strabo, and Josephus identify some rocks off of the coast of modern Tel Aviv as the place where Andromeda was chained.
Andromeda, -ae (f): Andromeda, princess of Ethiopia
Apollo, Apollōnis (m): Apollo
bēlua, -ae (f): sea monster
Cassiopēa, -ae (f): Cassiopeia or Cassiope, queen of Ethiopia
Cēpheus, -ī (m): Cepheus, king of Ethiopia
Cētus, -ī (m): Cetus, a sea monster (more generally can mean a large sea animal such as a whale or dolphin)
convolūtō (1): to whirl around, thrash
expōnō, -ere, -posuī, -positum I land (on), put/set out
gravis, -e: heavy
Medūsa, -ae (f): Medusa
nympha, -ae (f): nymph
ōrāculum, -ī (n): oracle
pennātus, -a, -um: winged
Perseus, -ī (m): Perseus
saccus, -ī (m): sack, bag
sacrificō (1): I sacrifice
solea, -ae (f): sandal
taceō, -ēre, -uī, -itum: I am silent

LESSON 8

Review and Test

Word List

No new words this lesson. Review vocabulary, especially from Lessons 3-7 (new words), but brush up on any old words from *KL1* as necessary.

Grammar

No new grammar this lesson. Review previous lessons.

Worksheet 8

A. Vocabulary

1. aedificō: _____
2. cōnfiteor: _____
3. cōnor: _____
4. ēgredior: _____
5. ēripiō: _____
6. impleō: _____
7. ingredior: _____
8. lābor: _____
9. loquor: _____
10. mīror: _____
11. misereor: _____
12. mōlior: _____
13. morior: _____
14. oblīvīscor: _____
15. operor: _____
16. orior: _____
17. patior: _____
18. percutiō: _____
19. proficīscor: _____
20. quaerō: _____
21. revertor: _____
22. sequor: _____
23. tendō: _____
24. trādō: _____
25. vereor: _____
26. blood: _____
27. sheep: _____
28. citadel: _____
29. place: _____
30. chief: _____
31. deed: _____
32. nobody: _____
33. year: _____
34. sacrifice: _____
35. citizen: _____
36. weapons: _____
37. divinity: _____
38. priest: _____
39. eye: _____
40. part: _____
41. spirit: _____
42. gate: _____
43. state: _____
44. pēius (adv.): _____
45. alius: _____
46. alter: _____
47. difficilis: _____
48. dissimilis: _____
49. excelsus: _____
50. multum: _____
51. fidēlis: _____
52. gracilis: _____
53. humilis: _____
54. īmus: _____

55. inferior: _____
56. inferus: _____
57. infimus: _____
58. ipse: _____
59. māior: _____
60. māximus: _____
61. melior: _____
62. minimus: _____
63. minor: _____
64. mortuus: _____
65. nūllus: _____
66. optimus: _____
67. pēior: _____
68. pessimus: _____
69. plēnus: _____
70. plūrimus: _____
71. plūs: _____
72. prior: _____
73. propior: _____
74. proximus: _____
75. quī: _____
76. reliquus: _____
77. sacer: _____
78. sapiēns: _____
79. similis: _____
80. sōlus: _____
81. summus: _____
82. superbus: _____
83. superior: _____
84. superus: _____
85. suprēmus: _____
86. tōtus: _____

87. trīstis: _____
88. ūllus: _____
89. ulterior: _____
90. ultimus: _____
91. vastus: _____
92. beyond: _____
93. prae (+_____) _____
94. less: _____
95. pessimē: _____
96. perchance: _____
97. tunc: _____
_____
98. expects "no": _____
99. expects "yes": _____
100. facile (adv.): _____
101. māne: _____
102. -ne: _____
_____
103. īta: _____
104. sīc: _____
105. melius (adv): _____
106. among: _____
107. least: _____
108. ob (+_____): _____
_____
109. magis: _____
110. prīmō: _____
111. optimē: _____
112. plurimum: _____
113. māximē: _____
114. quidem: _____
115. parum: _____

B. Grammar

1. Do a synopsis of *trādō* in the 2nd person singular, giving principal parts first:

   _____

		ACTIVE		PASSIVE	
		LATIN	ENGLISH	LATIN	ENGLISH
INDICATIVE	PRES.				
	IMPF.				
	FUT.				
	PERF.				
	PLUPF.				
	FT.PF.				
INF.	PRES.				
IMP.	SING.				
	PL.				

2. Give the appropriate Latin or English for the following verbs.

   they will have arisen: _____

   you (sg.) will have pity: _____

   cōnfitentur: _____

   she had marched out: _____

   aedificāta sunt: _____

   I will fill up: _____

   cōnābāminī: _____

we followed: _____
mīrābuntur: _____
I had respected: _____
quaesītus est: _____
you (pl.) will have suffered: _____
lapsī estis: _____
she had forgotten: _____
it is stretched: _____
passus est: _____
they set out: _____
loquitur: _____
percutitur: _____
you (sg.) will return: _____

3. Noun-Adjective Combinations: Give the Gender (Masc., Fem., or Neut.), Number (Sg. or Pl.), and Case (Nom., Gen., Dat., Acc., Abl., or Voc.) of the following noun and adjective combinations. There may be more than one answer for each phrase, so give all possible answers. Then translate each option.

PHRASE	GENDER, NUMBER, CASE	TRANSLATION
pēiorēs cīvitātēs		
ūllī locō		
istō prīncipe superbissimō		
ocule trīstior		
infimōrum operum		

sōlae animae sacrae		
tōtīus ovis humillimae		
alia arma meliōra		
annus excelsior		
nūllīs nūminibus proximīs		

4. Fill in the blanks of the following comparison sets of adjectives and adverbs, then draw pictures to illustrate each set. (Continued on next page.)

	POSITIVE	COMPARATIVE	SUPERLATIVE
ADJECTIVE #1		melior, **-ius**	
ADJECTIVE PICTURE			
ADVERB #1	bene		
ADVERB PICTURE			
ADJECTIVE #2	facilis, -e		
ADJECTIVE PICTURE			

ADVERB #2		facilius	
ADVERB PICTURE			
ADJECTIVE #3			plūrimus, **-a, -um**
ADJECTIVE PICTURE			
ADVERB #3		plūs	
ADVERB PICTURE			
ADJECTIVE #4	magnus, **-a, -um**		māximus, **-a, -um**
ADJECTIVE PICTURE			
ADVERB #4			
ADVERB PICTURE			
ADJECTIVE #5		minor, **minus**	
ADJECTIVE PICTURE			

ADVERB #5	parum		
ADVERB PICTURE			

C. Memorization

Write out in full the Prologue through Tenth Commandment.

D. Latin to English Translation

1 **Homo Qui Caecus Natus Est (adapted from John 9)***

Et Iesus vidit hominem caecum a *nativitate*. Et interrogaverunt eum discipuli eius: "Rabbi, *quis peccavit*, hic aut *parentes* eius—quia caecus natus est?" Respondit Iesus: "Neque hic peccavit neque parentes eius, sed *manifestabitur* opera Dei in illo. Dixerat et *expuit* in terram et fecit *lutum* et posuit
5 *lutum* super oculos eius. Et dixit ei: "*Vade, lava* in *natatoria Siloae*!" *Abiit* ergo et lavit et venit et videt. Itaque qui videbant eum prius quia* *mendicus* erat dicebant: "Nōnne hic est qui sedebat et *mendicabat*?" Alii* dicebant: "Hic est!" Alii* autem dicebant: "*Nequaquam*, sed similis* est eius!" Ille dicebat: "Ego sum!" Dicebant ergo ei: "Quomodo aperti sunt oculi tibi*?" Respondit ille: "Homo qui dicitur Iesus *lutum* fecit et posuit oculos meos et dixit mihi, "*Vade* ad *natatoriam Siloae* et *lava*," et abii et *lavi* et
10 vidi." Dixerunt ei: "Ubi est ille?" Ait: "Nescio."

Adducunt eum ad *Pharisaeos* qui caecus fuerat. Erat autem *sabbatum* quando lutum fecit Iesus et aperuit oculos eius. Iterum ergo *interrogabant* eum *Pharisaei*, "Quomodo vidis?" Ille autem dixit eis: "*Lutum* posuit mihi super oculos et *lavi* et video." Dicebat ergo ex Pharisaeis ūnus: "Non est hic homo a Deo, quia sabbatum non *custodit*!" Alii dicebant: "Quomodo potest homo *peccator* haec *signa*
15 facere?" Et *schisma* erat in eis. Dicunt ergo caeco iterum: "Tu *quid* dicis dē eo qui aperuit oculos tuos?" Ille autem dixit, "Propheta est."

Non crediderunt ergo *Iudaei* dē illo et vocaverunt *parentes* eius. Et interrogaverunt eos: "Hic est filius vester quem vos dicitis quia caecus natus est? Quomodo ergo nunc videt?" Responderunt eis parentes eius et dixerunt: "Scimus quia hic est filius noster et quia caecus nātus est. *Quis* autem eius
20 aperuit oculos nos nescimus; ipsum interrogate." Haec dixerunt parentes eius quia timebant Iudaeos. Vocaverunt ergo *rursum* hominem qui fuerat caecus et dixerunt ei: "Da gloriam Deo! Nos scimus quia hic homo *peccator* est." Dixit ergo ille: "Si *peccator* est, nescio; unum scio quia caecus eram, sed modo* video." Dixerunt ergo illi: "Quid fecit tibi? Quomodo aperuit tibi oculos?" Respondit eis: "Dixi vobis iam et non audivistis; *quid* iterum *vultis* audire? Num et vos *vultis* discipuli eius fieri*?" Rēsponderunt
25 et dixerunt ei: "In *peccatis* natus es totus* et tu doces nos?" Et *eiecerunt* eum *foras*.

Audivit Iesus quia eiecerunt eum foras et invenit eum et dixit ei: "Tu credis in Filium Dei?" Respondit ille et dixit: "Quis est, Domine? Credam in eum." Et dixit ei Iesus: "Et vidisti eum; et qui loquitur *tecum* ipse est." Et ille ait: "Credo, Domine!" Et *adoravit* eum. Dixit ei Iesus: "In* *iudicium* ego in hunc *mundum* veni. Qui non vident, videbunt; et qui vident, caeci fient."

Notes:
* Since this is adapted from the Vulgate, you get to practice reading Latin without macrons again. You'll be used to it next time.
* *quia*: Remember that quia also means "that"
* *aliī...aliī*: some...others
* *similis*: Followed by genitive or dative when meaning "similar to"
* *tibi*: a Dative of Reference (see *KL3*, Lesson 1); here translate as a possessive adjective (*oculī tibi = oculī tuī*)
* *modo*: In this context it means "now"
* *fierī*: Remember this one? It's the infinitive of *fiō, fierī, factus sum*, "I am made/done, become"

* *tōtus*: Here it sounds better to translate it as an adverb, "wholly" or "totally."
* *in*: Here it has a meaning of purpose, "for"

Glossary:
abeō, -ire, -iī/-ivī, -itum: I go away, depart
addūcō, -ere, -dūxī, -ductum: I lead to (notice that Latin prefers to use the preposition ad as well even though it is already a prefix on this verb)
adōrō (1): I worship, honor
custōdiō, -īre, -īvī, -ītum: I keep, guard

ēiciō, -ere, ēiēcī, ēiectum: I throw/cast out
expuō, -ere, -puī, -putum: I spit out
forās (adv.): out(side)
interrogō (1): I ask, interrogate
Iudaeus, -ī (m): a Jew
iūdicium, -ī (n): judgment
lavō, -āre, lavī, lavātum/lōtum/lautum: I wash
lutum, -i (n): mud, clay
manifestō (1): I reveal, make clear, manifest
mendīcō (1): I beg (for)
mendīcus, -ī (m): beggar
natātōria, -ae (f): pool, place for swimming
nātīvitās, -tātis (f): birth, nativity
nēquāquam: by no means, not at all

parēns, -ntis (m/f): parent, father, mother
peccātor, -tōris (m): sinner
peccō (1): I sin, err, make a mistake
Pharisaeus, -ī (m): Pharisee
quid (interrogative pronoun): what? why?
quis, quid (interrogative pronoun): who? what?
rursum: back(ward), again
sabbatum, -ī (m): Sabbath
schisma, -matis (n): schism, division
Siloam (indecl.): Siloam, a pool near Jerusalem
tēcum: cum te
vādō, -ere, ——, ——: I go, rush, hurry
vultis: 2nd person plural present active indicative of the irregular verb *volō, velle, voluī, ——,* "I wish, want"

[This page intentionally left blank]

Unit Two

UNIT 2: GOALS

Lessons 9–16

By the end of Unit 2, students should be able to . . .

- Decline and translate interrogative pronouns and adjectives
- Decline present, future, and perfect participles
- Translate participles as simple adjectives
- Translate participles when used in the ablative absolute construction
- Conjugate and translate the irregular verb *ferō*
- Decline and translate various indefinite pronouns
- Understand and translate the passive periphrastic with dative of agent
- Recognize and translate the locative case
- Conjugate and translate the irregular verbs *volō*, *nōlō*, and *mālō*
- Differentiate between and translate gerunds and gerundives

LESSON 9

Interrogative Pronoun and Adjective

Word List

Verbs

1. abeō, -īre, -iī (-īvī), -itum *I go away (from), depart*
2. ascendō, -ere, -scendī, -scēnsum *I go up, ascend, climb*
3. gignō, -ere, genuī, genitum *I beget, create* (in pass., *I am born*)
4. nōscō, -ere, nōvī, nōtum *I learn, get to know;* pf. tense, *I know*
5. respondeō, -ēre, -spondī, -spōnsum *I respond, answer*
6. vādō, -ere, vāsī, —— *I go, proceed*

Nouns/Pronouns

7. altāre, -tāris (n) *altar, burnt offering* (pl. forms often used with sg. meaning)
8. cōnspectus, -ūs (m) *sight, view, appearance*
9. iūdicium, -ī (n) *judgment, decision, trial*
10. nix, nivis (f) *snow*
11. pluvia, -ae (f) *rain*
12. quis, quid (interrog. pron.) *who? what? why?*
13. sermō, -ōnis (m) *speech, talk, conversation*

Adjectives

14. cūnctus, -a, -um *all (of), every*
15. quī? quae? quod? (interrog. adj.) *what (kind of)? which?*

Adverbs/Conjnctions

16. igitur *therefore, then*
17. nam *for; certainly*
18. numquid (emphatic form of *num*, interrogative adv. expecting a no answer) *surely...not?, is it really possible that...?*
19. simul *together, at the same time; simul atque/ac as soon as*
20. vel *or, or rather*

Memorization

LATIN	LITERAL ENGLISH
Veni, redemptor gentium,	Come, Redeemer of nations,
Ostende partum virginis,	Show forth the virgin's birth,
Miretur omne saeculum:	Let every age marvel:
Talis decet partus Deum.	Such a birth befits God.

Grammar

In *KL3*, Lesson 7 you were introduced to some basic Latin interrogatives: *-ne*, *num*, and *nōnne*. In this lesson you will expand your knowledge of questions with the interrogative pronoun and adjective.

Interrogative Pronoun

Like other Latin pronouns, the interrogative pronoun stands in the place of a noun. And, just like the English interrogative pronouns *who?* and *what?*, *quis?* and *quid?* are asking about that *person* and *thing*, respectively. The English interrogative pronoun only has a few forms:

Who are you? (subject)

Whom do you seek? What do you want? (object)

Whose sword is that? (possessive)

However, the Latin interrogative pronoun declines fully through the singular and plural in nominative, genitive, dative, accusative, and ablative cases:

	SINGULAR		PLURAL		
	MASC. / FEM.	NEUT.	MASC.	FEM.	NEUT.
NOM.	quis?	quid?	quī?	quae?	quae?
GEN.	cuius?	cuius?	quōrum?	quārum?	quōrum?
DAT.	cui?	cui?	quibus?	quibus?	quibus?
ACC.	quem?	quid?	quōs?	quās?	quae?
ABL.	quō?	quō?	quibus?	quibus?	quibus?

A few exciting things to note here. First off, the masculine and feminine singular forms are identical, so you really don't have to write them twice (I laid them out for you just this once for clarity's sake). In the chant chart on the sheet with this lesson's word list, they are listed together.

Second, in the plural, the chant is identical to the plural of the relative pronoun, so you don't have to learn an entirely new chant. Although this is very handy, it can also be confusing, so make sure you are aware of the unique forms in the singular. I have added questions marks after each word of this chant as a reminder that you are dealing with an interrogative word here (and not the relative pronoun), but these questions marks are not really necessary for you to include every time you write out the chant.

And one more thing: the neuter singular accusative form *quid* can also mean "why?" This is called an adverbial accusative, and context will help you determine whether quid means "what?" (regular old direct object accusative) or "why?" (adverbial accusative).

Here are some examples of the interrogative pronoun:

Quis dracōnem necāvit? Who killed the dragon?

Cuius gladius est? Whose sword is this?

Cui rēx aurum dedit? To whom did the king give the gold?

Quid Oswaldus necāvit? What did Oswald kill?

Quid Oswaldus dracōnem necāvit? Why did Oswald kill the dragon? (Note adverbial use of *quid* here, meaning "why.")

Ab quō dracō necātus est? By whom was the dragon killed?

More examples will be given in a bit to help you distinguish between the relative pronoun, the interrogative pronoun, and the interrogative adjective.

Interrogative Adjective

As its name implies, the interrogative adjective asks a question and modifies a noun or pronoun: *which* dragon? *what* animal? *which/what kind of* beast? Conveniently, **the forms of the interrogative adjective are identical to those of the relative pronoun**. In the chant below I have again added question marks to each word to help show its interrogativity (this may not be a word, but it definitely should be).

	SINGULAR			PLURAL		
	MASC.	FEM.	NEUT.	MASC.	FEM.	NEUT.
NOM.	quī?	quae?	quod?	quī?	quae?	quae?
GEN.	cuius?	cuius?	cuius?	quōrum?	quārum?	quōrum?
DAT.	cui?	cui?	cui?	quibus?	quibus?	quibus?
ACC.	quem?	quam?	quod?	quōs?	quās?	quae?
ABL.	quō?	quā?	quō?	quibus?	quibus?	quibus?

Since these forms are pretty self-explanatory, let's move on to some examples of this adjective.

Quem dracōnem Oswaldus necāvit? Which dragon did Oswald kill?

Quō gladiō dracō necātus est? By what kind of sword was the dragon killed?

Quās fēminās dracō terrēbat? Which women was the dragon frightening?

By this point you may be panicking about how you will be able to distinguish the relative pronoun from the interrogative pronoun from the interrogative adjective, since other than the obvious forms *quis* and *quid*, all the other words look alike. The answer is context again! Here is a whole slew of examples covering each case (in the singular) to show the differences.

NOM.	RELATIVE PRON.	*Vir **quī** dracōnem necāvit fortis est.* The man who killed the dragon is brave.
	INTERROG. PRON.	***Quis** dracōnem necāvit?* Who killed the dragon?
	INTERROG. ADJ.	***Quī** vir dracōnem necāvit?* Which man killed the dragon?
GEN.	RELATIVE PRON.	*Oswaldus, **cuius** gladius māximus est, dracōnem necāvit.* Oswald, whose sword is very large, killed the dragon.
	INTERROG. PRON.	***Cuius** gladius dracōnem necāvit?* Whose sword killed the dragon?
	INTERROG. ADJ.	*Gladius **cuius** virī dracōnem necāvit?* Which man's sword killed the dragon?
DAT.	RELATIVE PRON.	*Oswaldus, **cui** rēx multum aurum dedit, dracōnem necāverat.* Oswald, to whom the king gave much gold, had killed the dragon.
	INTERROG. PRON.	***Cui** rēx multum aurum dedit?* To whom did the king give much gold?
	INTERROG. ADJ.	***Cui** virō rēx multum aurum dedit?* To which man did the king give much gold?
ACC.	RELATIVE PRON.	*Dracō **quem** Oswaldus necāvit ācer erat.* The dragon that Oswald killed was fierce.
	INTERROG. PRON.	***Quem** Oswaldus necāvit?* Whom (or, in this case, "what") did Oswald kill?
	INTERROG. ADJ.	***Quem** dracōnem Oswaldus necāvit?* Which dragon did Oswald kill?
ABL.	RELATIVE PRON.	*Oswaldus, ab **quō** dracō necātus erat, rēx factus est.* Oswald, by whom the dragon had been killed, became king.
	INTERROG. PRON.	*Ab **quō** dracō necātus erat?* By whom had the dragon been killed?
	INTERROG. ADJ.	*Ab **quō** virō dracō necātus erat?* By which man had the dragon been killed?

Again, this may seem like a lot to go over, but remember you already learned most of these forms when you learned the relative pronoun, so the biggest challenge will just be using context to know when a word is being used as a relative pronoun, as an interrogative pronoun, or as an interrogative adjective. And once you get the hang of it, it's easy.

Review

Be sure to review passive forms if you are still having trouble with them, since now we have deponents to keep track of too (remember how to form the imprative and infinitive). Review the irregular adjectives *solus, miser, pulcher, celer, difficilis, facilis, similis, dissimilis, gracilis, humilis,* and *plus.*

Worksheet 9

A. Vocabulary

1. what kind of?: _____
2. gignō, -___, genuī, _____: _____
3. nam: _____
4. I get to know: _____
5. simul: _____
6. simul ac: _____
7. vādō, -ere, vāsī, ——: _____
8. rain: _____
9. abeō, -īre, -iī (-īvī), -itum: _____
10. burnt offering: _____
11. nix: _____
12. respondeō, _____ -sponsum: _____
13. igitur: _____
14. quis? quid?: _____
15. vel: _____
16. sermō: _____
17. appearance: _____
18. cunctus: _____
19. I go up: _____
20. surely...not?: _____
21. citizenship: _____

B. Grammar

1. In the following English sentences, determine whether each underlined word is a relative pronoun, interrogative pronoun, or interrogative adjective.

   _____ of the three tigers escaped? _____

   And then I saw something _____ terrified me. _____

109

Will we see the man ____ does magic tricks? _____

Just _____ is going on here? _____

_____ girl over there is the princess? _____

_____ dirty sock is this? _____

The boy _____ dirty sock was draped in the oatmeal looked guilty. _____

2. Decline *which sacred conversation?*

	LATIN SINGULAR	LATIN PLURAL
NOM.		
GEN.		
DAT.		
ACC.		
ABL.		
VOC.		

3. Do a synopsis of *respondeō* in the 3rd person singular, giving principal parts first:

_____ .

		ACTIVE		PASSIVE	
		LATIN	ENGLISH	LATIN	ENGLISH
INDICATIVE	PRES.				
	IMPF.				
	FUT.				
	PERF.				
	PLUPF.				
	FT.PF.				
INF.	PRES.				
IMP.	SG.				
	PL.				

C. Memorization

Fill in the blanks for the first stanza of Ambrose's *Hymnus IV*.

Veni, _____,

_____ partum _____,

Miretur _____ saeculum:

_____ decet _____ Deum.

D. English to Latin Translation Translation

1. The priests who will have ascended unto the altar will suddenly be frightened by the sight of a very angry bull.

2. Why did you forget that man's citizenship as soon as he set out to the farthest places?

3. Therefore all the rest of the spirits will attempt to follow the greedy man, who will certainly not answer them.

4. Who begets the snow, or from what place does the rain depart?

5. Surrender this tower to me immediately or die!

6. We citizens have suffered many things; who or what can help us now?

7. Which foolish speech proceeded from the smallest girl's mouth?

8. What things did the very proud women answer at the same time? Surely they spoke, didn't they?

9. I am learning new things about animals but I know two or perhaps three dragons that will respect my conversation.

10. You will have mercy on this most wretched citizen in his trial, won't you?

E. Latin to English Translation Translation

Excerpts from Job 38 and 39

1   Respondit autem Dominus *Iob* de *turbine* et dixit, "Quis est iste qui *involvit sententias* sermonibus *inperitis*? *Accinge* sicut vir *lumbos* tuos; rogabo te et responde mihi. Ubi eras quando ponebam *fundamenta* terrae? Quis posuit *mensuras* eius si novisti, vel quis tetendit super eam *lineam*? Super quo *bases* illius *solidatae sunt* aut quis dimisit* lapidem *angularem* eius, ubi me laudabant simul stella
5   *matutina* et gaudebant omnes filii Dei? Quis *conclusit* ostiis mare quando egrediebatur? Numquid ingressus es *profunda* maris et in infimis *abyssis* ambulavisti? Numquid apertae tibi sunt portae mortis et ostia *tenebrosa* vidisti? Numquid cogitavisti de *latitudinibus* terrae? Dic mihi, si nosti* omnia. In qua via habitat lux et tenebrarum qui locus est? Numquid ingressus es *thesauros* nivis aut *thesauros grandinis* spectavisti, quae paravi in* tempus hostis in* diem pugnae et belli? Per quam viam
10 *spargitur* lux et *dividitur aestus* super terram? Quis dedit *vehementissimo imbri* iter et viam tonitrui? Quis est pluviae pater vel quis genuit *rorem*? De cuius *utero* egressa est *glacies* et *gelu* de caelo quis genuit?" Et Dominus locutus est ad Iob, "Numquid qui *contendit* cum Deo *tam* facile *conquiescit*? Nonne qui *arguit* Deum debet respondere ei?" Respondens autem Iob Domino dixit, "Qui *leviter* locutus sum respondere quid possum? Manum meam ponam super os meum. Unum locutus sum et
15 alterum ultra non *addam*."

Notes:
* *dīmīsit*: also can mean "I put/set down"
* *nōstī*: syncopated form of *nōvistī*
* *in*: also can mean "for"

Glossary:
accingō, -ere, -cinxī, -cinctum: I gird on/about, equip, prepare
abyssus, -ī (f): abyss, deep, infernal pit
aestus, -ūs (m): heat, fire, passion
angulāris, -e: corner, placed at corners
arguō, -ere, arguī, argūtus: I accuse
basis, -is (f): pedestal, base, foundation
conclūdō, -ere, -clūsī, -clūsum: I shut up, close
conquiēscō, -ere, -quiēvī, -quiētum: I fall silent, am still
contendō, -ere, -tendī, -tentum: I contend, strive with
divīdō, -ere, -vīsī, -vīsum: I divide
fundāmentum, -ī (n): foundation
gelū, -ūs (n): frost
glaciēs, -eī (f): ice
grandō, -dinis (f): hail
imber, -bris (m): rain(storm), shower
inperītus, -a, -um: unskilled, inexperienced, ignorant
involvō, -ere, -volvī, -volūtum: I wrap (in)
Iob: Job
lātitūdō, -dinis (f): width, extent, latitude
leviter: lightly
līnea, -ae (f): line, string
lumbus, -ī (m): loin
mātūtīnus, -a, -um: of the (early) morning, early
mensūra, -ae (f): measure(ment)
profundum, -ī (n): depth, chasm
rōs, rōris (m): dew
sententia, -ae (f): thought, opinion, sentence
solidō (1): I make firm, strengthen
spargō, -ere, sparsī, sparsum: I scatter, sprinkle
tam: so
tenebrōsus, -a, -um: gloomy, dark
thēsaurus, -ī (m): treasure (house), hoard
turbō, -binis (m): whirlwind
uterus, -ī (m): womb
vehemēns, -mentis: violent, vehement

Lesson 10

Participles

Word List

Verbs

1. adeō, -īre, -iī, -itum *I go to(ward), approach*
2. bibō, -ere, bibī, potum *I drink*
3. canō, -ere, cecinī, cāntum *I sing, play, prophesy*
4. cōgnōscō, -ere, -nōvī, -nitum *I learn, get to know;* pf. tense, *I know*
5. emō, -ere, ēmī, emptum *I buy*
6. premō, -ere, pressī, pressum *I press, crush, overpower*
7. solvō, -ere, solvī, solūtum *I loose, set free, pay*
8. serviō, -īre, -īvī, -ītum (+dat.) *I serve, am a slave to*
9. sumō, -ere, sūmpsī, sūmptum *I take, assume*

Nouns

10. inīquitās, -tātis (f) *injustice, unfairness, iniquity*
11. lēx, lēgis (f) *law, covenant*
12. mandātum, -ī (n) *command(ment), order*
13. misericordia, -ae (f) *mercy, pity*
14. sapientia, -ae (f) *wisdom*
15. templum, -ī (n) *temple*
16. testimōnium, -ī (n) *testimony, evidence, witness*

Adverbs/Conjunctions

17. propquam *therefore*
17. entries are: proptereā *therefore*
18. inde *from there, thence*
19. postquam *after*
20. valde *very, exceedingly*

Memorization

LATIN	LITERAL ENGLISH
Veni, redemptor gentium,	Come, Redeemer of nations,
Ostende partum virginis,	Show forth the virgin's birth,
Miretur omne saeculum:	Let every age marvel:
Talis decet partus Deum.	Such a birth befits God.
Non ex virili semine,	Not from man's seed,
Sed mystico spiramine,	But of mystic breath,
Verbum Dei factum caro,	The Word of God was made flesh,
Fructusque ventris floruit.	And the womb's fruit has flourished.

Grammar

This is a very important lesson for us. The Latin participle is a big deal, being used quite often and in many splendid ways. A participle is a verbal adjective (that's right, a hybrid of a verb and an adjective). In English, we take verbs and add -ing to them to make them a participle (as well as other suffixes like -ed, for passive participles). A participle either describes a noun (functioning as an adjective) or it describes an action the noun is doing (functioning as a verb). Make sure you don't freak out: it is actually very similar to what we do in English.

Forms and Declensions of Participles

Happily, participles are fairly easy to decline (it's just the translation of them that can get a bit sticky). They will even use endings you have already learned!

	PARTICIPLE			
	ACTIVE		PASSIVE	
	LATIN	ENGLISH	LATIN	ENGLISH
PRES.	pres. stem + -ns, -ntis	X-ing		
PF.			4th principal part	X-ed, having been X-ed
FUT.	4th p. p. stem + -ūrus, -ūra, -ūrum	about to X	pres. stem + -ndus, -nda, -ndum	(about) to be X-ed

The **present active participle** is (not surprisingly) formed off of the present stem. You simply add -ns, -ntis and now, lo and behold, you have a third declension adjective. Like third declension adjectives, it will decline like a third declension i-stem. Here is an assortment of verbs from each conjugation to illustrate this transformation.

necāre → present stem *neca-* → *necāns, necantis* killing

vidēre → present stem *vidē-* → *vidēns, videntis* seeing

dūcere → present stem *duce-* → *ducēns, ducentis* leading

capere → present stem *cape-* → *capiēns, capientis* capturing

audīre → present stem *audī-* → *audiēns, audientis* hearing

	MASC./FEM. SG.	NEUT. SG.	MASC./FEM. PL.	NEUT. PL.
NOM.	necāns	necāns	necantēs	necantia
GEN.	necantis	necantis	necantium	necantium
DAT.	necantī	necantī	necantibus	necantibus
ACC.	necantem	necāns	necantēs	necantia
ABL.	necantī, necante	necantī, necante	necantibus	necantibus
VOC.	[Ō] necāns	[Ō] necāns	[Ō] necantēs	[Ō] necantia

Note that the ablative has two alternate endings, *-ī* or *-e*. There is a fine distinction between the two. Basically, when the participle is acting like a verb, you would choose the *-e* form: *Ambulāvit ab Oswaldō dracōnem necante*, "She walked away from Oswald killing the dragon" (or, ". . . away from Oswald as he was killing the dragon"; or, ". . . away from Oswald who was killing the dragon.") However, when the participle is simply being an adjective modifying a noun (an attributive adjective), use the *-ī* form: *Ambulāvit ab Oswaldō manducantī*, "She walked away from Oswald eating" (or, ". . . away from Oswald while he was eating"; or, ". . . away from Oswald who was eating"). This won't come up very often though.

The **perfect passive participle** is even easier to form. You already know it as the 4th principal part! So all you will need to do is take that 4th principal part and decline it just like any ordinary 1st/2nd declension adjective. (Remember that when the dictionary lists that 4th principal part as *necātus* or sometimes *necātum*, it stands for *necātus, -a, -um*.)

necātus, -a, -um (4th p.p.) killed, having been killed

vīsus, -a, -um (4th p.p.) seen, having been seen

ductus, -a, -um (4th p.p.) led, having been led

captus, -a, -um (4th p.p.) captured, having been captured

audītus, -a, -um (4th p.p.) heard, having been heard

	SINGULAR			PLURAL		
	MASC.	FEM.	NEUT.	MASC.	FEM.	NEUT.
NOM.	necātus	necāta	necātum	necātī	necātae	necāta
GEN.	necātī	necātae	necātī	necātōrum	necātārum	necātōrum
DAT.	necātō	necātae	necātō	necātīs	necātīs	necātīs
ACC.	necātum	necātam	necātum	necātōs	necātās	necāta
ABL.	necātō	necātā	necātō	necātīs	necātīs	necātīs
VOC.	necāte	necāta	necātum	necātī	necātae	necāta

The **future active participle** is rather unexpectedly formed from the perfect passive participle (or 4th principal part), and not from the present stem as we might suppose. Remove the *-us, -a, -um* endings from the perfect passive participle, and then add *-ūrus, -ūra, -ūrum*, and there you have the future active participle.

necātus, -a, -um → *necāt-* → *necātūrus, necātūra, necātūrum* about to kill

vīsus, -a, -um → *vīs-* → *vīsūrus, vīsūra, vīsūrum* about to see

ductus, -a, -um → *duct-* → *ductūrus, ductūra, ductūrum* about to lead

captus, -a, -um → *capt-* → *captūrus, captūra, captūrum* about to capture

audītus, -a, -um → *audīt-* → *audītūrus, audītūra, audītūrum* about to hear

	SINGULAR			PLURAL		
	MASC.	FEM.	NEUT.	MASC.	FEM.	NEUT.
NOM.	necātūrus	necātūra	necātūrum	necātūrī	necātūrae	necātūra
GEN.	necātūrī	necātūrae	necātūrī	necātūrōrum	necātūrārum	necātūrōrum
DAT.	necātūrō	necātūrae	necātūrō	necātūrīs	necātūrīs	necātūrīs
ACC.	necātūrum	necātūram	necātūrum	necātūrōs	necātūrās	necātūra
ABL.	necātūrō	necātūrā	necātūrō	necātūrīs	necātūrīs	necātūrīs
VOC.	necātūre	necātūra	necātūrum	necātūrī	necātūrae	necātūra

The **future passive participle**, also known as the **gerundive**, is formed by taking the present stem and adding *-ndus, -nda, -ndum*. This will also follow the usual 1st/2nd declension adjective path.

necāre → present stem *neca-* → *necandus, -a, -um* (about) to be killed

vidēre → present stem *vide-* → *videndus, -a, -um* (about) to be seen

dūcere → present stem *dūce-* → *dūcendus, -a, -um* (about) to be led

capere → present stem *cape-* → *capiendus, -a, -um* (about) to be captured

audīre → present stem *audi-* → *audiendus, -a, -um* (about) to be heard

	SINGULAR			PLURAL		
	MASC.	FEM.	NEUT.	MASC.	FEM.	NEUT.
NOM.	necandus	necanda	necandum	necandī	necandae	necanda
GEN.	necandī	necandae	necandī	necandōrum	necandārum	necandōrum
DAT.	necandō	necandae	necandō	necandīs	necandīs	necandīs
ACC.	necandum	necandam	necandum	necandōs	necandās	necanda
ABL.	necandō	necandā	necandō	necandīs	necandīs	necandīs
VOC.	necande	necanda	necandum	necandī	necandae	necanda

Now that we've shown you participles and how they work in a sentence, you may want to know how to parse them. Remember, they are verb-adjective hybrids, so when you parse them, you will need to parse them partially like verbs and partialy like adjectives.

Because it is made from a verb stem, the participle has tense and voice, but no mood, so if you are asked to parse it like a verb put "participle" under mood, even though it does not have one. This means that it can function in a sentence like a verb, taking an object or being modified by adverbs. As an adjective, the participle has gender, number, and case (just like regular old adjectives). This means it can function as an adjective, modifying nouns or stands in for a noun if need be, like substantive adjectives. Thus to parse a participle, you will need to give Gender Number Case Tense Voice Mood.

As we have seen, the participle only comes in present, perfect, and future tenses. The **present participle** *only* exists in the **active** voice. The **perfect participle** *only* exists in the **passive** voice. The **future participle** is more agreeable and comes in both **active and passive** forms. You will perhaps wonder why this is the case—and I do not have an answer for you. You should just rejoice that there are fewer forms to learn!

Participles in a Synopsis

Your new synopsis will look like this example below. Note that no matter what person and number is asked for, you can simply give the nominative case of the participle—although, in this book when I ask for a verb in the plural, I will require the plural nominative of the participles (see below).

necō, -āre, -āvī, -ātum in the 2nd person plural

		ACTIVE		PASSIVE	
		LATIN	ENGLISH	LATIN	ENGLISH
INDICATIVE	PRES.	necātis	you (pl.) kill, are killing	necāminī	you are (being) killed
	IMPF.	necābātis	you were killing	necābāminī	you were (being) killed
	FUT.	necābitis	you will kill	necābiminī	you will be killed
	PERF.	necāvistis	you (have) killed	necātī/ae/a estis	you were/have been killed
	PLUPF.	necāverātis	you had killed	necātī/ae/a erātis	you had been killed
	FT.PF.	necāveritis	you will have killed	necātī/ae/a eritis	you will have been killed
INF.	PRES.	necāre	to kill	necārī	to be killed
PART.	PRES.	necantēs, -ium	killing		
	PERF.			necātī, -ae, -a	killed, having been killed
	FUT.	necātūrī, -ae, -a	about to kill	necandī, -ae, -a	(about) to be killed
IMP.	SG.	necā!	kill!	necāre!	be killed!
	PL.	necāte!	kill! (pl.)	necāminī!	be killed! (pl.)

Translation of Participles

When you come to translate participles, one of the most important things to remember that **the tense of the participle is relative to the main verb**; that is, it depends upon the tense of the main verb. By this I mean the following:

Present Participle: happens *at the same time* as the main verb

Perfect Participle: happens *before* the main verb does (in the main verb's past)

Future Participle: happens *after* the main verb does (in the main verb's future)

Another significant aspect of translating Latin participles is that very often we will use some kind of subordinate clause in English to get across the meaning, and not necessarily use an English participle. This concept-for-concept type of translating rather than a literal, word-for-word translating can be VERY difficult to grasp. This is why in the exercises for the next few chapters, I will be asking you to first give a more literal (often wooden-sounding) translation, and then smooth it out with a more readable English version (which usually involves a clause of some sort).

Here are a few examples of how to translate a Latin participial phrase into English. First I will give a literal translation, then an adverbial English clause, then an adjectival English clause. Pay attention to how the tense of the participle is translated relative to the main verb! (Latin participial phrases are italicized along with their corresponding English translations.)

PRT.	LATIN SENTENCE	ENGLISH TRANSLATION(S)
PRESENT	Fīlia rēgis Oswaldum *dracōnem necantem* amat.	The princess loves Oswald *killing the dragon*. The princess loves Oswald *while he is killing the dragon*. The princess loves Oswald *who is killing the dragon*.
	Fīlia rēgis Oswaldum *dracōnem necantem* amāvit.	The princess loved Oswald *killing the dragon*. The princess loved Oswald *while he was killing the dragon*. The princess loved Oswald *who was killing the dragon*.
	Fīlia rēgis Oswaldum *dracōnem necantem* amābit.	The princess will love *Oswald killing the dragon*. The princess will love *Oswald when he will kill (is about to kill) the dragon*. The princess will love *Oswald who will kill (is about to kill) the dragon*.
PERFECT	Fīlia rēgis *dracōnem necātum* nōn amat.	The princess does not love *the killed dragon*. The princess does not love *the dragon after it has been killed*. The princess does not love *the dragon that has been killed*.
	Fīlia rēgis *dracōnem necātum* nōn amāvit.	The princess did not love *the killed dragon*. The princess did not love *the dragon after it had been killed*. The princess did not love *the dragon that had been killed*.
	Fīlia rēgis *dracōnem necātum* nōn amābit.	The princess will not love *the killed dragon*. The princess will not love *the dragon after it has been killed*. The princess will not love *the dragon that has been killed*.
FUTURE ACTIVE	Fīlia rēgis Oswaldum *dracōnem necātūrum* amat.	The princess loves Oswald *about to kill the dragon*. The princess loves Oswald *when he is about to kill (will kill) the dragon*. The princess loves Oswald *who is about to kill (will kill) the dragon*.
	Fīlia rēgis Oswaldum *dracōnem necātūrum* amāvit.	The princess loved Oswald *about to kill the dragon*. The princess loved Oswald *when he was about to kill (would kill) the dragon*. The princess loved Oswald *who was about to kill (would kill) the dragon*.
	Fīlia rēgis Oswaldum *dracōnem necātūrum* amābit.	The princess will love Oswald *about to kill the dragon*. The princess will love Oswald *when he will kill (is about to kill) the dragon*. The princess will love Oswald *who will kill (is about to kill) the dragon*.
FUTURE PASSIVE	Fīlia rēgis *dracōnem necandum* nōn amat.	The princess does not love *the dragon (about) to be killed*. The princess does not love *the dragon when it is (about) to be killed*. The princess does not love *the dragon that is (about) to be killed*.
	Fīlia rēgis *dracōnem necandum* nōn amāvit.	The princess did not love *the dragon (about) to be killed*. The princess did not love *the dragon when it was (about) to be killed*. The princess did not love *the dragon that was (about) to be killed*.
	Fīlia rēgis *dracōnem necandum* nōn amābit.	The princess will not love *the dragon (about) to be killed*. The princess will not love *the dragon when it will be killed (is [about] to be killed)*. The princess will not love *the dragon that will be killed (is [about] to be killed)*.

Notes on the Future Participles:

1. The future active participle can sometimes indicate likelihood or purpose. (Context, of course, will help you determine this.)

    Vīdimus Oswaldum necātūrum dracōnem. We saw Oswald who would kill the dragon.

    Oswaldus necātūrus dracōnem ex castellō ēgressus est. Oswald left the castle to kill the dragon.

2. The future passive participle usually indicates obligation or necessity rather than simple future-passive-ness.

    Hic est dracō necandus. This is the dragon to be killed (which ought to be / should be killed).

Participles of Deponent Verbs

Yes, deponent verbs have participles too. Interestingly, although deponent verbs are usually lacking in all or most of their active indicative forms, they do have the two active participles. All their participles are formed in the same way as non-deponent verbs. The only other trick with deponent verbs is that although generally you will translate the passive forms actively, as in *sequitur*, "he follows" (NOT "he is followed"), passive deponent participles are translated passively. Here is a sample synopsis to illustrate these features.

Synopsis of a Deponent Verb, Including Participles: *sequor, -quī, secūtus sum* in 3rd person singular.

		ACTIVE		PASSIVE	
		LATIN	ENGLISH	LATIN	ENGLISH
INDICATIVE	PRES.			sequitur	he/she/it follows
	IMPF.			sequēbātur	he was following
	FUT.			sequētur	he will follow
	PERF.			secūtus/a/um est	he (has) followed
	PLUPF.			secūtus/a/um erat	he had followed
	FT.PF.			secūtus/a/um erit	he will have followed
INF.	PRES.			sequī	to follow
PRT.	PRES.	sequēns, -entis	following		
	PERF.			secūtus, -a, -um	having followed
	FUT.	secūtūrus, -a, -um	about to follow	sequendus, -a, -um	(about) to be followed
IMP.	SG.			sequere!	follow!
	PL.			sequiminī!	follow! (pl.)

Participles of Irregular Verbs

Generally, irregular verbs form their participles regularly—but often, some of their participles simply do not exist. (I don't know why, so don't ask). Below are the irregular verbs used most commonly in this book along with their existent participles.

sum, esse, fuī, futūrum

PRT.	PRES.	————			
	PERF.			————	
	FUT.	futūrus, -a, -um	about to be	————	

possum, posse, potuī, ———

PRT.	PRES.	potēns, -tentis	*lit.,* "being able", *but most commonly used as the adj.,* "powerful"		
	PERF.			————	
	FUT.	————		————	

eō, īre, iī (īvī), itum

PRT.	PRES.	iēns, euntis	going		
	PERF.			itus, -a, -um	(these passive forms work in transitive compound verbs formed from *eō*)
	FUT.	itūrus, -a, -um	about to go	eundus, -a, -um	

fiō, fierī, factus sum

PRT.	PRES.	————			
	PERF.			factus, -a, -um	having been made
	FUT.	————		faciendus, -a, -um	(about) to be made

Review

Be sure to reivew the question words that are different from the relative pronoun, and be careful not to get them mixed up. Also see if you can remember how to form adverbs from the words *potens, facilis, celer, multum/plus/plurimum, bonus/melior/optimus, malus/peior/pessimus, magnus/maior/maximus,* and *parvus/minor/minimus.*

Worksheet 10

A. Vocabulary

1. adeō, _____ : _____
2. abeō, _____ _____
3. solvō: _____
4. I buy: _____
5. I climb: _____
6. premō, -ere, _____
7. testimōnium: _____
8. inde: _____
9. cōgnōscō, _____ _____
10. sumō, ____, sūmpsī, _____
11. who?: _____
12. inīquitās: _____
13. bibō, _____
14. lēx: _____
15. postquam: _____
16. misericordia: _____
17. commandment: _____
18. igitur: _____
19. sapientia: _____
20. valde: _____
21. templum: _____
22. I serve (+_____): _____
23. nam: _____
24. intereā: _____
25. canō, _____ : _____

B. Grammar

1. Give the correct form of the Latin participle, then translate (literal English is fine, even if it sounds awkward).

   a. Feminine Singular Accusative Future Active Participle of *ascendō*:

   b. Neuter Plural Ablative Perfect Passive Participle of *emō*:

   c. Masculine Singular Dative Present Active Participle of *serviō*:

   d. Neuter Singular Nominative Future Passive Participle of *cōgnōscō*:

   e. Feminine Singular Ablative Perfect Passive Participle of *trādō*:

   f. Masculine Plural Accusative Present Active Deponent Participle of *mīror*:

   g. Neuter Plural Genitive Future Passive Deponent Participle of *sequor*:

   h. Neuter Singular Dative Future Active Participle of *premō*:

   i. Masculine Nominative Singular Perfect Passive Deponent Participle of *patior*:

   j. Feminine Plural Genitive Present Active Participle of *tendō*:

2. Parse the following participles, giving Gender, Number, Case, Tense, Voice (identify deponents as such), and Mood, as well as the first principle part of the verb of origin. Some participles have more than one correct answer, so give all the possibilities.

PARTICIPLE	GENDER(S)	NBR(S)	CASE(S)	TENSE	VOICE	MOOD	1ST PRIN. PART
solūtūrōs							
orientia							
cantīs							
ēreptam							
adeuntēs							
conātus							
quaerendō							
mortua							
abitūrārum							
ēgredientibus							

3. Do a synopsis of *percutiō* in the 1st person plural, first giving principal parts:

		ACTIVE		PASSIVE	
		LATIN	ENGLISH	LATIN	ENGLISH
INDICATIVE	PRES.				
	IMPF.				
	FUT.				
	PERF.				
	PLUPF.				
	FT.PF.				
INFIN.	PRES.				

			ACTIVE		PASSIVE	
			LATIN	ENGLISH	LATIN	ENGLISH
PART.	PRES.					
	PERF.					
	FUT.					
IMP.	SG.					
	PL.					

4. Do a synopsis of *misereor* in the 2nd person singular, first giving principal parts:

		ACTIVE		PASSIVE	
		LATIN	ENGLISH	LATIN	ENGLISH
INDICATIVE	PRES.				
	IMPF.				
	FUT.				
	PERF.				
	PLUPF.				
	FT.PF.				
INF.	PRES.				
PART.	PRES.				
	PERF.				
	FUT.				
IMP.	SG.				
	PL.				

C. Memorization

Fill in the blanks for the first two stanzas of Ambrose's *Hymnus IV*.

Veni, _____

Ostende _____

Miretur _____

Talis _____

Non _____ semine,

Sed mystico _____

_____ Dei _____ caro,

_____ ventris floruit.

D. Latin to English Translation

Learning how to translate participles accurately yet readably can take some time. First translate each sentence literally/woodenly, then finesse it into a readable (yet still accurate) translation.

1. Nōs, cōnātī ponere sacrificia sancta in altārī, dē summā arce reversī sumus.

    a. Literal Translation: _____

    b. Readable Translation: _____

2. Minimae puellae ab caprō māximō eās percussūrō fūgērunt.

    a. Literal Translation: _____

    b. Readable Translation: _____

3. Quis est iste oriēns et male respondēns verbīs mandātisque nostrī prīncipis magnī?

    a. Literal Translation: _____

    b. Readable Translation: _____

4. Rēx ipse quī moritūrus erat mihi locūtus est, "Hī sunt dracōnēs interficiendī et illae sunt fīliae rēgis serviendae."

   a. Literal Translation: _____

   b. Readable Translation: _____

5. Ō vōs passī pēiora, vōbīs dabunt deī ab hīs quoque pacem.

   a. Literal Translation: _____

   b. Readable Translation: _____

6. Ex fenestrā lapsī, līberī avārī crūstula ērepta inde manducāvērunt.

   a. Literal Translation: _____

   b. Readable Translation: _____

7. Trīstēs labōrantēs sub montem mirātī erant dīvitiās aurī ibī inventās.

   a. Literal Translation: _____

   b. Readable Translation: _____

8. Proptereā, iūvistis nautās nantēs ab nāvēs eōrum fractās suprā saxa.

   a. Literal Translation: _____

   b. Readable Translation: _____

9. Rēgī, "Castellum," loquēbāmur, "aedificātum in agrō perdī potest facilius quam castellum aedificātum in monte."

   a. Literal Translation: _____

   b. Readable Translation: _____

10. Pressus inīquitāte, intereā servit lēgī sed misericordiā solvētur.

    a. Literal Translation: _____

    b. Readable Translation: _____

E. English to Latin

Translate the following sentences into Latin (you only have five this lesson). The italicized phrases should be rendered by a Latin participle.

1. We exceedingly feared the priests *who had been seen* in the dark cave.

2. "Beware!" we shouted to the pirates *who were about to drink* the wine *prepared* with poison.

3. The leader was *about to lose* [his] whole army in the woods but found all the men after two days.

4. She pitied that citizen *after he had fallen* on the snow and gave the *wounded* man food and water.

5. Jesus was begotten, not made; *begotten* from the Father before all worlds.

Lesson 11

Ablative Absolute; Irregular Verb *Ferō*

Word List

Nouns

1. fōns, fontis (m) *fountain, spring, source*
2. mūrus, -ī (m) *wall*

Verbs

3. crēscō, -ere, crēvī, crētum *I grow, increase*
4. ferō, ferre, tulī, lātum *I bear, carry*
5. lavō, -āre, lāvī, lōtum/lavātum *I wash, bathe*
6. offerō, offerre, obtulī, oblātum *I offer, bring/carry to*
7. perveniō, -īre, -vēnī, -ventum *I arrive, come through to, reach*
8. vertō, -ere, vertī, versum *I turn (around)*

Adjective

9. tenuis, -e *thin, slender*

Conjunctions/Adverbs

10. dum/dummodo (conj.) *while, during, provided that*
11. hīc *here, in this place*
12. hinc *from here, hence, from/on this side*
13. hūc *to this place, hither*
14. illīc *there, in that place*
15. illinc *from there, thence, from/on that side*
16. illūc *to that place, thither*
17. procul *at/from a distance, (a)far*
18. quō *to what place (?), whither (?), where (?)*
19. sērō, sērius, sērissimē (adv.) *late*
20. unde *from where (?), whence (?)*

Memorization

LATIN	LITERAL ENGLISH
Veni, redemptor gentium,	Come, Redeemer of nations,
Ostende partum virginis,	Show forth the virgin's birth,
Miretur omne saeculum:	Let every age marvel:
Talis decet partus Deum.	Such a birth befits God.
Non ex virili semine,	Not from man's seed,
Sed mystico spiramine,	But of mystic breath,
Verbum Dei factum caro,	The Word of God was made flesh,
Fructusque ventris floruit.	And the womb's fruit has flourished.
Alvus tumescit virginis.	The womb of the virgin swelled,
Claustrum pudoris permanet,	The barrier of chastity remains,
Vexilla virtutum micant,	Banners of virtues/miracles glitter,
Versatur in templo Deus.	God dwells in His temple.

Grammar

Ablative Absolute

At this point, you may be coming to grips with the participle, and you might be just beginning to feel comfortable translating participial phrases a bit more freely into English. Or, you may still feel a bit uncertain about the whole thing. Thankfully, in this lesson we're not going to learn any new grammar: we're just going to learn another way of using the participles we have already learned.

This lesson is about an exciting usage of the participle in Latin—the Ablative Absolute. This is a phrase in the ablative case (obviously), and the "absolute" comes from the Latin verb *absolvō* (a compound of the last lesson's verb *solvō*), meaning "I loosen from." Thus the Ablative Absolute is a construction consisting of a noun and a participle in the ablative case (or sometimes just a noun and a noun, or a noun and an adjective), loosely connected to the rest of the sentence. It is grammatically independent of the main sentence, but describes the circumstances in which the sentence occurs. You will not be learning any new participial forms in this lesson—they've already learned all the forms. This is simply another way to use participles. And now for some examples:

1. *Dracōne interfectō, Oswaldus rēx factus est.* Literal: "The dragon having been killed, Oswald will become king." Better: "Because/After the dragon had been killed, Oswald became king."

2. *Dracōne perveniente, Oswaldus gladium rapuit.* Literal: "The dragon arriving, Oswald seized [his] sword." Better: "Because/while the dragon was arriving, Oswald seized [his] sword."

3. *Oswaldō rēge, nōs dracōnes numquam timēbimus.* Literal: "Oswald being king, we will never fear dragons." Better: "Since Oswald is king, we will never fear dragons."

If you are still not comfortable with plunging in and translating ablative absolutes with a clause (e.g., "because the dragon had been killed"), you may translate these initially with the literal "the dragon having been killed." It's a bit clunky in English, but still gets the point across.

Also, notice two other things about the ablative absolute from the examples above: 1) the words in the ablative absolute generally *don't* refer to the subject or object of the main sentence; 2) the participle's tense still depends on the main clause. Hence, the present participle in the ablative absolute phrase occurs at the same time as the main verb, the perfect participle occurs before the main verb, and the future participle will occur after the main verb.

Irregular Verb *Ferō*

Periodically I have introduced irregular verbs, such as *sum, possum, faciō, fiō,* and *eō*. Like these words, the verb *ferō*, meaning "I bear, carry" is unusual and needs to have its particular forms memorized. To begin with, its principal parts are not exactly predictable: *ferō, ferre, tulī, lātum*. You may wonder why these are so wildly different. One possibility is that once upon a time two different verbs meaning the same or similar things combined to form this bold new hybrid verb. *Ferō* is a 3rd conjugation verb, and although there are a few oddities in the present system, its perfect system and participles are formed regularly off the appropriate (if somewhat strange) principal parts.

Present Active and Passive Indicatives of *ferō*

	PRESENT ACTIVE		PRESENT PASSIVE	
1ST	ferō	ferimus	feror	ferimur
2ND	fers	fertis	ferris	feriminī
3RD	fert	ferunt	fertur	feruntur

Basically, *ferō* follows the 3rd conjugation vowel pattern of *o, i, i, i, i, u* in the present, except in a few of the forms (in bold) the vowel has been dropped altogether. The imperfect is much more predictable:

Imperfect Active and Passive Indicatives of *ferō*

	PRESENT ACTIVE		PRESENT PASSIVE	
1ST	ferēbam	ferēbāmus	ferēbar	ferēbāmur
2ND	ferēbās	ferēbātis	ferēbāris	ferēbāminī
3RD	ferēbat	ferēbant	ferēbātur	ferēbantur

Nothing really surprising there in the imperfect. Nor is there in the future, provided that one remembers that in the 3rd conjugation the future uses a vowel change to *a, e, e, e, e, e* rather than *-bo, -bis, -bit*, etc.:

Future Active and Passive Indicatives of *ferō*

	PRESENT ACTIVE	
1ST	feram	ferēmus
2ND	ferēs	ferētis
3RD	feret	ferent

	PRESENT PASSIVE	
1ST	ferar	ferēmur
2ND	ferēris	ferēminī
3RD	ferētur	ferentur

Because the perfect system and even the participles are formed regularly from those strange principal parts, I have not conjugated them in full here. However, here is a sample synopsis to prove how easy *ferō* is once you actually learn its principal parts.

Synopsis of *ferō* in the 2nd person singular

		ACTIVE		PASSIVE	
		LATIN	ENGLISH	LATIN	ENGLISH
INDICATIVE	PRES.	fers	you carry	ferris	you are carried
	IMPF.	ferēbās	you were carrying	ferēbāris	you were (being) carried
	FUT.	ferēs	you will carry	ferēris	you will be carried
	PERF.	tulistī	you (have) carried	lātus/a/um es	you were/have been carried
	PLUPF.	tulerās	you had carried	lātus/a/um erās	you had been carried
	FT.PF.	tuleris	you will have carried	lātus/a/um eris	you will have been carried
INF.	PRES.	ferre	to carry	ferrī	to be carried
PRT.	PRES.	ferēns, -entis	carrying		
	PERF.			lātus, -a, -um	(having been) carried
	FUT.	lātūrus, -a, -um	about to carry	ferendus, -a, -um	(about) to be carried
IMP.	SG.	fer!	carry!	ferre!	be carried!
	PL.	ferte!	carry! (pl.)	ferimini!	be carried! (pl.)

Review

Be sure to review the question word differences again, and if you're rusty, practice your passive/deponent forms.

Worksheet 11

A. Vocabulary

1. fountain: _____
2. procul: _____
3. hūc: _____
4. illūc: _____
5. quō: _____
6. here: _____
7. tenuis, -e: _____
8. agō, agere, ēgī, actum: _____
9. crēscō, _____, _____, crētum: _____
10. deinde: _____
11. illīc: _____
12. hinc: _____
13. wall: _____
14. illinc: _____
15. _____ offerre, _____ _____ _____
16. ferō, ferre, tulī, lātum: _____
17. lātē (adv.): _____
18. cupiō, cupere, _____: _____
19. I wash: _____
20. āiō: _____
21. perveniō, _____, _____, _____: _____
    _____
22. dum/dummodo (conj.): _____
23. unde: _____
24. I turn: _____
25. cēdō, cēdere, cessī, cessum: _____

B. Grammar

1. Do a synopsis of *offerō* in the 3rd person singular, first giving principal parts:

   _____

		ACTIVE		PASSIVE	
		LATIN	ENGLISH	LATIN	ENGLISH
INDICATIVE	PRES.				
	IMPF.				
	FUT.				
	PERF.				
	PLUPF.				
	FT.PF.				
INF.	PRES.				
PART.	PRES.			███	███
	PERF.	███	███		
	FUT.				
IMP.	SG.				
	PL.				

2. Translate these Ablative Absolute phrases (literal is fine here):

   puellā inventā: _____

   illīs factīs: _____

   sapientiā crēscente: _____

   cibō ēmptō: _____

   hōc audītō: _____

   armīs latīs: _____

exercitū ēgrediente: _____

sacerdōtibus cognitīs: _____

oculō lōtō: _____

dracōne percussō: _____

C. Memorization

Memorization: Fill in the blanks in the first three stanzas of Ambrose's *Hymnus IV*.

_____

_____

_____

_____

N_____ _____ _____ _____,

S_____ _____ _____ _____,

V_____ _____ _____ _____,

F_____ _____ _____

Alvus _____ _____.

_____ _____ permanet,

_____ _____ micant,

_____ _____ templo _____.

D. English to Latin Translation

Translate the words in italics with participles.

1. The wine *having been drunk*, from there the foolish pirates quickly followed the dragon *flying* over the ship.

_____

_____

2. *Confessing* the truth, the disciples had been killed by wicked men on account of Jesus' name.

_____

_____

3. Because the tree *was growing* well in this place, the farmer kept thanking the gods and thought about better fruit.

4. Which women sought the best things for [their] children after these strong words *had been spoken*?

5. I was hearing a large animal *following* me here in the woods after the sun *had slipped* down from the sky.

6. Who are the men who wash the farmer's sheep in the fountain of the temple since the wall *has* not yet *been completed*?

7. The mountain being in the middle, on this side rain and snow fell on the hills; on that side, there was no water in the desolate places.

8. Because our large family *is arriving* soon, my mother has been preparing the most food possible, *bought* in the city and *carried* hither by me and my brother.

9. Whither you go, I will go, and from there I will never return to the rest of my country.

10. From where have you come? Will you offer me gold and riches *brought* from afar?

E. Latin to English Translation

Pyramus and Thisbe (Ovid's Metamorphoses IV.55-166)

1 *Pȳramus*, qui adulēscēns pulcherrimus erat, et *Thisbē*, *praelāta* puella, proximās tenuērunt domōs. Tempore crēvit amor, sed patres eōrum matrimōnium *vetuērunt*. Erat *rīma* tenuis et antiqua, occultāta in mūris inter domōs—sed quid nōn sentit amor? *Rīmā* inventā, amantēs verba amōris per eam saepe loquēbantur. Saepe, ubī stetērunt hinc Thisbē, Pȳramus illinc, "*Invide*," dicēbant, "mūre, quid amantibus *obstās*? Quid
5 nōn ad *ōscula* danda aperīre potēs? Sed grātī tibi sumus, nam nōbīs viam verbōrum nostrōrum dās."

    Unō diē, prīmā lūce, *cōnstituērunt* ex urbe illā nocte clam exīre, et tum convenīre ad *tumulum Nīnī*. Arbor, altus *mōrus*, ibi albīs *uberrima* pōmīs erat, et gelidus fōns.

    Clam per tenebrās versō *cardine* Thisbē ēgreditur, et pervēnit ad *tumulum* et sub arbōre sēdit. *Audācem* eam faciēbat amor. Vēnit ecce ab *recentī caede* boum* *lea* potātūra ex fonte, quam procul vīdit
10 et atram fūgit in speluncam. Dumque fugit, *vēlāmina* lapsa reliquit. Ubi lea saeva potāverat, dum redit in silvas, inventum ōre *cruentātō* manducāvit vēlāmen.

    Sērius ēgressus Pȳramus *vestīgia* leae vīdit, et vēlāmen cruentātum invēnit. "Unā duo," inquit, "nocte perdentur amantēs. *Nocēns* ego tē, miseranda, interfēcī, quod in haec loca perīculōrum nec prior tē hūc vēnī. Meum invenīte corpus et manducāte, Ō leōnēs!" Hīs dictīs, *suō* gladiō *sē* percussit et moriēns, eum
15 ē vulnere trāxit. Sanguis eius mōrum lāvit et alba *pōma* in purpurea mutāvit.

    Ecce metū *nōndum* positō, Thisbē ex spēluncā ēgressa est, sed *color* pōmī *morī* eam *incertam* facit. Deinde corpus amantis cognōvit, et *amplexa* amātum, "Pȳrame," clamāvit, "Quis tē ab mē ēripuit? Pȳrame, respondē! Tua tē cārissima Thisbē vocat!" Ad nōmen Thisbēs* Pȳramus vīsam illam cognōvit et tunc mortuus est. Ea vēlāmen *suum* et gladium eius cognōvit et, "Tua tē manus," inquit, "amorque
20 perdiderunt, miser! Egō etiam fortis sum, et sequar tē ad mortem. Hoc tamen rogō, Ō miserī nostrī parentēs—pōnite nōs duo in unō tumulō, et tū, arbor, semper habē pōma purpurea, *monumentum* sanguinis nostrī." Dīxit, et in gladiō eius lapsa est. Verba eius tetigerunt deōs, tetigerunt parentēs; nam color pōmī est hodiē āter, et *cinis* amantium unā *requiēscit* in *urnā*."

Notes:
* *boum*: irregular genitive plural of *bos, bovis*.
* *Thisbēs*: Latinized Greek genitive singular form.

Glossary:
amplector, amplectī, amplexus sum: I embrace, hug
audāx, -ācis: bold, courageous, daring
caedēs, -is (f): slaughter, killing
cardō, -dinis (m): hinge
cinis, -eris (m): ashes
color, -ōris (m): color
cōnstituō, -ere, -stituī, -stitūtum: I decide, establish, arrange
cruentō (1): I stain with blood, make bloody
incertus, -a, -um: uncertain, unsure
invidus, -a, -um: envious, unfavorable (to)
lea, -ae (f): lioness
monumentum, -ī (n): monument, memorial
mōrus, -ī (f): mulberry tree
nocēns, -ntis: harmful, injurious
Nīnus, -ī (m): Ninus, an Assyrian king, possibly after whom Nineveh is named

nōndum: not yet
obstō, -stāre, -stitī, -stātūrum (+dat.): I stand in the way, hinder, obstruct
ōsculum, -ī (n): a kiss
pōmum, -ī (n): fruit, apple; here, "berry"
praeferō, -ferre, -tulī, -lātum: I seek after, prefer
Pȳramus, -ī (m): Pyramus
recēns, -centis: fresh, recent
requiēscō, -ere, -quiēvī, -quiētum: I rest
rīma, -ae (f): crack, fissure
saevus, -a, -um: savage, cruel, fierce
sē: accusative of the reflexive pronoun, "himself, herself, itself"
suus, -a, -um (reflexive possessive adj.): his (own), her (own), its (own)
Thisbē, -ēs (f): Thisbe
tumulus, -ī (m): tomb, grave mound
ūber, -eris: rich, fruitful, abundant
urna, -ae (f): urn
vetō, -āre, vetuī, vetitum: I forbid, prevent
vēlāmen, -minis (n): veil, covering

UNIT ONE \\ LESSON 11

E. For Fun: Word Scramble

Unscramble the letters to form a Latin participle, then translate it. (Macrons omitted to make things a bit easier).

1. SERNTEEF: _____

2. BADINBE: _____

3. SOTABIL: _____

4. ETIIPNNVEER: _____

5. RAVEMURS: _____

6. SEERCCNS: _____

7. OLDNAVA: _____

8. NUTSIDEA: _____

9. RATUNCA: _____

10. BOGTENCOCSINUS: _____

11. PETMUM: _____

12. SOPSERS: _____

13. TENVIRMESE: _____

143

14. MAPUSTE: _____

_____

15. NOPRUSSRUES: _____

_____

Lesson 12

Indefinite Pronouns and Adjectives;
Review of Participles

Word List

Nouns

1. foedus, -deris (n) *treaty, covenant, agreement*
2. fortitūdō, -tūdinis (f) *strength, bravery*
3. multitūdō, -tūdinis (f) *multitude, crowd*
4. nuntius, -ī (m) *messenger*
5. puteus, -ī (m) *a well, pit*

Pronouns/Adjectives

6. aliēnus, -a, -um *of another, foreign, alien*; as noun, aliēnus, -ī (m) *stranger, foreigner*
7. aliquī, aliqua, aliquod (adj.) *some, any*
8. aliquis, aliquid (pron.) *someone, something, anyone, anything*
9. quīcumque, quaecumque, quodcumque (rel. pron./adj.) *whoever, whichever, whatever; whosoever, etc.*
10. quīdam, quaedam, quiddam (pron.) *a certain one/thing; someone, something* (do NOT confuse with *quidem*, KL2, Lesson 3)
11. quīdam, quaedam, quoddam (adj.) *a certain; some* (do NOT confuse with *quidem*, KL2, Lesson 3)
12. quisquis, quidquid (quicquid) (pron.) *whoever, whichever, whatever* (only nominatives used commonly)

Verbs

13. caedō, -ere, cecīdī, caesum *I cut (down), kill* (do not confuse with *cadō, -ere, cecidī, casum,* "I fall, sink, drop," *KL1*, Lesson 27)
14. exeō, -īre, -iī (-īvī), -itum *I go out, go away*
15. nāscor, -scī, nātus sum *I am born, am begotten, arise*
16. petō, -ere, -īvi (-iī), -ītum *I seek, ask (for); attack*
17. rumpō, -ere, rūpī, ruptum *I burst, break*

Adverbs

18. continuō *immediately, at once*
19. intereā *in the meantime, meanwhile*
20. invicem *in turn, by turns*; often translated *one another, each other*

Memorization

LATIN	LITERAL ENGLISH
Veni, redemptor gentium,	*Come, Redeemer of nations,*
Ostende partum virginis,	*Show forth the virgin's birth,*
Miretur omne saeculum:	*Let every age marvel:*
Talis decet partus Deum.	*Such a birth befits God.*
Non ex virili semine,	*Not from man's seed,*
Sed mystico spiramine,	*But of mystic breath,*
Verbum Dei factum caro,	*The Word of God was made flesh,*
Fructusque ventris floruit.	*And the womb's fruit has flourished.*
Alvus tumescit virginis.	*The womb of the virgin swelled,*
Claustrum pudoris permanet,	*The barrier of chastity remains,*
Vexilla virtutum micant,	*Banners of virtues/miracles glitter,*
Versatur in templo Deus.	*God dwells in His temple.*
Procedens dē thalamo suo,	*Coming forth from his bedchamber,*
Pudoris aula regia,	*The royal palace of purity,*
Geminae Gigas substantiae,	*A giant of twin substance*
Alacris ut currat viam.	*Eager to run a race.*

Grammar

Indefinite Pronouns and Adjectives

To allow participles and ablative absolutes time to marinate, this lesson will cover a relatively easy concept, indefinite pronouns and adjectives. The only tricky thing about these words is that quite a lot of them look alike (and involve the letter "q"), so remember to review the forms!

In both English and Latin, an indefinite pronoun is simply that—a pronoun that refers to a non-specific entity. All the pronouns we've studied so far have been definite, referring to a specific noun.

Definite Pronoun: Oswald fought the dragon and killed *it*.

Indefinite Pronoun: Oswald killed *something*.

Adjectives work along these same lines—definite adjectives are specific; indefinite adjectives are not.

Definite Adjective: Oswald killed *five* dragons.

Indefinite Adjective: Oswald killed *some* dragons.

You may remember that *a* and *the* are definite and indefinite articles. Oswald killed *the* dragon. Oswald killed *a* dragon. Remember, these don't really exist in Latin.

Latin has several different indefinite adjectives and pronouns, and although their usage is straightforward, there are a few tricks to the forms. In this lesson's word list, I have separated out *aliquī, aliqua, aliquod* (adj.) from *aliquis, aliquid* (pron.), and *quīdam, quaedam, quiddam* (pron.) from *quīdam, quaedam, quoddam* (adj.). These pairs are obviously very similar, and their differences will be discussed below.

Aliquis (pron.) and *Aliquī* (adj.)

Aliquis is a pronoun, and means someone, something, or anyone or anything, depending on the context. Again, the idea is that it's an indefinite pronoun. Thus it's a word that is vague on purpose! The word *aliquī* is the adjective version of this.

Conveniently, the *aliquis* chant generally follows that of the interrogative pronoun *quis, quid*, while *aliquī* declines a whole lot like the relative pronoun *quī, quae, quod*. The few exceptions to these are in bold:

aliquis, aliquid (pron.)

	SINGULAR			PLURAL		
	MASC.	FEM.	NEUT.	MASC.	FEM.	NEUT.
NOM.	aliquis	aliquis	aliquid	aliquī	aliquae	**aliqua**
GEN.	alicuius	alicuius	alicuius	aliquōrum	aliquārum	aliquōrum
DAT.	alicui	alicui	alicui	aliquibus	aliquibus	aliquibus
ACC.	aliquem	aliquem	aliquid	aliquōs	aliquās	**aliqua**
ABL.	aliquō	aliquō	aliquō	aliquibus	aliquibus	aliquibus

aliquī, aliqua, aliquod (adj.)

	SINGULAR			PLURAL		
	MASC.	FEM.	NEUT.	MASC.	FEM.	NEUT.
NOM.	aliquī	**aliqua**	aliquod	aliquī	aliquae	**aliqua**
GEN.	alicuius	alicuius	alicuius	aliquōrum	aliquārum	aliquōrum
DAT.	alicui	alicui	alicui	aliquibus	aliquibus	aliquibus
ACC.	aliquem	aliquam	aliquod	aliquōs	aliquās	**aliqua**
ABL.	aliquō	aliquā	aliquō	aliquibus	aliquibus	aliquibus

One quirk about *aliquis* can be summed up by this memorization help, taught to Latin students for generations (if I knew the author, I'd tell you!): "After *si*, *nisi*, *num* or *ne*, *ali*-takes a holiday." Even though you haven't learned *nisi* or *ne* yet, you should know this for *si* and *num*. Thus if you had the sentence, "If anyone sees a dragon, he ought to call Oswald," you should translate it like this: *Si quis* [NOT *aliquis*] *dracōnem vidit, Oswaldum vocāre debet*.

Quīdam (pron.) and *Quīdam* (adj.)

While the word *aliquis/aliquī* is very vague, the word *Quīdam* (both as an pronoun and adjective) is very specific: it refers to a particular item, and is usually translated in English with "a certain one" or "a certain thing," but in certain contexts you wouldn't get in trouble for translating it like "someone" or "something." Hopefully you see it's vague like *aliquis*, but it's just a tad more particular. The two words are otherwise very similar.

Both *quīdam* the pronoun and *quīdam* the adjective generally follow the relative pronoun chant, simply adding the suffix *-dam*. This pronoun and adjective are declined identically with the exception of the neuter singular nominative and accusative. One other slight oddity is found in the genitive plural and accusative singular. Rather than *quōrumdam, quārumdam, quōrumdam*, we have *quōrundam, quārundam, quōrundam*.

This change from "m" to "n" is simply a matter of ease of pronunciation. To see this, say an "m" followed by a "d" several times: "m-d, m-d, m-d," and then try it with "n": "n-d, n-d, n-d." Notice that while the "m" sound is made with the lips, the "n" and "d" are formed with the tongue in the same place in the mouth (called the alveolar ridge). Because our mouths are lazy, it's simply easier to go from "n" to "d" rather than the extra effort of "m" to "d." This same phenomenon occurs in the masculine and feminine accusaive singular.

	SINGULAR			PLURAL		
	MASC.	FEM.	NEUT.	MASC.	FEM.	NEUT.
NOM.	quīdam	quaedam	quiddam/ quoddam*	quīdam	quaedam	quaedam
GEN.	cuiusdam	cuiusdam	cuiusdam	**quōrundam**	**quārundam**	**quōrundam**
DAT.	cuidam	cuidam	cuidam	quibusdam	quibusdam	quibusdam
ACC.	**quendam**	**quandam**	quiddam/ quoddam*	quōsdam	quāsdam	quaedam
ABL.	quōdam	quādam	quōdam	quibusdam	quibusdam	quibusdam

*_quiddam_ is the pronoun form, _quoddam_ is the adjective

Quīcumque and *Quisquis* (prons.)

Quīcumque and *quisquis* are both indefinite relative pronouns, and they mean "whoever, whatever, or whichever." They will usually introduce a clause and act just like our beloved relative pronoun *quī, quae, quod*.

Since *quisquis, quidquid* most commonly appears in the nominative, you are not required to learn its forms in this book. For your information though, since it's formed by repeating *quis*, both *quis*es do decline, so its genitive would be *cuiuscuius*, dative *cuicui*, etc. (very fun to say, incidentally). The alternate spelling *quicquid* of the neuter occurs for the same ease of pronunciation discussed above ("c" and "q" are both made in the back of the throat while "d" is up front on that alveolar ridge).

Quīcumque is declined just like the relative pronoun *quī, quae, quod* with the suffix *-cumque* attached:

	SINGULAR			PLURAL		
	MASC.	FEM.	NEUT.	MASC.	FEM.	NEUT.
NOM.	quīcumque	quaecumque	quodcumque	quīcumque	quaecumque	quaecumque
GEN.	cuiuscumque	cuiuscumque	cuiuscumque	quōrumcumque	quārumcumque	quōrumcumque
DAT.	cuicumque	cuicumque	cuicumque	quibuscumque	quibuscumque	quibuscumque
ACC.	quemcumque	quamcumque	quodcumque	quōscumque	quāscumque	quaecumque
ABL.	quōcumque	quācumque	quōcumque	quibuscumque	quibuscumque	quibuscumque

Again, you don't need to know the above forms!

Review

Be sure to review the word *fero* in this lesson. It's mostly normal, but note carefully the places where it diverges from the norm. Also, practice making a few present participles.

Worksheet 12

A. Vocabulary

1. aliēnus: _____
2. aliquī, aliqua, aliquod (adj.): _____
3. quīdam, quaedam, quiddam (pron.): _____
4. petō, petere, petīvī (petiī), _____: _____
5. fortitūdō: _____
6. nāscor, -scī, nātus sum: _____
7. rumpō, _____, rūpī, _____: _____
8. I hasten: _____
9. exeō, exīre, exiī (exīvī), exitum: _____
10. caedō, _____: _____
11. messenger: _____
12. quīcumque, quaecumque, quodcumque: _____
13. puteus: _____
14. multitūdō: _____
15. intereā: _____
16. quisquis, quidquid (quicquid) (pron.): _____
17. doceō, _____ doctum: _____
18. continuō: _____
19. I hear: _____
20. aliquis, aliquid (pron.): _____
21. foedus: _____
22. vel: _____
23. invicem: _____
24. diū: _____
25. quīdam, quaedam, quoddam (adj.): _____

B. Grammar

1. Translate these phrases into English or Latin as appropriate.

of certain treaties: _____

whoever (singular, subject): _____

aliquī puteus: _____

aliēnae misericordiae: _____

some temple (direct object): _____

aliqua fortitudō: _____

a certain crowd (subject): _____

quibusdam nuntiīs: _____

of whatever [thing]: _____

certain fountains (direct object): _____

2. Do a synopsis of *rumpō* in the 3rd person singular, first giving principal parts:

_____

		ACTIVE		PASSIVE	
		LATIN	ENGLISH	LATIN	ENGLISH
INDICATIVE	PRES.				
	IMPF.				
	FUT.				
	PERF.				
	PLUPF.				
	FT.PF.				
INF.	PRES.				

PART.	PRES.				
	PERF.				
	FUT.				
IMP	SG.				
	PL.				

3. Do a synopsis of *nāscor* in the 1st person plural, first giving principal parts:

_____

		ACTIVE		PASSIVE	
		LATIN	ENGLISH	LATIN	ENGLISH
INDICATIVE	PRES.				
	IMPF.				
	FUT.				
	PERF.				
	PLUPF.				
	FT.PF.				
INF.	PRES.				
PART.	PRES.				
	PERF.				
	FUT.				

IMP.	SG.				
	PL.				

C. Memorization

Fill in the blanks in the first four stanzas of Ambrose's *Hymnus IV*.

_____

_____

_____

_____

___ ___ ___ _____,

___ ___ _____,

___ ___ ___ _____,

___ ___ ___ _____.

A_____.

C_____,

V_____,

V_____.

_____ _____ thalamo _____,

Pudoris _____ _____,

_____ Gigas _____,

_____ ut _____ _____.

D. English to Latin Translation

Translate italicizied English phrases with Latin participles or participial phrases:

1. Whoever believes in the Son of God will not die but will have eternal life because [his] evil works *have been forgiven*.

_____

_____

_____

2. After the foreign messenger *had been cut down*, the very evil throng went out and threw his body into a certain well.

   _____
   _____

3. Ask of me and I will immediately give you all the troops that you desire because of our treaty.

   _____
   _____

4. Meanwhile, if anyone says anything to you, say, "Are we not following the kraken's road in the sea?"

   _____
   _____

5. Because the fountain's waters *were bursting* through the walls of house, they were talking to one another about a certain man who indeed ought to help.

   _____
   _____

E. Latin to English Translation

Jesus and the Woman at the Well (adapted from John 4:5–34)

1   Venit ergo in civitatem *Samariae*, quae dicitur *Sychar*, iuxta agrum quod dedit *Iacob Ioseph* filio suo. Erat autem ibi fons Iacob. Iesus ergo *fatigatus* ex itinere sedebat sic super fontem. Venit quaedam mulier dē *Samaria haurire* aquam.

   Dicit ei Iesus: "Da mihi aliquid bibere"; discipuli enim eius abierant in civitatem et cibos emebant.

5   Dicit ergo ei mulier illa *Samaritana*: "Quomodo tu *Iudaeus* aliquid bibere a me *poscis*, quae sum mulier *Samaritana*?" Non enim *coutuntur Iudaei Samaritanis*.

   Respondit Iesus et dixit ei, "Pete a me et dabo tibi aquam vivam."

   Dicit ei mulier: "Domine, neque aliquid in quo haurire potes habes et puteus altus est; unde ergo habes aquam vivam? Numquid tu maior es patre nostro *Iacob* qui dedit nobis puteum et ipse ex eo bibit
10 et filii eius et *pecora* eius?"

   Respondit Iesus et dixit ei: "Omnis qui bibit ex aqua hac *sitiet* iterum; qui autem biberit ex aqua quam ego dabo ei, non sitiet in aeternum. Sed aqua quam dabo ei fiet in eo fons aquae *salientis* in vitam aeternam."

   Dicit ad eum mulier: "Domine, da mihi hanc aquam, et non sitiam neque veniam huc haurire."

   Dicit ei Iesus: "Vade, voca virum* tuum et veni huc."

15 Respondit mulier et dixit: "Non habeo virum." Dicit ei Iesus: "Bene dixisti quia* 'non habeō virum'; quinque enim viros habuisti et nunc quem habes non est tuus vir. Hoc *vere* dixisti."

Dicit ei mulier: "Domine, video quia propheta es tu. Et scio quia *Messias* venit qui dicitur Christus. Cum ergo venerit ille nobis nuntiabit omnia."

Dicit ei Iesus: "Ego sum qui loquor tecum." Et continuo venerunt discipuli eius et mirabantur quia
20 cum muliere loquebatur; nemo tamen dixit "quid quaeris?" aut "quid loqueris cum ea?"

Reliquit ergo *hydriam* suam mulier et abiit in civitatem et dicit illis hominibus: "Venite videte hominem qui dixit mihi omnia quaecumque feci. Numquid ipse est Christus?" Exierunt dē civitate et veniebant ad eum.

Interea rogabant eum discipuli dicentes, "*Rabbi* manduca." Ille autem dixit eis, "Ego cibum habeo man-
25 ducare quem vos nescitis." Dicebant ergo discipuli ad invicem, "Numquid aliquis *adtulit* ei manducare?"
Dicit eis Iesus, "Meus cibus est ut faciam *voluntatem* eius qui misit me ut *perficiam opus* eius."

Notes:
* *virum:* here *vir* is better translated as "husband"
* *quia:* Translate as "that" here.

Glossary:
Indeclinable names: *Sychar, Iacob, Ioseph*
adferō, adferre, adtulī, adlātum: I carry over, towards
coūtor, -ūtī, —, —(+abl.): I associate with, have dealings with
fatigō (1): I weary, tire
hauriō, -īre, hausī, haustum: I draw up, draw out
hydria, -ae (f): jug
Iudaeus, -ī (m): a Jew

Messīā(s), -ae (m): Messiah, Anointed One
opus: work, task
pecus, -ōris (n): cattle; herd, flock
perficiō, -ere, -fēcī, -fectum: I finish, complete, perfect
poscō, -ere, pōposcī, —: I request, ask earnestly
rabbi (m, indecl.): from Hebrew "rabbi," master, teacher
saliō, -īre, saluī, saltum: I spring, leap, jump
Samarīa, -ae: Samaria
Samaritanus, -a, -um: Samaritan
sitiō, -īre, -īvī, —: I thirst (for), am thirsty
vērē: adverb from *vērus, -a, -um*
vōluntās, -tātis (f): will, wish

Lesson 13

Passive Periphrastic with Dative of Agent

Word List

Nouns

1. clāmor, -mōris (m) *shout, cry, noise*
2. comes, comitis (m) *companion, comrade*
3. fama, -ae (f) *rumor, report; fame, reputation*
4. fātum, -ī (n) *fate; oracle, prophecy*
5. genus, generis (n) *birth, origin, race, kind*
6. imperium, -iī (n) *command, authority, empire*
7. līgnum, -ī (n) *wood, tree*
8. mōs, mōris (m) *manner, custom;* (pl.) *character, morals*
9. nepōs, nepōtis (m/f) *descendant, grandson/granddaughter, nephew/niece*
10. sepulcrum, -ī (n) *grave, tomb*
11. socius, -iī (m) *ally, companion*

Adjectives

12. pactus, -a, -um *agreed upon, covenanted, appointed*
13. singulī, -ae, -a *one at a time, single, separate*

Verbs

14. parcō, -ere, pepercī, parsum (+dat.) *I spare*
15. sternō, -ere, strāvī, strātum *I spread (out), scatter, extend*
16. tollō, -ere, sustulī, sublātum *I lift (up), raise (up); take away, destroy*

Prepositions and Adverbs

17. circā (adv. and prep. +acc.) *around, about*
18. praeter (prep. +acc.) *beside, beyond, past*
19. quondam *ever, once, formerly*
20. passim *everywhere, far and wide*

Memorization

LATIN	LITERAL ENGLISH
Veni, redemptor gentium,	Come, Redeemer of nations,
Ostende partum virginis,	Show forth the virgin's birth,
Miretur omne saeculum:	Let every age marvel:
Talis decet partus Deum.	Such a birth befits God.
Non ex virili semine,	Not from man's seed,
Sed mystico spiramine,	But of mystic breath,
Verbum Dei factum caro,	The Word of God was made flesh,
Fructusque ventris floruit.	And the womb's fruit has flourished.
Alvus tumescit virginis.	The womb of the virgin swelled,
Claustrum pudoris permanet,	The barrier of chastity remains,
Vexilla virtutum micant,	Banners of virtues/miracles glitter,
Versatur in templo Deus.	God dwells in His temple.
Procedens dē thalamo suo,	Coming forth from his bedchamber,
Pudoris aula regia,	The royal palace of purity,
Geminae Gigas substantiae,	A giant of twin substance
Alacris ut currat viam.	Eager to run a race.
Egressus eius a Patre,	He has gone forth from His Father,
Regressus eius ad Patrem;	Returned to His Father;
Excursus usque ad inferos,	Sallying forth even unto the dead,
Recursus ad sedem Dei.	Going back to the seat of God.

Grammar

Passive Periphrastic with Dative of Agent

You do not need to learn any new forms in this lesson! Instead, you will continue to delve deeper into the riches of the Latin participle. As we have already seen with the Ablative Absolute, the Latin participle is used far more often and in far more ways than its English counterpart. The Passive Periphrastic may sound intimidating, but the concept is not as tricky as you might think. "Periphrastic" is a word of Greek origin, with the *peri-* meaning "around" (as in *perimeter*), and "-phrastic" referring to a way of speaking (like the English *phrase*). The Latin equivalent of this word is "circumlocutory," and both of these long fancy-sounding words simply mean "roundabout way of saying." Think of the Passive Periphrastic like a politician who is trying very hard not to answer your question and be as indirect as possible. The Passive Periphrastic employs the future passive participle (also known as the gerundive) along with a form of *sum*. And that's why it's roundabout—it uses two words to convey one idea.

First let's brush up on the future passive participle. Add *-ndus, -a, -um* to the present stem (2nd principal part): *necāre* → *necā-* → *necandus, -a, -um*. So far we have translated this very literally as "about to be killed," as in *Videō dracōnem necandum*, "I see the dragon about to be killed." However, we could also translate this as "I see the dragon to be killed," and when you put it that way, notice how a sense of necessity or obligation creeps in—this is the dragon to be killed; the one that *should* be or *ought* to be killed. The gerundive's flavor of necessity can come directly into English. An agenda (from *agō*), is a list of "things to be done"—not just things about to be done in the future, but things that *should* be done. Thus, if context calls for it, feel free to translate the isolated future passive participle with that flavor of necessity.

When the gerundive (aka the future passive participle) is combined with a form of *sum*, then we will for sure include that taste of necessity in our translation. Below I have given possible translations for each tense (but this is not an exhaustive list of examples):

Dracō necandus est. The dragon is to be killed. The dragon should be killed. The dragon ought to be killed. The dragon has to be killed.

Dracō necandus erat. The dragon was to be killed. The dragon had to be killed.

Dracō necandus erit. The dragon will have to be killed. The dragon must be killed.

Thus far with indicative passives we have used the ablative of agent (*ab* + ablative) for a person performing the action, and ablative of means/instrument (plain ablative) for a thing:

Dracō ab Oswaldō necātus est. The dragon was killed by Oswald.

Dracō ab equite necātus est. The dragon was killed by the knight.

Dracō gladiō necātus est. The dragon was killed by a sword.

When you have an agent with the passive periphrastic, however, **that agent will be in the dative case rather than in ablative case with *ab*.** (You can still use the ablative of means/instrument.)

Dracō Oswaldō necandus est. The dragon should be killed by Oswald.

Dracō equitī necandus est. The dragon ought to be killed by the knight.

Dracō mihi necandus est. The dragon must be killed by me.

Although these examples sound just fine in English, oftentimes the translation can be pretty awkward. Therefore, it is perfectly acceptable to swap things around when putting the Latin into English, and make the verb active, with the agent as the subject and the passive verb's subject as the direct object.

Dracō Oswaldō necandus est. Oswald should kill the dragon.

Dracō equitī necandus est. The knight ought to kill the dragon.

Dracō mihi necandus est. I must kill the dragon.

Review

Be sure to review the words *aliquis, aliquī, quīdam,* and *quīcumque*. They're weird in places.

Worksheet 13

A. Vocabulary

1. ally: _____
2. gerō, gerere, gessī, gestum: _____
3. passim: _____
4. ibī: _____
5. shout: _____
6. mōs: _____
7. priest: _____
8. praeter (+_____): _____
9. sword: _____
10. pactus: _____
11. quondam: _____
12. fama: _____
13. genus: _____
14. nepōs: _____
15. fate: _____
16. singulī: _____
17. parcō, _____, pepercī, parsūrum (+_____): _____
18. opus: _____
19. around (_____): _____
20. sternō, _____, _____, strātum: _____
21. companion: _____
22. tollō, _____: _____
23. grave: _____
24. līgnum: _____
25. imperium: _____

B. Grammar

1. Do a synopsis of *tollō* in the 3rd person plural, first giving principal parts:

   _____

		ACTIVE		PASSIVE	
		LATIN	ENGLISH	LATIN	ENGLISH
INDICATIVE	PRES.				
	IMPF.				
	FUT.				
	PERF.				
	PLUPF.				
	FT.PF.				
INF.	PRES.				
PART.	PRES.			▓	▓
	PERF.	▓	▓		
	FUT.				
IMP.	SG.				
	PL.				

2. Translate these participial phrases.

   nepōtēs parcendī: _____

   _____

   clamōribus ex puteō exitūrīs: _____

   _____

sacrificia offerenda:_____

līgnīs strātīs: _____
_____

aliēnōs caedendōs:_____

nūminum proficīscentium: _____

comes tollēns: _____

fātī petītī: _____

aliquis parsūrus dracōnī: _____

quibusdam cognitīs: _____

nuntium hūc vertentem: _____

sociō sternente: _____

pluviae lōtūrae: _____

imperiō sublātō: _____
_____

ovēs emendās: _____

C. Memorization

Fill in the blanks in the first five stanzas of Ambrose's *Hymnus IV*.

_____
_____
_____
_____
_____
_____
_____
_____
_____ _____ _____ _____.
_____ _____ _____ _____,
_____ _____ _____ _____,
_____ _____ _____ _____.

P_____ _____ _____ _____,
P_____ _____ _____ _____,
G_____ _____ _____ _____,
A_____ _____ _____ _____.
_____ eius _____ _____,
_____ eius _____ _____;
_____ _____ _____ inferos,
Recursus _____ _____ _____.

D. English to Latin Translation

Translate the italicized verbs with participles (whether regular participles, ablative absolutes, or passive periphrastics!)

1. We *must spare* the lives of your grandchildren, since an agreed upon covenant *has* formerly *been made*.

2. Will anything grow in that place since the trees *were destroyed* and *scattered* everywhere by the dragon that *flew* around?

3. All the allies *had to believe* the prophesied prophecy about the race of kings and the empire *about to be born*.

4. Certain companions, one at a time, *must follow* the customs of these strangers or they will be cut down beside the Very Old Well of Fate.

5. At the appointed time we heard certain shouts, which told us where the citizens had burst through the enemy's walls.

_____

_____

_____

E. Latin to English Translation

Visit to the Underworld: Aeneas learns of Rome's future greatness from his father Anchises (adapted from Vergil's *Aeneid*, Book VI.850-900)

1   "Tu, Romane, rege imperio populos pacisque *impone* morem, parce victis et supera superbos." Sic dixit pater *Anchises*, atque haec *Aeneae* miranti loquitur: "Specta, quam Marcellus* insignis spoliis opimis* ingreditur *victorque* viros *supereminet* omnes. Hic rem *Romanam* magno *turbante* belloaedificabit eques, sternet hostes feros, tertiaque arma patri dabit capta *Romulo*."

5   Atque hic Aeneas dicit (simul nam videbat pulchrum adulescentem *fulgentibus* armis, sed trīsti facie), "Quis, pater, est ille*, qui sic sequitur virum euntem? Estne filius, aut aliquis magno dē genere nepotum? Qui* clamores sunt circa eum comitum! Quod *instar* est in ipso! Sed nox atra caput trīsti *umbra circumvolat*."

    Tum pater Anchises *lacrimis* ortis incipit: "O nate*, ingentem *luctum* ne* quaere tuorum; nec fata hunc
10 in terris diu vivere *sinent*. Nonne *nimium* potens vobis Romanum genus visum est, O dei superi, itaque haec dona rapuistis? *Quantas* lacrimas ille virum campus magnam *Martis* ad urbem offeret! Vel quae, *Tiberine*, videbis *funera*, praeter sepulcrum labens novum! Nec aliqui puer Romanus dē gente *Troiana Latinos* in *tanta* spe tollet avos, nec terra *Romuli* quondam tantum laudabit nepotem. Heu *pietas*, heu antiqua fides *invictaque* bello dextera manus! Heu, miserende puer, tu verus Marcellus eris—sed *aspera* fata non rumpes.
15 Manibus date *lilia* plenis, purpureos ponam flores, animamque nepotis his laudabo donis."

    Sic Anchises et Aeneas *Sibyllaque* per totam passim terram vadunt *aeris* in agris latis atque omnia spectant. Quae* postquam Anchises natum per singula dūxit *incenditque* animum famae venientis amore, tunc narrat bella quae deinde viro gerenda sunt, Latinosque docet populos urbemque magnam, et in terra et in mari laborem.

20   Sunt geminae *Somni* portae, quarum altera* facta est ex cornu, qua veris facilis datur *exitus* umbris; altera* candido facta elephanto*, sed per eam *falsa* ad caelum mittuntur *insomnia*. His dictis ibi tum natum Anchises unaque Sibyllam sequitur, ex portaque mittit candida. Ille viam tendit ad naves sociosque iterum videt.

    Tum ad *Caietae* portum navigat praeter litus. *Ancora* dē *prora* iacitur; stant in litore naves.

Notes:
* *Marcellus, -ī (m)*: Marcellus the Elder (c. 268–208 B.C.), a famous Roman general who won the *spolia opima* in the battle of Clastidium (222 B.C.) by killing the enemy king Viridomarus in hand-to-hand combat, and who fought somewhat successfully against Hannibal and the Carthaginians in the Second Punic War.
* *spolia opīma (spolium, -iī (n) + opīmus, -a, -um,* rich spoils*)*: The most honorable war trophy a general could earn in battle, when he defeated the opposing general or leader and took the armor from him. These spoils were taken only three times in Roman history by Romulus, Aulus Cornelius Cossus, and Marcellus.
* *ille*: Refers to Marcellus the Younger (42–23 B.C.), Emperor Augustus' nephew (and descendent of Marcellus the Elder) who was presumed by many to be a successor to the throne but who died at the age of 19.
* *quī*: Here *quī* (also *quod* in the next sentence) the interrogative adjective *what…?* is more of an exclamatory adjective, *what…!*
* *nāte*: From *nātus*, the fourth principal part of *nāscor*. Any guesses? Yes, it's the vocative of that participle, meaning "O one who was born"; in other words, "son." (It's poetic, alright?)
* *nē*: not; used here with *quaere* as a prohibition (negative command): "Do not…"
* *Quae*: When the relative pronoun begins a sentence like this, often it sounds better translated with a demonstrative pronoun like *haec*—"These things" instead of "Which things."
* *altera…altera*: When two forms of *alter* appear in this way, translate as "the one…the other."
* *elephantō*: Here it means "ivory" (the shining white part of the elephant).

Glossary:
Aenēas, -ae (m): Aeneas, son of Anchises and Venus who fled the destruction of Troy to found the kingdom from which Rome would arise
aer, aeris (m): air, mist; *terram aeris* here is referring to the Underworld
Anchises, -ae (m): Anchises, father of Aeneas; he died on their journey from the destruction of Troy
ancora, -ae (f): anchor
asper, -era, -erum: harsh, fierce
Caieta, -ae (f): Caieta, a coastal city of Italy near Rome
circumvolō (1): I fly around
exitus, -ūs (m): exit
falsus, -a, -um: false, deceitful
fulgeō, -ēre, fulsī, ——: I shine, glitter
fūnus, -neris (n): funeral (rites)
impōnō, -ere, -posuī, -positum: I put on, establish
incendō, -ere, -cendī, -censum: I kindle, set on fire
īnsōmnium, -iī (n): dream
īnstar: likeness, appearance, worth
invīctus, -a, -um: unconquered, invincible
lacrima, -ae (f): tear
Latīnus, -a, -um: Latin, of Latium, the region in which Rome is located
līlium, -iī (n): lily
lūctus, -ūs (m): grief, sorrow, mourning
Mars, Martis (m): Mars, god of war and father of Romulus
nimium: too much, too, excessively
pietās, -tātis (f): duty, piety, loyalty
prōra, -ae (f): prow
quantus, -a, -um: how much, how many, how great
Rōmānus, -a, -um: Roman; here with *rēs* it means "the Roman state"
Rōmulus, -ī (m): Romulus, the legendary founder of Rome
Sibylla, -ae (f): the Sibyl, a prophetess and priestess of Apollo at Cumae who guided Aeneas through the Underworld
sinō, -ere, sīvī, situs: I let, allow
Somnum, -ī (n): Sleep, in classical mythology, sleep has two gates; true dreams come through the gate of horn and false dreams from the gate of ivory
superēmineō, -ēre, ——, ——: I rise above, surpass
tantus, -a, -um: so great, such
Tiberīnus, -ī (m): the Tiber (river)
Trōiānus, -a, -um: Trojan, of Troy, the city from which Aeneas fled
turbō (1): I disturb, trouble
umbra, -ae (f): shadow, shade, ghost
victor, -tōris (m): victor, conqueror

Lesson 14

Nouns: Locative Case and Other Place Constructions; Verbs: *Volō, Nōlō, Mālō*

Word List

Nouns

1. aetās, -tātis (f) *age, (time of) life*
2. Athēnae, -ārum (f, pl) *Athens* (the leading city of ancient Greece)
3. Carthāgo, -ginis (f) *Carthage* (city in north Africa, now a suburb of Tunis, Tunisia)
4. cubitum, -ī (n) *elbow; a cubit* (distance from elbow to tip of middle finger; approximately 18 inches)
5. humus, -ī (f) *ground, soil, earth*
6. iūdicium, -ī (n) *judgment, decision*
7. lapis, lapidis (m) *stone, jewel*
8. lēx, lēgis (f) *law, rule*
9. malitia, -ae (f) *malice, wickedness*
10. mēnsūra, -ae (f) *measurement, measure*
11. Rōma, -ae (f) *Rome* (capital city of ancient and modern Italy)
12. rūs, rūris (n) *country, farm*
13. vestīmentum, -ī (n) *clothing, garment*

Adjective

14. modicus, -a, -um *moderate, ordinary, little*

Verbs

15. congregō (1) *I collect (into a flock/herd), assemble*
16. ēiciō, -ere, -iēcī, -iectum *I throw out, cast out, drive out*
17. induō, -ere, -duī, dūtum *I put on, clothe, wear*
18. iūdicō (1) *I judge, decide*
19. mālō, mālle, māluī, —— *I prefer, want more/instead*
20. mētior, -īrī, mēnsus sum *I measure, traverse*
21. nōlō, nōlle, nōluī, —— *I do not wish, do not want, am unwilling*
22. pascō, -ere, pāvī, pastum *I feed, pasture*

23. rēspiciō, -ere, -spēxī, -spectum *I look back, regard*

24. volō, velle, voluī, —— *I wish, want, will*

Adverb

25. ideo *therefore, for that reason*

Memorization

LATIN	LITERAL ENGLISH
Veni, redemptor gentium,	Come, Redeemer of nations,
Ostende partum virginis,	Show forth the virgin's birth,
Miretur omne saeculum:	Let every age marvel:
Talis decet partus Deum.	Such a birth befits God.
Non ex virili semine,	Not from man's seed,
Sed mystico spiramine,	But of mystic breath,
Verbum Dei factum caro,	The Word of God was made flesh,
Fructusque ventris floruit.	And the womb's fruit has flourished.
Alvus tumescit virginis.	The womb of the virgin swelled,
Claustrum pudoris permanet,	The barrier of chastity remains,
Vexilla virtutum micant,	Banners of virtues/miracles glitter,
Versatur in templo Deus.	God dwells in His temple.
Procedens dē thalamo suo,	Coming forth from his bedchamber,
Pudoris aula regia,	The royal palace of purity,
Geminae Gigas substantiae,	A giant of twin substance
Alacris ut currat viam.	Eager to run a race.
Egressus eius a Patre,	He has gone forth from His Father,
Regressus eius ad Patrem;	Returned to His Father;
Excursus usque ad inferos,	Sallying forth even unto the dead,
Recursus ad sedem Dei.	Going back to the seat of God.
Aequalis aeterno Patri	Equal to the eternal Father
Carnis tropaeo accingere	To gird the trophy [captured armor] of flesh
Infirma nostri corporis	Strengthening the weak parts
Virtute firmans perpeti.	Of our body with eternal strength.

Grammar

Locative Case

We have long been comfortable with noun cases and our dear friends the Nominative, Genitive, Dative, Accusative, and Ablative. Even the Vocative is familiar territory. There is one more tiny case to add to the repertoire—the Locative. As its name implies, the locative is used when referring to a *locus*, a place, and therefore it only appears on nouns having to do with place. Usually these are proper nouns—names of cities, towns, and small islands, and with a few ordinary nouns, such as *domus* (KL2, Ls. 9), *rūs*, and *humus* (the latter two in this lesson's Word List).

Conveniently, the locative does not have completely new forms. In the 1st and 2nd declension singular, the locative is the same as the genitive. In the plurals and 3rd declension, the locative is identical to the Dative/Ablative. The 4th and 5th Declension locatives are not common, but happily, when they do occur they are also the same as the Dative/Ablative.

1ST DECL.		2ND DECL.		3RD DECL.	
SG.	PL.	SG.	PL.	SG.	PL.
-ae	-īs	-ī	īs	-ī/-e	-ibus

Because the locative does not appear on all nouns, it will not be added to our noun charts that include the other cases. Although it might take a bit of remembering to form it from English to Latin, when you encounter a word in the locative in Latin, you shouldn't have any difficulty understanding or translating it.

Speaking of translation, since the Locative refers to "place where," it can be translated with "in" or "at." Here are some examples, using our new vocabulary words. (Note that some city names, such as *Athēnae* for "Athens," are born plural.)

Oswaldus trēs dracōnēs Carthāginī/Carthāgine interfēcit. Oswald killed three dragons in Carthage.

Oswaldus fīliam rēgis prīmum Rōmae vīdit. Oswald first saw the princess at Rome.

Oswaldus mortuum dracōnem humī vīdit. Oswald saw the dead dragon on the ground.

Oswaldus rūrī nātus est. Oswald was born in the country.

Oswaldus Athēnīs dē dracōnibus nōscet. Oswald will learn about dragons in Athens.

Oswaldus domī* nōn saepe est. Oswald is not often at home.

In all of these examples, notice that we do **not** need to use a Latin preposition (such as *in*); we simply put these nouns in the locative case and then translate with an English preposition.

Other Place Constructions

The Locative is used for "place where" with this group of nouns (cities, towns, small islands, and *domus* and *rūs*), but with these particular nouns we can do some other fun things. If we wish to express "place to which," we can simply put the special place noun in the accusative case and do **not** need a preposition such as *ad*. In English, we can also do this with a noun like "home", as in "I went home"; we don't need to use a preposition and say, "I went to home." For "place from which" we can do the same thing with the ablative, no preposition required.

Place to Which: Regular noun—*Dracō ad castellum volāvit. The dragon flew to the castle.*

Special place noun—*Dracō Rōmam volāvit. The dragon flew to Rome.*

Dracō domum volāvit. The dragon flew home.

Place from Which: Regular noun—*Dracō ab castellō abiit. The dragon left the castle.*

Special place noun—*Dracō Rōmā abiit. The dragon left Rome.*

Dracō domō abiit. The dragon left home.

---

* Recall that *domus* has forms belonging to both the 2nd and 4th declension. Its locative follows the 2nd declension locative form.

Irregular *Volō*, *Nōlō*, and *Mālō*

In this lesson you will learn three very common but somewhat irregular verbs. You have probably wanted these verbs for a long time.

Nōlō is formed from *nē* ("not") + *volō*; *mālō* from *magis* ("more, rather") + *volō*. They are only a bit strange in the present active indicative (notice they don't have passives in any tense), and elsewhere in the indicative are regular. I have given all the forms, though, just to reassure you. The present infinitives are a little strange as well. Also they often don't exist as participles, infinitives, and imperatives do not exist, but make sure you do learn the few that do exist.

These verbs often appear with the complementary infinitive to complete their meaning: *Mālō pānem mandūcāre*, "I prefer to eat bread." However, the infinitive is not necessarily required: *Mālō pānem*, "I prefer bread."

A special note on the imperatives of *nōlō*: *Nōlī* (singular) and *nōlīte* (plural) are used with that complementary infinitive to express negative commands (also called prohibitions). If Oswald told the dragon, "Do not kill the king," in Latin he would say, *"Nōlī rēgem necāre."* Literally this means "Be unwilling to kill the king," but since that is quite an awkward command, you can simply translate the *Nōlī* as "Do not."

The present active forms are the most important, so they're bolded.

volō, velle, voluī——I wish, want, will

nōlō, nōlle, nōluī——I do not wish, do not want, am unwilling

mālō, mālle, māluī——I prefer, want more/instead

			VOLŌ		NŌLŌ		MĀLŌ	
			SG.	PL.	SG.	PL.	SG.	PL.
INDICATIVE	PRES.	1ST	**volō**	**volumus**	**nōlō**	**nōlumus**	**mālō**	**mālumus**
		2ND	**vīs**	**vultis**	**nōn vīs**	**nōn vultis**	**māvīs**	**māvultis**
		3RD	**vult**	**volunt**	**nōn vult**	**nōlunt**	**māvult**	**mālunt**
	IMPERF.	1ST	volēbam	volēbāmus	nōlēbam	nōlēbāmus	mālēbam	mālēbāmus
		2ND	volēbās	volēbātis	nōlēbās	nōlēbātis	mālēbās	mālēbātis
		3RD	volēbat	volēbant	nōlēbat	nōlēbant	mālēbat	mālēbant
	FUT.	1ST	volam	volēmus	nōlam	nōlēmus	mālam	mālēmus
		2ND	volēs	volētis	nōlēs	nōlētis	mālēs	mālētis
		3RD	volet	volent	nōlet	nōlent	mālet	mālent
	PERF.	1ST	voluī	voluimus	nōluī	nōluimus	māluī	māluimus
		2ND	voluistī	voluistis	nōluistī	nōluistis	māluistī	māluistis
		3RD	voluit	voluērunt	nōluit	nōluērunt	māluit	māluērunt
	PLUPF.	1ST	volueram	voluerāmus	nōlueram	nōluerāmus	mālueram	māluerāmus
		2ND	voluerās	voluerātis	nōluerās	nōluerātis	māluerās	māluerātis
		3RD	voluerat	voluerant	nōluerat	nōluerant	māluerat	māluerant
	FUT. PF.	1ST	voluerō	voluerimus	nōluerō	nōluerimus	māluerō	māluerimus
		2ND	volueris	volueritis	nōlueris	nōlueritis	mālueris	mālueritis
		3RD	voluerit	voluerint	nōluerit	nōluerint	māluerit	māluerint

		ACTIVE	PASSIVE	ACTIVE	PASSIVE	ACTIVE	PASSIVE
INF.	PRES.	velle	—	nōlle	—	mālle	—
PRT.	PRES.	volēns, -entis		nōlēns, -entis		—	
	PERF.		—		—		—
	FUT.	—	—	—	—	—	—
		SG.	PL.	SG.	PL.	SG.	PL.
IMP.		—	—	nōlī	nōlīte	—	—

Obviously these are very important words. If you want to do something, now all you have to do is add a infinitive to the verb *volo*. "I want to eat" would be *volo edere*, "I want to drink," would be *volo bibere*, and so on. Since it's so important, make sure you work on learning this verb.

Review

Be sure to review *ferō* as well as all those weird words we recently learned (*aliquis/aliquī, quīdam, quīcumque*). Review question words if you've gotten rusty.

Worksheet 14

A. Vocabulary

1. modicus: _____
2. _____, _____, ēiēcī, ēiectum: _____
3. cubitum: _____
4. I do not wish: _____
5. lapis: _____
6. interim: _____
7. Carthage: _____
8. induō, _____, _____, indūtum: _____
9. mēnsūra: _____
10. mētior, mentīrī, mēnsus sum: _____
11. mālō, mālle, māluī, ——: _____
12. ipse, ipsa, ipsum: _____
13. iūdicium: _____
14. I feed: _____
15. Rome: _____
16. quidem: _____
17. aetās: _____
18. militia: _____
19. rūs: _____
20. law: _____
21. quī, quae, quod: _____
22. iūdicō: _____
23. Athens: _____
24. vestīmentum: _____
25. rēspiciō, _____
26. quaerō, _____, _____, quaesītum (-situm): _____

27. volō, velle, voluī, ——: _____

28. humus: _____

29. congregō: _____

B. Grammar

Translate these verb forms from Latin to English or English to Latin as appropriate.

1. nōluērunt: _____
2. to wish: _____
3. she prefers: _____
4. you (pl.) are unwilling: _____
5. mālam: _____
6. you (sg.) wish: _____
7. they will have preferred: _____
8. we do not want: _____
9. vultis: _____
10. mālumus: _____
11. they don't wish: _____
12. you (pl.) will wish: _____
13. I will prefer: _____
14. mālle: _____
15. we were wanting: _____

Locative Practice: Put the following nouns into the locative case.

16. at home: _____
17. in Carthage: _____
18. in Rome: _____
19. on the ground: _____
20. at Athens: _____

21. Do a synopsis of *nōlō* in the 3rd person singular, first giving principal parts:

_____

		ACTIVE		PASSIVE	
		LATIN	ENGLISH	LATIN	ENGLISH
INDICATIVE	PRES.				
	IMPF.				
	FUT.				
	PERF.				
	PLUPF.				
	FT.PF.				
INF.	PRES.				
PART.	PRES.			▓▓▓	▓▓▓
	PERF.	▓▓▓	▓▓▓		
	FUT.				
IMP.	SG.				
	PL.				

22. Do a synopsis of *ēiciō* in the 2nd person plural, first giving principal parts:

_____

| | | ACTIVE || PASSIVE ||
		LATIN	ENGLISH	LATIN	ENGLISH
INDICATIVE	PRES.				
	IMPF.				
	FUT.				
	PERF.				
	PLUPF.				
	FT.PF.				
INF.	PRES.				
PART.	PRES.			■	■
	PERF.	■	■		
	FUT.				
IMP.	SG.				
	PL.				

C. Memorization

Fill in the blanks in the first six stanzas of Ambrose's *Hymnus IV*.

_____

_____

_____

_____

_____
_____
_____
_____
_____
_____
_____
_____
_____
_____
_____ ___ _____ _____,
_____ _____ _____,
_____ _ _____,
_____ ___ _____ _____.

E_____ _____ ___ _____,
R_____ _____ ___ _____;
E_____ _____ ___ _____,
R_____ ___ _____ _____.

_____ aeterno _____.
_____ _____ accingere
_____ nostri _____
_____ _____ perpeti.

D. English to Latin Translation

Use participles to translate italicized verbs.

1. You *must pasture* my sheep in the country, since they are unwilling to eat the grass in Carthage.

   _____
   _____

2. Once the purple garments *have been put on*, the queen wishes to go out from Rome to the foreigner's tomb.

   _____
   _____

3. Do not cast stones out of that window or someone will be wounded or killed!

4. Surely, O king, you do not prefer to regard certain prophecies of malice and to assemble the worst possible men in Athens?

5. Although the tree *had* a measurement of twenty cubits, the ordinary boy had climbed it and then was unwilling to descend to the ground.

E. Latin to English Translation

An Excerpt from the Sermon on the Mount (adapted from Matthew 6:25–7:12)

1 Ideo dico vobis: Nolite *solliciti* esse animae* vestrae, dicentes, "Quid manducabimus?" neque corpori* vestro, "Quid induemus?" Nonne anima plus est quam *esca*, et corpus quam vestimentum? Respicite aves caeli, quoniam* non *serunt* neque *metunt* neque congregant in *horrea*, et Pater vester in caelo pascit illas. Nonne vos magis pluris estis illis? Quis autem vestrum cogitans potest *adicere* ad aetatem suam cubitum
5 unum? Et dē vestimento quid *solliciti* estis? *Considerate lilia* agri quomodo crescunt: non laborant neque *nent*. Dico autem vobis quoniam nec *Salomon* in omni gloria sua indutus est sicut unum ex istis. Si autem *fenum* agri, quod hodie est et cras in *clibanum* mittitur, Deus sic induit, quanto magis, vos modicae fidei?
   Nolite ergo solliciti esse dicentes: "Quid manducabimus?" aut "Quid bibemus?" aut "Quo induemur?" Haec enim omnia gentes quaerunt; scit enim Pater vester in caelo quia his omnibus *indigetis*. Quaerite
10 autem primum regnum Dei et *iustitiam* eius, et haec omnia *adicientur* vobis. Nolite ergo esse *solliciti* in *crastinum*; crastinus enim dies *sollicitus* erit *sibi* ipse. *Sufficit* diei malitia *sua*.
   Nolite iudicare, aut iudicabimini; in quo enim iudicio iudicaveritis, iudicabimini, et in qua mensura mensi eritis, metietur vobis. Quid autem vides *festucam* in oculo fratris tui, et *trabem* in oculo tuo non vides? Aut quomodo dices fratri tuo: "Sine, eiciam *festucam* dē oculo tuo," et ecce *trabes* est in oculo
15 tuo? *Hypocrita*, eice primum *trabem* dē oculo tuo, et tunc videbis eicere *festucam* dē oculo fratris tui. Nolite dare sanctum canibus neque mittere* margaritas vestras ante porcos, aut forte *conculcabunt* eas pedibus suis et versi *dirumpent* vos.
   Petite, et dabitur vobis; quaerite et invenietis; *pulsate*, et aperietur vobis. Omnis enim qui petit, accipit; et, qui quaerit, invenit; et pulsanti aperietur. Aut qui homo est ex vobis, quem si petiverit filius

20 suus panem, numquid lapidem dabit ei? Aut si piscem petiverit, numquid *serpentem* dabit ei? Si ergo vos, mali, novistis dona bona dare filiis vestris, quanto magis Pater vester, qui in caelis est, dabit bona petentibus se. Omnia ergo, quaecumque vultis facere vobis homines, ita et vos facite eis; haec est enim Lex et *Prophetae*.

Notes:
* *animae* and *corporī*: dative of reference (see *KL3*, Lesson 1) with *sollicitī*; lit., "anxious with regard to…" but "anxious in…" works well.
* *quoniam*: like *quia*, it can also mean "that"
* *mittere*: *mittō* can mean "I throw, cast" as well as "send"

Glossary:
adiciō, -ere, -iecī, -iectum: I throw to, add, increase
clibanum, -ī (n): oven
conculcō (1): I trample, tread underfoot
cōnsiderō (1): I inspect, examine, consider
crāstinus, -a, -um: tomorrow's, next; *in crāstinum* = for tomorrow
dirumpō, -ere, -rūpī, -ruptum: I burst asunder, tear asunder
esca, -ae (f): food
fēnum [faenum], -ī (n): hay
festūca, -ae (f): straw
horreum, -ī (n): barn, granary, storehouse
hypocrita, -ae (m): hypocrite

indigeō, -ēre, -diguī, —— (+ gen./abl.): I need, require, lack
iūstitia, -ae (f): justice, righteousness
līlium, -ī (n): lily
metō, -ere, messuī, messum: I reap, harvest
neō, nēre, nēvī, nētus: I spin, weave
pulsō (1): I strike, knock
prophēta, -ae (m): prophet
quantō (adv.): (by) how much
serō, -ere, sēvī, satum: I sow, plant
Salomon, -mōnis (m): Solomon
serpēns, -pentis (m/f): serpent, snake
sibi: from reflexive pronoun *sui* (gen.), *sibi* (dat.), *sē* (acc.), *sē* (abl.), himself, herself, itself
sinō, -ere, sīvī, situs: I let, allow
sollicitus, -a, -um: anxious, troubled
sufficiō, -ere, -fēcī, -fectum: I am sufficient, suffice
suus, -a, -um (reflexive possessive adj.): his (own), her (own), its (own)
trabēs, -is (m): tree trunk, beam

F. For Fun: Matching

In honor of learning the Locative Case this lesson, match the names of the ancient cities to their modern equivalents.

ANCIENT NAME	MODERN NAME
Brundisium	a. Florence
Caietae Portus	b. Venice
Cannae	c. Gaeta
Comum	d. Pisa
Florentia	e. Rome
Forum Fulvii	f. Taranto
Mantua	g. Milan
Mediolanum	h. Como
Narnia	i. Mentana
Neapolis	j. Perugia
Nomentum	k. Brindisi
Panormus	l. Narni
Perusia	m. Mantova
Pisae	n. Siena
Regium	o. Villa del Foro
Roma	p. Palermo
Saena Julia	q. Canne della Battaglia
Tarentum	r. Reggio Calabria
Urbs Vetus	s. Naples
Venetiae	t. Orvieto

Lesson 15
Gerund vs. Gerundive

Word List

Nouns

1. causa, -ae (f) *cause, reason*; the abl. causā (+gen.) *on account of, for the sake of* [usually follows its gen. object]
2. ferrum, -ī (n) *iron, sword*
3. īnsidiae, -ārum (f, pl) *ambush, plot*
4. iūs, iūris (n) *justice, right, duty*
5. lēgātus, -ī (m) *ambassador, envoy, lieutenant*
6. mūnus, -neris (n) *office, duty, gift*
7. ōrdō, -dinis (m) *line, row, order*
8. praeda, -ae (f) *spoil, booty, plunder*
9. sensus, -ūs (m) *sense, feeling, understanding*

Adjectives

10. uter, utra (ūtra), utrum (ūtrum) (interrog.) *which (of two)?*; (relat.) *whichever (of two), the one which*; (indef.) *either, one (of two)*
11. neuter, -tra, -trum *neither*
12. cēterus, -a, -um *the other, the rest* (usually used in pl.)
13. Rōmānus, -a, -um *Roman*; (subst.) *a Roman*

Verbs

14. cōnstituō, -ere, -stituī, -stitūtum *I set up, establish, decide*
15. ignōrō (1) *I do not know, am ignorant of*
16. iūrō (1) *I swear, vow, take an oath* (iūs iūrandum [*or as one word*, iūsiūrandum] *an oath*)
17. trānseō, -īre, -iī, -itum *I go across/over, cross (over)*

Adverbs, Prepositions

18. intrā (prep. +acc.; adv.) *within, inside, inwardly*
19. undique *from all sides, on all sides, everywhere*
20. vērō *truly, certainly* [can also be used to say "yes"]

Memorization

LATIN	LITERAL ENGLISH
Veni, redemptor gentium,	Come, Redeemer of nations,
Ostende partum virginis,	Show forth the virgin's birth,
Miretur omne saeculum:	Let every age marvel:
Talis decet partus Deum.	Such a birth befits God.
Non ex virili semine,	Not from man's seed,
Sed mystico spiramine,	But of mystic breath,
Verbum Dei factum caro,	The Word of God was made flesh,
Fructusque ventris floruit.	And the womb's fruit has flourished.
Alvus tumescit virginis.	The womb of the virgin swelled,
Claustrum pudoris permanet,	The barrier of chastity remains,
Vexilla virtutum micant,	Banners of virtues/miracles glitter,
Versatur in templo Deus.	God dwells in His temple.
Procedens dē thalamo suo,	Coming forth from his bedchamber,
Pudoris aula regia,	The royal palace of purity,
Geminae Gigas substantiae,	A giant of twin substance
Alacris ut currat viam.	Eager to run a race.
Egressus eius a Patre,	He has gone forth from His Father,
Regressus eius ad Patrem;	Returned to His Father;
Excursus usque ad inferos,	Sallying forth even unto the dead,
Recursus ad sedem Dei.	Going back to the seat of God.
Aequalis aeterno Patri	Equal to the eternal Father
Carnis tropaeo accingere	To gird the trophy [captured armor] of flesh
Infirma nostri corporis	Strengthening the weak parts
Virtute firmans perpeti.	Of our body with eternal strength.
Praesepe iam fulget tuum,	Now your manger flashes forth,
Lumenque nox spirat novum,	And night breathes out new light,
Quod nulla nox interpolet,	Which no night may falsify,
Fideque iugi luceat.	And which shines with eternal faith.

Grammar

Gerund vs. Gerundive

In this lesson we are exploring the wonderful world of participles further. At this point it is also probably an opportune time to remember that Latin and English are different languages. This may sound a little more than obvious, but often we expect another language to behave exactly as our own does, and it simply will not. We can't translate Latin into English word-for-word without quickly sounding ridiculous, and so that's when we need to translate Latin idiom with English idiom. With this in mind, let's learn gerunds.

First off, remember that the "gerundive" is simply another name for the future passive participles (e.g., *necandus, -a, -um*). The Latin gerund is the neuter gerundive used as a noun, and only appears in the singular in genitive, dative, accusative, and ablative:

	SG.	PL.
NOM.	————	————
GEN.	-ī	————
DAT.	-ō	————
ACC.	-um	————
ABL.	-ō	————

Thus where the gerund*ive* is a verbal adjective, the gerund is a verbal noun. You may recall the term "gerund" from English grammar, where a gerund is simply the *-ing* form of the verb, as in "*Slaying* dragons is difficult." The Latin gerund is similar, but since it's another language, after all, it differs from the English gerund at several points.

Why is there no nominative? In English we can say, "Slaying dragons is difficult" using a gerund to do so. In Latin, however, that usage is already supplied by the infinitive: *Necāre dracōnēs difficile est*. (Note that the infinitive is a neuter verbal noun and is therefore modified by a neuter adjective.) We can translate this sentence either as "To slay dragons is difficult" or "Slaying dragons is difficult." So a nominative gerund would be redundant. Here are some examples of the Latin gerund being used in the other cases (fancy term: oblique cases).

1. Genitive

    Ex castellō Oswaldus necandī dracōnem causā ēgressus est. Oswald went out from the castle for the sake of slaying the dragon.

2. Dative

    Occīdere cētōs simile necandō dracōnēs est. Killing krakens is similar to slaying dragons.

3. Accusative

    Ex castellō Oswaldus ad servandum fīliam rēgis ēgressus est. Oswald went out from the castle to save the princess. (Note this special use of *ad* with a gerund to express purpose.)

Important Note: The gerund in the accusative is usually not used as a pure direct object, as in the English "Oswald loves slaying dragons." For that, Latin would again use that infinitive: *Oswaldus necāre dracōnēs amat*, which can also be translated "Oswald loves to slay dragons."

4. Ablative

    Oswaldus fīliam rēgis necandō dracōnem servāvit. Oswald saved the princess by slaying the dragon.

The third example above for the accusative, *Ex castellō Oswaldus ad servandum filiam rēgis ēgressus est*, is actually "bad" Latin: the Romans would almost never have said that! For some reason, the Romans did not like the gerund (*servandum*) to take a direct object (*filiam*). Therefore, they preferred to swap out the gerund (verbal noun) for the gerundive (future passive participle). When they did so they changed the gerundive to match its direct object in gender and number, and make the direct object match the case of the gerundive. For instance, the above example becomes: *Ex castellō Oswaldus ad **servandam** filiam rēgis ēgressus est*. Think of it as though the two switch clothes: the gerundive takes on *filiam*'s gender (feminine) and its number (in this case, singular, so no change there).

This may seem complicated, but fortunately, you can translate this version **exactly** like the gerund one: "Oswald went out from the castle to save the princess."

If you try to translate it literally, things get awkward pretty fast: "Oswald went out of the castle for the purpose of the princess to be saved." (So yes, if you were wondering, we are indeed authorized to translate the *passive* gerundive as though it were an *active* gerund.) Once in a while you do find these gerunds taking objects (particularly the genitive, dative, and ablative ones; but when *ad* + accusative is used, there aren't any examples out there of a gerund with a direct object). So if we were to fix our above examples to the preferred mode of expression, we would get the following:

1. Genitive

    Gerund with object (okay Latin): *Ex castellō Oswaldus necandī dracōnem causā ēgressus est.* Oswald went out from the castle for the sake of slaying the dragon.

    Gerundive phrase (preferred by Romans): *Ex castellō Oswaldus necandī dracōnis causā ēgressus est.* Oswald went out from the castle for the sake of slaying the dragon. The gerundive *necandī* is already masculine and singular, and *dracōnem* takes on the case of the gerundive, in this case genitive.

2. Dative

    Gerund with object (okay Latin): *Occidere cētōs simile necandō dracōnēs est.* Killing krakens is similar to slaying dragons.

    Gerundive phrase (preferred by Romans): *Occidere cētōs simile necandīs dracōnibus est.* Killing krakens is similar to slaying dragons. Again, notice how the gerundive *necandō* has become plural (it is already masculine), and the direct object *dracōnēs* takes on the case of the gerundive, in this case dative.

3. Accusative

    Gerund with object (bad Latin): *Ex castellō Oswaldus ad servandum filiam rēgis ēgressus est.* Oswald went out from the castle to save the princess.

Gerundive phrase (preferred by Romans): *Ex castellō Oswaldus ad servandam fīliam rēgis ēgressus est.* Oswald went out from the castle to save the princess. We have seen this example before. Note that we use *ad* here to signfiy purpose; it usually doesn't work this way, so be sure you don't use *ad* to express purpose unless you use a gerundive.

4. Ablative:

   Gerund with object (okay Latin): *Oswaldus fīliam rēgis necandō dracōnem servāvit.* Oswald saved the princess by slaying the dragon.

   Gerundive phrase (preferred by Romans): *Oswaldus fīliam rēgis necandō dracōne servāvit.* Oswald saved the princess by slaying the dragon. Last time, but hopefully you see that the gerundive is already the number and case of the direct object (masculine and singular) and that the direct object has become ablative.

You might feel like panicking at this point because it all sounds so complicated. Trust me. When you are translating merrily along, you will not be fazed by this. You will not stop to flounder in doubt about whether this word is a gerund or gerundive. You will simply translate the phrase in a way that sounds like real English and makes sense. Of course, it is a little trickier to generate the proper form when translating English to Latin, but since most of your time will probably be spent going from Latin to English, you will be able to overcome the gerund vs. gerundive dilemma.

Synopsis and the Gerund

The addition of this new concept of a gerund won't change our synopsis at all since the gerund is taken straight from the gerundive (future passive participle). A separate box for it in the synopsis chart will *not* be added; carry on as before.

Summary of Differences between the Gerund and the Gerundive

Here is a chart highlighting the basic differences between the two, even though sometimes we will translate them into English in the same way.

	GERUND	GERUNDIVE
PT. OF SPEECH	verbal noun	verbal adjective
GENDER	neuter only	masculine, feminine, and neuter
NUMBER	singular only	singular and plural
CASE	genitive, dative, accusative, and ablative	nominative, genitive, dative, accusative, ablative
VOICE	active	passive (but can be translated actively if need be)

Review

Be sure to review the words *volō*, *nolō*, and *malō*.

Worksheet 15

A. Vocabulary

1. ignōrō: _____
2. ambassador: _____
3. soon: _____
4. modo: _____
5. Roman (adj.): _____
6. iron: _____
7. intrā (prep. _____ adv.): _____
8. spoil: _____
9. cēterus: _____
10. sensus: _____
11. cause: _____
12. neuter, -tra, -trum: _____
13. magnoperē: _____
14. mūnus: _____
15. undique: _____
16. vērō: _____
17. uter, utra, utrum (interrog.): _____
18. trānseō, _____ transitum: _____
19. ambush: _____
20. anima: _____
21. ōrdō: _____
22. inveniō, _____ inventum: _____
23. iūs: _____
24. iūrō: _____
25. _____, cōnstituere, cōnstituī, constitūtum: _____

B. Grammar

1. Translate the following participial phrases. Identify gerunds and gerundives; some are neither.

LATIN PHRASE	ENGLISH TRANSLATION	GERUND OR GERUNDIVE?
īnsidiīs cōnstitūtīs		
ad lēgātōs congregandōs		
iūs iūrandum		
Deō volente		
cubitōs mētiendī causā		
vestīmenta indūta		
ignorandō ōrdinem		
sublātīs ferrīs		
praedā sternendā		
lēgatī trānseuntis		

2. Do a synopsis of *iūrō* in the 3rd person singular, first giving principal parts:

		ACTIVE		PASSIVE	
		LATIN	ENGLISH	LATIN	ENGLISH
INDICATIVE	PRES.				
	IMPF.				
	FUT.				
	PERF.				
	PLUPF.				
	FT.PF.				

INF.	PRES.				
PART.	PRES.				
PART.	PERF.				
PART.	FUT.				
IMP.	SG.				
IMP.	PL.				

C. Memorization

Write out all of Ambrose's *Hymnus IV* in Latin.

_____
_____
_____
_____
_____
_____
_____
_____
_____
_____
_____
_____
_____
_____
_____
_____
_____ _____ _____ _____,

_____ _____ _____ _____;
_____ _____ _____,
_____ _____ _____ _____.
A_____ _____ _____.
C_____ _____ _____
I_____ _____ _____
V_____ _____ _____ _____.
_____ _____ fulget _____,
_____ _____ spirat _____,
_____ _____ nox _____,
_____ iugi _____.

D. English to Latin Translation

Translate the following sentences into Latin; italics indicate a Latin participle should be used.

1. The pirate vowed, *saying*, "I will give my life to *fighting*, *seeking* spoil, *drinking*, and *loving* beautiful women!"

2. Which duty will the Roman lieutenant decide to do for the sake of *cutting down* the ambush?

3. By *not knowing* the custom in Carthage, we were unwilling to wear certain clothes and therefore were sent home.

4. After some jewels and spoils *were scattered* within the tomb, the companions assembled in a line to *carry* the rest to the ship.

5. Your nephew *must lift up* the sword against the malice in Athens, or justice and good sense will die there.

E. Latin to English Translation

The Story of Scaevola, based on Livy's *Ab Urbe Condita* II.12–13

1 *Obsidio* autem manebat et erat frumentum parum, nam obsidendo capere urbem *Porsinna* magnopere volebat. *Gaius Mucius*, adulescens *nobilis*, voluit superare obsidentes *Etruscos* quos populus Romanus saepe quondam vicit. Itaque, cogitans "Magno *audacique* aliquo opere ea *indignitas* removenda est," clam ingredi in hostium castra constituit et tunc *senatum* adit. "Transire *Tiberim*," inquit, "patres, et
5 ingredi castra hostium volo. Non praedam quaero; maius opus conabor." Volebant patres; occultato intra vestimentum ferro proficiscitur.

Ubi illuc venit, in *confertissima* turba prope regis *tribunal* constitit. Ibi *stipendium* militibus forte dabatur, et *scriba*, cum rege sedens indutusque simillimis vestimentis regis, multa agebat eumque milites undique adiebant. Timens quaerere, "Uter Porsinna est?"—quod (cogitat) "Ignorando regem, mihi hostis
10 dicet 'Num regem scis? Quis es? Es hostis!'"—percussit *temere* quo fortuna constitit et scribam pro rege interficit. Vadens inde per turbam *cruento* ferro *effugere* conabatur, sed clamore audito captus est ab militibus regis et ante *tribunal* regis tractus est.

Ibi, etiam in maximo periculo timendus, magis quam timens, "Romanus sum," inquit, "civis; me *Gaium Mucium* vocant. Hostis hostem occidere volui; mori volo sicut occidere volebam. Et facere et
15 pati fortia Romanum est. Nec solus ego te occidere conatus sum; est longus post me ordo petentium hanc gloriam. Ergo para esse in periculo in singulas* horas et habere ferrum hostis in ostio tuo. Hoc tibi nos, *iuventus* Romana, declaramus bellum."

Rex simul ira *infensus* periculoque territus "Tu," inquit, "ignibus daberis nisi *expromes* has insidias!" *Mucius* "Ecce," inquit, "quam *vile* corpus est eis qui magnam gloriam vident!"; dextramque manum
20 *accenso* ad sacrificium *foculo* inicit. Eam torrebat sicut *alienato* ab sensu animo, et tunc mirans rex removeri ab altaribus adulescentem *iussit*. "Tu vero abi," inquit, "maior hostis in te* quam in me* fuisti. Tua virtus maxima est; ergo *intactum inviolatumque* hinc dimitto." Tunc Mucius, "quando quidem," inquit, "miraris virtutem, nos *trecenti* iuravimus principes iuventutis Romanae: 'Nos *Porsinnam* ferro occidemus!' Ego primus fui, sed ceteri adibunt *quoad* tu mortuus fueris."
25 Legati *Mucium* dimissum—cui postea "Scaevolae" a *clade* dextrae manus *cognomen* datum est—a *Porsinna* Romam secuti sunt. Rex periculo vitae motus est et itaque pacis *condiciones* ferebat Romanis. Facta pace, exercitum ab *Ianiculo* duxit *Porsinna* et agro Romano abiit. Patres *Gaio Mucio* virtutis causa trans *Tiberim* agrum dono dederunt, quae postea sunt "*Mucia prata*" appellata.

Notes:
* *singulās*: Here it sounds better to translate *singulās* as "each" or "each and every."
* *in*: + acc. can also mean "against"

Glossary:
accendō, -ere, -cēnsī, -cēnsum: I kindle, light, set on fire
aliēnō (1): I alienate, estrange
audāx, audācis (adj.): bold, daring
clādēs, -is (f): destruction, ruin, loss
cognōmen, -minis (n): surname, family name, cognomen, Roman cognomina often began as nicknames based on achievements or physical appearance and then were passed down as a family name
condiciō, -ōnis (f): condition, demand, agreement
confertus, -a, -um: crowded, thick, dense
cruentus, -a, -um: bloody
effugiō, -ere, -fūgī, -fugitum: I escape
Etruscus, -a, -um: Etruscan; (subst.) an Etruscan
exprōmō, -ere, -mpsī, -mptum: I take out, reveal, disclose
foculus, -ī (m): fire-pan, brazier
Gāius Mūcius, Gāiī Mūciī (m): Gaius Mucius, Roman youth renowned for his bravery as recounted in this story. After this incident he became known as Gaius Mucius Scaevola ("left-handed"); the name Scaevola was handed down to his descendents as well.

Iāniculum, -ī (n): the Janiculum, a hill just outside Rome
indīgnitās, -tātis (f): unworthiness, indignity
īnfēnsus, -a, -um: enraged, hostile
iniciō, -ere, -iēcī, -iectum: I throw in, put in, cast in
intāctus, -a, -um: untouched, uninjured
iubeō, -ēre, iussī, iūssum: I order, command
iuventūs, -tūtis (f): youth
inviolātus, -a, -um: unharmed, unhurt
Mucius, -a, -um: Mucian; of the Roman gens Mucius
nōbilis: noble, famous
obsidiō, -ōnis (f): siege, blockade
Porsinna, -ae (m): Lars Porsena, king of the Etruscan city of Clusium, who besieged Rome around 509 B.C.
prātum, -ī (n): meadow, plain
quoad: until
senātus, -ūs (m): senate
Scaevola, -ae (m): the left-handed (from *scaevus, -a, -um*, "left")
scrība, -ae (m): clerk, secretary, scribe
stīpendium, -iī (n): pay, stipend, tax
temere: rashly, at random, by chance
Tiberis, -is [acc. -berim; abl. -berī] (m): the Tiber river
tribūnal, -ālis (n): judgment seat, tribunal, a raised platform where magistrates sat to administer justice
trecentī (tres + centum): three hundred
vīlis, -e: cheap, worthless

Lesson 16

Review and Test

Word List

No new words this lesson. Review vocabulary from Lessons 9-15.

Grammar

No new chant this lesson. Review chants from Lessons 9-15.

Memorization

No new memorization this lesson. Review the entirety of Ambrose's *Hymnus IV*.

Worksheet 16

A. Vocabulary

1. īnsidiae: _____
2. aetās: _____
3. aliēnus (noun): _____
4. altāre: _____
5. Athens: _____
6. Carthage: _____
7. nepōs: _____
   _____
8. cubitum: _____
9. causa: _____
10. clāmor: _____
11. comes: _____
12. cōnspectus: _____
13. fātum: _____
14. ferrum: _____
15. caedō: _____
16. fountain: _____
17. abeō: _____
18. genus: _____
19. ground: _____
20. imperium: _____
    _____
21. cognōscō: _____
22. iūdicium: _____
23. iūs: _____
24. covenant: _____
25. stone: _____

26. lēgātus: _____
27. law: _____
28. wood: _____
29. malitia: _____
30. cōnstituō: _____
31. mandātum: _____
32. mēnsūra: _____
33. mercy: _____
34. mōs: _____
    _____
35. multitude: _____
36. canō: _____
37. mūnus: _____
38. mūrus: _____
39. rumōr: _____
40. snow: _____
41. messenger: _____
42. ōrdō: _____
43. exeō: _____
44. a well: _____
45. ferō: _____
46. pluvia: _____
47. praeda: _____
48. wisdom: _____
49. ignōrō: _____
    _____
50. sensus: _____

51. sermō: _____
52. grave: _____
53. socius: _____
54. temple: _____
55. Rome: _____
56. rēspiciō: _____
57. testimōnium: _____
_____
58. rūs: _____
59. mētior: _____
60. clothing: _____
61. I buy: _____
62. adeō: _____
63. I go up: _____
64. bibō: _____
65. parcō: _____
66. congregō: _____
_____
67. inīquitās: _____
_____
68. slender: _____
69. I grow: _____
70. ēiciō: _____
71. gignō: _____
72. induō: _____
73. I swear: _____
74. iūdicō: _____
75. I wash: _____
76. mālō: _____
77. I am born: _____

78. nōlō: _____
_____
79. nōscō: _____
80. offerō: _____
81. I feed: _____
82. singulī: _____
83. hīc: _____
84. perveniō: _____
_____
85. hinc: _____
_____
86. petō: _____
87. premō: _____
88. respondeō: _____
89. I burst: _____
90. I serve: _____
91. quō: _____
_____
92. I loose: _____
93. sternō: _____
94. sumō: _____
95. tollō: _____
_____
96. trānseō: _____
97. illinc: _____
_____
98. vādō: _____
99. vertō: _____
100. volō: _____
101. aliēnus (adj.): _____

102. aliquī, aliqua, aliquod (adj.): _____
103. cēterus: _____
_____
104. cunctus: _____
105. modicus: _____
106. neither: _____
107. illīc: _____
108. pactus: _____
_____
109. quī? quae? quod?: _____
_____
110. quīdam, quaedam, quoddam (adj.): _____
_____
111. Roman: _____
112. uter, utra, utrum (interrog.): _____
_____
_____
113. intereā: _____
114. aliquis, aliquid (pron.): _____
_____
115. continuō: _____
116. circā (adv. and prep. +_____): _____
117. undique: _____
_____
118. dum/dummodo (conj.): _____
_____
119. hūc: _____
120. igitur: _____
121. illūc: _____

122. inde: _____
123. simul: _____
124. quisquis, quidquid (quicquid) (pron.): _____
_____
125. intereā: _____
_____
126. intrā (prep. +_____; adv.): _____
_____
127. procul: _____
128. invicem: _____
_____
129. sērō, sērius, sērissimē (adv.): _____
130. nam: _____
131. quīcumque, quaecumque, quodcumque: _____
_____
132. vel: _____
133. numquid (interrogative adv.): _____
_____
134. passim: _____
135. postquam: _____
136. praeter (prep. +_____): _____
_____
137. quīdam, quaedam, quiddam (pron.): _____
_____
138. quis, quid (interrog. pron.): _____
139. quondam: _____
140. unde: _____
141. very: _____
142. truly: _____

B. Grammar

1. Do a synopsis of *ferō* in the 2nd person singular, first giving principal parts:

		ACTIVE		PASSIVE	
		LATIN	ENGLISH	LATIN	ENGLISH
INDICATIVE	PRES.				
	IMPF.				
	FUT.				
	PERF.				
	PLUPF.				
	FT.PF.				
INF.	PRES.				
PART.	PRES.				
	PERF.				
	FUT.				
IMP.	SG.				
	PL.				

2. Do a synopsis of *nāscor* in the 1st person plural, first giving principal parts:

_____

		ACTIVE		PASSIVE	
		LATIN	ENGLISH	LATIN	ENGLISH
INDICATIVE	PRES.				
	IMPF.				
	FUT.				
	PERF.				
	PLUPF.				
	FT.PF.				
INF.	PRES.				
PART.	PRES.				
	PERF.				
	FUT.				
IMP.	SG.				
	PL.				

3. Do a synopsis of *volō* in the 3rd person singular, first giving principal parts:

		ACTIVE		PASSIVE	
		LATIN	ENGLISH	LATIN	ENGLISH
INDICATIVE	PRES.				
	IMPF.				
	FUT.				
	PERF.				
	PLUPF.				
	FT.PF.				
INF.	PRES.				
PART.	PRES.			■	■
	PERF.	■	■		
	FUT.				
IMP.	SG.				
	PL.				

4. Decline the following noun-adjective pairs. Some of the adjectives may not have a vocative.

which custom? *quī mōs?*

	LATIN SINGULAR	LATIN PLURAL
NOM.		
GEN.		
DAT.		
ACC.		
ABL.		
VOC.		

the singing tree, *canēns līgnum*

	LATIN SINGULAR	LATIN PLURAL
NOM.		
GEN.		
DAT.		
ACC.		
ABL.		
VOC.		

the assembled multitude, *congregāta multitūdō*

	LATIN SINGULAR	LATIN PLURAL
NOM.		
GEN.		
DAT.		
ACC.		
ABL.		
VOC.		

certain soil, *quaedam humus*

	LATIN SINGULAR	LATIN PLURAL
NOM.		
GEN.		
DAT.		
ACC.		
ABL.		
VOC.		

some sense, *aliquī sensus*

	LATIN SINGULAR	LATIN PLURAL
NOM.		
GEN.		
DAT.		
ACC.		
ABL.		
VOC.		

*Note: Although I suppose the indefinite pronoun could have a vocative, it seems probable that if one were addressing something, that would make the indefinite thing definite. Thus I have put it in brackets.

oath, *iūs iūrandum*

	LATIN SINGULAR	LATIN PLURAL
NOM.		
GEN.		
DAT.		
ACC.		
ABL.		
VOC.		

5. Noun-Adjective Identification: Give Gender, Number, and Case (in all possible combinations) for each phrase, then translate the phrase.

NOUN/ ADJECTIVE PHRASE	GENDER, NUMBER, CASE	TRANSLATION

6. Verb Parsing: Parse each of the verbs given below, identify the verb it comes from (1st principal part), and translate the form. For Indicatives, give Person, Number, Tense, Voice, and Mood. For Participles, give Gender, Number, Case, Tense, Voice, and Mood. For Infinitives and Imperatives, give Tense, Voice, and Mood. If the verb is a deponent, identify it as such.

VERB	PNTVM OR GNCTVM OR TVM	1ST PR. PT.	TRANSLATION
indūtīs			
transit			
respiciēs			
māvultīs			
adeuntī			
strātōs			

crēvērunt			
nāscitur			
genitum			
sustuleris			

C. Memorization

Write out Ambrose's *Hymnus IV*. The first word in each line has been given to you.

Veni, _____

Ostende _____

Miretur _____

Talis _____

Non _____

Sed _____

Verbum _____

Fructusque _____

Alvus _____

Claustrum _____

Vexilla _____

Versatur _____

Procedens _____

Pudoris _____

Geminae _____

Alacris _____

Egressus _____

Regressus _____

Excursus _____

Recursus _____

Aequalis _____

Carnis _____

Infirma _____

Virtute _____

Praesepe _____

Lumenque _____

Quod _____

Fideque _____

D. English to Latin Translation

As is our custom, translate italicized words with participles.

1. "Don't drink the water!" the pirate said as we *were arriving* in Rome. "Drink the wine—which do you prefer?"

   _____
   _____

2. By *casting* out evil spirits God's messenger pitied the crowds, and they marveled to one another at His mercy.

   _____
   _____
   _____

3. Therefore mother sent the boys in a line to the well for the sake of *washing*, their clothes *having been destroyed* in the appointed place.

   _____
   _____

4. Someone *must measure* twenty cubits from Carthage, and there in the ground we will seek the ambassador's jewels <u>which had been snatched from his wife.</u> [First translate the underlined clause with a participle, then translate it again with a relative clause.]

5. Who heard shouts within the tomb from a distance and thence spread rumors about the *living* dead?

6. At the first sight of snow, go from here to Athens and offer a hundred sheep on the altars *to pay* for your wickedness.

7. *Departing* from home, I then bought a farm in which was once an old Roman fountain.

8. Indeed, certain men *about to arrive* here will establish the treaty for the sake of the empire as soon as the rest have been assembled.

9. After these things *were known*, the priest immediately decided with wisdom about the *broken* wall and the foreigner's sheep *pasturing* everywhere in my fields.

10. Surely your grandsons will not do this injustice in the temple by *being ignorant* of all our gods?

E. Latin to English Translation

Translate these sentences into literal English (if necessary), then into readable English. After that parse the requested verbs in each sentence. For indicative verbs, give Person, Number, Tense, Voice, and Mood; for participles, give Gender, Number, Case, Tense, Voice, and Mood. For infinitives and imperatives, give Tense, Voice, and Mood. If a verb is deponent, identify it as such.

1. Rēx, moritūrus ob fortitūdinem contrā dracōnem, hoc iūdicium mihi dedit: "Nam hic dracō tibi māximē caedendus est, et nōlī parcere cētō!"

   a. Literal English: _____

   b. Readable English: _____

   c. Parse *moritūrus*: _____

   d. Parse *caedendus est*: _____

   e. Parse *nōlī*: _____

2. Postquam Thisbe clamāvit, "Quis tē ab mē ēripuit? Pȳrame, respondē! Tua tē cārissima Thisbe vocat!", Pȳramus vīsam illam cōgnōvit et tunc mortuus est.

   a. Literal English: _____

   b. Readable English: _____

   c. Parse *ēripuit*: _____

   d. Parse *vīsam*: _____

   e. Parse *mortuus est*: _____

3. Intereā rogābant eum discipulī dicentēs: "Domine, manducā," et tum sērius dicēbant ergo ad invicem, "Numquid aliquis obtulit ei aliquid manducāre?"

   a. Literal English: _____

   b. Readable English: _____

   c. Parse *rogābant*: _____

   d. Parse *dicentēs*: _____

   e. Parse *obtulit*: _____

4. "Tū, Rōmāne, rēge imperiō populōs pacisque cōnstitue mōrem, parce victīs, et superā superbōs," sīc Aenēae mīrantī loquitur pater Anchises.

   a. Literal English: _____

b. Readable English: _____

_____

_____

c. Parse *cōnstitue*: _____

d. Parse *mīrantī*: _____

e. Parse *loquitur*: _____

5. Nōbīs singulīs arcem ascendentibus, pars ex comitibus nostrīs sūmptum tōtum panem nostrum in pluviā mandūcāvērunt.

   a. Literal English: _____

   _____

   _____

   b. Readable English: _____

   _____

   _____

   c. Parse *ascendentibus*: _____

   d. Parse *sūmptum*: _____

   e. Parse *mandūcāvērunt*: _____

6. Nōlīte iūdicāre, aut iūdicābiminī; in quō enim iūdiciō iūdicāveritis, iūdicābiminī, et in quā mensurā mensī eritis, mētiētur vōbīs.

   a. Literal English: _____

   _____

   _____

   b. Readable English: _____

   _____

   _____

   c. Parse *iūdicābiminī*: _____

   d. Parse *mensī eritis*: _____

   e. Parse *mētiētur*: _____

215

7. Quisquis pessimō dominō dandīs eī mūneribus servit Modicō Ferrō Fātī moriētur, et quaecumque mūnera dāta vērō tollentur.

   a. Literal English: _____

   b. Readable English: _____

   c. Parse *dandīs*: _____
   d. Parse *moriētur*: _____
   e. Parse *tollentur*: _____

8. Īnsidiīs contrā sociōs cōgnōtīs, Rōmānī vertentēs hostēs praeter flūmen pressērunt dum fēminae liberīque congregātam praedam Rōmam tulērunt.

   a. Literal English: _____

   b. Readable English: _____

   c. Parse *vertentēs*: _____
   d. Parse *congregātam*: _____
   e. Parse *tulērunt*: _____

9. Ibī, etiam in māximō perīculō timendus magis quam timēns, "Rōmānus sum," inquit, "cīvis; mē Gaium Mucium vocant. Hostis hostem occidere voluī; morī volō sīcut occīdere volēbam."

   a. Literal English: _____

b. Readable English: _____

c. Parse *timendus*: _____
d. Parse *timēns*: _____
e. Parse *volēbam*: _____

10. Vāsī ad spēluncam ad sermōnēs fatōrum audiendōs, sed pervenientī mihi illūc locūta sunt: "Quis es? Unde exiistī et quō adis? Ī hinc!"

   a. Literal English: _____

   b. Readable English: _____

   c. Parse *vāsī*: _____
   d. Parse *audiendōs*: _____
   e. Parse *pervenientī*: _____

Appendices

- Appendix A: Chant Charts
- Appendix B: Latin to English Glossary
- Appendix C: English to Latin Glossary
- Appendix D: Sources and Helps
- Appendix E: Verb Formation Chart

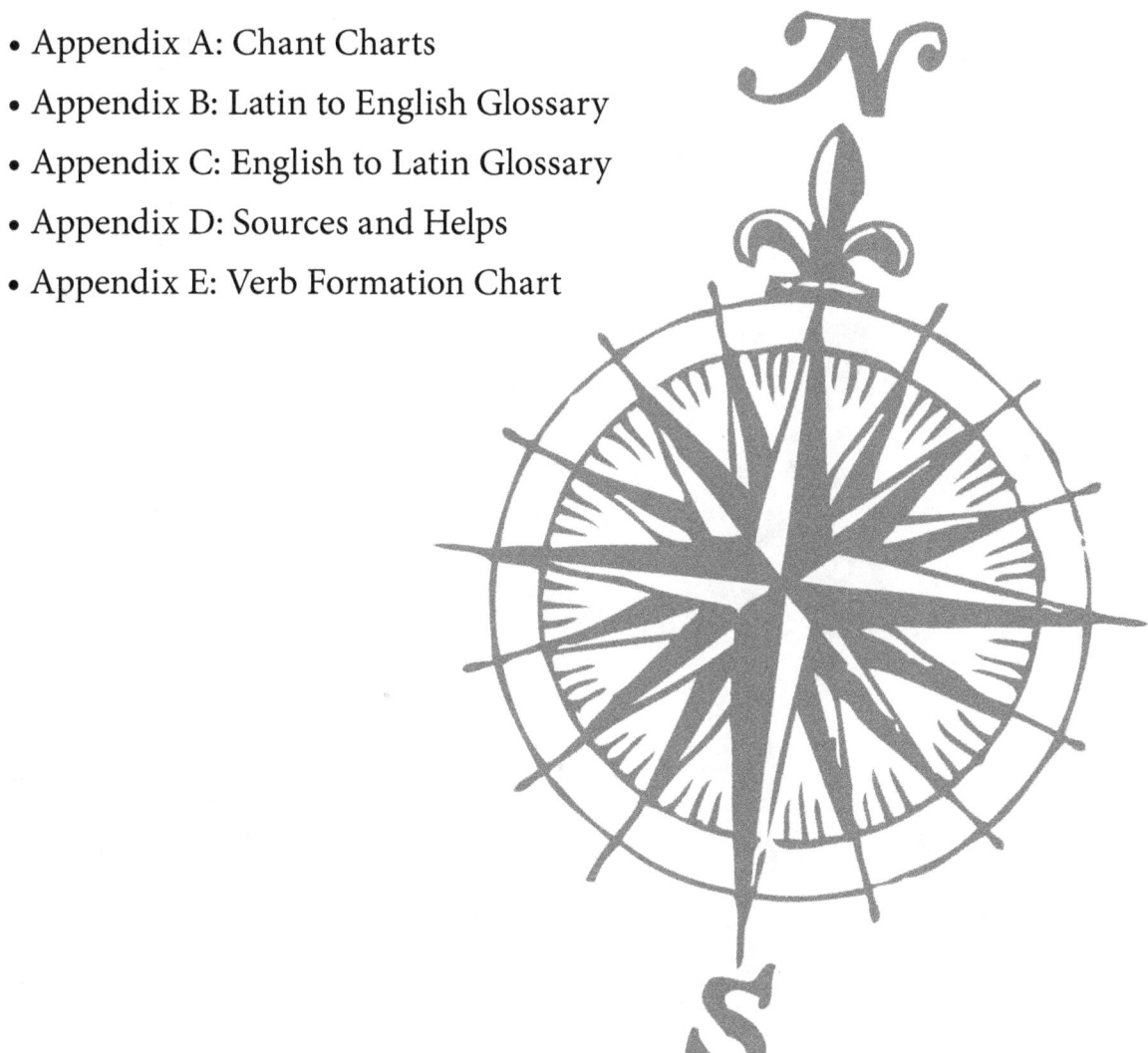

[This page intentionally left blank]

Appendix A
Chant Charts

Verbs

Indicative

Present Active Indicative Verb Endings (*KL1*, Lesson 1)

	LATIN SINGULAR	ENGLISH SINGULAR	LATIN PLURAL	LATIN PLURAL
1ST	-ō	I am *verbing*, I *verb*	-mus	we are *verbing*
2ND	-s	you are *verbing*	-tis	you all are *verbing*
3RD	-t	he/she/it is *verbing*	-nt	they are *verbing*

Present Passive Indicative Verb Endings (*KL1*, Lesson 20)

	LATIN SINGULAR	ENGLISH SINGULAR	LATIN PLURAL	ENGLISH PLURAL
1ST	-r	I am (being) *verbed*	-mur	we are (being) *verbed*
2ND	-ris	you are (being) *verbed*	-minī	you (pl.) are (being) *verbed*
3RD	-tur	he/she/it is (being) *verbed*	-ntur	they are being *verbed*

Imperfect Active Indicative Verb Endings (*KL1*, Lesson 6)

	LATIN SINGULAR	ENGLISH SINGULAR	LATIN PLURAL	ENGLISH PLURAL
1ST	-bam	I was *verbing*	-bāmus	we were *verbing*
2ND	-bās	you were *verbing*	-bātis	you all were *verbing*
3RD	-bat	he/she/it was *verbing*	-bant	they were *verbing*

Imperfect Passive Indicative Verb Endings (*KL1*, Lesson 20)

	LATIN SINGULAR	ENGLISH SINGULAR	LATIN PLURAL	ENGLISH PLURAL
1ST	-bar	I was (being) *verbed*	-bāmur	we were (being) *verbed*
2ND	-bāris	you were (being) *verbed*	-bāminī	you (pl.) were (being) *verbed*
3RD	-bātur	he/she/it was (being) *verbed*	-bantur	they were (being) *verbed*

Future Active Indicative Verb Endings (*KL1*, Lesson 6)

	LATIN SINGULAR	ENGLISH SINGULAR	LATIN PLURAL	ENGLISH PLURAL
1ST	-bō	I will *verb*	-bimus	we will *verb*
2ND	-bis	you will *verb*	-bitis	you all will *verb*
3RD	-bit	he/she/it will *verb*	-bunt	they will *verb*

Future Passive Indicative Verb Endings (*KL1*, Lesson 20)

	LATIN SINGULAR	ENGLISH SINGULAR	LATIN PLURAL	ENGLISH PLURAL
1ST	-bor	I will be **verbed**	-bimur	we will be **verbed**
2ND	-beris	you will be **verbed**	-biminī	you (pl.) will be **verbed**
3RD	-bitur	he/she/it will be **verbed**	-buntur	they will be **verbed**

Perfect Active Indicative Verb Endings (*KL1*, Lesson 14)

	LATIN SINGULAR	ENGLISH SINGULAR	LATIN PLURAL	ENGLISH PLURAL
1ST	-ī	I **verbed**, have **verbed**	-imus	we **verbed**, have **verbed**
2ND	-istī	you **verbed**, have verbed	-istis	you (pl.) **verbed**, have **verbed**
3RD	-it	he/she/it **verbed**, has **verbed**	-ērunt	they **verbed**, have **verbed**

Perfect Passive Indicative (*KL1*, Lesson 22, p. 330)

	LATIN SINGULAR	ENGLISH SINGULAR	LATIN PLURAL	ENGLISH PLURAL
1ST	4th principal part (sg.) + sum	I was/have been **verbed**	4th p.p. (pl.) + sumus	we were/have been **verbed**
2ND	4th p.p. (sg.) + ēs	you were/have been **verbed**	4th p.p. (pl.) + estis	you (pl.) were/have been **verbed**
3RD	4th p.p. (sg.) + est	he/she/it was/has been **verbed**	4th p.p. (pl.) + sunt	they were/have been **verbed**

Pluperfect Active Indicative Verb Endings (*KL1*, Lesson 15)

	LATIN SINGULAR	ENGLISH SINGULAR	LATIN PLURAL	ENGLISH PLURAL
1ST	-eram	I had **verbed**	-erāmus	we had **verbed**
2ND	-erās	you had **verbed**	-erātis	you (pl.) had **verbed**
3RD	-erat	he/she/it had **verbed**	-erant	they had **verbed**

Pluperfect Passive Indicative (*KL1*, Lesson 22)

	LATIN SINGULAR	ENGLISH SINGULAR	LATIN PLURAL	ENGLISH PLURAL
1ST	4th principal part (sg.) + eram	I had been **verbed**	4th p.p. (pl.) + erāmus	we had been **verbed**
2ND	4th p.p. (sg.) + erās	you had been **verbed**	4th p.p. (pl.) + erātis	you (pl.) had been **verbed**
3RD	4th p.p. (sg.) + erat	he/she/it had been **verbed**	4th p.p. (pl.) + erant	they had been **verbed**

Future Perfect Active Indicative Verb Endings (*KL1*, Lesson 15)

	LATIN SINGULAR	ENGLISH SINGULAR	LATIN PLURAL	ENGLISH PLURAL
1ST	-erō	I will have **verbed**	-erimus	we will have **verbed**
2ND	-eris	you will have **verbed**	-eritis	you (pl.) will have **verbed**
3RD	-erit	he/she/it will have **verbed**	-erint	they will have **verbed**

Future Perfect Passive Indicative (*KL1*, Lesson 22)

	LATIN SINGULAR	ENGLISH SINGULAR	LATIN PLURAL	ENGLISH PLURAL
1ST	4th principal part (sg.) + erō	I will have been **verb**ed	4th p.p. (pl.) + erimus	we will have been **verb**ed
2ND	4th p.p. (sg.) + eris	you will have been **verb**ed	4th p.p. (pl.) + eritis	you (pl.) will have been **verb**ed
3RD	4th p.p. (sg.) + erit	he/she/it will have been **verb**ed	4th p.p. (pl.) + erunt	they will have been **verb**ed

Imperative

Present Active and Passive Imperative Endings (*KL2*, Lesson 6; *KL1*, Lesson. 11)

	ACTIVE		PASSIVE	
	LATIN	ENGLISH	LATIN	ENGLISH
SING.	present stem	**verb**!	present stem + *-re*	Be **verb**ed!
PLUR.	present stem + *-te*	**verb**! (pl.)	present stem + *-minī*	Be **verb**ed! (pl.)

Participle

(*KL2*, Lesson 10)

	ACTIVE LATIN	ACTIVE ENGLISH	PASSIVE LATIN	PASSIVE ENGLISH
PRES.	-ns, -ntis	*verb*-ing		
PF.			4th principal part	*verb*-ed, having been *verb*-ed
FUT.	4th p. p. stem + -ūrus, -ūra, -ūrum	about to *verb*	pres. stem + -ndus, -nda, -ndum	(about) to be *verbed*-ed

Infinitive

(*KL3*, Lesson 1)

	INFINITIVE			
	LATIN ACTIVE	ENGLISH ACTIVE	LATIN PASSIVE	ENGLISH PASSIVE
PRES.	-re (2nd p.p.)	to **verb**	-rī/-ī	to be **verb**ed
PF.	perf. stem + -isse	to have **verb**ed	4th p.p. + esse	to have been **verb**ed
FUT.	fut. act. prt. + esse	to be about to **verb**	(uncommon)	

Subjunctive

Present Active Subjunctive Endings (*KL3*, Lesson 4)

	LATIN SINGULAR	ENGLISH SINGULAR	LATIN PLURAL	ENGLISH PLURAL
1ST	stem vowel change + *-m*	[depends on context]	stem vowel change + *-mus*	[depends on context]
2ND	stem vowel change + *-s*	[depends on context]	stem vowel change + *-tis*	[depends on context]
3RD	stem vowel change + *-t*	[depends on context]	stem vowel change + *-nt*	[depends on context]

Present Passive Subjunctive Endings (*KL1*, Lesson 4)

	LATIN SINGULAR	ENGLISH SINGULAR	LATIN PLURAL	ENGLISH PLURAL
1ST	stem vowel change + -*r*	[depends on context]	stem vowel change + -*mur*	[depends on context]
2ND	stem vowel change + -*ris*	[depends on context]	stem vowel change + -*minī*	[depends on context]
3RD	stem vowel change + -*tur*	[depends on context]	stem vowel change + -*ntur*	[depends on context]

Imperfect Active Subjunctive Endings (*KL1*, Lesson 5)

	LATIN SINGULAR	ENGLISH SINGULAR	LATIN PLURAL	ENGLISH PLURAL
1ST	present active infinitive + -*m*	[depends on context]	present active infinitive + -*mus*	[depends on context]
2ND	present active infinitive + -*s*	[depends on context]	present active infinitive + -*tis*	[depends on context]
3RD	present active infinitive + -*t*	[depends on context]	present active infinitive + -*nt*	[depends on context]

Imperfect Passive Subjunctive Endings (*KL1*, Lesson 5)

	LATIN SINGULAR	ENGLISH SINGULAR	LATIN PLURAL	ENGLISH PLURAL
1ST	present active infinitive + -*r*	[depends on context]	present active infinitive + -*mur*	[depends on context]
2ND	present active infinitive + -*ris*	[depends on context]	present active infinitive + -*minī*	[depends on context]
3RD	present active infinitive + -*tur*	[depends on context]	present active infinitive + -*ntur*	[depends on context]

Perfect Active Subjunctive Endings (*KL1*, Lesson 6)

	LATIN SINGULAR	ENGLISH SINGULAR	LATIN PLURAL	ENGLISH PLURAL
1ST	perfect active stem + -*eri*- + -*m*	[depends on context]	perfect active stem + -*eri*- + -*mus*	[depends on context]
2ND	perfect active stem + -*eri*- + -*s*	[depends on context]	perfect active stem + -*eri*- + -*tis*	[depends on context]
3RD	perfect active stem + -*eri*- + -*t*	[depends on context]	perfect active stem + -*eri*- + -*nt*	[depends on context]

Perfect Passive Subjunctive Endings (*KL1*, Lesson 6)

	LATIN SINGULAR	ENGLISH SINGULAR	LATIN PLURAL	ENGLISH PLURAL
1ST	perfect passive participle + *sim*	[depends on context]	perfect passive participle + *sīmus*	[depends on context]
2ND	perfect passive participle + *sīs*	[depends on context]	perfect passive participle + *sītis*	[depends on context]
3RD	perfect passive participle + *sit*	[depends on context]	perfect passive participle + *sint*	[depends on context]

Pluperfect Active Subjunctive Endings (*KL1*, Lesson 6)

	LATIN SINGULAR	ENGLISH SINGULAR	LATIN PLURAL	ENGLISH PLURAL
1ST	perfect active stem + -*isse*- + -*m*	[depends on context]	perfect active stem + -*isse*- + -*mus*	[depends on context]
2ND	perfect active stem + -*isse*- + -*s*	[depends on context]	perfect active stem + -*isse*- + -*tis*	[depends on context]
3RD	perfect active stem + -*isse*- + -*t*	[depends on context]	perfect active stem + -*isse*- + -*nt*	[depends on context]

Pluperfect Passive Subjunctive Endings (*KL1*, Lesson 6)

	LATIN SINGULAR	ENGLISH SINGULAR	LATIN PLURAL	ENGLISH PLURAL
1ST	perfect passive participle + *essem*	[depends on context]	perfect passive participle + *essēmus*	[depends on context]
2ND	perfect passive participle + *essēs*	[depends on context]	perfect passive participle + *essētis*	[depends on context]
3RD	perfect passive participle + *esset*	[depends on context]	perfect passive participle + *essent*	[depends on context]

Verb Chants, applied to *amō*, *videō*, *dūcō*, *capiō*, and *audiō*

1st Conjugation: *amō, amāre, amāvī, amātum*
2nd Conjugation: *videō, vidēre, vīdī, vīsum*
3rd Conjugation: *dūcō, dūcere, dūxī, ductum*
3rd -iō Conjugation: *capiō, capere, cēpī, captum*
4th Conjugation: *audiō, audīre, audīvī, audītum*

Indicative

	1ST	2ND	3RD	3RD -iō	4TH
PRESENT ACTIVE	amō	videō	dūcō	capiō	audiō
	amās	vidēs	dūcis	capis	audīs
	amat	videt	dūcit	capit	audit
	amāmus	vidēmus	dūcimus	capimus	audīmus
	amātis	vidētis	dūcitis	capitis	audītis
	amant	vident	dūcunt	capiunt	audiunt
IMPERFECT ACTIVE	amābam	vidēbam	dūcēbam	capiēbam	audiēbam
	amābās	vidēbās	dūcēbās	capiēbās	audiēbās
	amābat	vidēbat	dūcēbat	capiēbat	audiēbat
	amābāmus	vidēbāmus	dūcēbāmus	capiēbāmus	audiēbāmus
	amābātis	vidēbātis	dūcēbātis	capiēbātis	audiēbātis
	amābant	vidēbant	dūcēbant	capiēbant	audiēbant
FUTURE ACTIVE	amābō	vidēbō	dūcam	capiam	audiam
	amābis	vidēbis	dūcēs	capiēs	audiēs
	amābit	vidēbit	dūcet	capiet	audiet
	amābimus	vidēbimus	dūcēmus	capiēmus	audiēmus
	amābitis	vidēbitis	dūcētis	capiētis	audiētis
	amābunt	vidēbunt	dūcent	capient	audient
PRESENT PASSIVE	amor	videor	dūcor	capior	audior
	amāris	vidēris	dūceris	caperis	audīris
	amātur	vidētur	dūcitur	capitur	audītur
	amāmur	vidēmur	dūcimur	capimur	audīmur
	amāminī	vidēminī	dūciminī	capiminī	audīminī
	amantur	videntur	dūcuntur	capiuntur	audiuntur

IMPERFECT PASSIVE	amābar	vidēbar	dūcēbar	capiēbar	audiēbar
	amābāris	vidēbāris	dūcēbāris	capiēbāris	audiēbāris
	amābātur	vidēbātur	dūcēbātur	capiēbātur	audiēbātur
	amābāmur	vidēbāmur	dūcēbāmur	capiēbāmur	audiēbāmur
	amābāminī	vidēbāminī	dūcēbāminī	capiēbāminī	audiēbāminī
	amābantur	vidēbantur	dūcēbantur	capiēbantur	audiēbantur
FUTURE PASSIVE	amābor	vidēbor	dūcar	capiar	audiar
	amāberis	vidēberis	dūcēris	capiēris	audiēris
	amābitur	vidēbitur	dūcētur	capiētur	audiētur
	amābimur	vidēbimur	dūcēmur	capiēmur	audiēmur
	amābiminī	vidēbiminī	dūcēminī	capiēminī	audiēminī
	amābuntur	vidēbuntur	dūcentur	capientur	audientur
PERFECT ACTIVE	amāvī	vīdī	dūxī	cēpī	audīvī
	amāvistī	vīdistī	dūxistī	cēpistī	audīvistī
	amāvit	vīdit	dūxit	cēpit	audīvit
	amāvimus	vīdimus	dūximus	cēpimus	audīvimus
	amāvistis	vīdistis	dūxistis	cēpistis	audīvistis
	amāvērunt	vīdērunt	dūxērunt	cēpērunt	audīvērunt
PLUPERFECT ACTIVE	amāveram	vīderam	dūxeram	cēperam	audīveram
	amāverās	vīderās	dūxerās	cēperās	audīverās
	amāverat	vīderat	dūxerat	cēperat	audīverat
	amāverāmus	vīderāmus	dūxerāmus	cēperāmus	audīverāmus
	amāverātis	vīderātis	dūxerātis	cēperātis	audīverātis
	amāverant	vīderant	dūxerant	cēperant	audīverant
FUTURE PERFECT ACTIVE	amāverō	vīderō	dūxerō	cēperō	audīverō
	amāveris	vīderis	dūxeris	cēperis	audīveris
	amāverit	vīderit	dūxerit	cēperit	audīverit
	amāverimus	vīderimus	dūxerimus	cēperimus	audīverimus
	amāveritis	vīderitis	dūxeritis	cēperitis	audīveritis
	amāverint	vīderint	dūxerint	cēperint	audīverint
PERFECT PASSIVE	amātus sum	vīsus sum	ductus sum	captus sum	audītus sum
	amātus ēs	vīsus ēs	ductus ēs	captus ēs	audītus ēs
	amātus est	vīsus est	ductus est	captus est	audītus est
	amātī sumus	vīsī sumus	ductī sumus	captī sumus	audītī sumus
	amātī estis	vīsī estis	ductī estis	captī estis	audītī sumus
	amātī sunt	vīsī sunt	ductī sunt	captī sunt	audītī sunt

PLUPERFECT PASSIVE	amāt**us eram**	vīs**us eram**	duct**us eram**	capt**us eram**	audīt**us eram**
	amāt**us erās**	vīs**us erās**	duct**us erās**	capt**us erās**	audīt**us erās**
	amāt**us erat**	vīs**us erat**	duct**us erat**	capt**us erat**	audīt**us erat**
	amāt**ī erāmus**	vīs**ī erāmus**	duct**ī erāmus**	capt**ī erāmus**	audīt**ī erāmus**
	amāt**ī erātis**	vīs**ī erātis**	duct**ī erātis**	capt**ī erātis**	audīt**ī erātis**
	amāt**ī erant**	vīs**ī erant**	duct**ī erant**	capt**ī erant**	audīt**ī erant**
FUT. PERFECT PASSIVE	amāt**us erō**	vīs**us erō**	duct**us erō**	capt**us erō**	audīt**us erō**
	amāt**us eris**	vīs**us eris**	duct**us eris**	capt**us eris**	audīt**us eris**
	amāt**us erit**	vīs**us erit**	duct**us erit**	capt**us erit**	audīt**us erit**
	amāt**ī erimus**	vīs**ī erimus**	duct**ī erimus**	capt**ī erimus**	audīt**ī erimus**
	amāt**ī eritis**	vīs**ī eritis**	duct**ī eritis**	capt**ī eritis**	audīt**ī eritis**
	amāt**ī erunt**	vīs**ī erunt**	duct**ī erunt**	capt**ī erunt**	audīt**ī erunt**

Imperative

		1ST	2ND	3RD	3RD -iō	4TH
ACT.	SING.	amā!	vidē!	dūc!*	cape!	audī!
	PLUR.	amāte!	vidēte!	dūcite!	capite!	audīte!
PASS.	SING.	amāre!	vidēre!	dūcere!	capere!	audīre!
	PLUR.	amāminī!	vidēminī!	dūciminī!	capiminī!	audīminī!

*The present active imperative of *dūcō* is slightly irregular since it drops the short *-e* that would appear on regular 3rd conjugation verbs (*agō* → *age!*, *mittō* → *mitte!* etc.). Other common verbs that are irregular in this form are *dīcō* → *dīc!* and *faciō* (a 3rd -iō) → *fac!*

Participle

		1ST	2ND	3RD	3RD -iō	4TH
ACT.	SING.	amāns	vidēns	dūcēns	capiēns	audiēns
	PLUR.	amātūrus	vīsūrus	ductūrus	captūrus	audītūrus
PASS.	SING.	amātus	vīsus	ductus	captus	audītus
	PLUR.	amandus	videndus	dūcendus	capiendus	audiendus

Infinitive

		1ST	2ND	3RD	3RD -iō	4TH
ACTIVE	PRES.	amāre	vidēre	dūcere	capere	audīre
	PF.	amāvisse	vīdisse	dūxisse	cēpisse	audīvisse
	FUT.	amātūrus esse	vīsūrus esse	ductūrus esse	captūrus esse	audītūrus esse
PASSIVE	PRES.	amārī	vidērī	dūcī	capī	audīrī
	PF.	amātus esse	vīsus esse	ductus esse	captus esse	audītus esse
	FUT.	(uncommon)				

Subjunctive

	1ST	2ND	3RD	3RD -iō	4TH
PRES. ACT. SUBJ.	amem	videam	dūcam	capiam	audiam
	amēs	videās	dūcās	capiās	audiās
	amet	videat	dūcat	capiat	audiat
	amēmus	videāmus	dūcāmus	capiāmus	audiāmus
	amētis	videātis	dūcātis	capiātis	audiātis
	ament	videant	dūcant	capiant	audiant
PRES. PASS. SUBJ.	amer	videar	dūcar	capiar	audiar
	amēris	videāris	dūcāris	capiāris	audiāris
	amētur	videātur	dūcātur	capiātur	audiātur
	amēmur	videāmur	dūcāmur	capiāmur	audiāmur
	amēminī	videāminī	dūcāminī	capiāminī	audiāminī
	amentur	videantur	dūcantur	capiantur	audiantur
IMP. ACT. SUBJ.	amārem	vidērem	dūcerem	caperem	audīrem
	amārēs	vidērēs	dūcerēs	caperēs	audīrēs
	amāret	vidēret	dūceret	caperet	audīret
	amārēmus	vidērēmus	dūcerēmus	caperēmus	audīrēmus
	amārētis	vidērētis	dūcerētis	caperētis	audīrētis
	amārent	vidērent	dūcerent	caperent	audīrent
IMP. PASS. SUBJ.	amārer	vidērer	dūcerer	caperer	audīrer
	amārēris	vidērēris	dūcerēris	caperēris	audīrēris
	amārētur	vidērētur	dūcerētur	caperētur	audīrētur
	amārēmur	vidērēmur	dūcerēmur	caperēmur	audīrēmur
	amārēminī	vidērēminī	dūcerēminī	caperēminī	audīrēminī
	amārentur	vidērentur	dūcerentur	caperentur	audīrentur
PERF. ACT. SUBJ.	amāverim	vīderim	dūxerim	cēperim	audīverim
	amāverīs	vīderīs	dūxerīs	cēperīs	audīverīs
	amāverit	vīderit	dūxerit	cēperit	audīverit
	amāverīmus	vīderīmus	dūxerīmus	cēperīmus	audīverīmus
	amāverītis	vīderītis	dūxerītis	cēperītis	audīverītis
	amāverint	vīderint	dūxerint	cēperint	audīverint
PERF. PASS. SUBJ.	amātus sim	vīsus sim	ductus sim	captus sim	audītus sim
	amātus sīs	vīsus sīs	ductus sīs	captus sīs	audītus sīs
	amātus sit	vīsus sit	ductus sit	captus sit	audītus sit
	amātī sīmus	vīsī sīmus	ductī sīmus	captī sīmus	audītī sīmus
	amātī sītis	vīsī sītis	ductī sītis	captī sītis	audītī sītis
	amātī sint	vīsī sint	ductī sint	captī sint	audītī sint

PLU. ACT. SUBJ.	amāvissem	vīdissem	dūxissem	cēpissem	audīverim
	amāvissēs	vīdissēs	dūxissēs	cēpissēs	audīverīs
	amāvisset	vīdisset	dūxisset	cēpisset	audīverit
	amāvissēmus	vīdissēmus	dūxissēmus	cēpissēmus	audīverīmus
	amāvissētis	vīdissētis	dūxissētis	cēpissētis	audīverītis
	amāvissent	vīdissent	dūxissent	cēpissent	audīverint
PLU. PASS. SUBJ.	amātus essem	vīsus essem	ductus essem	captus essem	audītus essem
	amātus essēs	vīsus essēs	ductus essēs	captus essēs	audītus essēs
	amātus esset	vīsus esset	ductus esset	captus esset	audītus esset
	amātī essēmus	vīsī essēmus	ductī essēmus	captī essēmus	audītī essēmus
	amātī essētis	vīsī essētis	ductī essētis	captī essētis	audītī essētis
	amātī essent	vīsī essent	ductī essent	captī essent	audītī essent

Deponent Verb Chants, applied to *cōnor, misereor, loquor, ēgredior,* and *mētior*

1st Conjugation: *cōnor, cōnārī, cōnātus sum*
2nd Conjugation: *misereor, miserērī, misertus sum*
3rd Conjugation: *loquor, loquī, locūtus sum*
3rd -iō Conjugation: *ēgredior, ēgredī, ēgressus sum*
4th Conjugation: *mētior, mētīrī, mēnsus sum*

Indicative

	1ST	2ND	3RD	3RD -iō	4TH
PRES. PASS. DEP. IND.	cōnor	misereor	loquor	ēgredior	mētior
	cōnāris	miserēris	loqueris	ēgrederis	mētīris
	cōnātur	miserētur	loquitur	ēgreditur	mētītur
	cōnāmur	miserēmur	loquimur	ēgredimur	mētīmur
	cōnāminī	miserēminī	loquiminī	ēgrediminī	mētīminī
	cōnantur	miserentur	loquuntur	ēgrediuntur	mētiuntur
IMP. PASS. DEP. IND.	cōnābar	miserēbar	loquēbar	ēgrediēbar	mētiēbar
	cōnābāris	miserēbāris	loquēbāris	ēgrediēbāris	mētiēbāris
	cōnābātur	miserēbātur	loquēbātur	ēgrediēbātur	mētiēbātur
	cōnābāmur	miserēbāmur	loquēbāmur	ēgrediēbāmur	mētiēbāmur
	cōnābāminī	miserēbāminī	loquēbāminī	ēgrediēbāminī	mētiēbāminī
	cōnābantur	miserēbantur	loquēbantur	ēgrediēbantur	mētiēbantur

FUT. PASS. DEP. IND.	cōnābor	miserēbor	loquar	ēgrediar	mētiar
	cōnāberis	miserēberis	loquēris	ēgrediēris	mētiēris
	cōnābitur	miserēbitur	loquētur	ēgrediētur	mētiētur
	cōnābimur	miserēbimur	loquēmur	ēgrediēmur	mētiēmur
	cōnābiminī	miserēbiminī	loquēminī	ēgrediēminī	mētiēminī
	cōnābuntur	miserēbuntur	loquentur	ēgredientur	mētientur
PERF. PASS. DEP. IND.	cōnātus sum	misertus sum	locūtus sum	ēgressus sum	mēnsus sum
	cōnātus ēs	misertus ēs	locūtus ēs	ēgressus ēs	mēnsus ēs
	cōnātus est	misertus est	locūtus est	ēgressus est	mēnsus est
	cōnātī sumus	misertī sumus	locūtī sumus	ēgressī sumus	mēnsī sumus
	cōnātī estis	misertī estis	locūtī estis	ēgressī estis	mēnsī estis
	cōnātī sunt	misertī sunt	locūtī sunt	ēgressī sunt	mēnsī sunt
PLU. PASS. DEP. IND.	cōnātus eram	misertus eram	locūtus eram	ēgressus eram	mēnsus eram
	cōnātus erās	misertus erās	locūtus erās	ēgressus erās	mēnsus erās
	cōnātus erat	misertus erat	locūtus erat	ēgressus erat	mēnsus erat
	cōnātī erāmus	misertī erāmus	locūtī erāmus	ēgressī erāmus	mēnsī erāmus
	cōnātī erātis	misertī erātis	locūtī erātis	ēgressī erātis	mēnsī erātis
	cōnātī erant	misertī erant	locūtī erant	ēgressī erant	mēnsī erant
FUT. PERF. PASS. DEP. IND.	cōnātus erō	misertus erō	locūtus erō	ēgressus erō	mēnsus erō
	cōnātus eris	misertus eris	locūtus eris	ēgressus eris	mēnsus eris
	cōnātus erit	misertus erit	locūtus erit	ēgressus erit	mēnsus erit
	cōnātī erimus	misertī erimus	locūtī erimus	ēgressī erimus	mēnsī erimus
	cōnātī eritis	misertī eritis	locūtī eritis	ēgressī eritis	mēnsī eritis
	cōnātī erunt	misertī erunt	locūtī erunt	ēgressī erunt	mēnsī erunt

Imperative

		1ST	2ND	3RD	3RD -iō	4TH
PASS.	SING.	cōnāre!	miserēre!	loquere!	ēgredere!	mēnsīre!
	PLUR.	cōnāminī!	miserēminī!	loquiminī!	ēgrediminī!	mēnsīminī!

Participle

		1ST	2ND	3RD	3RD -iō	4TH
ACT.	PRES.	amāns	vidēns	dūcēns	capiēns	audiēns
	FUT.	amātūrus	vīsūrus	ductūrus	captūrus	audītūrus
PASS.	PERF.	amātus	vīsus	ductus	captus	audītus
	FUT.	amandus	videndus	dūcendus	capiendus	audiendus

Infinitive

		1ST	2ND	3RD	3RD -iō	4TH
ACT.	FUT.	cōnātūrus esse	misertūrus esse	locūtūrus esse	ēgressūrus esse	mēnsūrus esse
PASS./DEP.	PRES.	cōnārī	miserērī	loquī	ēgressī	mētīrī
PASS./DEP.	PERF.	cōnātus esse	misertus esse	locūtus esse	ēgressus esse	mēnsus esse

Subjunctive

	1ST	2ND	3RD	3RD -iō	4TH
PRES. PASS. DEP. SUBJ.	cōner	miserear	loquar	ēgrediar	mētiar
	cōnēris	misereāris	loquāris	ēgrediāris	mētiāris
	cōnētur	misereātur	loquātur	ēgrediātur	mētiātur
	cōnēmur	misereāmur	loquāmur	ēgrediāmur	mētiāmur
	cōnēminī	misereāminī	loquāminī	ēgrediāminī	mētiāminī
	cōnentur	misereantur	loquantur	ēgrediantur	mētiantur
IMP. PASS. DEP. SUBJ.	cōnārer	miserērer	loquerer	ēgrederer	metīrer
	cōnārēris	miserērēris	loquerēris	ēgrederēris	metīrēris
	cōnārētur	miserērētur	loquerētur	ēgrederētur	metīrētur
	cōnārēmur	miserērēmur	loquerēmur	ēgrederēmur	metīrēmur
	cōnārēminī	miserērēminī	loquerēminī	ēgrederēminī	metīrēminī
	cōnārentur	miserērentur	loquerentur	ēgrederentur	metīrentur
PERF. PASS. DEP. SUBJ.	cōnātus sim	misertus sim	locūtus sim	ēgressus sim	mēnsus sim
	cōnātus sīs	misertus sīs	locūtus sīs	ēgressus sīs	mēnsus sīs
	cōnātus sit	misertus sit	locūtus sit	ēgressus sit	mēnsus sit
	cōnātī sīmus	misertī sīmus	locūtī sīmus	ēgressī sīmus	mēnsī sīmus
	cōnātī sītis	misertī sītis	locūtī sītis	ēgressī sītis	mēnsī sītis
	cōnātī sint	misertī sint	locūtī sint	ēgressī sint	mēnsī sint
PLU. PASS. DEP. SUBJ.	cōnātus essem	misertus essem	locūtus essem	ēgressus essem	mēnsus essem
	cōnātus essēs	misertus essēs	locūtus essēs	ēgressus essēs	mēnsus essēs
	cōnātus esset	misertus esset	locūtus esset	ēgressus esset	mēnsus esset
	cōnātī essēmus	misertī essēmus	locūtī essēmus	ēgressī essēmus	mēnsī essēmus
	cōnātī essētis	misertī essētis	locūtī essētis	ēgressī essētis	mēnsī essētis
	cōnātī essent	misertī essent	locūtī essent	ēgressī essent	mēnsī essent

Irregular Verbs *sum, possum, eō, volō, nōlō, mālō*

sum, esse, fuī, futūrum
possum, posse, potuī, ——
eō, īre, iī (īvī), itum
volō, velle, voluī, ——
nōlō, nōlle, nōluī, ——
mālō, mālle, māluī, ——

Indicative

	SUM	POSSUM	EŌ	VOLŌ	NŌLŌ	MĀLŌ
PRES. ACT. IND.	sum	possum	eō	volō	nōlō	mālō
	ēs	potēs	is	vīs	nōn vīs	māvīs
	est	potest	it	vult	nōn vult	māvult
	sumus	possumus	īmus	volumus	nōlumus	mālumus
	estis	potestis	ītis	vultis	nōn vultis	māvultis
	sunt	possunt	eunt	volunt	nōlunt	mālunt
IMP. ACT. IND.	eram	poteram	ībam	volēbam	nōlēbam	mālēbam
	erās	poterās	ībās	volēbās	nōlēbās	mālēbās
	erat	poterat	ībat	volēbat	nōlēbat	mālēbat
	erāmus	poterāmus	ībāmus	volēbāmus	nōlēbāmus	mālēbāmus
	erātis	poterātis	ībātis	volēbātis	nōlēbātis	mālēbātis
	erant	poterant	ībant	volēbant	nōlēbant	mālēbant
FUT. ACT. IND.	erō	poterō	ībō	volam	nōlam	mālam
	eris	poteris	ībis	volēs	nōlēs	mālēs
	erit	poterit	ībit	volet	nōlet	mālet
	erimus	poterimus	ībimus	volēmus	nōlēmus	mālēmus
	eritis	poteritis	ībitis	volētis	nōlētis	mālētis
	erunt	poterint	ībunt	volent	nōlent	mālent
PERF. ACT. IND.	fuī	potuī	iī (īvī)	voluī	nōluī	māluī
	fuistī	potuistī	īstī	voluistī	nōluistī	māluistī
	fuit	potuit	iit	voluit	nōluit	māluit
	fuimus	potuimus	iimus	voluimus	nōluimus	māluimus
	fuistis	potuistis	īstis	voluistis	nōluistis	māluistis
	fuērunt	potuērunt	iērunt	voluērunt	nōluērunt	māluērunt

PLU. ACT. IND.	fueram	potueram	ieram	volueram	nōlueram	mālueram
	fuerās	potuerās	ierās	voluerās	nōluerās	māluerās
	fuerat	potuerat	ierat	voluerat	nōluerat	māluerat
	fuerāmus	potuerāmus	ierāmus	voluerāmus	nōluerāmus	māluerāmus
	fuerātis	potuerātis	ierātis	voluerātis	nōluerātis	māluerātis
	fuerant	potuerant	ierant	voluerant	nōluerant	māluerant
FUT. PERF. ACT. IND.	fuerō	potuerō	ierō	voluerō	nōluerō	māluerō
	fueris	potueris	ieris	volueris	nōlueris	mālueris
	fuerit	potuerit	ierit	voluerit	nōluerit	māluerit
	fuerimus	potuerimus	ierimus	voluerimus	nōluerimus	māluerimus
	fueritis	potueritis	ieritis	volueritis	nōlueritis	mālueritis
	fuerint	potuerint	ierint	voluerint	nōluerint	māluerint

Imperative

		SUM	POSSUM	EŌ	VOLŌ	NŌLŌ	MĀLŌ
ACT.	SING.	es!	——	ī!	——	nōlī!	——
	PL.	este!	——	īte!	——	nōlīte!	——

Participle

		SUM	POSSUM	EŌ	VOLŌ	NŌLŌ	MĀLŌ
ACT.	PRES.	——	potēns	iēns, *gen.* euntis	volēns	nōlēns	——
	FUT.	fūtūrus	——	itūrus	——	——	——
PASS.	PERF.	——	——	itum	——	——	——
	FUT.	——	——	eundus	——	——	——

Infinitive

		SUM	POSSUM	EŌ	VOLŌ	NŌLŌ	MĀLŌ
ACT.	PRES.	esse	posse	īre	velle	nōlle	mālle
	PERF.	fuisse	potuisse	īsse	voluisse	nōluisse	māluisse
	FUT.	futūrus esse (*or* fore)	——	itūrus esse	——	——	——

Subjunctive

	SUM	POSSUM	EŌ	VOLŌ	NŌLŌ	MĀLŌ
PRES. ACT. SUBJ.	sim	possim	eam	velim	nōlim	mālim
	sīs	possīs	eās	velīs	nōlīs	mālīs
	sit	possit	eat	velit	nōlit	mālit
	sīmus	possīmus	eāmus	velīmus	nōlīmus	mālīmus
	sītis	possītis	eātis	velītis	nōlītis	mālītis
	sint	possint	eant	velint	nōlint	mālint
IMP. ACT. SUBJ.	essem	possem	īrem	vellem	nōllem	māllem
	essēs	possēs	īrēs	vellēs	nōllēs	māllēs
	esset	posset	īret	vellet	nōllet	māllet
	essēmus	possēmus	īrēmus	vellēmus	nōllēmus	māllēmus
	essētis	possētis	īrētis	vellētis	nōllētis	māllētis
	essent	possent	īrent	vellent	nōllent	māllent
PERF. ACT. SUBJ.	fuerim	potuerim	ierim	voluerim	nōluerim	māluerim
	fuerīs	potuerīs	ierīs	voluerīs	nōluerīs	māluerīs
	fuerit	potuerit	ierit	voluerit	nōluerit	māluerit
	fuerīmus	potuerīmus	ierīmus	voluerīmus	nōluerīmus	māluerīmus
	fuerītis	potuerītis	ierītis	voluerītis	nōluerītis	māluerītis
	fuerint	potuerint	ierint	voluerint	nōluerint	māluerint
PLU. ACT. SUBJ.	fuissem	potuissem	īssem	voluissem	nōluissem	māluissem
	fuissēs	potuissēs	īssēs	voluissēs	nōluissēs	māluissēs
	fuisset	potuisset	īsset	voluisset	nōluisset	māluisset
	fuissēmus	potuissēmus	īssēmus	voluissēmus	nōluissēmus	māluissēmus
	fuissētis	potuissētis	īssētis	voluissētis	nōluissētis	māluissētis
	fuissent	potuissent	īssent	voluissent	nōluissent	māluissent

Irregular Verb *ferō*

ferō, ferre, tulī, lātum

Indicative

	ACTIVE	PASSIVE
PRESENT	ferō	feror
	fers	ferris
	fert	fertur
	ferimus	ferimur
	fertis	feriminī
	ferunt	feruntur
IMPERFECT	ferēbam	ferēbar
	ferēbās	ferēbāris
	ferēbat	ferēbātur
	ferēbāmus	ferēbāmur
	ferēbātis	ferēbāminī
	ferēbant	ferēbantur
FUTURE	feram	ferar
	ferēs	ferēris
	feret	ferētur
	ferēmus	ferēmur
	ferētis	ferēminī
	ferent	ferentur

	ACTIVE	PASSIVE
PERFECT	tulī	lātus sum
	tulistī	lātus ēs
	tulit	lātus est
	tulimus	lātī sumus
	tulistis	lātī estis
	tulērunt	lātī sunt
PLUPERFECT	tuleram	lātus eram
	tulerās	lātus erās
	tulerat	lātus erat
	tulerāmus	lātī erāmus
	tulerātis	lātī erātis
	tulerant	lātī erant
FUTURE PERFECT	tulerō	lātus erō
	tuleris	lātus eris
	tulerit	lātus erit
	tulerimus	lātī erimus
	tuleritis	lātī eritis
	tulerint	lātī erint

Imperative

	ACTIVE	PASSIVE
SG.	es!	----------
PL.	este!	----------

Imperative

	ACTIVE	PASSIVE
PRES.		----------
PERF.	----------	
FUT.		

Infinitive

	ACTIVE	PASSIVE
PRES.	ferre	ferrī
PERF.	tulisse	lātus esse
FUT.	lātūrus esse	(uncommon)

Subjunctive

<table>
<tr><th></th><th>ACTIVE</th><th>PASSIVE</th></tr>
<tr><td rowspan="6">PRESENT</td><td>feram</td><td>ferar</td></tr>
<tr><td>ferās</td><td>ferāris</td></tr>
<tr><td>ferat</td><td>ferātur</td></tr>
<tr><td>ferāmus</td><td>ferāmur</td></tr>
<tr><td>ferātis</td><td>ferāminī</td></tr>
<tr><td>ferant</td><td>ferantur</td></tr>
<tr><td rowspan="6">IMPERFECT</td><td>ferrem</td><td>ferrer</td></tr>
<tr><td>ferrēs</td><td>ferrēris</td></tr>
<tr><td>ferret</td><td>ferrētur</td></tr>
<tr><td>ferrēmus</td><td>ferrēmur</td></tr>
<tr><td>ferrētis</td><td>ferrēminī</td></tr>
<tr><td>ferrent</td><td>ferrentur</td></tr>
</table>

<table>
<tr><th></th><th>ACTIVE</th><th>PASSIVE</th></tr>
<tr><td rowspan="6">PERFECT</td><td>tulerim</td><td>lātus sim</td></tr>
<tr><td>tulerīs</td><td>lātus sīs</td></tr>
<tr><td>tulerit</td><td>lātus sit</td></tr>
<tr><td>tulerīmus</td><td>lātī sīmus</td></tr>
<tr><td>tulerītis</td><td>lātī sītis</td></tr>
<tr><td>tulerint</td><td>lātī sint</td></tr>
<tr><td rowspan="6">PLUERFECT</td><td>tulissem</td><td>lātus essem</td></tr>
<tr><td>tulissēs</td><td>lātus essēs</td></tr>
<tr><td>tulisset</td><td>lātus esset</td></tr>
<tr><td>tulissēmus</td><td>lātī essēmus</td></tr>
<tr><td>tulissētis</td><td>lātī essētis</td></tr>
<tr><td>tulissent</td><td>lātī essent</td></tr>
</table>

Nouns

First Declension (*KL1*, Lesson. 2)

	ENDINGS		EXAMPLE NOUN	
	SINGULAR	PLURAL	SINGULAR	PLURAL
NOM.	-a	-ae	bēlua	bēluae
GEN.	-ae	-ārum	bēluae	bēluārum
DAT.	-ae	-īs	bēluae	bēluīs
ACC.	-am	-ās	bēluam	bēluās
ABL.	-ā	-īs	bēluā	bēluīs
VOC.	-a	-ae	bēlua	bēluae
LOC.	-ae	īs	[bēluae]*	[bēluīs]*

Second Declension Masculine (*KL1*, Lesson. 4)

	ENDINGS		EXAMPLE NOUN	
	SINGULAR	PLURAL	SINGULAR	PLURAL
NOM.	-us/-r/-ius	-ī	mūrus	mūrī
GEN.	-ī	-ōrum	mūrī	mūrōrum
DAT.	-ō	-īs	mūrō	mūrīs
ACC.	-um	-ōs	mūrum	mūrōs
ABL.	-ō	-īs	mūrō	mūrīs
VOC.	-e/-r/-ī	-ī	mūre	mūrī
LOC.	-ī	-īs	[mūrī]*	[mūrīs]*

APPENDIX A \\ CHANT CHARTS

Second Declension Neuter (*KL1*, Lesson. 5)

	ENDINGS		EXAMPLE NOUN	
	SINGULAR	PLURAL	SINGULAR	PLURAL
NOM.	-um	-a	fātum	fāta
GEN.	-ī	-ōrum	fātī	fātōrum
DAT.	-ō	-īs	fātō	fātīs
ACC.	-um	-a	fātum	fāta
ABL.	-ō	-īs	fātō	fātīs
VOC.	-um	-a	fātum	fāta
LOC.	-ī	-īs	[fātī]*	[fātīs]*

Third Declension Masculine/Feminine (*KL1*, Lesson. 12)

	ENDINGS		EXAMPLE NOUN	
	SINGULAR	PLURAL	SINGULAR	PLURAL
NOM.	X	-ēs	clāmor	clāmorēs
GEN.	-is	-um	clāmoris	clāmorum
DAT.	-ī	-ibus	clāmorī	clāmoribus
ACC.	-em	-ēs	clāmorem	clāmorēs
ABL.	-e	-ibus	clāmore	clāmoribus
VOC.	X	-ēs	clāmor	clāmorēs
LOC.	-e	-ibus	[clāmore]*	[clāmoribus]*

Third Declension Neuter (*KL1*, Lesson. 13)

	ENDINGS		EXAMPLE NOUN	
	SINGULAR	PLURAL	SINGULAR	PLURAL
NOM.	X	-a	genus	genera
GEN.	-is	-um	generis	generum
DAT.	-ī	-ibus	generī	generibus
ACC.	X	-a	genus	genera
ABL.	-e	-ibus	genere	generibus
VOC.	X	-a	genus	genera
LOC.	-e	-ibus	[genere]*	[generibus]*

Third Declension Masculine/Feminine i-Stem (*KL1*, Lesson. 18)

	ENDINGS		EXAMPLE NOUN	
	SINGULAR	PLURAL	SINGULAR	PLURAL
NOM.	X	-ēs	collis	collēs
GEN.	-is	-ium	collis	collium
DAT.	-ī	-ibus	collī	collibus
ACC.	-em	-ēs	collem	collēs
ABL.	-e	-ibus	colle	collibus
VOC.	X	-ēs	collis	collēs
LOC.	-e	-ibus	[colle]*	[collibus]*

Third Declension Neuter i-Stem (*KL1*, Lesson. 18)

	ENDINGS		EXAMPLE NOUN	
	SINGULAR	PLURAL	SINGULAR	PLURAL
NOM.	X	-ia	altāre	altāria
GEN.	-is	-ium	altāris	altārium
DAT.	-ī	-ibus	altārī	altāribus
ACC.	X	-ia	altāre	altāria
ABL.	-ī	-ibus	altārī	altāribus
VOC.	X	-ia	altāre	altāria
LOC.	-ī	-ibus	[altārī]*	[altāribus]*

Fourth Declension Masculine/Feminine (*KL1*, Lesson. 25)

	ENDINGS		EXAMPLE NOUN	
	SINGULAR	PLURAL	SINGULAR	PLURAL
NOM.	-us	-ūs	adventus	adventūs
GEN.	-ūs	-uum	adventūs	adventuum
DAT.	-uī	-ibus	adventuī	adventibus
ACC.	-um	-ūs	adventum	adventūs
ABL.	-ū	-ibus	adventū	adventibus
VOC.	-us	-ūs	adventus	adventūs
LOC.	-ū	-ībus	[adventū]*	[adventibus]*

Fourth Declension Neuter (*KL1*, Lesson. 25)

	ENDINGS		EXAMPLE NOUN	
	SINGULAR	PLURAL	SINGULAR	PLURAL
NOM.	-ū	-ua	cornū	cornua
GEN.	-ūs	-uum	cornūs	cornuum
DAT.	-ū	-ibus	cornū	cornibus
ACC.	-ū	-ua	cornū	cornua
ABL.	-ū	-ibus	cornū	cornibus
VOC.	-ū	-ua	cornū	cornua
LOC.	-ū	-ibus	[cornū]*	[cornibus]*

Fifth Declension (*KL1*, Lesson. 28)

	ENDINGS		EXAMPLE NOUN	
	SINGULAR	PLURAL	SINGULAR	PLURAL
NOM.	-ēs	-ēs	aciēs	aciēs
GEN.	-eī/-ēī	-ērum	aciēī	aciērum
DAT.	-eī/-ēī	-ēbus	aciēī	aciēbus
ACC.	-em	-ēs	aciem	aciēs
ABL.	-ē	-ēbus	aciē	aciēbus
VOC.	-ēs	-ēs	aciēs	aciēs
LOC.	-ē	-ēbus	[aciē]*	[aciēbus]*

*Recall that the Locative case (*KL2*, Lesson 14) is used to indicate place, so it wouldn't necessarily work with these example nouns (thus they are in brackets). Normally you'd see names of cities, towns, and small islands, along with a few ordinary nouns, such as **domus**, **rūs**, and **humus**.

Irregular Nouns

nēmō (*KL2*, Lesson 4)

NOM.	nēmō
GEN.	nēminis [*or* nūllīus]
DAT.	nēminī
ACC.	nēminem
ABL.	nēmine [*or* nūllō]

vīs, vīs (f) (*KL3*, Lesson 5)

	SG.	PL.
NOM.	vīs	vīrēs
GEN.	vīs	vīrium
DAT.	vī	vīribus
ACC.	vim	vīrēs (-īs)
ABL.	vī	vīribus

Pronouns

Personal Pronouns (KL1, Lesson 17)

First Person

	LATIN SINGULAR	ENGLISH SINGULAR	LATIN PLURAL	ENGLISH PLURAL
NOM.	ego	I [subject]	nōs	we [subject]
GEN.	meī	of me	nostrum	of us
DAT.	mihi	to/for me	nōbīs	to/for us
ACC.	mē	me [direct object]	nōs	us [direct object]
ABL.	mē	by/with/from me	nōbīs	by/with/from us

Second Person

	LATIN SINGULAR	ENGLISH SINGULAR	LATIN PLURAL	ENGLISH PLURAL
NOM.	tū	you [subject]	vōs	you (pl.) [subject]
GEN.	tuī	of you	vestrum	of you (pl.)
DAT.	tibi	to/for you	vōbīs	to/for you (pl.)
ACC.	tē	you [direct object]	vōs	you (pl.) [direct object]
ABL.	tē	by/with/from you	vōbīs	by/with/from you (pl.)

Third Person Singular

	MASCULINE	FEMININE	NEUTER	ENGLISH
	HE/HIS/HIM	SHE/HERS/HER	IT/ITS	
NOM.	is	ea	id	he/she/it (this/that, etc.) [subject]
GEN.	eius	eius	eius	of him/his, of her/hers, of it/its
DAT.	eī	eī	eī	to/for him, to/for her, to/for it
ACC.	eum	eam	id	him/her/it [direct object]
ABL.	eō	eā	eō	by/with/from him/her/it

Third Person Plural

	MASCULINE	FEMININE	NEUTER	ENGLISH
	HE/HIS/HIM	SHE/HERS/HER	IT/ITS	
NOM.	eī	eae	ea	they (these/those, etc.) [subject]
GEN.	eōrum	eārum	eōrum	of them, their
DAT.	eīs	eīs	eīs	to/for them
ACC.	eōs	eās	ea	them [direct object]
ABL.	eīs	eīs	eīs	by/with/from them

Demonstrative Pronouns (KL1, Lesson 17)

Hic, haec, hoc—this; (pl.) these

	SINGULAR			PLURAL		
	MASCULINE	FEMININE	NEUTER	MASCULINE	FEMININE	NEUTER
NOM.	hic	haec	hoc	hī	hae	haec
GEN.	huius	huius	huius	hōrum	hārum	hōrum
DAT.	huic	huic	huic	hīs	hīs	hīs
ACC.	hunc	hanc	hoc	hōs	hās	haec
ABL.	hōc	hāc	hōc	hīs	hīs	hīs

Ille, illa, illud—that; (pl.) those; that famous

	SINGULAR			PLURAL		
	MASCULINE	FEMININE	NEUTER	MASCULINE	FEMININE	NEUTER
NOM.	ille	illa	illud	illī	illae	illa
GEN.	illīus	illīus	illīus	illōrum	illārum	illōrum
DAT.	illī	illī	illī	illīs	illīs	illīs
ACC.	illum	illam	illud	illōs	illās	illa
ABL.	illō	illā	illō	illīs	illīs	illīs

Iste, ista, istud—that (of yours); such

	SINGULAR			PLURAL		
	MASCULINE	FEMININE	NEUTER	MASCULINE	FEMININE	NEUTER
NOM.	iste	ista	istud	istī	istae	ista
GEN.	istīus	istīus	istīus	istōrum	istārum	istōrum
DAT.	istī	istī	istī	istīs	istīs	istīs
ACC.	istum	istam	istud	istōs	istās	ista
ABL.	istō	istā	istō	istīs	istīs	istīs

Intensive Pronouns

ipse, ipsa, ipsum (KL2, Lesson 3)

	SINGULAR			PLURAL		
	MASC.	FEM.	NEUT.	MASC.	FEM.	NEUT.
NOM.	ipse	ipsa	ipsum	ipsī	ipsae	ipsa
GEN.	ipsīus	ipsīus	ipsīus	ipsōrum	ipsārum	ipsōrum
DAT.	ipsī	ipsī	ipsī	ipsīs	ipsīs	ipsīs
ACC.	ipsum	ipsam	ipsum	ipsōs	ipsās	ipsa
ABL.	ipsō	ipsā	ipsō	ipsīs	ipsīs	ipsīs

quī, quae, quod (*KL2*, Lesson 3)

	SINGULAR			PLURAL		
	MASC.	FEM.	NEUT.	MASC.	FEM.	NEUT.
NOM.	quī	quae	quod	qu**ī**	qu**ae**	quae
GEN.	cuius	cuius	cuius	qu**ōrum**	qu**ārum**	qu**ōrum**
DAT.	cui	cui	cui	quibus	quibus	quibus
ACC.	quem	qu**am**	quod	qu**ōs**	qu**ās**	quae
ABL.	qu**ō**	qu**ā**	qu**ō**	quibus	quibus	quibus

aliquis, aliquid (*KL2*, Lesson 12)

	SINGULAR			PLURAL		
	MASC.	FEM.	NEUT.	MASC.	FEM.	NEUT.
NOM.	aliquis	aliquis	aliquid	aliquī	aliquae	aliqua
GEN.	alicuius	alicuius	alicuius	aliquōrum	aliquārum	aliquōrum
DAT.	alicui	alicui	alicui	aliquibus	aliquibus	aliquibus
ACC.	aliquem	aliquem	aliquid	aliquōs	aliquās	aliqua
ABL.	aliquō	aliquō	aliquō	aliquibus	aliquibus	aliquibus

quīdam, quaedam, quiddam (*KL2*, Lesson 12)

	SINGULAR			PLURAL		
	MASC.	FEM.	NEUT.	MASC.	FEM.	NEUT.
NOM.	quīdam	quaedam	**quiddam**/quoddam*	quīdam	quaedam	quaedam
GEN.	cuiusdam	cuiusdam	cuiusdam	quōrundam	quārundam	quōrundam
DAT.	cuidam	cuidam	cuidam	quibusdam	quibusdam	quibusdam
ACC.	quendam	quandam	**quiddam**/quoddam*	quōsdam	quāsdam	quaedam
ABL.	quōdam	quādam	quōdam	quibusdam	quibusdam	quibusdam

*quiddam is the pronoun form, quoddam is the adjective

Indefinite Relative Pronoun

quīcumque, quaecumque, quodcumque (*KL2*, Lesson 12)

	SINGULAR			PLURAL		
	MASC.	FEM.	NEUT.	MASC.	FEM.	NEUT.
NOM.	quīcumque	quaecumque	quodcumque	quīcumque	quaecumque	quaecumque
GEN.	cuiuscumque	cuiuscumque	cuiuscumque	quōrumcumque	quārumcumque	quōrumcumque
DAT.	cuicumque	cuicumque	cuicumque	quibuscumque	quibuscumque	quibuscumque
ACC.	quemcumque	quamcumque	quodcumque	quōscumque	quāscumque	quaecumque
ABL.	quōcumque	quācumque	quōcumque	quibuscumque	quibuscumque	quibuscumque

APPENDIX A \\ CHANT CHARTS

Interrogative Pronoun

quis, quid (*KL2*, Lesson 9)

	SINGULAR			PLURAL		
	MASC.	FEM.	NEUT.	MASC.	FEM.	NEUT.
NOM.	quis?	quis?	quid?	quī?	quae?	quae?
GEN.	cuius?	cuius?	cuius?	quōrum?	quārum?	quōrum?
DAT.	cui?	cui?	cui?	quibus?	quibus?	quibus?
ACC.	quem?	quem?	quid?	quōs?	quās?	quae?
ABL.	quō?	quō?	quō?	quibus?	quibus?	quibus?

Reflexive Pronoun (*KL3*, Lesson 2)

	MEĪ, TUĪ				SUĪ
	1ST PERSON		2ND PERSON		
	SING.	PL.	SING.	PL.	SING. OR PL.
NOM.	—	—	—	—	—
GEN.	meī	nostrī	tuī	vestrī	suī
DAT.	mihi	nōbīs	tibi	vōbīs	sibi
ACC.	mē	nōs	tē	vōs	sē
ABL.	mē	nōbīs	tē	vōbīs	sē

Adjectives

First and Second Declension Adjectives

Endings (*KL1*, Lesson 7)

	SINGULAR			PLURAL		
	MASC.	FEM.	NEUT.	MASC.	FEM.	NEUT.
NOM.	-us / -r	-a	-um	-ī	-ae	-a
GEN.	-ī	-ae	-ī	-ōrum	-ārum	-ōrum
DAT.	-ō	-ae	-ō	-īs	-īs	-īs
ACC.	-um	-am	-um	-ōs	-ās	-a
ABL.	-ō	-ā	-ō	-īs	-īs	-īs
VOC.	-e / -r	-a	-um	-ī	-ae	-a

Example

	SINGULAR			PLURAL		
	MASC.	FEM.	NEUT.	MASC.	FEM.	NEUT.
NOM.	vastus	vasta	vastum	vastī	vastae	vasta
GEN.	vastī	vastae	vastī	vastōrum	vastārum	vastōrum
DAT.	vastō	vastae	vastō	vastīs	vastīs	vastīs
ACC.	vastum	vastam	vastum	vastōs	vastās	vasta
ABL.	vastō	vastā	vastō	vastīs	vastīs	vastīs
VOC.	vaste	vasta	vastum	vastī	vastae	vasta

Third Declension Adjectives

Endings (*KL1*, Lesson 19)

	SINGULAR		PLURAL	
	MASC./FEM.	NEUTER	MASC./FEM.	NEUTER
NOM.	X	X	-ēs	-ia
GEN.	-is	-is	-ium	-ium
DAT.	-ī	-ī	-ibus	-ibus
ACC.	-em	X	-ēs	-ia
ABL.	**-ī**	-ī	-ibus	-ibus
VOC.	X	X	-ēs	-ia

Example

	SINGULAR		PLURAL	
	MASC./FEM.	NEUTER	MASC./FEM.	NEUTER
NOM.	trīstis	trīste	trīstēs	trīstia
GEN.	trīstis	trīstis	trīstium	trīstium
DAT.	trīstī	trīstī	trīstibus	trīstibus
ACC.	trīstem	trīste	trīstēs	trīstia
ABL.	trīstī	trīstī	trīstibus	trīstibus
VOC.	trīstis	trīste	trīstēs	trīstia

Irregular Adjectives

-ius Adjectives (KL2, Lesson 4)

alius, alter, neuter, nūllus, sōlus, tōtus, ūllus, unus, uter are all declined like *sōlus* below:

	SINGULAR			PLURAL		
	MASC.	FEM.	NEUT.	MASC.	FEM.	NEUT.
NOM.	sōlus	sōla	sōlum	sōlī	sōlae	sōla
GEN.	sōlīus	sōlīus	sōlīus	sōlōrum	sōlārum	sōlōrum
DAT.	sōlī	sōlī	sōlī	sōlīs	sōlīs	sōlīs
ACC.	sōlum	sōlam	sōlum	sōlōs	sōlās	sōla
ABL.	sōlō	sōlā	sōlō	sōlīs	sōlīs	sōlīs

plūs (KL2, Lesson 5)

	MASC./FEM. SG.	NEUT. SG.	MASC./FEM. PL.	NEUT. PL.
NOM.	——	plūs	plūrēs	plūra
GEN.	——	plūris	plūrium	plūrium
DAT.	——	——	plūribus	plūribus
ACC.	——	plūs	plūrēs	plūra
ABL.	——	plūre	plūribus	plūribus
VOC.	——	plūs	plūrēs	plūra

Comparison of Adjectives

Regular Comparison of Adjectives (KL2, Lesson 4)

	POSITIVE	COMPARATIVE	SUPERLATIVE
3-TERMINATION	superbus, -a, -um *proud*	superbior, -ius *prouder*	superbissimus, -a, -um *proudest*
2-TERMINATION	fortis, -e *brave*	fortior, -ius *braver*	fortissimus, -a, -um *bravest*
SINGLE TERMINATION	sapiēns, -entis *wise*	sapientior, -ius *wiser*	sapientissimus, -a, -um *wisest*

Slightly Irregular Comparison of Adjectives (KL2, Lesson 5)

	POSITIVE	COMPARATIVE	SUPERLATIVE
ENDING IN -ER	miser, -era, -erum *wretched*	miserior, -ius *more wretched*	miserrimus, -a, -um *most wretched*
	pulcher, -chra, -chrum *beautiful*	pulchrior, -ius *more beautiful*	pulcherrimus, -a, -um *most beautiful*
	celer, -eris, -e *swift*	celerior, -ius *swifter*	celerrimus, -a, -um *swiftest*

	POSITIVE	COMPARATIVE	SUPERLATIVE
6 ENDING IN -LIS	similis, -e *similar, like*	similior, -ius *more similar*	simillimus, -a, -um *most similar*
	dissimilis, -e *dissimilar, unlike, different*	dissimilior, -ius *more dissimilar*	dissimillimus, -a, -um *most dissimilar*
	facilis, -e *easy*	facilior, -ius *easier*	facillimus, -a, -um *easiest*
	difficilis *difficult*	difficilior, -ius *more difficult*	difficillimus, -a, -um *most difficult*
	gracilis, -e *slender, thin*	gracilior, -ius *thinner*	gracillimus, -a, -um *thinnest*
	humilis, -e *humble, low(ly)*	humilior, -ius *more humble*	humillimus, -a, -um *most humble*

Irregular Comparison of Adjectives (*KL2*, Lesson 5)

	POSITIVE	COMPARATIVE	SUPERLATIVE
JUST PLAIN IRREGULAR	magnus, -a, -um *big, great*	māior, māius *bigger, greater*	māximus, -a, -um *biggest, greatest*
	parvus, -a, -um *small*	minor, minus *smaller*	minimus, -a, -um *smallest*
	bonus, -a, -um *good*	melior, melius *better*	optimus, -a, -um *best*
	malus, -a, -um *bad, evil*	pēior, pēius *worse, more evil*	pessimus, -a, -um *worst, most evil*
	īnferus, -a, -um *below*	īnferior, -ius *lower*	īnfimus, -a, -um *or* īmus, -a, -um* *lowest, deepest*
	superus, -a, -um *above, high*	superior, -ius *higher*	suprēmus, -a, -um *or* summus, -a, -um* *highest, greatest*
	multus, -a, -um *much*	——, plūs *more*	plūrimus, -a, -um *most*
	——- [prō or prae (adv. & prep. + abl., *below*]	prior, prius *former*	prīmus, -a, -um *first*
	——- [prope (adv.) *near*]	propior, -ius *nearer*	proximus, -a, -um *next, nearest*
	——- [ultrā (adv.) *beyond*]	ulterior, -ius *farther*	ultimus, -a, -um *farthest*

*īmus and summus are often regarded as alternate superlatives of *īnferus* and *superus* respectively, even though they are technically not from these positive forms.

Indefinite Adjective *aliquī, aliquae, aliquod* (KL2, Lesson 12)

	SINGULAR			PLURAL		
	MASC.	FEM.	NEUT.	MASC.	FEM.	NEUT.
NOM.	aliquis	aliquis	aliquid	aliquī	aliquae	aliqua
GEN.	alicuius	alicuius	alicuius	aliquōrum	aliquārum	aliquōrum
DAT.	alicui	alicui	alicui	aliquibus	aliquibus	aliquibus
ACC.	aliquem	aliquem	aliquid	aliquōs	aliquās	aliqua
ABL.	aliquō	aliquō	aliquō	aliquibus	aliquibus	aliquibus

	SINGULAR			PLURAL		
	MASC.	FEM.	NEUT.	MASC.	FEM.	NEUT.
NOM.	aliquī	aliqua	aliquod	aliquī	aliquae	aliqua
GEN.	alicuius	alicuius	alicuius	aliquōrum	aliquārum	aliquōrum
DAT.	alicui	alicui	alicui	aliquibus	aliquibus	aliquibus
ACC.	aliquem	aliquam	aliquod	aliquōs	aliquās	aliqua
ABL.	aliquō	aliquā	aliquō	aliquibus	aliquibus	aliquibus

Indefinite Adjective *quīdam, quaedam, quoddam* (KL2, Lesson 12)

	SINGULAR			PLURAL		
	MASC.	FEM.	NEUT.	MASC.	FEM.	NEUT.
NOM.	quīdam	quaedam	quiddam	quīdam	quaedam	quaedam
GEN.	cuiusdam	cuiusdam	cuiusdam	quōrundam	quārundam	quōrundam
DAT.	cuidam	cuidam	cuidam	quibusdam	quibusdam	quibusdam
ACC.	quendam	quandam	quiddam	quōsdam	quāsdam	quaedam
ABL.	quōdam	quādam	quōdam	quibusdam	quibusdam	quibusdam

Interrogative Adjective *quī? quae? quod?* (KL2, Lesson 9)

	SINGULAR			PLURAL		
	MASC.	FEM.	NEUT.	MASC.	FEM.	NEUT.
NOM.	quī?	quae?	quod?	quī?	quae?	quae?
GEN.	cuius?	cuius?	cuius?	quōrum?	quārum?	quōrum?
DAT.	cui?	cui?	cui?	quibus?	quibus?	quibus?
ACC.	quem?	quam?	quod?	quōs?	quās?	quae?
ABL.	quō?	quā?	quō?	quibus?	quibus?	quibus?

Adverbs

Regular and Irregular Comparison of Adverbs

	ORIGINAL ADJECTIVE	POSITIVE ADVERB	COMPARATIVE ADVERB	SUPERLATIVE ADVERB
REGULAR	superbus, -a, -um *proud*	superbē *proudly*	superbius *more proudly*	superbissimē *most proudly*
	miser, -era, -erum *wretched*	miserē *wretchedly*	miserius *more wretchedly*	miserrimē *most wretchedly*
	pulcher, -chra, -chrum *beautiful*	pulchrē *beautifully*	pulchrius *more beautifully*	pulcherrimē *most beautifully*
	celer, -eris, -ere *swift*	celeriter *swiftly*	celerius *more swiftly*	celerrimē *most swiftly*
	potēns, -entis *powerful*	potenter *powerfully*	potentius *more powerfully*	potentissimē *most powerfully*
IRREGULAR	facilis, -e *easy*	facile *easily*	facilius *more easily*	facillimē *most easily*
	magnus, -a, -um *large, great*	magnoperē *greatly*	magis *more, rather*	māximē *most, especially, very*
	parvus, -a, -um *small, little*	parum *(too) little, not enough*	minus *less*	minimē *least, not at all*
	bonus, -a, -um *good*	bene *well*	melius *better*	optimē *best*
	malus, -a, -um *bad*	male *badly*	pēius *worst*	pessimē *worst*
	multus, -a, -um *much*	multum *much*	plūs *more*	plūrimum *most*
	———	[prō]	prius *before, earlier*	prīmō/prīmum *(at) first*
	———	diū *for a long time*	diūtius *longer*	diūtissimē *very long*

Appendix B
English-Latin Glossary

Here you will find the words for the English-Latin sections of your worksheets. When using any glossary, always keep in mind that two languages don't always mesh perfectly. For example, if you look up "land" you will find *patria*, *tellūs*, and *terra*. They all can mean "land," but you'll have to use good judgment to decide which is correct in a given context! In brackets you will find the volume of the text (KL1, 2, or 3) and the number of the lesson (L) or worksheet (W) where each word is introduced.

A

a long way off *longē* [KL3, L3]

abandon *relinquō, -ere, -līquī, -lictum* [KL1, L28]

abduction *raptus, -ūs (m)* [KL1, W31]

abide (in) *permaneō, -ēre, -mansī, -mansum* [KL3, L7]

able (am able) *possum, posse, potuī, ——* [KL1, L11]

above *super (+ acc. & + abl.)* [KL1, L6]; *suprā (adv. & prep. + acc.)* [KL1, L14]

about (adv.) *quasi* [KL3, L11]

about (prep.) *circā* [KL2, L13]

above (adj.) *superus, -a, -um* [KL2, L5]

absent (I am absent) *absum, -esse, āfuī, āfutūrum* [KL3, L3]

abundance *cōpia, -ae (f)* [KL1, L15]

abundant *plēnus, -a, -um* [KL2, L4]; *ūber, -eris* [KL2, W11]

accept *accipiō, -ere, -cēpī, -ceptum* [KL1, L31]

accomplish *pātrō* [KL3, W4]

according to *secundum (adv. & prep. + acc.)* [KL1, L28]

accordingly *ergo (adv.)* [KL1, L18]

accuse *arguō, -ere, arguī, argutus* [KL2, W9]; *accūsō* [KL3, W1]

accustomed (am accustomed to) *soleō, -ēre, ——, solitus sum (semi-deponent)* [KL3, L9]

across *trāns* [KL1, L11] **upon** *pactus, -a, -um* [KL2, L13]

agreement *foedus, -deris (n)* [KL2, L12]; *placitum, -ī (n)* [KL3, W9]

aid *auxilium, -ī (n)* [KL1, L5]

aim *tendō, -ere, tetendī, tentum* [KL2, L4]

air *aura, -ae (f)* [KL3, L3]

alas! *heu (ēheu)* [KL1, L22]

alchemy *alchemia, -ae (f)* [KL1, W27]

alder *alnus, -ī (f)* [KL1, L4]

alien (adj.) *aliēnus, -a, -um* [KL2, L12]

all *omnis, -e* [KL1, L19]; *tōtus, -a, -um* [KL2, L3]; **(all of)** *cunctus, -a, -um* [KL2, L9]; **(all together)** *ūniversus, -a, -um* [KL3, L4]

all the way up to *usque* [KL3, L4]

allow *permittō, -ere, -mīsī, -missum* [KL1, W30]; *sinō, -ere, sīvī, situs* [KL2, W13]; *concēdō, -ere, -cessī, -cessum* [KL3, W9]

allowed (it is allowed) *licet, licuit, -* (impers. + dat./acc.) [KL1, W26; KL3, L1]

ally *socius, -iī (m)* [KL2, L13]

almighty *omnipotēns, -tentis* [KL3, W2]

almost *paene (adv.)* [KL1, L19]; *quasi* [KL3, L11]; *ferē* [KL3, L3]

alone (adv.) *sōlum* [KL3, L7]

alone (adj.) *sōlus, -a, -um* [KL1, W12; KL2, L4]

already *iam* [KL1, L15]

also *et* [KL1, L1]; *etiam* [KL1, L22]; *quoque* [KL1, L29]

altar *altāre, -tāris (n)* [KL2, L9]

although *cum* [KL3, L7]; *etsi* [KL3, W2]

altogether *omnīnō* [KL3, L5]

always *semper* [KL1, L5]

am a slave to *serviō, -īre, -īvī, -ītum (+ dat.)* [KL2, L10]

am absent *absum, -esse, āfuī, āfutūrum* [KL3, L3]

am accustomed (to) *soleō, -ēre, ——, solitus sum (semi-deponent)* [KL3, L9]

am afraid of *metuō, -ere, -uī, -ūtum* [KL3, L15]

am amazed at *mīror, -ārī, ——, mīrātus sum* [KL2, L6]

am away (from) *absum, -esse, āfuī, āfutūrum* [KL3, L3]

am begotten *nāscor, -scī, ——, nātus sum* [KL2, L12]

am born *gignō, -ere, genuī, genitum (in pass.)* [KL2, L9]; *nāscor, -scī, ——, nātus sum* [KL2, L12]; *orior, -īrī, ——, ortus sum* [KL2, L6]

am busy *operor, -ārī, ——, operātus sum* [KL2, L6]

am created *orior, -īrī, ——, ortus sum* [KL2, L6]

am (I am) *sum, esse, fuī, futūrum* [KL1, L3]

am ignorant (of) *nesciō, -īre, -īvī, -ītum* [KL1, L30; KL3, L3]; *ignōrō* [KL2, L15]

am in the habit of *soleō, -ēre, ——, solītus sum (semi-deponent)* [KL3, L9]

am pleasing *placeō, -ēre, -cuī, -citum* [KL3, L1]

am unwilling *nōlō, nōlle, nōluī, ——* [KL2, L14]

am visible *appareō, -ēre, -uī, -itum (+ dat.)* [KL3, L4]

am without *careō, -ēre, -uī, -itum (+ abl.)* [KL3, L6]

amazement *stupor, -ōris (m)* [KL1, W28]

ambassador *lēgātus, -ī (m)* [KL2, L15]

ambush *īnsidiae, -ārum (f, pl)* [KL2, L15]

among *inter (+ acc.)* [KL1, L19]; *apud (+ acc.)* [KL2, L4]

ancestor *avus, -ī (m)* [KL1, L22]

anchor *ancora, -ae* [KL2, W12]

ancient *antīquus, -a, -um* [KL1, L7]

and *ac (atque)* [KL1, L27]; *et* [KL1, L1]; *-que (enclitic)* [KL1, L10]

and also *ac (atque)* [KL1, L27]

and not *nec (neque)* [KL1, L14]

and so *itaque* [KL1, L2]

angel *angelus, -ī (m)* [KL3, W5]

anger *furor, -ōris (m)* [KL3, W6]

be angry *furō, -ere, -uī, ——* [KL2, W13]; *īrāscor, -scī, ——, īrātus sum* [KL3, W9]

anger *īra, -ae (f)* [KL1, L2]

angry *īrātus, -a, -um* [KL1, L15]; *īnfēnsus, -a, -um* [KL2, W15]

animal *animal, -ālis (n)* [KL1, L18]

ankle *tālāria, -ium (n, pl)* [KL3, W16]

announce *nuntiō (1)* [KL1, L14]; *adnūntiō* [KL3, L7]

annoy *vexō (1)* [KL1, L19]

Anointed One *Messīā(s), -ae (m)* [KL2, W12]

anointing *ūnctiō, -ōnis (f)* [KL3, W12]

another *alius, -a, -um* [KL1, W21; KL2, L4]; *aliēnus, -a, -um* [KL2, L12]

answer *respondeō, -ēre, -spondī, -sponsum* [KL1, L9]

anticipate *praecipiō, -ere, -cēpī, -ceptum* [KL3, W5]

any *ūllus, -a, -um* [KL1, W27; KL2, L4]; *aliquī, aliquae, aliquod (adj.)* [KL2, L12]

anyhow *saltem* [KL3, W5]

anyone *ūllus, -a, -um* [KL1, W27]; *aliquis, aliquid (pron.)* [KL2, L12]; *quisquam, quidquam/quicquam* [KL3, L1]

anything *ūllus, -a, -um* [KL1, W27]; *aliquis, aliquid (pron.)* [KL2, L12]; *quisquam, quidquam/quicquam* [KL3, L1]

anywhere *usquam* [KL3, L9]

anxious *sollicitus, -a, -um* [KL2, W14]

Apollo *Apollō, -inis (m)* [KL1, W20]

apostle *apostolus, -ī (m)* [KL1, L11]

apparent (it is apparent) *apparet* [KL3, L4]

appear *appareō, -ēre, -uī, -itum (+ dat.)* [KL3, L4]

appearance *cōnspectus, -ūs (m)* [KL2, L9]; *speciēs, -ēī (f)* [KL3, W4]

apple *pōmum, -ī (n)* [KL3, W11]

apply *referō, -ferre, -(t)tulī, -(l)lātum* [KL3, W9]

appointed *pactus, -a, -um* [KL2, L13]

apprentice *discipulus, -ī (m)* [KL1, L5]

approach *appropinquō (1)* [KL1, L25]; *adeō, -īre, -iī, -itum* [KL2, L10]; *propinquō (+ dat./acc.)* [KL2, W3]; *aggredior, -ī, ——, -gressus sum* [KL3, W7]

approve (of) *probō* [KL3, L14]

arch *arcus, -ūs (m)* [KL1, L27]

Ares *Mars, Martis (m)* [KL2, W13]

Argus *Argus, -ī (m)* [KL1, W21]

Ariadne *Ariadna, -ae (f)* [KL1, W30]

arise *nāscor, -scī, ——, nātus sum* [KL2, L12]; *orior, -īrī, ——, ortus sum* [KL2, L6]

arise *surgō, -ere, surrēxī, surrēctum* [KL1, L28]

arm *bracchium, -ī (n)* [KL1, W13; KL3, W3]

armor *arma, -ōrum (n, pl)* [KL1, W32]

arms *arma, -ōrum (n, pl)* [KL1, W32; KL2, L3]

army (on the march) *exercitus, -ūs (m)* [KL1, L25]; *āgmen, -minis (n)* [KL3, L6]; *cohors, -hortis (f)* [KL3, W2]

around *circā* [KL2, L13]

arrange *collocō (1)* [KL1, W21]

arrival *adventus, -ūs (m)* [KL3, L12]

arrive *perveniō, -īre, -vēnī, -ventum* [KL2, L11]

arrogance *superbia, -ae (f)* [KL2, L12]

arrow *sagitta, -ae (f)* [KL1, L3]

as far as *usque* [KL3, L4]

as *quam* [KL1, L28]; *sīcut* [KL1, L20]; *ut (+ indic.)* [KL3, L5]

as if *quasi* [KL3, L11]

as long as *quamdiu* [KL3, L9]

as (rel. adj.) *quālis* [KL3, L9]

as soon as *simul atque* [KL2, L9]

ascend *ascendō, -ere, -scendī, -scensum* [KL2, L9]

ascertain *perspiciō, -ere, -spēxī, -spectum* [KL3, W2]

ashes *cinis, -neris (m)* [KL3, L10]

ask *rogō (1)* [KL1, L6]; *interrogō* [KL2, W8]; *postulō* [KL3, L10]; *quaerō, -ere, quaesīvī, quaesītum (-situm)* [KL2, L3]

ask for *petō, -ere, -īvī, -ītum* [KL2, L12]

assemble *congregō* [KL2, L14]

assemble (trans. verb) *convocō* [KL3, W5]

assert *āiō* [KL1, L14]

assume *sumō, -ere, sūmpsī, sūmptum* [KL2, L10]

astonished (be) *stupeō, -ēre, -uī, ——* [KL3, W16]

astonishment *stupor, -ōris (m)* [KL1, W28]

at *ad (+ acc.)* [KL1, L3]

at a distance *procul* [KL2, L11]

at all *omnīno* [KL3, L5]

at any time *umquam* [KL3, L14]

at first *prīmum/prīmō* [KL2, L7]

at last *tandem* [KL3, L15]

at least *saltem* [KL3, W5]
at once *continuō* [KL2, L12]
at that place *ibī* [KL1, L5]
at that time *tum* [KL1, L15]; *tunc* [KL2, L4]
at the foot of *sub (+ abl.)* [KL1, L14]
at the house of *apud (+ acc.)* [KL2, L4]
at the same time *simul* [KL2, L9]
at/in any place *usquam* [KL3, L9]
Athena *Minerva, -ae (f)* [KL3, W6]; *Pallas, -adis (f)* [KL3, W6]
Athenian *Athēniensis, -is (m/f)* [KL1, W30]
Athens *Athēnae, -ārum (f, pl)* [KL1, W30; KL2, L14]
atonement *propitiātiō, -ōnis (f)* [KL2, W11]
attack (noun) *impetus, -ūs (m)* [KL3, L9]
attack (verb) *oppugnō (1)* [KL1, L4]; *petō, -ere, -īvī, -ītum* [KL2, L12]; *aggredior, -ī, ——, -gressus sum* [KL3, W7]
attempt *cōnor, -ārī, ——, cōnātus sum* [KL2, L6]; *temptō* [KL1, W27; KL3, L7]
attendant *minister, -strī (m)* [KL3, L10]
aunt *amita, -ae (f)* [KL1, L22]
authority *imperium, -iī (n)* [KL2, L3]; *diciō, -ōnis (f)* [KL3, W10]
avoid *vītō (1)* [KL1, L30]
away from *ā, ab (+ abl.)* [KL1, L3]
awaken *suscitō* [KL3, W5]
away (I am away [from]) *absum, -esse, āfuī, āfutūrum* [KL3, L3]
awful *horrendus, -a, -um* [KL1, L13]

B

baby *īnfāns, -fantis (adj. & noun, m/f)* [KL1, W31; KL3, L12]
Bacchus *Bacchus, -ī (m)* [KL1, W27]
back (adv.) *retrō* [KL1, W23; KL3, W3]; *rursum/rursus* [KL3, L3];
back (noun) *tergum, -ī (n)* [KL3, L6]
back(ward) *retrō* [KL1, W23]

backwards *rursum/rursus* [KL3, L3]; *resupīnus, -a, -um* [KL3, W7]
bad *malus, -a, -um* [KL1, L7]
badly *male* [KL1, L1]
bag *pēra, -ae (f)* [KL1, W32]; *saccus, -ī (m)* [KL2, W6]
ball *pila, -ae (f)* [KL1, W30]
banquet *convīvium, -iī (n)* [KL3, L10]
barbarian *barbarus, -ī (m)* [KL1, L31]
barber *tonsor, -ōris (m)* [KL1, W28]
bare *nūdus, -a, -um* [KL3, W7]
barn *horreum, -ī (n)* [KL2, W14]
barrier *spīna, -ae (f)* [KL1, W23]
bathe *lavō, -āre, lāvī, lōtum/lavātum* [KL1, W27; KL2, L11]
batter (verb) *quassō* [KL3, W1]
battle *proelium, -ī (n)* [KL1, L15]; *pugna, -ae (f)* [KL2, W9]
battle line *aciēs, -ēī (f)* [KL3, L14]
be *sum, esse, fuī, futūrum* [KL1, L3]
be silent *taceō, -ēre, -uī, -itum* [KL1, W26]
be strong *valeō, -ēre, -uī, valitūrum* [KL1, L9]
be well *salveō, -ēre, ——, ——* [KL1, L9]; *valeō, -ēre, -uī, valitūrum* [KL1, L9]
beach *harēna, -ae (f)* [KL1, L3]
beam *trabēs, -is (m)* [KL2, W14]
bear (noun) *ursus, -ī (m)* [KL1, W32]
bear (verb) *gerō, -ere, gessī, gestum* [KL1, L28]; *ferō, ferre, tulī, lātum (irreg. 3rd conj.)* [KL1, W32] *ferō, ferre, tulī, lātum* [KL1, W32; KL2, W11]; **bear across** *trānsferō, -ferre, -tūlī, -lātum* [KL3, L13]; **bear over** *trānsferō, -ferre, -tūlī, -lātum* [KL3, L13]
beast *bēstia, -ae (f)* [KL1, L2]; *bēlua, -ae (f)* [KL3, L15]; **(of burden)** *iūmentum, -ī (n)* [KL3, W4]
beat *percutiō, -ere, -cussī, -cussum* [KL1, W32; KL2, L3]
beautiful *pulcher, -chra, -chrum* [KL1, L7]
beauty *forma, -ae (f)* [KL3, W16]

because (conj.) *quandō* [KL1, L12]; *quia* [KL1, L18]; *quod* [KL1, L10]; *quoniam* [KL1, L26]
because of *propter (+ acc.)* [KL1, L25]
become *fīō, fierī, ——, factus sum* [KL1, L31]
bed *cubīle, -is (n)* [KL3, W9]; *lectulus, -ī (m)* [KL3, W5]
before (adj.) *prior, prius* [KL2, L5]
before (conj.) *ante (+ acc.)* [KL1, L17]; *cōram (+ abl.)* [KL1, L27]; *pro (+ abl.)* [KL1, L18]; *antequam* [KL3, L15]; *priusquam* [KL3, L15]
beg *mendicō* [KL2, W8]; *obsecrō* [KL3, L13]
began *coepī, coepisse, ——, coeptum (defective)* [KL3, L1]
beget *gignō, -ere, genuī, genitum* [KL2, L9]; *pariō, -ere, peperī, par(i)tum* [KL3, L13]
begetting *generātiō, -ōnis (f)* [KL3, L7]
beggar *mendicus, -ī (m)* [KL2, W8]
begin *incipiō, -ere, -cēpī, -ceptum* [KL1, L31]; *ineō, -īre, -iī (-īvī), -ītum* [KL3, L4]
beginning *initium, -iī (n)* [KL3, L7]; *prīncipium, -iī (n)* [KL3, L4]
begotten (am begotten) *nāscor, -scī, ——, nātus sum* [KL2, L12]
behind *retrō* [KL1, W23; KL3, W3]; *post (+ acc.)* [KL1, L17]
behold! *ecce* [KL1, L17]
believe *crēdō, -ere, -didī, -ditum* [KL1, L26]
belly *uterus, -ī (m)* [KL2, W9]
beloved *cārus, -a, -um* [KL1, L13]; *dīlēctus, -a, -um* [KL3, L1]
below (adj.) *īnferus, -a, -um* [KL2, L5]
below (adv./prep.) *sub (+ abl.)* [KL1, L14]; *īnfrā* [KL3, W16]; *prae* [KL2, L5]
bereft *orbus, -a, -um* [KL1, L22]
beseech *dēprecor, -ārī, ——, -ātus sum* [KL3, L10]; *obsecrō* [KL3, L13]
beseige *obsideō, -ēre, -sēdī, -sessum* [KL1, L10]

251

beside (prep.) *praeter* [KL2, L13]

besides (adv.) *etiam* [KL1, L22]; *amplius* [KL3, L9]; *extrā* [KL3, L15]

best (adj.) *optimus, -a, -um* [KL2, L5]

best (adv.) *optimē* [KL2, L7]

Bethlehem *Bethleem (indecl.)* [KL1, W32]

better (adj.) *melior, -ius* [KL1, W28; KL2, L5]

better (adv.) *melius, -ius* [KL2, L7]

between *inter (+ acc.)* [KL1, L19]

beware (of) *caveō, -ēre, cāvī, cautum* [KL1, L12]

beyond *super (+ acc./+ abl.)* [KL1, L26]; *extrā* [KL3, L15]; *praeter* [KL2, L13]; *ultrā* [KL2, L5]

Bible (Holy Bible) *Biblia Sacra, Bibliae Sacrae (f)* [KL1, L11]

big *magnus, -a, -um* [KL1, L7]

bigger *māior, -ius* [KL1, W31; KL2, L5]

biggest *māximus, -a, -um* [KL1, W31; KL2, L5]

billy goat *caper, -prī (m)* [KL1, L4]

bind *vinciō, -īre, vīnxī, vīnctum* [KL1, L30]

bird *avis, avis (f)* [KL1, L18]

birth *genus, -neris (n)* [KL2, L13]; *nātīvitās, -tātis (f)* [KL2, W8]

bit by bit *minūtātim* [KL1, L20]

bite *mordeō, -ēre, momordī, morsum* [KL1, L9]

black (dead black) *āter, -tra, -trum* [KL1, L17]; **(shining black)** *niger, -gra, -grum* [KL1, L17]

blanket *strātum, -ī (n)* [KL2, L13]

blasphemy *blasphēmia, -ae (f)* [KL3, W1]

blaze *ardeō, ardēre, arsī, ——* [KL1, L20]

bless *benedīcō, -ere, -dīxī, -dictum (+ dat.)* [KL3, L4]

blessed *beātus, -a, -um* [KL1, L7]

blind *caecus, -a, -um* [KL1, L27]

blind *obcaecō* [KL3, W12]

blockade *obsidiō, -ōnis (f)* [KL2, W15]

blood *sanguis, -guinis (m)* [KL2, L3]

to make **bloody** *cruentō* [KL2, W11]

bloody *cruentus, -a, -um* [KL2, W15]

blow (noun) *plāga, -ae (f)* [KL3, L14]; *ictus, -ūs (m)* [KL3, W5]

blow (verb) *spīrō* [KL2, W3]

blue *caeruleus, -a, -um* [KL1, L17]; *hyacinthinus, -a, -um* [KL1, L17]

boat *nāvicula, -ae (f)* [KL1, W31]

body *corpus, corporis (n)* [KL1, L13]; **(dead body)** *cadaver, -veris (n)* [KL1, W32]

bold *magnanimus, -a, -um* [KL1, W9]

bone *os, ossis (n)* [KL3, L15]

book *liber, librī (m)* [KL1, L11]; *cōdex, -dicis (m)* [KL3, W9]

booty *praeda, -ae (f)* [KL2, L15]

born (am born) *gignō, -ere, genuī, genitum (in pass.)* [KL2, L9]; *nāscor, -scī, ——, nātus sum* [KL2, L12]

both...and *et...et* [KL1, L1]

bottom (lowest part) *fundus, -ī (m)* [KL2, W10]

bound(ary) *fīnis, -is (m)* [KL1, W4]; *regiō, -ōnis (f)* [KL3, W2]; *terminus, -ī (m)* [KL3, L15]

boundless *infīnītus, -a, -um* [KL3, W2]

bow *arcus, -ūs (m)* [KL1, L27]

box *arca, -ae (f)* [KL2, W6]

boy *puer, puerī (m)* [KL1, L5]

branch *virga, -ae (f)* [KL3, L10]

brandish *quatiō, -ere, quassī, quassus* [KL3, W5]

bravery *fortitūdō, -tudinis (f)* [KL2, L12]

brave *fortis, -e* [KL1, L19]; *magnanimus, -a, -um* [KL1, W9]; *audāx, -ācis* [KL2, W11]

braver *fortior, -tius (gen. fortioris)* [KL1, W31]

bravest *fortissimus, -a, -um* [KL1, W32]

bread *pānis, -is (m)* [KL1, L29]

break *frangō, -ere, frēgī, fractum* [KL1, L27]; *rumpō, -ere, rūpī, ruptum* [KL2, L12]

break (forth) *prōrumpō, -ere, -rūpī, -ruptum* [KL2, W9]

breath *spīritus, -ūs (m)* [KL1, L25]; *anima, -ae (f)* [KL2, L4]

breathe *spīrō* [KL2, W3]

breeze *aura, -ae (f)* [KL3, L3]

bridge *pōns, pontis (m)* [KL1, W19]

brief *brevis, -e* [KL1, L19]

bright (adj.; very bright) *clārus, -a, -um* [KL3, W3]; *limpidissimus, -a, -um* [KL1, W32]

bright (verb; am bright) *lūceō, lūcēre, lūxī, ——* [KL1, L11]

bring—(to) *afferō (adf-), -ferre (adf-), attulī (adt-), allātum (adl-)* [KL3, L5]; **(across)** *trānsferō, -ferre, -tūlī, -lātum* [KL3, L13]; **(back)** *referō, -ferre, -(t)tulī, -(l)lātum* [KL3, W9]; **(forth)** *ferō, ferre, tulī, lātum (irreg. 3rd conj.)* [KL1, W32]; *pariō, -ere, peperī, par(i)tum* [KL3, L13]; **(in)** *inferō, -ferre, intulī, illātum (+ dat. or + ad/ in + acc.)* [KL3, L2]; **(out)** *ēdūcō, -ere, -dūxī, -ductum* [KL3, L5]; **(over)** *trānsferō, -ferre, -tūlī, -lātum* [KL3, L13]; **(to)** *offerō, offerre, obtulī, oblātum* [KL2, L11]

broad *lātus, -a, -um* [KL1, L20]

broad way *platēa, -ae (f)* [KL3, L1]

bronze *aēneus, -a, -um* [KL2, W6]

brother *frāter, frātris (m)* [KL1, L12]; *germānus, -ī (m)* [KL1, L4]

brown (dark-brown) *purpureus, -a, -um* [KL1, L17]

build *aedificō* [KL2, L4]; *mōlior, -īrī, ——, mōlītus sum* [KL2, L6]

bull *bōs, bovis (m)* [KL1, L19]

business (mind one's own business) *suum negōtium agere* [KL1, W29]

burden *onus, oneris n.* [KL1, L13; KL3, L3]

burdensome *gravis, -e* [KL3, L6]

burn (intransit.) *ardeō, ardēre, arsī,* —— [KL1, L20]; *torreō, -ēre, torruī, tostum* [KL1, L17]

burn (transit.) *cremō (1)* [KL1, L2]

burnt offering *altāre, -tāris (n)* [KL2, L9]

burst *rumpō, -ere, rūpī, ruptum* [KL2, L12]

burst (forth) *prōrumpō, -ere, -rūpī, -ruptum* [KL2, W9]

business *negōtium, -iī (n)* [KL3, W9]

but *modo* [KL1, L27]; *sed* [KL1, L1]; *at* [KL3, L1]; *tantum* [KL3, L14]

buy *emō, -ere, ēmī, ēmptum* [KL2, L10]

by *iūxta (adv. & prep. + acc.)* [KL1, L28]

by chance *forte* [KL2, L3]; *temere* [KL2, W15]

by no means *haud* [KL3, L1]; *nequaquam* [KL2, W8]

by turns *invicem* [KL2, L12]

by what means? *quārē* [KL3, L9]

C

cabin (of a ship) *diaeta, -ae (f)* [KL1, W18]

call *appellō (1)* [KL1, L15]; *vocō (1)* [KL1, L1]

call (back/again) *revocō* [KL3, W2]

calm (verb) *mītigō* [KL3, W7]

calm (adj.) *placidus, -a, -um* [KL1, W29]; *tranquillus, -a, -um* [KL3, W9]

camel *camēlus, -ī (m/f)* [KL1, L4]

camp *castra, -ōrum (n, pl)* [KL1, L15]

can *possum, posse, potuī,* —— [KL1, L11]

capture *capiō, -ere, cēpī, captum* [KL1, L31]

carcass *cadaver, -veris (n)* [KL1, W32]

care for *cūrō (1)* [KL1, L15]

careless *immemor, -oris* [KL2, W6]

carpenter *faber, -brī (m)* [KL3, W2]

carry on *gerō, -ere, gessī, gestum* [KL1, L28]

carry *ferō, ferre, tulī, lātum* [KL1, W32; KL2, W11]; *portō (1)* [KL1, L4]; *vehō, -ere, vexī, vectum* [KL1, L27]; **(to)** *afferō (adf-), -ferre (adf-), attulī (adt-), allātum (adl-)* [KL3, L5]; *offerō, offerre, obtulī, oblātum* [KL2, L11]; **(across)** *trānsferō, -ferre, -tūlī, -lātum* [KL3, L13]; **(in)** *īnferō, -ferre, intulī, illātum (+ dat. or + ad/ in + acc.)* [KL3, L5]; *importō* [KL3, W2]; **(off/away)** *rapiō, -ere, rapuī, raptum* [KL1, L31]; *auferō, -ferre, abstulī, ablatum* [KL1, W32; KL3, L10]; **(over)** *trānsferō, -ferre, -tūlī, -lātum* [KL3, L13]

Carthage *Carthāgo, -ginis (f)* [KL2, L14]

cast *iaciō, -ere, iēcī, iactum* [KL1, L31]

cast down *dēiciō, -icere, -iēcī, iectum* [KL1, W23]

cast out *ēiciō, -ere, -iēcī, -iectum* [KL2, L14]

castle *castellum, -ī (n)* [KL1, L5]

cattle plural of *bōs, bovis (m/f)* [KL1, L19]; *pecus, -coris (n)* [KL3, L2]

cause (verb) *efficiō, -ere, -fēcī, -fectum* [KL3, W10]

cause (noun) *causa, -ae (f)* [KL2, L15]

cause of offense *scandalum, -ī (n)* [KL3, L12]

cavalry *equitātus, -ūs (m)* [KL3, W2]

cavalryman *eques, -quitis (m)* [KL1, L20]

cave *spēlunca, -ae (f)* [KL1, L3]; *caverna, -ae (f)* [KL2, W6]

censure *reprehendō, -ere, -hendī, -hēnsum* [KL3, W13]

centaur *centaurus, -ī (m)* [KL1, L10]

certain (adj.) *quīdam, quaedam, quiddam* [KL2, L12]; *certus, -a, -um* [KL3, L6]

certain one *quīdam, quaedam, quiddam* [KL2, L12]

certain thing *quīdam, quaedam, quiddam* [KL2, L12]

certainly *enim (postpositive conj.)* [KL1, L17]; *certe* [KL3, L6]; *nam* [KL1, W32; KL2, L9]; *quidem* [KL2, L3]; *vērō* [KL2, L15]; *utique* [KL3, L12]

chair *sella, -ae (f)* [KL1, L31]

challenge *provocō (1)*

chance (by chance) *forte* [KL2, L3]

chance *sors, -rtis (f)* [KL3, L6]

change *mūtō (1)* [KL1, L20]; *vertō, -ere, vertī, versum* [KL1, L28]; *convertō, -ere, -vertī, -versum* [KL3, L9]

chant *carmen, -inis (n)* [KL1, L13]

chapter *capitulum, -ī (n)* [KL3, W9]

character *faciēs, -ēī (f)* [KL1, L28]; *mōs, mōris (m) (pl.)* [KL2, L13]

chariot (four-horse chariot) *quadrīgae, -ārum (f)* [KL1, W23]

charioteer *aurīga, -ae (m/f)* [KL1, W23]

chasm *profundum, -ī (n)* [KL3, W9]

cheap *vīlis, -e* [KL2, W15]

cheese *cāseus, -a, -um* [KL2, W4]

cherish *foveō, -ēre, fōvī, fōtum* [KL1, L25]

chew *mandūcō (1)* [KL1, L6]

chief *prīnceps, -cipis (m)* [KL2, L3]

children *līberī, -ōrum (m, pl)* [KL1, L10]

choice *optio, optiōnis (f)* [KL1, W12]

choose *dēligō, -ere, lēgī, -lēctum* [KL1, L28]; *legō, -ere, lēgī, lēctum* [KL1, L28]; *ēligō, -ere, -lēgī, -lectum* [KL3, L1]

choose out *dīligō, -ere, -lēxī, -lēctum* [KL3, L1]

Christ *Christus, -ī (m)* [KL1, L4]

church *ecclēsia, -ae (f)* [KL1, L11]

Circus Maximus *Circus Maximus, Circī Maximī (m)* [KL1, W23]

citadel *arx, arcis (f)* [KL2, L7]

citizen *cīvis, -is (m/f)* [KL2, L7]

citizenship *cīvitās, -tātis (f)* [KL2, L7]

city *urbs, urbis (f)* [KL1, L18]; *cīvitās, -tātis (f)* [KL2, L7]

city walls *moenia, -ium (n, pl)* [KL1, L18]

clan *gens, -ntis (f)* [KL1, L31]

class *classis, -is (f)* [KL1, L30]

clay *lutum, -ī (n)* [KL3, W8]

clean (verb) *mundō* [KL3, L5]

clean (adj.) *mundus, -a, -um* [KL3, L5]

cleanse *mundō* [KL3, L5]; *ēmundō, -āre, ——, -ātum* [KL3, W11]

clear (make) *manifestō* [KL2, W8]

clear (it is clear) *scīlicet* [KL3, L6]

clear (very clear) *limpidissimus, -a, -um* [KL1, W32]

clemency *clēmentia, -ae (f)* [KL1, W21]

clerk *scrība, -ae (f)* [KL3, L10]

cliff *cautēs, -is (f)* [KL3, W16]; *scopulus, -ī (m)* [KL1, W30]

climb *ascendō, -ere, -scendī, -scēnsum* [KL2, L9]

cloak *pallium, -ī (n)* [KL3, W7]

close (adv. & prep. + acc.) *iūxta* [KL1, L28]

close (verb) *claudō, -ere, clausī, clausum* [KL3, W15]; *conclūdō, -ere, -clūsī, -clūsum* [KL2, W9]

close to *sub (+ acc.)* [KL1, L14]

clothe *induō, -ere, -duī, -dūtum* [KL2, L14]

clothing *vestis, vestis (f)* [KL1, L18]; *vestīmentum, -ī (n)* [KL2, L14]

cloud *nūbēs, nūbis (f)* [KL1, L18]

coil *spīra, -ae (f)* [KL3, W6]

coin *nummus, -ī (m)* [KL1, W22]

cold *gelidus, -a, -um* [KL1, L31]

collect (into a flock/herd) *congregō* [KL2, L14]

colonnade *porticus, -ūs (f)* [KL3, W5]

color *color, -ōris (m)* [KL2, W11]

come *veniō, -īre, vēnī, ventum* [KL1, L29]

come—(back) *redeō, -īre, -iī, -itum* [KL3, L2]; **(down)** *dēscendō, -ere, -scendī, -scēnsum* [KL3, L7]; **(forth)** *prōdeō, -īre, -iī, -itum* [KL3, L12]; **(through to)** *perveniō, -īre, -vēnī, -ventum* [KL2, L11]; **(near)** *propinquō (+ dat./acc.)* [KL2, W3]; **(to pass)** *accidō, -ere, -cīdī, ——* [KL3, L10]; **(upon)** *inveniō, -īre, -vēnī, -ventum* [KL1, L29]

coming *adventus, -ūs (m)* [KL3, L12]

command (noun) *imperium, -iī (n)* [KL2, L3]; *mandātum, -ī (n)* [KL2, L10]

command (verb) *iubeō, -ēre, iussī, iussum* [KL3, L2]; *imperō* [KL3, L10]; *mandō* [KL3, L10]; *praecipiō, -ere, -cēpī, -ceptum* [KL3, W5]

commandment *mandātum, -ī (n)* [KL2, L10]

commence *incipiō, -ere, -cēpī, -ceptum* [KL1, L31]

commencement *initium, -iī (n)* [KL3, L7]

commit *mandō* [KL3, L10]

common *commūnis, -e* [KL3, W2]

community *societās, -tātis (f)* [KL3, W11]

companion *comes, -mitis (m)* [KL2, L13]; *socius, -iī (m)* [KL2, L13]

compel *cōgō, -ere, -ēgī, -āctum* [KL1, L28]

complete *perficiō, -ere, -fēcī, -fectum* [KL1, W23]; *contendō, -ere, -tendī, -tentum* [KL2, W9]

complaint *gemitus, -ūs (m)* [KL3, W6]

complete *impleō, -ēre, -plēvī, -plētum* [KL2, L7]; *rēpleō, -ēre, -plēvī, -plētum* [KL3, L5]; *perficiō, -ere, -fēci, -fectum* [KL1, W23; KL3, L14]

comrade *comes, -mitis (m)* [KL2, L13]

conceal *occultō (1)* [KL1, L22]; *obcaecō* [KL3, W12]

concerning *dē (+ abl.)* [KL1, L4]

confess *cōnfiteor, -ērī, ——, -fessus sum (+ dat./acc.)* [KL2, L6]

confidence *fidūcia, -ae (f)* [KL3, L7]

confound *cōnfundō, -ere, -fūdī, -fūsum* [KL3, L12]

confuse *cōnsternō* [KL3, W7]

conquer *superō (1)* [KL1, L2]; *vincō, -ere, vīcī, victum* [KL1, L26]

conqueror *victor, -tōris (m)* [KL2, L13]

consecrated *sanctus, -a, -um* [KL1, L25]

consequently *ergō (adv.)* [KL1, L18]

consider *putō* [KL3, L3]

constantly *usque* [KL3, L4]

constellation *sīdus, sīderis (n)* [KL3, L15]

consume *consūmō, -ere, -sūmpsī, -sūmptum* [KL3, L2]

consume by fire *cremō (1)* [KL1, L2]

contest *certāmen, -minis (n)* [KL1, W23]

continent *continēns, -entis (f)* [KL3, W2]

continue *permaneō, -ēre, -mansī, -mansum* [KL3, L7]

continuously *usque* [KL3, L4]

on the contrary *immō* [KL3, W7]

conversation *sermō, -ōnis (m)* [KL2, L9]

convert *convertō, -ere, -vertī, -versum* [KL3, L9]

convey *vehō, -ere, vexī, vectum* [KL1, L27]

cookie *crustulum, -ī (n)* [KL1, L5]

corner *angulāris, -e* [KL2, W9]

couch (pallet) *grabātus, -ī (m)* [KL3, W5]

council *concilium, -iī (n)* [KL3, L5]

counsel *cōnsilium, -iī (n)* [KL1, L30]

counterfeit *mendācium, -iī (n)* [KL3, L6]

countless *innumerus, -a, -um* [KL3, W16]

country house *villa, -ae (f)* [KL1, L2]

country(side) *rūs, rūris (n)* [KL2, L14]

countryside (adj.) *rūsticus, -a, -um* [KL3, W7]

courage *virtūs, virtūtis (f)* [KL1, L12]

course *curriculum, -ī (n)* [KL1, W23]; *āgmen, -minis (n)* [KL3, L6]

court *ātrium, -iī (n)* [KL3, L10]

cousin (on the father's side) *patruēlis, -is (m/f)* [KL1, L22]; **(on the mother's side)** *consōbrīna, -ae (f)* & *consōbrīnus, -ī (m)* [KL1, L22]

covenant *foedus, -deris (n)* [KL2, L12]; *lēx, lēgis (f)* [KL2, L10]

covenanted *pactus, -a, -um* [KL2, L13]

cover (verb) *obumbrō* [KL3, W4]

covering *strātum, -ī (n)* [KL2, L13]; *vēlāmen, -minis (n)* [KL2, W11]

cow *bōs, bovis (m/f)* [KL1, L19]

crack *rīma, -ae (f)* [KL2, W11]
crash *naufragium, -ī (n)* [KL1, W23]
crawl *reptō (1)* [KL1, L14]
crazy (adj.) *insānus, -a, -um* [KL3, W3]
be **crazy (verb)** *furō, -ere, -uī, ——* [KL2, W13]
create *creō (1)* [KL1, L6]
creep *reptō (1)* [KL1, L14]
creeping *reptilis, -e* [KL3, W4]
create *gignō, -ere, genuī, genitum* [KL2, L9]
Crete *Crēta, -ae (f)* [KL1, W30]
crime *nefās (n, indecl.)* [KL3, W2]; *scelus, -leris (n)* [KL3, L6]; *crīmen, -minis (n)* [KL3, W1]
crops *plural of frūmentum, -ī (n)* [KL1, L15]
cross *crux, crucis (f)* [KL1, L15]
cross (over) *trānseō, -īre, -iī, -itum* [KL2, L15]
crowd *turba, -ae (f)* [KL1, L2]; *multitūdō, -tudinis (f)* [KL2, L12]; *congregātiō, -ōnis (f)* [KL3, W4]
crowded *confertus, -a, -um* [KL2, W15]
crown *corōna, -ae (f)* [KL1, L2]
cruel *crūdēlis, -e* [KL3, L10]; *saevus, -a, -um* [KL2, W11]
crush *premō, -ere, pressī, pressum* [KL2, L10]
cry (noun) *clāmor, -oris (m)* [KL1, W20]; *clāmor, -oris (m)* [KL1, W20; KL2, L13]; *gemitus, -ūs (m)* [KL3, W6]; *planctus, -ūs (m)* [KL3, W8]
cubit *cubitum, -ī (n)* [KL2, L14]
cultivate *colō, -ere, coluī, cultum* [KL1, L29]; *incolō, -ere, -coluī, -cultum* [KL3, L2]
cultivated field *arvum, -ī (n)* [KL3, L15]
Cupid *Cupīdō, -dinis (m)* [KL1, W20]
curse *maledīcō, -ere, -dīxī, -dictum (+ dat.)* [KL1, W30; KL3, L4]
curved *uncus, -a, -um* [KL3, W16]
custom *mōs, mōris (m)* [KL2, L13]

cut *scindō, -ere, scidī, scissum* [KL3, L10]; *dissecō* [KL2, W5]; **cut (down)** *occīdō, -ere, -cīdī, -cīsum* [KL1, L30]; *percutiō, -ere, -cussī, -cussum* [KL1, W32]; *caedō, -ere, cecīdī, caesum* [KL2, L12]; **(off)** *praecīdō, -ere, -cīdī, -cīsum* [KL1, W32; KL2, W6]
cyclops *Cȳclōps, Cȳclōpis (m)* [KL2, W4]

D

Daedalus *Daedalus, -ī (m)* [KL1, W30]
dagger *sīca, -ae (f)* [KL1, L3]
danger *perīculum, -ī (n)* [KL1, L5]
Daphne *Daphne, -ēs (f)* [KL1, W20]
dare *audeō, -ēre, ——, ausus sum* [KL1, L11]
dark *āter, -tra, -trum* [KL1, L17]; *tenebrōsus, -a, -um* [KL2, W15]
dark-colored *niger, -gra, -grum* [KL1, L17]
darken *obcaecō* [KL3, W12]
darkness *tenēbrae, -ārum (f, pl)* [KL1, L11]
daughter *fīlia, -ae (f)* [KL1, L6]
David *David (indecl.)* [KL1, W32]
day *diēs, diēī (m/f)* [KL1, L28]
dead *mortuus, -a, -um* [KL2, L3]
dead body *cadāver, -veris (n)* [KL1, W32]
deadly *fātālis, -e* [KL3, W6]
dear *cārus, -a, -um* [KL1, L13]
death *mors, mortis (f)* [KL1, L18]; *nex, necis (f)* [KL3, W10]
deceit *dolus, -ī (m)* [KL3, L6]
deceitful *falsus, -a, -um* [KL2, W13]
deceive *mentior, -īrī, ——, -ītus sum* [KL3, L6]; *sēdūcō, -ere, -dūxī, -ductum* [KL3, W11]
decide *cōnstituō, -ere, -stituī, -stitūtum* [KL2, L15]; *iūdicō* [KL2, L14]
decision *iūdicium, -ī (n)* [KL2, L9]
declare *dēclārō (1)* [KL1, L10]; *nuntiō (1)* [KL1, L14]; *indicō* [KL3, L11]; *ostendō, -ere, -dī, -sum/tum* [KL3, L5]; *praedicō* [KL3, W7]; *polliceor, -ērī, ——, pollicitus sum* [KL3, L7]

declaration *ēdictum, -ī (n)* [KL3, W10]
dedicate *dēdicō* [KL3, W7]
deed *opus, operis (n)* [KL2, L3]
deep *altus, -a, -um* [KL1, L19]
deepest *īmus, -a, -um* [KL2, L5]; *īnfimus, -a, -um* [KL2, L5]
deer *cervus, -ī (m)* [KL1, L10]
defeat *superō (1)* [KL1, L2]; *vincō, -ere, vīcī, victum* [KL1, L26]
defend *dēfendō, -ere, -fendī, -fēnsum* [KL1, L28]; *custōdiō, -īre, -iī/-īvī, -ītum* [KL3, L3]
defender *custōs, -ōdis (m/f)* [KL3, L3]
delay *cunctātiō, -ōnis (f)* [KL3, W9]
delay (verb) *cunctor, -ārī, ——, -ātus sum* [KL3, W9]
deliverance *salūs, -ūtis (f)* [KL3, W7]
demand (verb) *postulō* [KL3, L10]
demand (noun) *condiciō, -ōnis (f)* [KL2, W15]
demon *daemonium, -iī (n)* [KL3, L1]
deny *negō* [KL3, L3]
depart *abeō, -īre, -iī, -itum* [KL1, W32; KL2, L9]
deprive of *viduō (1)* [KL1, W19]
deprived of parents/children *orbus, -a, -um* [KL1, L22]
depth *profundum, -ī (n)* [KL3, W9]
descend *dēscendō, -ere, -scendī, -scensum* [KL3, L7]
descendant *nepōs, -pōtis (m/f)* [KL2, L13]
desert places *dēserta, -ōrum (n, pl)* [KL3, L4]
deserted *dēsertus, -a, -um* [KL3, L4]
deserve *mereō, -ēre, -uī, -itum* [KL1, L15; KL3, W6]
desire (noun) *voluntās, -tātis (f)* [KL3, L12]
desire (verb) *cupiō, -ere, cupīvī, cupītum* [KL1, L31]; *postulō* [KL3, L10]
desolate *vastus, -a, -um* [KL2, L6]

despise *despiciō, -ere, -spexī, -spectum* [KL1, W32]

destiny *sors, -rtis (f)* [KL3, L6]

destroy *dēleō, -ēre, -lēvī, -lētum* [KL1, L9]; *interficiō, -ere, -fēcī, -fectum* [KL1, L31]; *perdō, -ere, perdidī, perditum* [KL1, L27]; *dissolvō, -ere, -solvī, -solūtum* [KL3, W5]; *ēvertō, -ere, -tī, -sum* [KL3, W7]; *tollō, -ere, sustulī, sublātum* [KL1, W25; KL2, L13]

destruction *plāga, -ae (f)* [KL3, L14]; *clādēs, -is (f)* [KL2, W15]

devastate *vastō (1)* [KL1, L14]

device *māchina, -ae (f)* [KL3, W6]

devil *diabolus, -ī (m)* [KL3, W13]; *Satanās, -ae (m)* [KL3, W1]

devour *edō, -ere, ēdī, ēsum* [KL3, L1]

dew *rōs, rōris (m)* [KL2, W9]

Diana *Diāna, -ae (f)* [KL1, W20]

die *morior, morī, ——, mortuus sum* [KL2, L6]

different *dissimilis, -e* [KL2, L5]

difficult *difficilis, -e* [KL1, L20; KL2, L5]

dig *fodiō, -ere, fōdī, fossum* [KL1, W28]

dinner *cēna, -ae (f)* [KL1, L20]

direct *gubernō (1)* [KL1, L25]

direction *pars, partis (f)* [KL2, L3]

dirty *immundus, -a, -um* [KL3, L5]

disciple *discipula, -ae (f); discipulus, -ī (m)* [KL1, L5]

discus *discus, -ī (m)* [KL2, W6]

disgust *odium, -iī (n)* [KL3, L4]

dishonor (verb) *violō* [KL3, W1]

dishonor (noun) *turpitūdō, -dinis (f)* [KL3, W9]

dislike *ōdī, ōdisse, [fut. prt.] ōsūrum* [KL3, L6]

dismal *trīstis, -e* [KL1, L20]

dismiss *dīmittō, -ere, -mīsī, -missum* [KL1, L30]

dissimilar *dissimilis, -e* [KL2, L5]

distance *intervāllum, -ī (n)* [KL3, W2]

distant *longinquus, -a, -um* [KL1, L7]

distress *miseria, -ae (f)* [KL3, W9]

disturb *confundō, -ere, -fūdī, -fūsum* [KL3, L12]; *turbō* [KL2, W13]

diverse *dīversus, -a, -um* [KL3, W7]

divine *dīvīnus, -a, -um* [KL3, W7]

divine law *fās (n, indecl.)* [KL3, L2]

divine will *nūmen, -minis (n)* [KL2, L7]

divinity *nūmen, -minis (n)* [KL2, L7]

division *schisma, -ae (f)* [KL2, W8]

do *agō, -ere, ēgī, actum* [KL1, L26]; *faciō, -ere, fēcī, factum* [KL1, L31]

do not know *ignōrō* [KL2, L15]; *nesciō, -īre, -īvī, -ītum* [KL1, L30; KL3, L3]

dog *canis, canis (m/f)* [KL1, L18]

done (be done) *fīō, fierī, ——, factus sum* [KL1, L31]

donkey *asinus, -ī (m)* [KL1, L27]

door *porta, -ae (f)* [KL1, L31]; *ōstium, -iī (n)* [KL2, L4]

doorway *līmen, -minis (n)* [KL3, L3]

doubt (verb) *dubitō* [KL3, W7]

doubt (noun) *dubitātiō, -ōnis (f)* [KL3, W9]

doubtful *dubius, -a, -um* [KL3, W7]

down from *dē (+ abl.)* [KL1, L4]

downfall *cāsus, -ūs (m)* [KL1, L28]

drag *trahō, -ere, trāxī, trāctum* [KL1, L30]

dragon *dracō, dracōnis (m)* [KL1, L12]

draw *trahō, -ere, trāxī, trāctum* [KL1, L30]

draw near *appropinquō (1)* [KL1, L25]

draw (up) *hauriō, -īre, hausī, haustum* [KL2, W12]; *subdūcō, -ere, -dūxī, -ductum* [KL2, W2]; **(out)** *stringō, -ere, strinxī, strictum* [KL3, W7]

dread (noun) *metus, -ūs (m)* [KL1, L26]

dread (verb) *paveō, -ēre, pavī, ——* [KL3, L15]

dreadful *horrendus, -a, -um* [KL1, L13]

dream (noun) *īnsōmnium, -iī (n)* [KL2, W13]

dream (verb) *somniō (1)* [KL1, W18]

drench *perfundō, -ere, -fūdī, -fūsus* [KL3, W6]

drink (verb) *bibō, -ere, bibī, potum* [KL2, L10]; *hauriō, -īre, hausī, haustum* [KL2, W12]

drink (heavily), *pōtō, -āre, -āvī, pōtātum* or *pōtum* [KL1, L6]

drip *mānō* [KL3, W16]

drive *agō, -ere, ēgī, actum* [KL1, L26]

drive (out) *ēiciō, -ere, -iēcī, -iectum* [KL2, L14]; **(back)** *repellō, -ere, reppulī, repulsum* [KL3, W2]

drive together *cōgō, -ere, -ēgī, -āctum* [KL1, L28]

driver *aurīga, -ae (m/f)* [KL1, W23]

drop *cadō, -ere, cecidī, casūrum* [KL1, L27]

drunk *ēbrius, -a, -um* [KL1, W13; KL2, W4]

dry *āridus, -a, -um* [KL1, L27]

dry up *torreō, -ēre, torruī, tostum* [KL1, L17]

dryness *ārida, -ae (f)* [KL3, W1]

duty *iūs, iūris (n)* [KL2, L15]; *mūnus, -neris (n)* [KL2, L15]; *pietās, -tātis (f)* [KL2, W13]

dye (verb) *inficiō, -ere, -fēcī, -fectum* [KL3, W2]

dwell *habitō (1)* [KL1, L3]

dwell in *incolō, -ere, -coluī, -cultum* [KL3, L2]

E

each (one) *quisque, quaeque, quidque* [KL3, L2]

each other *invicem* [KL2, L12]

eager *ācer, ācris, ācre* [KL1, L20]; *cupidus, -a, -um* [KL3, W2]

eagerly *certātim* [KL1, L20]

ear *auris, -is (f)* [KL1, W28]

ear of corn *spīca, -ae (f)* [KL3, W1]

early (in the morning) *māne* [KL1, W19; KL2, L6]; *mātūtīnus, -a, -um* [KL3, W9]

earn *mereō, -ēre, -uī, -itum* [KL1, L15; KL3, W6]

earth *tellūs, tellūris (f)* [KL1, L14]; *terra, -ae (f)* [KL1, L4]; *humus, -ī (f)* [KL2, L14]

easily *facile* [KL2, L7]

easy *facilis, -e* [KL1, L20; KL2, L5]

eat *mandūcō (1)* [KL1, L6]; *edō, -ere, ēdī, ēsum* [KL3, L1]; *comedō, -ere, -ēdī, -ēsus* [KL3, W1]

echo *īnsonō, -āre, -uī, -ītum* [KL2, W6]

eight *octō* [KL1, L21]

eighteen *duodēvīgintī* [KL1, L21]

eighteenth *duodēvīcēsimus, -a, -um* [KL1, L23]

eighth *octāvus, -a, -um* [KL1, L23]

either *uter, utra (ūtra), utrum (ūtrum) (interrog.)* [KL2, L15]

elbow *cubitum, -ī (n)* [KL2, L14]

elder (adj.) *senior, -ōris* [KL3, L5]

elder (noun) *senior, -ōris* [KL3, L5]

elect *ēligō, -ere, -lēgī, -lectum* [KL3, L1]

elegant *mundus, -a, -um* [KL3, L5]

elephant *elephantus, -ī (m)* [KL1, L19]

eleven *ūndecim* [KL1, L21]

eleventh *ūndecimus, -a, -um* [KL1, L23]

empire *imperium, -iī (n)* [KL2, L3]

empty *inānis, -e* [KL3, W4]; *vacuus, -a, -um* [KL3, W4]

end *fīnis, -is (m)* [KL1, W4]; *terminus, -ī (m)* [KL3, L15]

endure *patior, -ī, ——, passus sum* [KL2, L6]

enemy (of the state) *hostis, -is (m)* [KL1, L18]; **(personal enemy)** *inimīcus, -ī (m)* [KL1, L10]

enjoy *ūtor, ūtī, ——, ūsus sum (+ abl.)* [KL3, L2]

enjoyment *voluptās, -tātis (f)* [KL3, W2]

enormous *ingēns, (gen.) -entis* [KL1, L19]; *immānis, -e* [KL3, L7]; *vastus, -a, -um* [KL2, L6]

enough *satis (adv./indecl., adj./noun)* [KL1, L30]

engine (military) *māchina, -ae (f)* [KL3, W6]

enraged *īnfēnsus, -a, -um* [KL2, W15]

entangle *implicō* [KL3, W5]

enter *intrō (1)* [KL1, L9]; *ineō, -īre, -iī (-īvī), -itum* [KL3, L4]

entire *ūniversus, -a, -um* [KL3, L4]

entrails *vīscus, -eris (n)* [KL3, L13]

entrance *initium, -iī (n)* [KL3, L7]; *ōstium, -iī (n)* [KL2, L4]

entrust *mandō* [KL3, L10]

entryway *ātrium, -iī (n)* [KL3, L10]

envious *invidus, -a, -um* [KL2, W11]

envoy *lēgātus, -ī (m)* [KL2, L15]

envy (noun) *aemulātiō, -ōnis (f)* [KL3, W7]

envy (verb) *invideō, -ēre, -vīdī, -vīsum* [KL1, W29]

Ephramite *Ephratheus, -ī (m)* [KL1, W32]

epistle *plural of littera, -ae (f)* [KL1, L26]

equally *pariter* [KL3, L1]

equipment (kit) *vās, vāsis (n)* [KL3, W1]

err *errō (1)* [KL1, L14]

error *error, -ōris (m)* [KL3, W7]

escape *effugiō, -ere, -fūgī, -fugitum* [KL1, W10]; *ēlābor, -lābī, ——, -lapsus sum* [KL2, L6]; *ēvādō, -ere, -vāsī, -vāsum* [KL3, L7]

especially *māximē* [KL2, L7]

essence *substantia, -ae (f)* [KL3, L13]

establish *cōnstituō, -ere, -stituī, -stitūtum* [KL2, L15]

esteem (noun) *cāritās, -tātis (f)* [KL3, L11]

esteem (verb) *foveō, -ēre, fōvī, fōtum* [KL1, L25]

eternal *aeternus, -a, -um* [KL1, L15]

evangelical *ēvangelicus, -a, -um* [KL3, W9]

even *et* [KL1, L1]; *etiam* [KL1, L22]; *quidem* [KL2, L3]

evening star *vesper, vesperis (m)* [KL1, L14]

evening *vesper, vesperis (m)* [KL1, L14]

event *cāsus, -ūs (m)* [KL1, L28]

ever *quandō* [KL1, L12]; *quondam* [KL2, L13]; *umquam* [KL3, L14]

every *omnis, -e* [KL1, L19]; *cunctus, -a, -um* [KL2, L9]; *tōtus, -a, -um* [KL2, L3]

every(one) *quisque, quaeque, quidque* [KL3, L2]

everywhere *ubīque* [KL1, W29]; *passim* [KL2, L13]; *undique* [KL1, L30; KL2, L15]

evidence *testimōnium, -ī (n)* [KL2, L10]

evident (verb, it is evident) *apparet* [KL3, L4]

evident (adj.) *manifestus, -a, -um* [KL3, W1]

evil *malus, -a, -um* [KL1, L7]; *malignus, -a, -um* [KL3, L13]

evil spirit *daemonium, -iī (n)* [KL3, L1]

exalt *exaltō* [KL3, W5]

examine *probō* [KL3, L14]

example *exemplum, -ī (n)* [KL3, W7]; *rēgula, -ae (f)* [KL3, W9]

exceedingly *nimium* [KL2, W13]; *valde* [KL2, L10]

excellent *ēgregius, -a, -um* [KL1, L29]

except *extrā* [KL3, L15]; *nisi* [KL3, L11]

excessively *nimis* [KL3, L4]; *nimium* [KL2, W13]

exercise *exerceō, ēre, -uī, -itum* [KL1, L14]

exile *exsilium, -iī (n)* [KL3, W3]

exit *exitus, -ūs (m)* [KL2, W13]

expect *exspectō (1)* [KL1, L3] *spērō* [KL3, L1]

expects a no answer *num* [KL2, L7]

expects a yes answer *nōnne* [KL2, L7]

expensive *pretiōsus, -a, -um* [KL2, W2]

explain *dēclārō (1)* [KL1, L10]

expose *aperiō, -īre, aperuī, apertum* [KL1, L29]

exposed *nūdus, -a, -um* [KL3, W7]

expression *vultus, -ūs (m)* [KL1, L25]

exstinguish *exstinguō, -ere, -stinxī, -stinctum* [KL3, W1]; *rēstinguō, -ere, -stinxī, -stinctum* [KL3, W3]

extend *extendō, -ere, -tendī, -tensum* [KL1, W26; KL3, W1]; *sternō, -ere, strāvī, strātum* [KL2, L13]

exult *exultō* [KL3, W9]; *triumphō* [KL3, W9]

eye *oculus, -ī (m)* [KL2, L3]

F

Fabius *Fabius, -iī (m)* [KL1, W19]

face *faciēs, -ēī (f)* [KL1, L28]; *vultus, -ūs (m)* [KL1, L25]

fair *iūstus, -a, -um* [KL1, L7]

faith *fidēs, -eī (f)* [KL1, L28]; *fidūcia, -ae (f)* [KL3, L7]

faithful *fīdus, -a, -um* [KL1, L7]; *fidēlis, -e* [KL2, L4]

fall *cadō, -ere, cecidī, cāsūrum* [KL1, L27]; *lābor, -ī, ——, lapsus sum* [KL2, L6]; **fall (down)** *dēscendō, -ere, -scendī, -scensum* [KL3, L7]; **fall down (violently)** *ruō, -ere, ruī, rutum* [KL3, L4]; **fall upon/out** *accidō, -ere, -cīdī, ——* [KL3, L10]

false *falsus, -a, -um* [KL2, W13]

falsehood *mendācium, -iī (n)* [KL3, L6]

fame *fāma, -ae (f)* [KL2, L13]

fame *glōria, -ae* [KL1, L15]; *fāma, -ae* [KL1, W23]

family *familia, -ae* [KL1, L22]

famous *nōbilis, -e* [KL2, W15]

famous (that famous) *ille, illa, illud* [KL1, L30]

far away *longinquus, -a, -um* [KL1, L7]

far and wide *passim* [KL2, L13]

far off *longē* [KL3, L3]

far *procul* [KL2, L11]

farm *rūs, rūris (n)* [KL2, L14]; *fundus, -ī (m)* [KL2, W10]

farmer *agricola, -ae (m)* [KL1, L3]

farmhouse *villa, -ae (f)* [KL1, L2]

farther *ulterior, -ius* [KL2, L5]

farthest *ultimus, -a, -um* [KL2, L5]

fast (verb) *iēiūnō* [KL3, W10]

fast (noun) *iēiūnium, -iī (n)* [KL3, W10]

fast (adv) *cito* [KL1, L27]

fasten in *infīgō, -ere, -fīxī, -fīxum* [KL1, W32]

fat *pinguis, -e* [KL1, W25]

fatal *fātālis, -e* [KL3, W6]

fate *fātum, -ī (n)* [KL1, L5; KL2, 13]

father *pater, patris (m)* [KL1, L12]; *parēns, -entis (m/f)* [KL1, W11; KL2, W8]

fault *peccātum, -ī (n)* [KL3, L11]

favor *grātia, -ae (f)* [KL1, L27]

favorable *dexter, -tra, -trum (or -tera, -terum)* [KL1, L30]

fear (noun) *metus, -ūs (m)* [KL1, L26]; *timor, -ōris (m)* [KL3, L14]

fear (verb) *timeō, -ēre, -uī, ——* [KL1, L9]; *paveō, -ēre, pavī, ——* [KL3, L15]; *metuō, -ere, -uī, -ūtum* [KL3, L15]; *vereor, -ērī, ——, veritus sum* [KL2, L6]

fearful *horrendus, -a, -um* [KL1, L13]

feast *epulae, -ārum (f, pl)* [KL1, L20]

feather *penna, -ae (f)* [KL3, W16]

feeble *īnfirmus, -a, -um* [KL3, W5]

feed *pascō, -ere, pāvī, pastum* [KL1, W32; KL2, W14]; *alō, alere, aluī, altum/alitum* [KL3, W2]

feel *sentiō, -īre, sēnsī, sēnsum* [KL3, L3]

feeling *sensus, -ūs (m)* [KL2, L15]

fellowship *societās, -tātis (f)* [KL3, W11]

female *fēmīnus, -a, -um* [KL3, W4]

female slave *ancilla, -ae (f)* [KL3, L10]

few *paucī, -ae, -a* [KL1, L7]

field *ager, agrī (m)* [KL1, L4]; *arvum, -ī (n)* [KL3, L15]

fierce *ācer, ācris, ācre* [KL1, L20]; *ferus, -a, -um* [KL1, L7]; *asper, -era, -erum* [KL2, W12]; *saevus, -a, -um* [KL2, W11]

fiery *caldus, -a, -um* [KL1, L7]

fifteen *quīndecim* [KL1, L21]

fifteenth *quīntus, -a, -um decimus, -a, -um* [KL1, L23]

fifth *quīntus, -a, -um* [KL1, L23]

fiftieth *quīnquāgēsimus, -a, -um* [KL1, L23]

fifty *quīnquāgintā* [KL1, L21]

fight (verb) *pugna, -ae (f)* [KL2, W9]

fight (noun) *pugnō (1)* [KL1, L1]

fill *rēpleō, -ēre, -plēvī, -plētum* [KL3, L5]

fill up *rēpleō, -ēre, -plēvī, -plētum* [KL3, L5]; *impleō, -ēre, -plēvī, -plētum* [KL2, L7]; *compleō, -ēre, -plēvī, -plētum* [KL2, W6]

fill again *rēpleō, -ēre, -plēvī, -plētum* [KL3, L5]

finally *dēnique* [KL1, L10]; *tandem* [KL3, L15]

find *inveniō, -īre, -vēnī, -ventum* [KL1, L29]

finish *perficiō, -ere, -fēci, -fectum* [KL1, W23; KL3, L14]

fire *ignis, ignis* [KL1, L18]; *aestus, -ūs (m)* [KL2, W9]

fire-pan *foculus, -ī (m)* [KL2, W15]

set on fire *accendō, -ere, -censī, -censum* [KL2, W15]; *incendō, -ere, -cendī, -censum* [KL2, W13]

first (adj.) *prīmus, -a, -um* [KL1, L23]

first (adv.) *prīmum/prīmō* [KL2, L7]

fish (noun) *piscis, -is (m)* [KL1, L19]

fish (verb) *piscor, -ārī, ——, -ātus sum (deponent)* [KL1, W29]

fisherman *piscātor, -ōris (m)* [KL3, W6]

fissure *rīma, -ae (f)* [KL2, W11]

fitting (it is fitting) *decet, -ēre, ——, decuit (impers. + acc.)* [KL3, L1]

five hundred *quīngentī* [KL1, L21]

five hundredth *quīngentēsimus, -a, -um* [KL1, L23]

five *quīnque* [KL1, L21]

fix in *infīgō, -ere, -fīxī, -fīxum* [KL1, W32]

flag (starting flag) *mappa, -ae (f)* [KL1, W23]

flank *latus, lateris (n)* [KL3, L6]

flash (verb) *micō, -āre, -uī, ——* [KL3, W3]

flee *fugiō, -ere, fūgī, fugitum* [KL1, L31]

fleet (of ships) *classis, -is (f)* [KL1, L30]

flicker *vibrō* [KL3, W6]

flesh *carō, carnis (f)* [KL1, L31]

flock *grex, gregis (m)* [KL1, L31]

flourish *flōreō, -ēre, -uī, ——* [KL1, L17]

flow *mānō* [KL3, W16]

flower *flōs, flōris (m)* [KL1, L15]

fly *volō (1)* [KL1, L10]; *circumvolō* [KL2, W12]

flying *volātilis, -e* [KL3, W4]

foam (verb) *spūmō* [KL3, W6]

fold *spīra, -ae (f)* [KL3, W6]

follow *sequor, sequī, ——, secūtus sum (deponent)* [KL1, W30; KL2, L6]

folly *stultitia, -ae (f)* [KL1, W27]

food *cibus, -ī (m)* [KL1, L4]; *esca, -ae (f)* [KL2, W14]

foolish *stultus, -a, -um* [KL1, L7]

foolishness *stultitia, -ae (f)* [KL1, W27]

foot *pēs, pedis (m)* [KL3, W3]

foot (at the foot of) *sub (+ abl.)* [KL1, L14]

footprint *vestīgium, -iī (n)* [KL2, W11]

for (conj.) *enim (postpositive conj.)* [KL1, L17]; *nam* [KL1, W32; KL2, L9]

for (prep.) *ob (+ acc.)* [KL2, L3]

for a long time *diū* [KL1, L13]

for that reason *ideō* [KL2, L14]

for (the sake of) *prō (+ abl.)* [KL1, L18]; *causā (+ gen.)* [KL2, L15]

forbid *vetō, -āre, vetuī, vetitum* [KL3, W11]

forbidden *nefās (n, indecl.)* [KL3, W2]

force (noun) *vīs, vīs (f)* [KL3, L5]

force (verb) *cōgō, -ere, -ēgī, -āctum* [KL1, L28]

forehead *frōns, -ntis (f)* [KL1, W32]

foreign *barbarus, -a, -um* [KL1, L31]; *aliēnus, -a, -um* [KL2, L12]

foreigner *aliēnus, -a, -um* [KL2, L12]; *barbarus, -ī (m)* [KL1, L31]

forever *perpetuō* [KL2, W2]

forest *silva, -ae (f)* [KL1, L3]

forethought *prōvidentia, -ae (f)* [KL2, W9]

forget *oblīvīscor, -vīscī, ——, oblītus sum (+ gen.)* [KL2, L7]

forgive *dīmittō, -ere, -mīsī, -missum* [KL1, L30]; *remittō, -ere, -mīsī, -missum* [KL3, L11]

forgiveness *remissiō, -ōnis (f)* [KL3, W5]; *venia, -ae (f)* [KL3, W12]

form *faciēs, -ēī (f)* [KL1, L28]; *īdōlum, -ī (n)* [KL3, L7]

former *prior, prius* [KL2, L5]

formerly *ōlim* [KL1, L6]; *quondam* [KL2, L13]

forsaken *dēsertus, -a, -um* [KL3, L4]

fort *arx, arcis (f)* [KL2, L7]

fortification *mūnītiō, -ōnis (f)* [KL3, W2]

fortifications *moenia, -ium (n, pl)* [KL1, L18]

forth *forās* [KL3, L6]

fortunate *fēlix, (gen.) -līcis* [KL1, L19]

fortune *substantia, -ae (f)* [KL3, L13]

foul *immundus, -a, -um* [KL3, L5]

fountain *fōns, fontis (m)* [KL1, L11]

foundation *basis, -is (f)* [KL2, W9]; *fundamentum, -ī (n)* [KL2, W9]

four *quattuor* [KL1, L21]

four times *quater* [KL3, W6]

four-horse chariot *quadrīgae, -ārum (f)* [KL1, W23]

fourteen *quattuordecim* [KL1, L21]

fourteenth *quārtus, -a, -um decimus, -a, -um* [KL1, L23]

fourth *quārtus, -a, -um* [KL1, L23]

fraud *dolus, -ī (m)* [KL3, L6]

free *līberō (1)* [KL1, L1]

frequent *crēber, -bra, -brum* [KL3, L2]

fresh *viridis, -e* [KL1, L17]; *recēns, -centis* [KL2, W11]

friend *amīca, -ae (f)* [KL1, L15]; *amīcus, -ī (m)* [KL1, L15]; *comes, -mitis (m)* [KL2, L13]

frighten *terreō, -ēre, -uī, -itum* [KL1, L9]

from a distance *procul* [KL2, L11]

from all sides *undique* [KL1, L30; KL2, L15]

from *ā, ab (+ abl.)* [KL1, L3]; *dē (+ abl.)* [KL1, L4]; *ē, ex (+ abl.)* [KL1, L3]

from all sides *undique* [KL1, L30]

from every direction *undique* [KL1, L30]

from here *hinc* [KL2, L11]

from that place *deinde* [KL1, L24]

from that side *illinc* [KL2, L11]

from there *illinc* [KL2, L11]; *inde* [KL2, L10]

from this side *hinc* [KL2, L11]

from where (?) *unde* [KL2, L11]

frost *gelū, -ūs (n)* [KL2, W9]

fruit *frūctus, -ūs (m)* [KL1, L25]; *pōmum, -ī (n)* [KL3, W11]

fruit-bearing *pōmifer, -era, -erum* [KL3, W6]

fruitful *ūber, -eris* [KL2, W11]

full *plēnus, -a, -um* [KL2, L4]

funeral *fūnus, -neris (n)* [KL2, W13]

funeral pyre *pyra, -ae (f)* [KL1, W8]

furrow *versus, -ūs (m)* [KL1, L27]

further *amplius* [KL3, L9]; *ultrā* [KL2, L5]

future (adj.) *futūrus, -a, -um* [KL2, W10]

G

garden *hortus, -ī (m)* [KL2, W6]

garment *vestis, vestis (f)* [KL1, L18]; *vestīmentum, -ī (n)* [KL2, L14]

gate *porta, -ae (f)* [KL1, L31]; *ōstium, -iī (n)* [KL2, L4]

gates (starting gates of a horse race) *plural of carcer, -eris (m)* [KL1, W23]
general *dux, ducis (m)* [KL1, L14]
generally *plērumque* [KL3, W7]
generation *saeculum, -ī (n)* [KL1, L6]; *generātiō, -ōnis (f)* [KL3, L7]
get to know *cognōscō, -ere, -nōvī, -nitum* [KL2, L10]; *nōscō, -ere, nōvī, nōtum* [KL2, L9]
ghost *umbra, -ae (f)* [KL3, L3]
giant *gigās, gigantis (m)* [KL1, L15]
gift *dōnum, -ī (n)* [KL1, L5]; *mūnus, -neris (n)* [KL2, L15]
girl *puella, -ae (f)* [KL1, L3]
give *dō, dare, dedī, datum* [KL1, L1]; *praebeō, -ēre, -uī, -itum* [KL3, W7]
give birth to *pariō, -ere, peperī, par(i)tum* [KL3, L13]
give over *trādō, -ere, -didī, -ditum* [KL1, W13; KL2, L4]
give thanks *grātiās agō (+ dat.)* [KL1, L27]
gladiator (in a chariot) *essedarius, -ī (m)* [KL3, W2]
gladness *laetitia, -ae (f)* [KL3, L7]
glide *lābor, -ī, ——, lapsus sum* [KL2, L6]
glitter *fulgeō, -ēre, fulsī, ——* [KL2, W13]; *micō, -āre, -uī, ——* [KL3, W3]
glad *laetus, -a, -um* [KL1, L7]
gloom *nūbēs, nūbis (f)* [KL1, L18]
gloomy *trīstis, -e* [KL1, L20; KL2, L3]; *tenebrōsus, -a, -um* [KL2, W15]
gloomy place *tenēbrae, -ārum (f, pl)* [KL1, L11]
glory *glōria, -ae* [KL1, L15]
go *cēdō, -ere, cessī, cessum* [KL1, L28]; *eō, īre, iī (īvī), itum* [KL1, L29]; *vādō, -ere, vāsī, ——* [KL2, L9]; **(across)** *trānseō, -īre, -iī, -itum* [KL2, L15]; **(apart)** *sēcēdō, -ere -cessī, -cessum* [KL3, W1]; **(away [from])** *abeō, -īre, -iī, -itum* [KL1, W32; KL2, L9]; **(away)** *exeō, -īre, -iī (-īvī), -itum* [KL2, L12]; **(back)** *redeō, -īre, -iī, -itum* [KL3, L2]; *regredior, -gredī, ——, -gressus sum* [KL3, L10]; *revertor, -vertī, ——, reversus sum* [KL2, L6]; **(forth)** *prōdeō, -īre, -iī, -itum* [KL3, L12]; **(in)** *ingredior, -gredī, ——, -gressus sum* [KL2, L6]; **(in[to])** *ineō, -īre, -iī (-īvī), -itum* [KL3, L4]; **(out)** *ēgredior, -gredī, ——, -gressus sum* [KL2, L6]; *exeō, -īre, -iī (-īvī), -itum* [KL2, L12]; **(over)** *trānseō, -īre, -iī, -itum* [KL2, L15]; **(to[ward])** *adeō, -īre, -iī, -itum* [KL2, L10]; **(up)** *ascendō, -ere, -scendī, -scensum* [KL2, L9]
goal *mēta, -ae (f)* [KL1, W23]
goat *caper, -prī (m)* [KL1, L4]
goblet *calix, calicis (m)* [KL1, W13]
god *deus, -ī (m)* [KL1, L4]; *nūmen, -minis (n)* [KL2, L7]
God *Deus, -ī (m)* [KL1, L4]
goddess *dea, -ae (f)* [KL1, L6]
gold (noun) *aurum, -ī (n)* [KL1, L5]
gold(en) *aureus, -a, -um* [KL1, L17]
good *bonus, -a, -um* [KL1, L7]
Good day! *salvē(te)* [KL1, L9]
good news *ēvangelium, -ī* [KL1, L5]
Goodbye! *valē(te)* [KL1, L9]
goose *ānser, -eris (m)* [KL3, W2]
Gorgon *Gorgō, -onis (f)* [KL2, L6]
gospel *ēvangelium, -ī* [KL1, L5]
govern *gubernō (1)* [KL1, L25]; *regnō (1)* [KL1, L6]
governor *satrapa, -ae (f)* [KL3, W10]
grace *grātia, -ae (f)* [KL1, L27]
gradually *minūtātim* [KL1, L20]; *paulātim* [KL3, W7]
grain (head) *frūmentum, -ī (n)* [KL1, L15]; *spīca, -ae (f)* [KL3, W1]
granddaughter *nepōs, -pōtis (m/f)* [KL2, L13]
grandfather *avus, -ī (m)* [KL1, L22]
grandmother *avia, -ae (f)* [KL1, L22]
grandson *nepōs, -pōtis (m/f)* [KL2, L13]
grass *grāmen, grāminis (n)* [KL1, L13]
grateful *grātus, -a, -um* [KL1, L27]
grave *sepulcrum, -ī (n)* [KL2, L13]; *tumulus, -ī (m)* [KL2, W11]
great (so/such great) *tantus, -a, -um* [KL3, L5]
greater *māior, -ius* [KL1, W31; KL2, L5]
greatest *māximus, -a, -um* [KL1, W31; KL2, L5]; *summus, -a, -um* [KL2, L5]; *suprēmus, -a, -um* [KL2, L5]
greatly *magnopere* [KL1, L29]
greedy *avārus, -a, -um* [KL1, L7]
Greek (adj.) *Graecus, -a, -um* [KL3, L6]
Greek (noun) *Graecus, -ī* [KL3, L6]
green *vīridis, -e* [KL1, L17]
greenery *grāmen, grāminis (n)* [KL1, L13]
grief *lūctus, -ūs (m)* [KL3, W13]
grim *trīstis, -e* [KL1, L20; KL2, L3]
groan *gemitus, -ūs (m)* [KL3, W6]
ground *tellūs, tellūris (f)* [KL1, L14]; *humus, -ī (f)* [KL2, L14]
group *classis, -is (f)* [KL1, L30]
grow *crēscō, -ere, crēvī, crētum* [KL2, L11]
guarantee *reprōmissiō, -ōnis (f)* [KL3, W12]
guard (noun) *custōs, -ōdis (m/f)* [KL3, L3]
guard (verb) *custōdiō, -īre, -iī/-īvī, -ītum* [KL3, L3]; *observō* [KL3, W11]
guard against *caveō, -ēre, cāvī, cautum* [KL1, L12]
guest *hospes, -pitis (m)* [KL2, W6]
guide (verb) *dūcō, -ere, duxī, ductum* [KL1, L26]
guide (noun) *dux, ducis (m)* [KL1, L14]

H

habit (am in the habit of) *soleō, -ēre, ——, solitus sum (semi-deponent)* [KL3, L9]
Hades *Plūto, -tōnis (m)* [KL2, W6]
hail *grandō, -dinis (f)* [KL2, W9]

hair *capillus, -ī (m)* [KL2, W6]; *coma, -ae (f)* [KL3, W3]

half (of) *dīmidius, -a, -um* [KL3, L10]

hall *ātrium, -iī (n)* [KL3, L10]; *aula, -ae (f)* [KL1, W13; KL3, W10]; *consistōrium, -iī (n)* [KL3, W10]

halt *resistō, -ere, -stitī, —* [KL3, W2]; *subsistō, -ere, -stitī, —* [KL3, W6]

hand *manus, -ūs (f)* [KL1, L25]; *palma, -ae (f)* [KL1, W13]

hand down *trādō, -ere, -didī, -ditum* [KL1, W13; KL2, L4]

hand over *trādō, -ere, -didī, -ditum* [KL1, W13; KL2, L4]

handle *temptō* [KL1, W27; KL3, L7]

handsome *pulcher, -chra, -chrum* [KL1, L7]

hang *suspendō, -ere, -pendī, -pensum* [KL3, W5]

happen *fīō, fierī, —, factus sum* [KL1, L31]; *accidō, -ere, -cīdī, —* [KL3, L10]; *ēveniō, -īre, -vēnī, -ventum* [KL3, W3]

happily ever after *felīciter in aeternum* [KL1, W6; KL2, W2]

happiness *gaudium, -ī (n)* [KL1, L5]

happy *beātus, -a, -um* [KL1, L7]; *felīx, (gen.) -līcis* [KL1, L19]; *laetus, -a, -um* [KL1, L7]; *festus, -a, -um* [KL3, W6]

harbor *portus, -ūs (m)* [KL1, L25]

hard *dūrus, -a, -um* [KL3, W16]

hardship *labor, labōris (m)* [KL1, L12]

hare *lepus, -oris (m)* [KL3, W2]

hardly *vix* [KL3, L3]

harmful *nocēns, -ntis* [KL2, W11]

harmless *innoxius, -a, -um* [KL3, W3]

harp *citara, -ae (f)* [KL2, W2]

harvest *metō, -ere, messuī, messum* [KL2, W14]

hasten *festīnō (1)* [KL1, L9]; *tendō, -ere, tetendī, tentum* [KL2, L4]

hate (verb) *ōdī, ōdisse, [fut. prt.] ōsūrum* [KL3, L6]

hatred *odium, -iī (n)* [KL3, L4]

haughty *superbus, -a, -um* [KL1, W18; KL2, L4]

haul up *subdūcō, -ere, -dūxī, -ductum* [KL2, W2]

have *habeō, -ēre, -uī, -itum* [KL1, L9]

have mercy on *misereor, -ērī, —, misertus sum (+ gen.)* [KL2, L6]

hay *fēnum, -ī (n)* [KL2, W14]; **(straw)** *festūca, -ae (f)* [KL2, W14]

he *is, ea, id* [KL1, L17]

head *caput, -itis (n)* [KL1, L13]

heal *curō* [KL1, L15]

health *salūs, -ūtis (f)* [KL3, W7]

healthy *sānus, -a, -um* [KL3, W1]

hear *audiō, -īre, -īvī, -ītum* [KL1, L29]

heart *cor, cordis (n)* [KL1, L13]

heart (metaphorically) *vīscus, -eris (n)* [KL3, L13]

heathen *gentīlis, -is (m/f)* [KL3, W7]

heaven *caelum, -ī (n)* [KL1, L5]; *aura, -ae (f)* [KL3, L3]

heavenly body *sīdus, sīderis (n)* [KL3, L15]

heaviness *gravitās, -tātis (f)* [KL3, W2]

heavy *gravis, -e* [KL3, L6]

heedless *immemor, -oris* [KL3, W6]

height *summitās, -tātis (f)* [KL2, W10]

Hello! *salvē(te)* [KL1, L9]

helmet *galea, -ae (f)* [KL2, W6]

help (noun) *auxilium, -ī (n)* [KL1, L5]

help (verb) *iuvō, -āre, iūvī, iūtum* [KL1, L22]

hen *gallīna, -ae (f)* [KL3, W2]

hence *hinc* [KL2, L11]

her (own) *suus, -a, -um* [KL1, W31; KL3, L2]

herd *grex, gregis (m)* [KL1, L31]; *pecus, -coris (n)* [KL3, L2]

here *hīc* [KL2, L11]

Hermes *Mercurius, -ī (m)* [KL1, W21; KL2, W6]

herself (pron./adj.) *ipse, ipsa, ipsum* [KL2, L3]; **(reflex. pron.)** *suī* [KL3, L2]

hide (noun) *pellis, -is (f)* [KL3, W2]

hide (verb) *occultō (1)* [KL1, L22]; *celō* [KL1, W28]

high *altus, -a, -um* [KL1, L19]; *excelsus, -a, -um* [KL2, L4]; *superus, -a, -um* [KL2, L5]

higher *superior, -ius* [KL2, L5]

highest *summus, -a, -um* [KL2, L5]; *suprēmus, -a, -um* [KL2, L5]

hill *arx, arcis* [KL2, L7]; *collis, collis (m)* [KL3, L2]

himself (pron./adj.) *ipse, ipsa, ipsum* [KL2, L3]; **(reflex. pron.)** *suī* [KL3, L2]

himself *sē (acc. reflexive pronoun)* [KL1, W8]

hinder *impediō, -īre, -īvī, -ītum* [KL1, L29]; *obstō, -stāre, -stitī, -stātūrum (+ dat.)* [KL2, W11]

hinge *cardō, -dinis (m)* [KL2, W11]

his (own) *suus, -a, -um* [KL1, W31; KL3, L2]

hissing *sībilus, -a, -um* [KL3, W6]

hit *pulsō* [K2L, W14]

hither *hūc* [KL2, L11]

hoard *thēsaurus, -ī (m)* [KL3, L11]

hold *habeō, -ēre, -uī, -itum* [KL1, L9]; *teneō, -ēre, tenuī, tentum* [KL1, L9]

hold back *reprehendō, -ere, -hendī, -hensum* [KL3, W13]; *reprimō, -ere, -pressī, -pressum* [KL3, W9]

hollow *lacus, -ūs (m)* [KL1, L27]

holy *sanctus, -a, -um* [KL1, L25]; *sacer, -cra, -crum* [KL2, L3]

Holy Bible *Biblia Sacra, Bibliae Sacrae (f)* [KL1, L11]

home *domus, -ūs (f)* [KL1, L25]

homicide *homicīda, -ae (m/f)* [KL3, L13]

hooked *uncus, -a, -um* [KL3, W16]

hope (noun) *spēs, speī (f)* [KL1, L28]

hope (verb) *spērō* [KL3, L1]

horn *cornū, -ūs (n)* [KL1, L25]
horrible *foedus, -a, -um* [KL1, L7]
horse *equus, -ī (m)* [KL1, L4]
horseman *eques, -quitis (m)* [KL1, L20]
hostile *īnfēnsus, -a, -um* [KL2, W15]
hot *caldus, -a, -um* [KL1, L7]
hour *hōra, -ae (f)* [KL1, L31]
house *domus, -ūs (f)* [KL1, L25]; *(country house) villa, -ae (f)* [KL1, L2]; *līmen, -minis (n)* [KL3, L3]
household *familia, -ae* [KL1, L22]
how (adv.) *quemadmodum* [KL3, L9]; **(conj.)** *ut (+ indic.)* [KL3, L5]
how (?) *quam* [KL1, L28]; *quōmodo* [KL1, L25]; *quārē* [KL3, L9]
how great *quantus, -a, -um* [KL2, W13]
how long? *quamdiū* [KL3, L9]
how many *quantus, -a, -um* [KL2, W13]
how much (adj.) *quantus, -a, -um* [KL2, W13]; **(by)** *quantō* [KL2, W14]
however *autem (postposit. conj.)* [KL1, L12] *vērumtamen* [KL3, L13]
howl *ululō (1)* [KL1, L6]
howling *ululātus, -ūs (m)* [KL3, W10]
hug *amplector, amplectī, ——, amplexus sum* [KL2, W11]; *complector, -plectī, ——, -plexus sum* [KL3, W3]
huge *ingēns, (gen.) -entis* [KL1, L19]
human *hūmānus, -a, -um* [KL3, W2]
human being *homō, hominis (m)* [KL1, L12]
humble *humilis, -e* [KL2, L5]
hungry *famēlicus, -a, -um* [KL1, L29]
be hungry *ēsuriō, -īre, -iī, -ītum* [KL3, W1]
hurl down *ruō, -ere, ruī, rutum* [KL3, L4]
hunt *captō (1)* [KL1, L10]
hunt down *persequor, -sequī, ——, -secūtus sum (deponent)* [KL1, W32]
hurl down *dēicio, -icere, -iēcī, -iectum* [KL1, W23]
hurl *iaciō, -ere, iēcī, iactum* [KL1, L31]

hurry *festīnō (1)* [KL1, L9]; *properō (1)* [KL1, L20]
husband *coniunx, -iugis (m)* [KL1, L22]
hypocrite *hypocrita, -ae (m)* [KL2, W14]

I

I *ego (sg)* [KL1, L17]
I wish that! *utinam* [KL3, L13]
ice: *gelū, -ūs (n)* [KL2, W9]
icy *gelidus, -a, -um* [KL1, L31]
idol *īdōlum, -ī (n)* [KL3, L7]; *simulācrum, -ī (n)* [KL3, L6]
if *sī (conj.)* [KL1, L16]
if not *nisi* [KL3, L11]
if only *dum, dummodo* [KL2, L11]
if only! *utinam* [KL3, L13]
ignorant (adj.) *inperitus* [KL2, W9]; *īnscius, -a, -um* [KL3, W16]
ignorant (am ignorant of) *ignōrō* [KL2, L15]; *nesciō, -īre, -īvī, -ītum* [KL1, L30; KL3, L3]
ill *male* [KL1, L1]
image *īdōlum, -ī (n)* [KL3, L7]; *imāgō, -ginis (f)* [KL3, L4]; *simulācrum, -ī (n)* [KL3, L6]
imagine *reor, rērī, ——, ratus sum* [KL3, W16]
immediately *statim* [KL1, L13]; *continuō* [KL2, L12]; *subitō/subitum* [KL3, L3]
immense *immānis, -e* [KL3, L7]
immorality *impudīcitia, -ae (f)* [KL3, W9]
immortal *immortālis, -e* [KL2, W6]
impartial *iūstus, -a, -um* [KL1, L7]
impetus *impetus, -ūs (m)* [KL3, L9]
impious *impius, -a, -um* [KL3, L1]
implore *obsecrō* [KL3, L13]
imprison *incarcerō* [KL2, W4]
in *in (+ abl.)* [KL1, L3]
in error *frustrā* [KL3, L3]
in front of *pro (+ abl.)* [KL1, L18]; *ob (+ acc.)* [KL2, L3]
in one *ūnā* [KL1, L29]

in order that/to *quō* [KL2, L11]; *ut (+ subj.)* [KL3, L5]
in that place *illīc* [KL2, L11]
in the presence of *cōram (+ abl.)* [KL1, L27]
in the meantime *intereā* [KL2, L12]
in the morning (early in the morning) *māne* [KL1, W19; KL2, L6]
in the same place *eōdem* [KL3, L2]
in this place *hīc* [KL2, L11]
in turn *invicem* [KL2, L12]
in vain *frustrā* [KL3, L3]
in what manner *quemadmodum* [KL3, L9]
in what way *quōmodo* [KL1, L25]
in which place *quō(?)* [KL2, L11]
in/to what/which place (?) *quō* [KL2, L11]
Inachus *Īnachus, -ī (m)* [KL1, W21]
inauspicious *sinister, -stra, -strum* [KL1, L30]
incident *cāsus, -ūs (m)* [KL1, L28]
increase *augeō -ēre, auxī, auctum* [KL1, L19]; *crēscō, -ere, crēvī, crētum* [KL2, L11]; *multiplicō* [KL3, W20]
indeed *enim (postpositive conj.)* [KL1, L17]; *quidem* [KL2, L3]
indicates a simple yes/no question *-ne* [KL2, L7]
indignity *indīgnitās, -tātis (f)* [KL2, W15]
inexperienced *inperitus, -a, -um* [KL2, W9]
infant *īnfāns, -fantis (adj. & noun, m/f)* [KL1, W31; KL3, L12]
infinite *infīnītus, -a, -um* [KL3, W2]
inhabit *colō, -ere, coluī, cultum* [KL1, L29]; *habitō (1)* [KL1, L3]; *incolō, -ere, -coluī, -cultum* [KL3, L2]
iniquity *inīquitās, -tātis (f)* [KL2, L10]
injury *nocēns, -ntis* [KL2, W11]
injustice *inīquitās, -tātis (f)* [KL2, L10]
inner *interior, -ius (gen. -teriōris)* [KL3, W2]
inner court *aula, -ae (f)* [KL1, W13]

innocent *inmeritus, -a, -um* [KL3, W16]

inquire *quaerō, -ere, quaesīvī, quaesītum (-situm)* [KL2, L3]

insane *insānus, -a, -um* [KL3, W3]

insanity *insānia, -ae (f)* [KL3, W6]

inside *intrā (prep. + acc.; adv.)* [KL2, L15]

instead of *prō (+ abl.)* [KL1, L18]

instruction *doctrīna, -ae (f)* [KL3, L5]

insult *contumēlia, -ae (f)* [KL3, W5]

intercede *dēprecor, -ārī, ——, -ātus sum* [KL3, L10]

interior *interior, -ius (gen. -teriōris)* [KL3, W2]

internal organs *vīscus, -eris (n)* [KL3, L13]

into *in (+ acc.)* [KL1, L3]

intoxicated *ēbrius, -a, -um* [KL1, W13]

invest *consūmō, -ere, -sūmpsī, -sūmptum* [KL3, L2]

invincible *invīctus, -a, -um* [KL3, W13]

invite *vocō (1)* [KL1, L1]

inward parts *vīscus, -eris (n)* [KL3, L13]

inwardly *intrā (prep. + acc.; adv.)* [KL2, L15]

Io *Īō, -ōnis (f)* [KL1, W21]

iron *ferrum, -ī (n)* [KL2, L15]

irreverent *impius, -a, -um* [KL3, L1]

island *īnsula, -ae (f)* [KL1, L3]

Israel *Israhel (indecl.) or Israhel, -is* [KL1, W32; KL2, W3]

Israelite *Israhelita, -ae (m)* [KL1, W32]

is it really possible that…? *numquid* [KL2, L9]

it *is, ea, id* [KL1, L17]

it is allowed *licet, licuit, - (impers. + dat./acc.)* [KL1, W26; KL3, L1]

it is apparent *apparet* [KL3, L4]

it is clear *scīlicet* [KL3, L6]

it is evident *apparet* [KL3, L4]

it is fitting *decet, decuit* [KL3, L1]

it is lawful *licet, licuit, - (impers. + dat./acc.)* [KL1, W26; KL3, L1]

it is necessary *necesse est* [KL3, L1]; *oportet, -ēre, -tuit, -tuitum (impers. + acc.)* [KL3, L1]

it is permitted *licet, licuit, - (impers. + dat./acc.)* [KL1, W26; KL3, L1]

it is proper *decet, -ēre, ——, decuit (impers. + acc.)* [KL3, L1]; *oportet, -ēre, -tuit, -tuitum (impers. + acc.)* [KL3, L1]

it is right *decet, -ēre, ——, decuit (impers. + acc.)* [KL3, L1]

it is suitable *decet, -ēre, ——, decuit (impers. + acc.)* [KL3, L1]

Italy *Ītalia, -ae (f)* [KL1, W8; KL2, W5]

its (own) *suus, -a, -um* [KL1, W31; KL3, L2]

itself (acc. reflexive pronoun) *sē* [KL1, W8]

itself (pron./adj.) *ipse, ipsa, ipsum* [KL2, L3]

itself (reflex. pron.) *suī* [KL3, L2]

Iulia *Iūlia, -ae (f)* [KL1, W11]

Iulius *Iūlius, -iī (m)* [KL1, W19]

Iunia *Iūnia, -ae (f)* [KL1, W11]

J

jail *carcer, -eris (m)* [KL1, W23; KL3, L5]

jar *vās, vāsis (n)* [KL3, W1]

jealousy *zēlus, -ī (m)* [KL3, W7]

Jerusalem *Hierusalem (indecl.)* [KL1, W32]

Jesse *Isai (indecl.)* [KL1, W32]

Jesus *Iēsus, -ūs (m)* [KL1, L25]

jewel *lapis, -idis (m)* [KL1, W27; KL2, L14]

Jew (Jewish) *Iudaeus, -a, -um* [KL2, W3]

job *negōtium, -iī (n)* [KL3, W9]

join (together) *coniungō, -ere, -iūnxī, -iūnctum* [KL3, L9]

joint *artus, -ūs (m)* [KL2, L6]

join *iungō, -ere, iūnxī, iunctum* [KL1, L27]

journey *iter, itineris (n)* [KL1, L13]

Jove *Iuppiter, Iovis (m)* [KL1, W21]

joy *gaudium, -ī (n)* [KL1, L5]; *laetitia, -ae (f)* [KL3, L7]

joyful *laetus, -a, -um* [KL1, L7]

judge (noun) *iūdex, -dicis (m)* [KL1, W28; KL3, L1]

judge (verb) *arbitror, -ārī, ——, -ātus sum* [KL3, L4]; *iūdicō* [KL2, L14]

judgment *iūdicium, -ī (n)* [KL2, L9]

judgment seat *tribūnal, -ālis (n)* [KL2, W15]

jug *hydria, -ae (f)* [KL2, W12]

Julia *Iūlia, -ae (f)* [KL1, W11]

Julius *Iūlius, -iī (m)* [KL1, W19]

jump *saliō, -īre, -uī, saltum* [KL1, W29; KL2, W12]

jump *saliō, -īre, saluī, saltum* [KL1, W29]

Junia *Iūnia, -ae (f)* [KL1, W11]

Juno *Iūno, -ōnis (f)* [KL1, W21; KL3, W3]

Jupiter *Iuppiter, Iovis (dat. Iovī, acc. Iovem, abl. Iove) (m)* [KL1, W21; KL2, W6]

just (adj.) *iūstus, -a, -um* [KL1, L7]

just (adv.) *modo* [KL1, L27]

just as *sīcut* [KL1, L20]; *quasi* [KL3, L11]

justice *iūs, iūris (n)* [KL2, L15]; *iūstitia, -ae (f)* [KL3, L12]

K

keep *custōdiō, -īre, -iī/-īvī, -ītum* [KL3, L3]; *observō* [KL3, W11]

kidnapping *raptus, -ūs (m)* [KL1, W31]

kill *interficiō, -ere, -fēcī, -fectum* [KL1, L31]; *necō (1)* [KL1, L1]; *occīdō, -ere, -cīdī, -cīsum* [KL1, L30]; *caedō, -ere, cecīdī, caesum* [KL2, L12]

kind (noun) *genus, -neris (n)* [KL2, L13]

kindle (verb) *accendō, -ere, -cēnsī, -cēnsum* [KL2, W15]; *incendō* [KL2, W13]

kindness *clēmentia, -ae (f)* [KL1, W21; KL3, W10]; *grātia, -ae (f)* [KL1, L27]

king *rēx, rēgis (m)* [KL1, L12]

kingdom *regnum, -ī (n)* [KL1, L5]

kingly *rēgālis, -e* [KL3, W10]

kiss *ōsculum, -ī (n)* [KL2, W11]

knee *genū, -ūs (n)* [KL1, L25]

knight *eques, -quitis (m)* [KL1, L20]

knock *pulsō* [K2L, W14]

know *sciō, -īre, sciī (scīvī), scītum* [KL1, L29]; *cognōscō (pf. tense)* [KL2, L10]; *noscō, -ere, nōvī, nōtum (pf. tense)* [KL2, L9]

kraken *cētus, -ī (m)* [KL1, L10]

L

labor (noun) *labor, labōris (m)* [KL1, L12]

labor (verb) *mōlior, -īrī, ——, mōlītus sum* [KL2, L6]; *operor, -ārī, ——, operātus sum* [KL2, L6]

labyrinth *labyrinthus, -ī (m)* [KL1, W30]

lack *careō, -ēre, -uī, -itum (+ abl.)* [KL3, L6]; *indigeō, -ēre, -diguī, —— (+ gen./abl.)* [KL2, W14]

lake *lacus, -ūs (m)* [KL1, L27]

lamp *lūmen, -minis (n)* [KL3, L11]

land *tellūs, tellūris (f)* [KL1, L14]; *terra, -ae (f)* [KL1, L4]; **(native land)** *patria, -ae (f)* [KL1, L3]

language *lingua, -ae* [KL1, L26]

lap (of a race) *curriculum, -ī (n)* [KL1, W23]

large *magnus, -a, -um* [KL1, L7]

late (adv.) *sērō, sērius, sērissimē (adv.)* [KL2, L11]

Latin (adj.) *Latīnus, -a, -um* [KL2, W13]

laugh *rīdeō, -ēre, rīsī, rīsum* [KL1, L9]

laurel (tree) *laurus, -ī (f)* [KL1, W20]

lay waste *vastō (1)* [KL1, L14]

laying on *impositiō, -ōnis (f)* [KL3, W7]

law *lēx, lēgis (f)* [KL2, L10]

lawful *fās (n, indecl.)* [KL3, L2]; **(it is lawful)** *licet, licuit, - (impers. + dat./acc.)* [KL1, W26; KL3, L1]

lead (adj) *plumbeus, -a, -um* [KL1, W20]

lead (verb) *dūcō, -ere, dūxī, ductum* [KL1, L26]

lead (out) *ēdūcō, -ere, -dūxī, -ductum* [KL3, L5]; **(to)** *addūcō* [KL2, L8]; **(forth)** *prōdūcō, -ere, -dūxī, -ductum* [KL3, W4]; **(aside/astray)** *sēdūcō, -ere, -dūxī, -ductum* [KL3, W11]

lead (metal) *plumbum, -ī (n)* [KL3, W2]

leaden *plumbeus, -a, -um* [KL1, W20]

leader *dux, ducis (m)* [KL1, L14]; *prīnceps, -cipis (m)* [KL2, L3]

leaf *folium, -ī (n)* [KL1, W20]; *frōns, -ontis (f)* [KL1, W32]

leaky *pertūsus, -a, -um* [KL1, W29]

leap *saliō, -īre, -uī, saltum* [KL1, W29; KL2, W12]

learn *cognōscō, -ere, -nōvī, -nitum* [KL2, L10]; *noscō, -ere, nōvī, nōtum* [KL2, L9]

learned *doctus, -a, -um* [KL1, L13]

least (adj.) *minimus, -a, -um* [KL1, W31]

least (adv.) *minimē* [KL2, L7]

leave *discēdō, -ere, -cessī, -cessum* [KL3, W5]

leave alone *dēsōlō* [KL3, W7]

leave behind *relinquō, -ere, -līquī, -lictum* [KL1, L28]

left(-handed) *sinister, -stra, -strum* [KL1, L30]

leg *crūs, crūris (n)* [KL1, W19]

legend *fābula, -ae (f)* [KL1, L2]

legion *legiō, -ōnis (f)* [KL3, W2]

less *minus* [KL2, L7]

lest *nē* [KL3, L4]

let *sinō, -ere, sīvī, situs* [KL2, W13]

let go *mittō, -ere, mīsī, missum* [KL1, L26]

letter (of the alphabet) *littera, -ae (f)* [KL1, L26]

letter *plural of littera, -ae (f)* [KL1, L26]

level surface *aequor, -oris (n)* [KL3, L6]

liar *mendāx, -dacis (m/f)* [KL3, L6]

lick *lambō, -ere, lambī, lambitum* [KL3, W3]

lie (noun) *mendācium, -iī (n)* [KL3, L6]

lie (verb) *mentior, -īrī, ——, -ītus sum* [KL3, L6]

lie down *iaceō, -ēre, -uī, ——* [KL1, L9]

lie flat *iaceō, -ēre, -uī, ——* [KL1, L9]

lieutenant *lēgātus, -ī (m)* [KL2, L15]

life *vīta, -ae* [KL1, L11]; *aetās, -tātis (f)* [KL2, L14]; *anima, -ae (f)* [KL2, L4]

lift (up) *levō* [KL3, W1]; *tollō, -ere, sustulī, sublātum* [KL1, W25; KL2, L13]

light (adj.) *levis, -e* [KL2, W6]

light (noun) *lux, lūcis (f)* [KL1, L12]; *lūmen, -minis (n)* [KL3, L11]; *lūmināre, -āris (n)* [KL3, W4]

light (up) *illūminō* [KL3, W4]

lightly *leviter* [KL2, W6]

lightning *fulgur, -uris (n)* [KL1, W25]

like (adj.) *similis, -e* [KL2, L5]

like (adv.) *sīcut* [KL1, L20]

likeness *imāgō, -ginis (f)* [KL3, L4]; *īnstar (indecl.)* [KL2, L13]; *simulācrum, -ī (n)* [KL3, L6]; *speciēs, -ēi (f)* [KL3, W4]

lily *līlium, -iī (n)* [KL3, W13]

limit *fīnis, -is (m)* [KL1, W4]; *terminus, -ī (m)* [KL3, L15]

lion *leō, leōnis (m)* [KL1, L12]

lioness *lea, -ae (f)* [KL2, W11]

line *ōrdō, -dinis (m)* [KL2, L15]

line (of poetry) *versus, -ūs (m)* [KL1, L27]

lion *leō, leōnis (m)* [KL1, L12]

lip *lābrum, -ī (n)* [KL3, W2]

listen to *audiō, -īre, -īvī, -ītum* [KL1, L29]

little (adj.) *parvus, -a, -um* [KL1, L7]; *modicus, -a, -um* [KL2, L14]

little (adv.) *parum* [KL2, L7]

little by little *paulātim* [KL3, W7]

little child *īnfāns, -fantis (adj. & noun, m/f)* [KL1, W31; KL3, L12]

live *habitō (1)* [KL1, L3]; *vīvō, -ere, vīxī, victum* [KL1, L27]

live in *incolō, -ere, -coluī, -cultum* [KL3, L2]

living *vīvus, -a, -um* [KL1, L20]

load *onus, oneris (n)* [KL1, L13; KL3, L3]

lofty *altus, -a, -um* [KL1, L19]; *excelsus, -a, -um* [KL2, L4]

loin *lumbus, -ī (m)* [KL2, W9]

loneliness *sōlitūdō, -dinis (f)* [KL3, W9]

long (adj.) *longus, -a, -um* [KL1, L20]

long (for) (verb) *cupiō, -ere, cupīvī, cupītum* [KL1, L31]

long way off (a long way off) *longē* [KL3, L3]

longer *amplius* [KL3, L9]

look at *spectō (1)* [KL1, L1]; *cōnspiciō, -ere, -spēxī, -spectum* [KL3, W16]

look back *rēspiciō, -ere, -spēxī, -spectum* [KL2, L14]

look down on *dēspiciō, -ere, -spexī, -spectum* [KL1, W32]

loose *solvō, -ere, solvī, solūtum* [KL2, L10]

lop *praecīdō, -ere, -cīdī, -cīsum* [KL1, W32]

lop off *praecīdō, -ere, -cīdī, -cīsum* [KL1, W32; KL2, W6]

lord *dominus, -ī (m)* [KL1, L4]

lose *perdō, -ere, perdidī, perditum* [KL1, L27]

lot *sors, -rtis (f)* [KL3, L6]

love (noun) *amor, amōris (m)* [KL1, L14]; *cāritās, -tātis (f)* [KL3, L11]

love (verb) *amō (1)* [KL1, L1]; *foveō, -ēre, fōvī, fōtum* [KL1, L25]; *dīligō, -ere, -lēxī, -lēctum* [KL3, L1]

low(ly) (adj.) *humilis, -e* [KL2, L5]

lower *īnferior, -ius* [KL2, L5]

lowest *īmus, -a, -um* [KL2, L5]; *īnfimus, -a, -um* [KL2, L5]

loyalty *pietās, -tātis (f)* [KL2, W13]

lucky *fēlix, (gen.) -līcis* [KL1, L19]

lust *concupiscentia, -ae (f)* [KL3, W9]

lying on one's back *resupīnus, -a, -um* [KL3, W7]

lyre *lyra, -ae (f)* [KL1, W28]

M

machine *māchina, -ae (f)* [KL3, W6]

made (am made) *fīō, fierī, ——, factus sum* [KL1, L31]

magic (adj.) *magicus, -a, -um* [KL2, W2]

maiden *virgō, virginis (f)* [KL1, L12]

maidservant *ancilla, -ae (f)* [KL3, L10]

magistrate *magistrātus, -ūs (m)* [KL3, W5]

make *faciō, -ere, fēcī, factum* [KL1, L31]; *aedificō* [KL2, L4]

make clear *dēclārō (1)* [KL1, L10]

make firm *solidō* [KL2, W9]

make holy *sanctificō* [KL3, L4]

make known *adnūntiō* [KL3, L7]; *indicō* [KL3, L11]

male *masculus, -a, -um* [KL3, W4]

malice *malitia, -ae (f)* [KL2, L14]

malicious *malignus, -a, -um* [KL3, L13]

malignant *malignus, -a, -um* [KL3, L13]

man (as opposed to animal) *homō, hominis (m)* [KL1, L12]; **(as opposed to woman)** *vir, virī (m)* [KL1, L4]

manifest (verb) *manifestō* [KL2, W8]

manifest (adj.) *manifestus, -a, -um* [KL3, W1]

manliness *virtūs, virtūtis (f)* [KL1, L12]

manslayer *homicīda, -ae (m/f)* [KL3, L13]

manner *modus, -ī (m)* [KL3, L7]; *mōs, mōris (m)* [KL2, L13]

many *multus, -a, -um* [KL1, L7]

marble *marmoreus, -a, -um* [KL3, W16]

march out *ēgredior, -gredī, ——, -gressus sum* [KL2, L6]

maritime *maritimus, -a, -um* [KL3, W2]

marriage (adj.) *nūptiālis, -e* [KL2, W2]

marriage (noun) *mātrimōnium, -ī (n)* [KL1, L20]

marry *nūbō, -ere, nūpsī, nūptum* [KL3, W2]

Mars *Mars, Martis (m)* [KL2, W13]

marvel at *mīror, -ārī, ——, mīrātus sum* [KL2, L6]

marvelous *mīrābilis, -e* [KL3, L3]

master *dominus, -ī (m)* [KL1, L4]

mat *grabātus, -ī (m)* [KL3, W9]

material *māteria, -ae (f)* [KL3, W2]

maybe *forsitan* [KL3, L13]

maze *labyrinthus, -ī (m)* [KL1, W30]

meadow *prātum, -ī (n)* [KL2, W15]

meager *exiguus, -a, -um* [KL3, W2]

meal *cēna, -ae (f)* [KL1, L20]

meantime (in the meantime) *interim* [KL1, L9]

meanwhile *interim* [KL1, L9]; *intereā* [KL2, L12]; *proptereā* [KL2, L10]

measure (noun) *mēnsūra, -ae (f)* [KL2, L14]; *modus, -ī (m)* [KL3, L7]

measure (verb) *mētior, -īrī, ——, mēnsus sum* [KL2, L14]

measurement *mēnsūra, -ae (f)* [KL2, L14]

meat *carō, carnis (f)* [KL1, L31]

mediterranean *mediterrāneus, -a, -um* [KL3, W2]

meeting *concilium, -iī (n)* [KL3, L5]

memorial *monumentum, -ī (n)* [KL2, W11]

memory *memoria, -ae (f)* [KL3, L2]

menace (verb) *minor, -ārī, ——, -ātus sum* [KL2, W5]

Mercury *Mercurius, -ī (m)* [KL1, W21; KL2, W6]

mercy *clēmentia, -ae (f)* [KL1, W21]; *misericordia, -ae (f)* [KL2, L10]; *venia, -ae (f)* [KL3, W12]

merely *modo* [KL1, L27]; *sōlum* [KL3, L7]; *tantum* [KL3, L14]

merit *mereō, -ēre, -uī, -itum* [KL1, L15; KL3, W6]

messenger *nuntius, -ī (m)* [KL2, L12]

Messiah *Messīā(s), -ae (m)* [KL2, W12]

Midas *Midās, -ae (m)* [KL1, W27]

middle (of) *medius, -a, -um* [KL1, L26]

midst (of) *medius, -a, -um* [KL1, L26]

milk *lac, lactis (n)* [KL1, L13]

mind *animus, -ī (m)* [KL1, L29]

mind one's own business *suum negōtium agere* [KL1, W29]

mindful *memor, -oris* [KL3, L9]

mine *meus, -a, -um* [KL1, L11]

Minerva *Minerva, -ae (f)* [KL3, W6]; *Pallas, -adis (f)* [KL3, W6]

minister *minister, -strī (m)* [KL3, L10]

Minos *Mīnōs, -ōnis (m)* [KL1, W30]

Minotaur *Mīnōtaurus, -ī (m)* [KL1, W30]

miracle *sīgnum, -ī (n)* [KL3, L4]

miserable *infēlix, (gen.) -līcis* [KL1, L19]; *miser, -era, -erum* [KL1, L7]

misery *miseria, -ae (f)* [KL3, W9]

misfortune *cāsus, -ūs (m)* [KL1, L28]

mistaken (am mistaken) *errō (1)* [KL1, L14]

mob *turba, -ae (f)* [KL1, L2]

moderate *modicus, -a, -um* [KL2, L14]

monastery *monastērium, -iī (n)* [KL3, W7]

money *aes, aeris (n)* [KL3, W2]; *argentum, -ī (n)* [KL1, L5]; *peccnia, -ae (f)* [KL1, L3]

monk *monachus, -ī (m)* [KL3, W7]

monster *mōnstrum* [KL1, W30]; *bēlua, -ae (f)* [KL3, L15]

monstrous *immānis, -e* [KL3, L7]

month *mensis, -is (m)* [KL3, L10]

monument *monumentum, -ī (n)* [KL2, W11]

moon *lūna, -ae* [KL1, L2]

morals *mōs, mōris (m) (pl.)* [KL2, L13]

more *amplius* [KL3, L9]; *magis* [KL2, L7]; *plūs* [KL2, L5]; *potius* [KL3, L7]

moreover *autem (postposit. conj.)* [KL1, L12]

morning (in the morning) *māne* [KL1, W19; KL2, L6]

mortal *mortālis, -e* [KL2, W6]

most (adj.) *plūrimus, -a, -um* [KL2, L5]

most (adv.) *plūrimum* [KL2, L7]; *māximē* [KL2, L7]

mother (noun) *māter, mātris (f)* [KL1, L12]; *parēns* [KL1, W11; KL2, W8]

mother (adj.) *māternus, -a, -um* [KLS, W16]

mountain *mōns, montis* [KL1, L18]

mourning *lūctus, -ūs (m)* [KL3, W13]

mouth *ōs, ōris (n)* [KL1, L13]

move (intransit.) *cēdō, -ere, cessī, cessum* [KL1, L28]

move (transit.) *moveō, -ēre, mōvī, mōtum* [KL1, L14]

movement *āgmen, -minis (n)* [KL3, L6]

much (adj.) *multus, -a, -um* [KL1, L7]

much (noun) *multum* [KL2, L7]

mud *lutum, -ī (n)* [KL3, W8]

mulberry *mōrus, -ī (f)* [KL2, W11]

multiply *multiplicō* [KL3, W20]

multitude *multitūdō, -tudinis (f)* [KL2, L12]

murder *nex, necis (f)* [KL3, W10]

murderer/-ess *homicīda, -ae (m/f)* [KL3, L13]

musician *musicus, -ī (m)* [KL3, W28]

mute *mūtus, -a, -um* [KL3, W1]

my *meus, -a, -um* [KL1, L11]

N

name (verb) *appellō (1)* [KL1, L15]; *nōminō* [KL3, W13]

name (noun) *nōmen, nōminis (n)* [KL1, L13]; *cognōmen, -minis (n)* [KL2, W15]

napkin *mappa, -ae (f)* [KL1, W23]

naked *nūdus, -a, -um* [KL3, W7]

nation *gens, -ntis (f)* [KL1, L31]; *populus, -ī (m)* [KL1, L11]

native land *patria, -ae (f)* [KL1, L3]

nativity *nātīvitās, -tātis (f)* [KL2, W8]

naturally *scīlicet* [KL3, L6]

near *ad (+ acc.)* [KL1, L3]; *prope (adv. & prep. + acc.)* [KL1, L19]; *propter (+ acc.)* [KL1, L25]

near(by) *vīcīnus, -a, -um* [KL3, L9]

near (to) *iūxta (adv. & prep. + acc.)* [KL1, L28]

nearer *propior, -ius* [KL2, L5]

nearest *proximus, -a, -um* [KL2, L5]

nearly *ferē* [KL3, L3]; *quasi* [KL3, L11]

neat *mundus, -a, -um* [KL3, L5]

necessary *necesse* [KL3, L1]; **(it is necessary)** *oportet, -ēre, -tuit, -tuitum (impers. + acc.)* [KL3, L1]

need *indigeō, -ēre, -diguī, —— (+ gen./abl.)* [KL2, W14]

neighbor(ing) *vīcīnus, -a, -um* [KL3, L9]

neither *neuter, -tra, -trum* [KL2, L15]

neither...nor *nec...nec* [KL1, L14]

nephew *nepōs, -pōtis (m/f)* [KL2, L13]

Neptune *Neptūnus, -ī (m)* [KL2, W7]

never *numquam* [KL1, L5]

nevertheless *tamen* [KL1, L30]; *vērumtamen* [KL3, L13]

new *novus, -a, -um* [KL1, L26]

next (adj.) *proximus, -a, -um* [KL2, L5]

next (adv.) *deinde* [KL1, L22]; *tum* [KL1, L15]

next to *prope (adv. & prep. + acc.)* [KL1, L19]

niece *nepōs, -pōtis (m/f)* [KL2, L13]

night *nox, noctis (f)* [KL1, L18]

nine *novem* [KL1, L21]

nineteen *ūndēvīgintī* [KL1, L21]

nineteenth *ūndēvīcēsimus, -a, -um* [KL1, L23]

ninth *nōnus, -a, -um* [KL1, L23]

no (adj.) *nūllus, -a, -um* [KL2, L4]

no (adv.) *nē* [KL3, L4]

no (expects a no answer) *num* [KL2, L7]; *numquid* [KL2, L9]

no longer *nōn iam* [KL1, L15]

no one *nēmō, neminis (m/f)* [KL2, L4]

noble *magnanimus, -a, -um* [KL1, W9]; *excelsus, -a, -um* [KL2, L4]; *nōbilis, -e* [KL2, W15]

nobody *nēmō, neminis (m/f)* [KL2, L4]

nod *nūtō* [KL3, W7]

noise *clāmor, -oris (m)* [KL1, W20; KL2, L13]; *fragor, -ōris (m)* [KL3, W7]; *sonitus, -ūs (m)* [KL3, W3]

none *nūllus, -a, -um* [KL2, L4]

noon *merīdiēs, -ēī (m)* [KL1, L28]
nor *nec (neque)* [KL1, L14]
not *nōn* [KL1, L1]; *nec (neque)* [KL1, L14]
not any *nūllus, -a, -um* [KL2, L4]
not at all *nihil (n. indecl.)* [KL1, L6]; *haud* [KL3, L1]; *minimē* [KL2, L7]; *nequaquam* [KL2, W8]
not enough *parum* [KL2, L7]
not know *nesciō, -īre, -īvī, -ītum* [KL1, L30]
not *nē* [KL3, L4]
nothing *nihil (n, indecl.)* [KL1, L6]
notice *attendō, -ere, -ndī, -ntum* [KL3, W9]
not want *nōlō, nōlle, nōluī, ——* [KL2, L14]
not wish *nōlō, nōlle, nōluī, ——* [KL2, L14]
not yet *nōndum* [KL3, L7]
now *iam* [KL1, L15]; *nunc* [KL1, L1]
number *numerus, -ī (m)* [KL3, L2]
numerous *crēber, -bra, -brum* [KL3, L2]
nymph *nympha, -ae (f)* [KL1, W20; KL2, W6]

O

oar *rēmus, -ī (m)* [KL2, W5]
oath *iūs iūrandum* [KL2, L15]; *iūsiūrandum* [KL2, L15]
obey *oboediō [obediō], -īre, -īvī, -ītum (+ dat.?)* [KL3, L5]
observe *observō* [KL3, W11]
obstruct *obstō, -stāre, -stitī, -stātūrum (+ dat.)* [KL2, W11]
occasion *occāsiō, -ōnis (f)* [KL3, W10]
occupation *negōtium, -iī (n)* [KL3, W9]
ocean *ōceanus, -ī (m)* [KL1, L4]
Odysseus *Ulixēs, -is (m)* [KL2, W5]
of course *scīlicet* [KL3, L6]
of such a sort (rel. adj.) *quālis* [KL3, L9]
of such size *tantus, -a, -um* [KL3, L5]
of what sort (interrog. adj.) *quālis* [KL3, L9]
offend *laedō, -ere, laesī, laesus* [KL3, W6]; *peccō* [KL3, L11]
offense *peccātum, -ī (n)* [KL3, L11]

offer (verb) *offerō, offerre, obtulī, oblātum* [KL2, L11]; *polliceor, -ērī, ——, pollicitus sum* [KL3, L7]
offering *sacrificium, -iī (n)* [KL2, L4]
office *mūnus, -neris (n)* [KL2, L15]
often *saepe* [KL1, L6]
oh! *heu (ēheu)* [KL1, L22]
oh that! *utinam* [KL3, L13]
ointment *ūnctiō, -ōnis (f)* [KL3, W12]
old man *senex, senis (m)* [KL1, L14]
old *vetus, -teris* [KL1, L30]
older *māior, māius (gen. māioris)* [KL1, W31]; *senior, -ōris* [KL3, L5]
oldest (son) *postnatus, -ī (m)* [KL1, W19]
oldest *māximus, -a, -um* [KL1, W31]
omen *mōnstrum, -ī (n)* [KL1, W13]; *prōdigium, -iī (n)* [KL3, W5]
omnipotent *omnipotēns, -tentis* [KL3, W2]
on *in (+ abl.)* [KL1, L3]
on account of *propter (+ acc.)* [KL1, L25]; *causā (+ gen.)* [KL2, L15]; *ob (+ acc.)* [KL2, L3]
on all sides *undique* [KL1, L30; KL2, L15]
on that side *illinc* [KL2, L11]
on the outside *extrā* [KL3, L15]
on this side *hinc* [KL2, L11]
once *quondam* [KL2, L13]
once upon a time *ōlim* [KL1, L6]
one *ūnicus, -a, -um* [KL1, W22]; *ūnus, -a, -um* [KL1, L21]
one another *invicem* [KL2, L12]
one at a time *singulī, -ae, -a* [KL2, L13]
one (in one) *ūnā* [KL1, L29]
one hundred *centum* [KL1, L21]
one hundredth *centēsimus* [KL1, L23]
one (of two) *uter, utra (ūtra), utrum (ūtrum) (interrog.)* [KL2, L15]
one which *uter, utra (ūtra), utrum (ūtrum) (interrog.)* [KL2, L15]
only (adj.) *sōlus, -a, -um* [KL1, W12; KL2, L4]; *ūnicus, -a, -um* [KL1, W22]

only (adv.) *modo* [KL1, L27]; *sōlum* [KL3, L7]; *tantum* [KL3, L14];
only-begotten *unigenitus, -a, -um* [KL2, W3]
onset *impetus, -ūs (m)* [KL3, L9]
open *aperiō, -īre, -uī, apertum* [KL1, L29]
openly *cōram* [KL1, L27]
opinion *cōgitātiō, -tiōnis (f)* [KL3, L1]; *sententia, -ae (f)* [KL3, L9]
opportunity *occāsiō, -ōnis (f)* [KL3, W10]
oppose *obsistō, -ere, -stitī, -stitum* [KL3, W7]
opposite *dīversus, -a, -um* [KL3, W7]
or *aut* [KL1, L1]; *sīve (seū)* [KL1, L30]; *an* [KL3, L9]; *vel* [KL2, L9]
or rather *vel* [KL2, L9]
or whether *an* [KL3, L9]
oracle *ōrāculum, -ī (n)* [KL1, W31]; *fātum, -ī (n)* [KL1, L5; KL2, 13]; *sors, -rtis (f)* [KL3, L6]
order (verb) *imperō* [KL3, L10]; *iubeō, -ēre, iussī, iussum* [KL3, L2]; *mandō* [KL3, L10]
order (noun) *mandātum, -ī (n)* [KL2, L10]; *ōrdō, -dinis (m)* [KL2, L15]
ordinary *mediōcris, -e* [KL1, L19]; *modicus, -a, -um* [KL2, L14]
origin *genus, -neris (n)* [KL2, L13]; *prīncipium, -iī (n)* [KL3, L4]
ornament *ornātus, -ūs (m)* [KL3, W6]
orphan *orba, -ae (f)/orbus, -ī (m)* [KL1, L22]
Oswald *Oswaldus, -ī (m)* [KL1, W19]
other *alius, -a, -um* [KL1, W21; KL2, L4]; *cēterus, -a, -um* [KL2, L15]; **the other (of two)** *alter, -era, -erum* [KL2, L4]
ought *dēbeō, -ēre, -uī, -itum* [KL1, L11]
our(s) *noster, -stra, -strum* [KL1, L11]
out of *ē, ex (+ abl.)* [KL1, L3]
out(side) *forās* [KL3, L6]
outside (of) *extrā* [KL3, L15]
outstanding *ēgregius, -a, -um* [KL1, L29]

over *super (+ acc./+ abl.)* [KL1, L26]; *suprā (adv./prep. + acc.)* [KL1, L14]

overpower *premō, -ere, pressī, pressum* [KL2, L10]

overshadow *obumbrō* [KL3, W4]

overturn *ēvertō, -ere, -tī, -sum* [KL3, W7]; *subvertō, -ere, -vertī, -versus* [KL3, W7]

owe *dēbeō, -ēre, -uī, -itum* [KL1, L11]

ox *bōs, bovis (m/f)* [KL1, L19]

P

pacify *mītigō* [KL3, W7]

Pactolus *Pactōlus, -ī (m)* [KL1, W27]

palace *rēgia, -ae (f)* [KL1, L2]

pale (verb) *palleō, -ēre, -uī, ——* [KL3, W7]

pale (adj.) *exsanguis, -e* [KL3, W6]

Pan *Pān, Pānos (acc. Pāna) (m)* [KL1, W28]

pan pipe *avēna, -ae (f)* [KL1, W21]

parch *torreō, -ēre, torruī, tostum* [KL1, L17]

pardon *venia, -ae (f)* [KL3, W12]

parent *parēns, -entis (m/f)* [KL1, W11; KL2, W8]

part *pars, partis (f)* [KL2, L3]

pass (by/over) *trānseō, -īre, -iī, -itum* [KL2, L15]

passages [in a book] *loca (n, pl)*

past (prep.) *praeter* [KL2, L13]

pastoral *pastorālis, -e* [KL1, W32]

pasture *pāscō, -ere, pāvī, pāstum* [KL1, W32; KL2, W14]

pattern *rēgula, -ae (f)* [KL3, W9]

pause *subsistō, -ere, -stitī, ——* [KL3, W6]

pay (noun) *stīpendium, -iī (n)* [KL2, W15]

pay (verb) *solvō, -ere, solvī, solūtum* [KL2, L10]

pay the penalty *poenās dō* [KL1, L27]

peace *pāx, pācis (f)* [KL1, L15]

peacock *pāvō, -ōnis (m)* [KL1, W21]

penalty *poena, -ae (f)* [KL1, L27]

people *populus, -ī (m)* [KL1, L11]

peradventure *forsitan* [KL3, L13]

perceive *intellegō, -ere, -lēxī, -lēctum* [KL3, L2]; *perspiciō, -ere, -spēxī, -spectum* [KL3, W2]; *sentiō, -īre, sēnsī, sēnsum* [KL3, L3]

perchance *forte* [KL2, L3]

perfect *perficiō, -ere, -fēcī, -fectum* [KL1, W23; KL3, L14]

perhaps *fortasse* [KL1, L26]; *forte* [KL2, L3]; *forsitan* [KL3, L13]

period of time *diēs, diēī (m/f)* [KL1, L28]

permit *permittō, -ere, -mīsī, -missum* [KL1, W30]

permitted *fās (n, indecl.)* [KL3, L2]; **(it is permitted)** *licet, licuit, - (impers. + dat./acc.)* [KL1, W26; KL3, L1]

personally *cōram* [KL1, L27]

persuade *persuādeō, -ere, -suāsī, -suāsum (+ dat.)* [KL1, W15; KL3, L10]

petition *petītiō, -ōnis (f)* [KL3, W16]

Pharisee *Pharisaeus, -ī (m)* [KL2, W3]

Philistine *Philistheus, -ī (m)*

phoenix *phoenīx, -nīcis (m)* [KL3, W3]

Phrygia *Phrygia, -ae (f)* [KL1, W27]

pick *dēligō, -ere, lēgī, -lēctum* [KL1, L28]

pick out *ēligō, -ere, -lēgī, -lectum* [KL3, L1]

pierce *percutiō, -ere, -cussī, -cussum* [KL1, W32; KL2, L3]

piety *pietās, -tātis (f)* [KL2, W13]

pig *porcus, -ī (m)* [KL1, L10]

pig-sty *hara, -ae (f)* [KL1, W25]

pine *pīnus, -ī (f)* [KL3, W7]

pipe (reed-pipe) *calamus, -ī (m)* [KL1, W28]

pirate *pīrāta, -ae (m)* [KL1, L2]

pit *abyssus, -ī (f)* [KL3, W9]; *fovea, -ae (f)* [KL3, W1]; *puteus, -ī (m)* [KL2, L12]

pity (verb) *misereor, -ērī, ——, misertus sum (+ gen.)* [KL2, L6]

pity (noun) *misericordia, -ae (f)* [KL2, L10]

place (noun) *locus, -ī (m)* [KL2, L7]

place (verb) *collocō (1)* [KL1, W21]; *pōnō, -ere, posuī, positum* [KL1, L26]

places [geographic] *locī (m, pl)*; **[in a book]** *loca (n, pl)* [KL2, L7]

plague *plāga, -ae (f)* [KL3, L14]

plain (noun) *prātum, -ī (n)* [KL2, W15]

planet *lūmināre, -āris (n)* [KL3, W4]

plan *cōnsilium, -iī (n)* [KL1, L30]

plant (verb) *serō, -ere, sēvī, satum* [KL2, W11]

play (music) *cantō (1)* [KL1, L1]; *canō, -ere, cecinī, cāntum* [KL2, L10]

play *lūdō, lūdere, lūsī, lūsum* [KL1, L26]

please (interj.) *obsecrō* [KL3, L13]

please (verb) *placeō, -ēre, -cuī, -citum* [KL3, L1]

pleasing *grātus, -a, -um* [KL1, L27]; *placitus, -a, -um* [KL3, W12]

pleasure *voluptās, -tātis (f)* [KL3, W2]

plenty *cōpia, -ae (f)* [KL1, L15]

plot *īnsidiae, -ārum (f, pl)* [KL2, L15]

pluck *vellō, -ere, vulsī/vellī, vulsum* [KL3, W1]

plump *plēnus, -a, -um* [KL2, L4]

plunder (noun) *praeda, -ae (f)* [KL2, L15]

plunder (verb) *dīripiō, -ere, -ripuī, -reptum* [KL3, W1]

Pluto *Plūtō, -tōnis (m)* [KL2, W6]

poem *carmen, -inis (n)* [KL1, L13]

poet *poēta, -ae* [KL1, L2]

point out *ostendō, -ere, -dī, -sum/tum* [KL3, L5]; *sīgnō* [KL3, W3]

poison *venēnum, -ī (n)* [KL1, L10; KL3, W6]

polite *urbānus, -a, -um* [KL1, W29]

Polyphemus *Polyphēmus, -ī (m)* [KL2, W4]

ponder *pendō, -ere, pependī, pensum* [KL3, L10]

pool *natātōria, -ae (f)* [KL2, W8]

poor *pauper, -eris* [KL3, L9]

porch *porticus, -ūs (f)* [KL3, W5]

port *portus, -ūs (m)* [KL1, L25]

portent *mōnstrum, -ī (n)* [KL1, W13]; *prōdigium, -iī (n)* [KL3, W5]

Poseidon *Neptūnus, -ī (m)* [KL2, W7]
possess *teneō, -ēre, tenuī, tentum* [KL1, L9]
possible *fās (n, indecl.)* [KL3, L2]
pour *fundō, -ere, fūdī, fūsum* [KL3, W3]; **(out/forth)** *effundō, -ere, -fūdī, -fūsum* [KL3, L9]; **(together)** *confundō, -ere, -fūdī, -fūsum* [KL3, L12]; **(in)** *infundō, -ere, -fūdī, -fūsum (+ dat.)* [KL3, W9]; **(over)** *perfundō, -ere, -fūdī, -fūsus* [KL3, W6]
power *vīs, vīs (f)* [KL3, L5]
powerful *potēns, (gen.) -entis* [KL1, L19]
praise (noun) *laus, laudis (f)* [KL1, L15]
praise (verb) *laudō (1)* [KL1, L1]; *benedīcō, -ere, -dīxī, -dictum (+ dat.)* [KL3, L4]
pray *ōrō (1) (takes double acc.)* [KL1, L6]; *obsecrō* [KL3, L13]; **(for)** *dēprecor, -ārī, ——, -ātus sum* [KL3, L10]
preach *ēvangelīzō* [KL3, W5]; *praedīcō* [KL3, W7]
predict *cantō (1)* [KL1, L1]; *praedīcō, -ere, -dīxī, -dictum* [KL1, W31]
prefer *mālō, mālle, māluī, ——* [KL2, L14]; *praeferō, -ferre, -tulī, -lātum* [KL2, W11]
pregnant *fētus, -a, -um* [KL3, W6]
preparation *ornātus, -ūs (m)* [KL3, W6]
prepare *parō (1)* [KL1, L14]; *accingō, -ere, -cinxī, -cinctum* [KL2, W9]
press *premō, -ere, pressī, pressum* [KL2, L10]
press on *īnstō, -āre, -stitī, -stātum* [KL2, W6]
prevent *vetō, -āre, vetuī, vetitum* [KL3, W11]
presence (in the presence of) *cōram (+ abl.)* [KL1, L27]
pride *superbia, -ae (f)* [KL3, L12]
priest *sacerdōs, -dōtis (m)* [KL2, L3]
prince *prīnceps, -cipis (m)* [KL2, L3]
principle *placitum, -ī (n)* [KL3, W9]
prison *carcer, -eris (m)* [KL1, W23; KL3, L5]

proclaim *praedīcō* [KL3, W7]
proceed *vādō, -ere, vāsī, ——* [KL2, L9]
produce (verb) *prōdūcō, -ere, -dūxī, -ductum* [KL3, W4]
profit *frūctus, -ūs (m)* [KL1, L25]
promise (verb) *polliceor, -ērī, ——, pollicitus sum* [KL3, L7]
promise (noun, formal) *reprōmissiō, -ōnis (f)* [KL3, W12]
proper (it is proper) *decet, -ēre, ——, decuit (impers. + acc.)* [KL3, L1]
property *substantia, -ae (f)* [KL3, L13]
prophecy *carmen, -inis (n)* [KL1, L13]; *ōrāculum, -ī (n)* [KL1, W31; KL2, W6]; *fātum, -ī (n)* [KL1, L5; KL2, 13]
prophesy *praedīcō, -ere, -dīxī, -dictum* [KL1, W31]
prophesy *canō, -ere, cecinī, cāntum* [KL2, L10]; *for, fārī, ——, fātus sum* [KL3, L3]
prophet *vātēs, -is (m)* [KL1, W31]; *prophēta, -ae (f)* [KL3, L4]; **(false)** *pseudoprophēta, -ae (f)* [KL3, W14]
prophetess *vātēs, -is (f)* [KL1, W31]
propitiation *propitiātiō, -ōnis (f)* [KL2, W11]
proposition *prōpositiō, -tiōnis (f)* [KL3, W1]
proud *superbus, -a, -um* [KL1, W18; KL2, L4]
prove *probō* [KL3, L14]
provided that *dum, dummodo* [KL2, L11]
providence *prōvidentia, -ae (f)* [KL2, W9]
province *prōvincia, -ae (f)* [KL3, W10]
provision *prōvidentia, -ae (f)* [KL2, W9]
prow *prōra, -ae (f)* [KL2, W13]
pull *stringō, -ere, strinxī, strictum* [KL3, W7]; **(pluck)** *vellō, -ere, vulsī/vellī, vulsum* [KL3, W1]
punishment *poena, -ae (f)* [KL1, L27]
pure *castus, -a, -um* [KL3, W9]
purple *purpureus, -a, -um* [KL1, L17]

purplish-blue *hyacinthinus, -a, -um* [KL1, L17]
pursue *persequor, -sequī, ——, -secutus sum (deponent)* [KL1, W32; KL2, W6]
push (back) *repellō, -ere, reppulī, repulsum* [KL3, W2]
put *pōnō, -ere, posuī, positum* [KL1, L26]
put (in) *inficiō, -ere, -fēcī, -fectum* [KL3, W2]; **(on)** *impōnō, -ere, -posuī, -positum* [KL2, W13]; *induō, -ere, -duī, dūtum* [KL2, L14]; **(out)** *rēstinguō, -ere, -stinxī, -stinctum* [KL3, W3]
putting on *impositiō, -ōnis (f)* [KL3, W7]
pyre *pyra, -ae (f)* [KL1, W8]

Q

quake *tremō, -ere, -uī, ——* [KL1, W25]
queen *rēgīna, -ae (f)* [KL1, L2]
quick *celer, celeris, celere* [KL1, L19]
quickly *cito* [KL1, L27]
quiet *placidus, -a, -um* [KL1, W29]; *tranquillus, -a, -um* [KL3, W9]

R

rabbit (hare) *lepus, -oris (m)* [KL3, W2]
race *certāmen, -minis (n)* [KL1, W23]; *genus, -neris (n)* [KL2, L13]
rain *imber, -bris (m)* [KL2, W9]; *pluvia, -ae (f)* [KL2, L9]
rainbow *arcus, -ūs (m)* [KL1, L27]
raise *tollō, -ere, sustulī, sublātum* [KL1, W25]
raise (up) *levō* [KL3, W1]; *tollō, -ere, sustulī, sublātum* [KL1, W25; KL2, L13]; **(from death)** *suscitō* [KL3, W5]
ram *ariēs, -ietis (m)* [KL1, W32]
randomly *temere* [KL3, W15]
rashly *temere* [KL3, W15]
rather *immō* [KL3, W7]; *magis* [KL2, L7]; *potius* [KL3, L7]; *priusquam* [KL3, L15]
ravage *vexō (1)* [KL1, L19]
rave *furō, -ere, -uī, ——* [KL2, W13]

reach perveniō, -īre, -vēnī, -ventum [KL2, L11]
read legō, -ere, lēgī, lēctum [KL1, L28]
receive accipiō, -ere, -cēpī, ceptum [KL1, L31]
recent recēns, -centis [KL2, W11]
reciprocally invicem [KL1, W26]
recount narrō (1) [KL1, L2]
red ruber, -bra, -brum [KL1, L17]; rūfus, -a, -um [KL1, W32]; **(dark-red)** purpureus, -a, -um [KL1, L17]
reed calamus, -ī (m) [KL1, W28]
relieve excipiō, -ere, -cēpī, -ceptum [KL3, W2]
reading lectiō, -ōnis (f) [KL3, W9]
realize sentiō, -īre, sēnsī, sēnsum [KL3, L3]
reap metō, -ere, messuī, messum [KL2, W14]
rear tergum, -ī (n) [KL3, L6]
reason causa, -ae (f) [KL2, L15]
rebuke reprehendō, -ere, -hendī, -hensum [KL3, W13]
receive recipiō, -ere, -cēpī, -ceptum [KL3, L11]
redeemer salvātor, -ōris (m) [KL3, L5]
reed arundō, -inis (f) [KL3, W1]
refer referō, -ferre, -(t)tulī, -(l)lātum [KL3, W9]
regal rēgālis, -e [KL3, W10]
regard rēspiciō, -ere, -spēxī, -spectum [KL2, L14]
region arvum, -ī (n) [KL3, L15]; regiō, -ōnis (f) [KL3, W2]
reign regnō (1) [KL1, L6]
rein habēna, -ae (f) [KL3, W8]
rejoice gaudeō, -ēre, ——, gāvīsus sum [KL1, L22]; exultō [KL3, W9]
relate narrō (1) [KL1, L2]
religion religiō, -ōnis (f) [KL3, W7]
remain maneō, -ēre, mansī, mansum [KL1, L10]; permaneō, -ēre, -mansī, -mansum [KL3, L7]

remain near obsideō, -ēre, -sēdī, -sessum [KL1, L10]
remaining reliquus, -a, -um [KL2, L6]
remake reficiō, -ere, -fēcī, -fectum [KL1, W29; KL3, W2]
remembering memor, -oris [KL3, L9]
remembrance memoria, -ae (f) [KL3, L2]
remission remissiō, -ōnis (f) [KL3, W5]
remove auferō, -ferre, abstulī, ablatum (3rd conj. irreg.) [KL1, W32]; removeō, -ēre, -mōvī, -mōtum [KL1, L14]; excipiō, -ere, -cēpī, -ceptum [KL3, W2]; remittō, -ere, -mīsī, -missum [KL3, L11]; **(myself)** auferō mē [KL3, L10]
replace succedō, -ere, -cessī, -cessum [KL3, W2]
reptile reptilis, -e [KL3, W4]
resist obsistō, -ere, -stitī, -stitum [KL3, W7]
rend scindō, -ere, scidī, scissum [KL3, L10]
repair reficiō, -ere, -fēcī, -fectum [KL1, W29; KL3, W2]
repeat repetō, -ere, -īvī/-iī, -ītum [KL3, W9]
repel repellō, -ere, reppulī, repulsum [KL3, W2]
repentance paenitentia, -ae (f) [KL3, W5]
report fāma, -ae (f) [KL2, L13]
reproach exprobrō (1) [KL1, W32]
reputation fāma, -ae (f) [KL2, L13]
request (verb) poscō, -ere, pōposcī, —— [KL3, W12]
request (noun) petītiō, -ōnis (f) [KL3, W16]
rescue ēripiō, -ere, -ripuī, -reptum [KL2, L3]
resolution prōpositiō, -tiōnis (f) [KL3, W1]
respect vereor, -ērī, ——, veritus sum [KL2, L6]
respond respondeō, -ēre, -spondī, -sponsum [KL1, L9]
rest (adj.) cēterus, -a, -um [KL2, L15]; **(of)** reliquus, -a, -um [KL2, L6]
rest (verb) quiēscō, -ere, quiēvī, quiētum [KL3, W7]; requiēscō, -ere, -quiēvī, -quiētum [KL3, L4]

restless turbulentus, -a, -um [KL3, W9]
restrain reprimō, -ere, -pressī, -pressum [KL3, W9]
restore restituō, -ere, -stituī, -stitutus [KL3, W1]
resume resūmō, -ere, -sūmpsī, -sūmptum [KL3, W16]
return redeō, -īre, -iī, -itum [KL3, L2]; revertor, -vertī, ——, reversus sum [KL2, L6]; regredior, -gredī, ——, -gressus sum [KL3, L10]
reveal exprōmō, -ere, -mpsī, -mptum [KL2, W15]; manifestō [KL2, W8]; revēlō [KL3, W9]
revere metuō, -ere, -uī, -ūtum [KL3, L15]
reverence (verb) vereor, -ērī, ——, veritus sum [KL2, L6]
reverence (noun) religiō, -ōnis (f) [KL3, W7]
revive restituō, -ere, -stituī, -stitutus [KL3, W1]
reward praemium, -ī (n) [KL1, W27]
riches dīvitiae, -ārum (f, pl) [KL1, L2]
riddle enigma, -matis (n) [KL1, W19]
ride vehō, -ere, vexī, vectum [KL1, L27]
right (adj.) iūstus, -a, -um [KL1, L7]
right (verb, it is right) decet, -ēre, ——, decuit (impers. + acc.) [KL3, L1]
right (noun) iūs, iūris (n) [KL2, L15]
right(-handed) dexter, -tra, -trum (or -tera, -terum) [KL1, L30]
righteous iūstus, -a, -um [KL1, L7; KL3, L7]
righteousness iūstitia, -ae (f) [KL3, L12]
ring ānulus, -ī (m) [KL3, W10]
rise surgō, -ere, surrēxī, surrēctum [KL1, L28]; orior, -īrī, ——, ortus sum [KL2, L6]
rise again resurgō, -ere, -surrēxī, -surrēctum [KL1, L29]
river flūmen, flūminis (n) [KL1, L13]
road iter, itineris (n) [KL1, L13]; via, -ae (f) [KL1, L11]

rock *saxum, -ī (n)* [KL1, L29]
rod *virga, -ae (f)* [KL3, L10]
roll *volvō, -ere, volvī, volūtum* [KL3, W1]
Roman (adj./noun) *Rōmānus, -a, -um* [KL2, L15]
Rome *Rōma, -ae (f)* [KL2, L14]
route *iter, itineris (n)* [KL1, L13]
row *versus, -ūs (m)* [KL1, L27]; *ōrdō, -dinis (m)* [KL2, L15]
royal court *aula, -ae (f)* [KL1, W13]
ruddy *ruber, -bra, -brum* [KL1, L17]; *rūfus, -a, -um* [KL1, W32]
ruin *perdō, -ere, perdidī, perditum* [KL1, L27]
rule (noun) *lēx, lēgis (f)* [KL2, L10]; *rēgula, -ae (f)* [KL3, W9]
rule (verb) *regnō (1)* [KL1, L6]; *regō, -ere, rexī, rectum* [KL1, L26]
ruin *subvertō, -ere, -vertī, -versus* [KL3, W7]
rumor *fāma, -ae (f)* [KL2, L13]
run *currō, -ere, cūcurrī, cursum* [KL1, L26]
run away *fugiō, -ere, fūgī, fugitum* [KL1, L31]
rush *properō (1)* [KL1, L20]
rush (down) *ruō, -ere, ruī, rutum* [KL3, L4]

S

Sabbath *sabbatum, -ī (n)* [KL3, L1]
sack *saccus, -ī (m)* [KL2, W6]
sacred *sanctus, -a, -um* [KL1, L25]; *sacer, -cra, -crum* [KL2, L3]
sacrifice *sacrificium, -iī (n)* [KL2, L4]
sad *amārus, -a, -um* [KL3, W9]; *flēbilis, -e* [KL3, W9]; *trīstis, -e* [KL1, L20; KL2, L3]
sad *trīstis, -e* [KL1, L20]
sadness *contrītio, -ōnis (f)* [KL3, W9]; *dolor, -ōris (m)* [KL3, L3]
safe *salvus, -a, -um* [KL1, L25]; *incolumis* [KL3, W2]; *tūtus, -a, -um* [KL3, L7]
safety *salūs, -ūtis (f)* [KL3, W7]

sail (noun) *vēlum, -ī (n)* [KL1, W30]
sail (verb) *nāvigō (1)* [KL1, L4]
sailor *nauta, -ae (m)* [KL1, L3]
salvation *salūs, -ūtis (f)* [KL3, W7]
same (the same) *īdem, eadem, idem* [KL3, L2]
same place (in the same place, to the same place/purpose) *eōdem* [KL3, L2]
sanctify *sanctificō* [KL3, L4]
sand *harēna, -ae (f)* [KL1, L3]
sandal *solea, -ae (f)* [KL2, W6]; **(winged)** *tālāria, -ium (n, pl)* [KL3, W16]
Satan *Satanās, -ae (f)* [KL3, W1]
satchel *pēra, -ae (f)* [KL1, W32]
satisfy *impleō, -ēre, -plēvī, -plētum* [KL2, L7]
Saul *Saul (indecl.)* [KL1, W32]
savage *barbarus, -a, -um* [KL1, L31]; *crūdēlis, -e* [KL3, L10]; *saevus, -a, -um* [KL2, W11]
save *conservō* [KL3, W15]; *servō (1)* [KL1, L6]
saved *salvus, -a, -um* [KL1, L25]
savior *salvātor, -ōris (m)* [KL3, L5]
say *āiō* [KL1, L14]; *dīcō, -ere, dīxī, dictum* [KL1, L26]; *for, fārī, ——, fātus sum* [KL3, L3]; *loquor, -quī, ——, locūtus sum* [KL2, L6]
say falsely *mentior, -īrī, ——, -ītus sum* [KL3, L6]
say no *negō* [KL3, L3]
scaly *squāmeus, -a, -um* [KL3, W6]
scarcely *vix* [KL3, L3]
scatter *spargō, -ere, sparsī, sparsum* [KL2, W9]; *sternō, -ere, strāvī, strātum* [KL2, L13]
scattered *fūsus, -a, -um* [KL3, W6]; *rārus, -a, -um* [KL3, W2]
schism *schisma, -ae (f)* [KL2, W8]
scream *ululō (1)* [KL1, L6]
scribe *scrība, -ae (f)* [KL3, L10]

sea *aequor, -oris (n)* [KL3, L6]; *sālum, -ī (n)* [KL3, W6]; *mare, maris (n)* [KL1, L18]
sea serpent *hydrus, -ī (m)*
seaside (adj.) *maritimus, -a, -um* [KL3, W2]
seat *sella, -ae (f)* [KL1, L31]; *solium, -iī (n)* [KL3, W10]
second (adj.) *alter, -era, -erum* [KL2, L4]; *secundus, -a, -um* [KL1, L23]
second (adv.; a second time) *iterum* [KL1, L25]
secretary *scrība, -ae (f)* [KL3, L10]
secret *sēcrētum, -ī (n)* [KL1, W28]
secretly *clam* [KL1, L29]
secure *tūtus, -a, -um* [KL3, L7]
see *videō, -ēre, vīdī, vīsum* [KL1, L9]
seek *petō, -ere, -īvī, -ītum* [KL2, L12]; *quaerō, -ere, quaesīvī, quaesītum (-situm)* [KL2, L3]; **(after)** *praeferō, -ferre, -tulī, -lātum* [KL2, L11]; **(again)** *repetō, -ere, -īvī/-iī, -ītum* [KL3, W9]
seize *capiō, -ere, cēpī, captum* [KL1, L31]; *occupō (1)* [KL1, L6]; *rapiō, -ere, rapuī, raptum* [KL1, L31]; *arripiō, -ere, -ripuī, -reptum* [KL3, W9]; *corripiō, -ere, -ripuī, -reptus* [KL3, W16]
-self (intensifying suffix on pers. pron.) *-met* [KL3, L7]
sell *vendō, -ere, -didī, -ditum* [KL3, W9]
senate *senātus, -ūs (m)* [KL3, W15]
send *mittō, -ere, mīsī, missum* [KL1, L26]
send (back) *remittō, -ere, -mīsī, -missum* [KL3, L11]; **(away)** *āmittō, -ere, -misī, -missum* [KL2, W6]; *dīmittō, -ere, -mīsī, -missum* [KL1, L30; KL2, W15]; **(forth)** *prōmittō, -ere, -mīsī, -missum* [KL3, W2]
sense *sensus, -ūs (m)* [KL2, L15]
sentence *sententia, -ae (f)* [KL3, L9]
separate (adj.) *singulī, -ae, -a* [KL2, L13]
separate (verb) *differō, -ferre, distulī, dīlātum* [KL3, W2]; *dīvidō, -ere, -vīsī, -vīsum* [KL2, W9]

271

serpent *anguis, -is (m)* [KL3, W5]; *serpēns, -pentis (m/f)* [KL2, W4]

servant *serva, -ae (f)* [KL1, L4]; *servus, -ī (m)* [KL1, L4]; *minister, -strī (m)* [KL3, L10]

serve *oboediō [obediō], -īre, -īvī, -ītum (+ dat.?)* [KL3, W5]; *serviō, -īre, -īvī, -ītum (+ dat.)* [KL2, L10]

set *collocō (1)* [KL1, W21]

set free *līberō (1)* [KL1, L1]; *solvō, -ere, solvī, solūtum* [KL2, L10]

set out *proficīscor, -ficīscī, ——, -fectus sum* [KL2, W7]

set up *cōnstituō, -ere, -stituī, -stitūtum* [KL2, L15]; *statuō, -ere, -uī, -ūtum* [KL2, W7]

seven *septem* [KL1, L21]

seventeen *septendecim* [KL1, L21]

seventeenth *septimus, -a, -um decimus, -a, -um* [KL1, L23]

seventh *septimus, -a, -um* [KL1, L23]

shade *umbra, -ae (f)* [KL3, L3]

shadow *umbra, -ae (f)* [KL3, L3]

shadows *tenēbrae, -ārum (f, pl)* [KL1, L11]

shake *nūtō* [KL3, W7]; *quatiō, -ere, quassī, quassus* [KL3, W5]; **(violently)** *quassō* [KL3, W1]; **(off)** *excutiō, -ere, -cussī, -cussum* [KL3, W3]; **(shiver)** *tremō, -ere, -uī, ——* [KL1, W25; KL3, W6]

shame *turpitūdō, -dinis (f)* [KL3, W9]

shape *forma, -ae (f)* [KL3, W16]; *faciēs, -ēī (f)* [KL1, L28]

share *commūnicō* [KL2, W6]

sharp *ācer, ācris, ācre* [KL1, L20]

sharp point *aciēs, -ēī (f)* [KL3, L14]

sharpness (esp. of sight) *aciēs, -ēī (f)* [KL3, L14]

shatter *frangō, -ere, frēgī, fractum* [KL1, L27]

shave *rādō, -ere, rāsī, rāsum* [KL3, W2]

she *is, ea, id* [KL1, L17]

shed *effundō, -ere, -fūdī, -fūsum* [KL3, L9]

sheep *ovis, ovis (f)* [KL2, L3]

shepherd *pastor, pastōris (m)* [KL1, L20]

shepherd (of/belonging to a shepherd) *pastorālis, -e* [KL3, W32]

shepherd's pipe *avēna, -ae (f)* [KL1, W21]

shield *clypeum, -ī (n)* [KL1, W32]; *scūtum, -ī (m)* [KL1, L10]; *clipeus (clypeus), -ī (m)* [KL3, W3]

shine *fulgeō, -ēre, fulsī, ——* [KL3, W13]; *lūceō, lūcēre, lūxī, ——* [KL1, L11]

ship *nāvis, -is (f)* [KL1, L18]; *alnus, -ī (f)* [KL1, L4]

shipwreck *naufragium, -ī (n)* [KL1, W23]

shiver *tremō, -ere, -uī, ——* [KL1, W25; KL3, W6]

shoot *petō, -ere, -īvī, -ītum* [KL1, W20]

shore *lītus, lītoris (n)* [KL1, L13]; *ōra, -ae (f)* [KL1, L13]

shoreline *lītus, lītoris (n)* [KL1, L13]

short *brevis, -e* [KL1, L19]

shortly *breviter* [KL3, W5]

shoulder *umerus, -ī (m)* [KL3, W3]

shout (noun) *clāmor, -oris (m)* [KL1, W20]

shout (verb) *clāmō (1)* [KL1, L1]

show *indicō* [KL3, L11]; *praebeō, -ēre, -uī, -ītum* [KL3, W7]; *ostendō, -ere, -dī, -sum/tum* [KL3, L5]

shrieking *ululātus, -ūs (m)* [KL3, W10]

shrine *templum, -ī (n)* [KL1, W25]

shun *vītō (1)* [KL1, L30]

shut (in/up) *claudō, -ere, clausī, clausum* [KL3, W15]; *inclūdō, -ere, -clūsī, -clūsum* [KL3, W6]

the Sibyl *Sibylla, -ae (f)* [KL2, W13]

Sicily *Sicilia, -ae (f)* [KL2, W5]

sick *aeger, -gra, -grum* [KL3, W5]

sickness *īnfirmitās, -tātis (f)* [KL3, W5]

side *lātus, -eris (n) pars, partis (f)* [KL2, L3]

siege *obsidiō, -ōnis (f)* [KL2, W15]

sight *cōnspectus, -ūs (m)* [KL2, L9]

sign *sīgnum, -ī (n)* [KL3, L4]; *prōdigium, -iī (n)* [KL3, W5]

signal *sīgnum, -ī (n)* [KL3, L4]

silence *silentium, -iī (n)* [KL3, W9]

silent (be silent) *taceō, ēre, -uī, -itum* [KL1, W26]; *conquiēscō, -ere, -quiēvī, -quiētum* [KL2, W9]; *conticēscō, -ere, -ticuī, ——* [KL3, W6]; *sileō, -ēre, -uī, ——* [KL3, W10]

Silenus *Sīlēnus, -ī (m)* [KL1, W27]

silver (adj.) *argenteus, -a, -um* [KL1, L17]

silver (noun) *argentum, -ī (n)* [KL1, L5]

similar *similis, -e* [KL2, L5]

sin (noun) *peccātum, -ī (n)*

sin (verb) *peccō* [KL3, L11]

sin *nefās (n, indecl.)* [KL3, W2]; *scelus, -leris (n)* [KL3, L6]

since *quandō* [KL1, L12]; *quia* [KL1, L18]; *quoniam* [KL1, L26]; *cum* [KL3, L7]

sing *cantō (1)* [KL1, L1]; *canō, -ere, cecinī, cāntum* [KL2, L10]; *cantitō* [KL3, W9]

singing *cantus, -ūs (m)* [KL1, L25]

single *sōlus, -a, -um* [KL1, W12]; *singulī, -ae, -a* [KL2, L13]

sinner *peccātor, -ōris (m)* [KL3, L5]; *peccātrīx, -trīcis (f)* [KL3, L5]

sink *cadō, -ere, cecidī, cāsūrum* [KL1, L27]

sister *germāna, -ae (f)* [KL1, L4]; *soror, sorōris (f)* [KL1, L12]

sit *sedeō, -ēre, sēdī, sessum* [KL1, L9]

six *sex* [KL1, L21]

sixteen *sēdecim* [KL1, L21]

sixteenth *sextus, -a, -um decimus, -a, -um* [KL1, L23]

sixth *sextus, -a, -um* [KL1, L23]

size (of such size) *tantus, -a, -um* [KL3, L5]

skilled *dexter, -tra, -trum (or -tera, -terum)* [KL1, L30]; *doctus, -a, -um* [KL1, L13]

skin *pellis, -is (f)* [KL3, W2]

sky *firmāmentum, -ī (n)* [KL3, W4]; *caelum, -ī (n)* [KL1, L5]

slander *maledīcō, -ere, -dīxī, -dictum (+ dat.)* [KL1, W30; KL3, L4]

slaughter *nex, necis (f)* [KL3, W10]

slave (noun) *serva, -ae (f)* [KL1, L4]; *servus, -ī (m)* [KL1, L4]

slave (verb, am a slave to) *serviō, -īre, -īvī, -ītum (+ dat.)* [KL2, L10]

slay *interficiō, -ere, -fēcī, -fectum* [KL1, L31]; *necō (1)* [KL1, L1]; *occīdō, -ere, -cīdī, -cīsum* [KL1, L30]

sleep *dormiō, -īre, -īvī, -ītum* [KL1, L29]; *somnus, -ī (n)* [KL3, W13]; **(deep)** *sopor, -ōris (m)* [KL3, W6]

slender *gracilis, -e* [KL2, L5]; *tenuis, -e* [KL2, L11]

sling *funda, -ae (f)* [KL1, W32]

slip *lābor, -ī, ——, lapsus sum* [KL2, L6]

small *brevis, -e* [KL1, L19]; *parvus, -a, -um* [KL1, L7]

small cake *crustulum, -ī (n)* [KL1, L5]

smaller *minor, -ārī, ——, -ātus sum* [KL2, W5]

smallest *minimus, -a, -um* [KL1, W31; KL2, L5]

smash *frangō, -ere, frēgī, fractum* [KL1, L27]

smile *rīdeō, -ēre, rīsī, rīsum* [KL1, L9]

smoke *fūmigō* [KL3, W1]

snake *anguis, -is (m)* [KL3, W5]; *serpēns, -pentis (m/f)* [KL2, W4]

snatch (away/from) *ēripiō, -ere, -ripuī, -reptum* [KL2, L3]

snare (noun) *fovea, -ae (f)* [KL3, W1]

snatch *rapiō, -ere, rapuī, raptum* [KL1, L31]

snow *nix, nivis (f)* [KL2, L9]

so great a number *tot (indecl. adj.)* [KL3, L9]

so great *tantus, -a, -um* [KL3, L5]

so greatly *tantum* [KL3, L14]

so *ita* [KL2, L6]; *sīc* [KL2, L4]; *tam* [KL3, L5]; *tantum* [KL3, L14]

so many *tot (indecl. adj.)* [KL3, L9]

so much *tam* [KL3, L5]; *tantum* [KL3, L14]

so that *ut (+ subj.)* [KL3, L5]

so...as *tam...quam* [KL3, L5]

social feast *convīvium, -iī (n)* [KL3, L10]

society *societās, -tātis (f)* [KL3, W11]

softly *leviter* [KL2, W6]

soil *humus, -ī (f)* [KL2, L14]

soldier *mīles, mīlitis (m)* [KL1, L12]

solitary *dēsertus, -a, -um* [KL3, L4]

solitude *sōlitūdō, -dinis (f)* [KL3, W9]

sole *ūnicus, -a, -um* [KL1, W22]

solo *canticum, -ī (n)* [KL3, L14]

some *aliquī, aliquae, aliquod (adj.)* [KL2, L12]; *quīdam, quaedam, quiddam (adj.)* [KL2, L12]

someone *aliquis, aliquid (pron.)* [KL2, L12]; *quīdam, quaedam, quiddam* [KL2, L12]; *quisquam, quidquam/quicquam* [KL3, L1]

something *aliquis, aliquid (pron.)* [KL2, L12]; *quīdam, quaedam, quiddam* [KL2, L12]; *quisquam, quidquam/quicquam* [KL3, L1]

son *fīlius, -ī (m)* [KL1, L4]

son (little) *fīliolus, -ī (m)* [KL3, W10]

song *cantus, -ūs (m)* [KL1, L25]; *carmen, -inis (n)* [KL1, L13]; *canticum, -ī (n)* [KL3, L14]

Song of Songs *Canticum Canticōrum* [KL3, L14]

soon *mox* [KL1, L15]

sooner *priusquam* [KL3, L15]

sooner than *antequam* [KL3, L15]

soothe (verb) *mītigō* [KL3, W7]

soothsayer *prophēta, -ae* [KL3, L4]

sorrow *lūctus, -ūs (m)* [KL3, W13]

sort (of what sort, of such a sort) *quālis* [KL3, L9]

sort *modus, -ī (m)* [KL3, L7]

soul *anima, -ae (f)* [KL2, L4]

sound (adj.) *salvus, -a, -um* [KL1, L25]

sound (noun) *sonitus, -ūs (m)* [KL3, W3]

source *fōns, fontis (m)* [KL2, L11]

sow (verb) *serō, -ere, sēvī, satum* [KL2, W11]

spare *parcō, -ere, pepercī, parsūrum (+ dat.)* [KL2, L13]

speak *dīcō, -ere, dīxī, dictum* [KL1, L26]; *ōrō (1) (takes double acc.)* [KL1, L6]; **for**, *fārī, ——, fātus sum* [KL3, L3]; *loquor, -quī, ——, locūtus sum* [KL2, L6]

speak ill of *maledīcō, -ere, -dīxī, -dictum (+ dat.)* [KL1, W30; KL3, L4]

speak well *benedīcō, -ere, -dīxī, -dictum (+ dat.)* [KL3, L4]

spear *hasta, -ae (f)* [KL1, L3]

species *speciēs, -ēī (f)* [KL3, W4]

speech *sermō, -ōnis (m)* [KL2, L9]

speedily *cito* [KL1, L27]

spend *consūmō, -ere, -sūmpsī, -sūmptum* [KL3, L2]

spin (wool) *neō, nēre, nēvī, nētus* [KL2, W14]

spine *spīna, -ae (f)* [KL1, W23]

spirit *spīritus, -ūs (m)* [KL1, L25]; *anima, -ae (f)* [KL2, L4]

spirit of the age *saeculum, -ī (n)* [KL1, L6]

spit out *expuō, -ere, -puī, -putum* [KL2, W8]

split *findō, -ere, fidī, fissum* [KL3, W16]

spoil *praeda, -ae (f)* [KL2, L15]

spray (verb) *spūmō* [KL3, W6]

spread (out) *sternō, -ere, strāvī, strātum* [KL2, L13]

spring (fountain) *fōns, fontis (m)* [KL2, L11]

spring (jump) *saliō, -īre, -uī, saltum* [KL1, W29; KL2, W12]

sprinkle *spargō, -ere, sparsī, sparsum* [KL2, W9]

sprout *germinō* [KL3, W4]

spurious *spurius, -a, -um* [KL1, W32]

staff *virga, -ae (f)* [KL3, L10]; *baculum, -ī (n)* [KL1, W32]

stag *cervus, -ī (m)* [KL1, L10]

stand *stō, stāre, stetī, statum* [KL1, L1]
stand (back/still) *resistō, -ere, -stitī, ——* [KL3, L2]; **(apart)** *distō* [KL3, W9]; **(in the way)** *obstō, -stāre, -stitī, -stātūrum (+ dat.)* [KL2, W11]; **(cause to)** *statuō, -ere, -uī, -ūtum* [KL2, W7]
star *stella, -ae* [KL1, L11]; *lūmināre, -āris (n)* [KL3, W4]; *sīdus, sīderis (n)* [KL3, L15]; **(evening)** *vesper, vesperis (m)* [KL1, L14]
start *proficīscor, -ficīscī, ——, -fectus sum* [KL3, W7]
starting gates (of a horse race) plural of *carcer, -eris (m)* [KL1, W23]
state *cīvitās, -tātis (f)* [KL2, L7]; **(USA)** *prōvincia, -ae (f)* [KL3, W10]
statue *simulacrum, -ī (n)* [KL1, W25]
steer *gubernō (1)* [KL1, L25]
step-mother *noverca, -ae (f)* [KL1, W22]
stick to *haereō, -ēre, haesī, haesum* [KL3, W3]
still *etiam* [KL1, L22]; *tamen* [KL1, L30]; *adhūc* [KL3, L12]
stillness *silentium, -iī (n)* [KL3, W9]
sting *mordeō, -ēre, momordī, morsum* [KL1, L9]
stone *lapis, -idis (m)* [KL1, W27; KL2, L14]
storm *tempestās, -tātis (f)* [KL1, L26]
stormy *turbulentus, -a, -um* [KL3, W9]
story *fābula, -ae (f)* [KL1, L2]
strange *barbarus, -a, -um* [KL1, L31]; *mīrus, -a, -um* [KL1, L7]
stranger *aliēnus, -a, -um* [KL2, L12]
stream *torrens, -ntis (m)* [KL1, W32]
strength *virtūs, virtūtis (f)* [KL1, L12]
street *platēa, -ae (f)* [KL3, L1]
stretch out *extendō, -ere, -tendī, -tensum* [KL1, W26]
strength *fortitūdō, -tudinis (f)* [KL2, L12]; *vīs, vīs (f)* [KL3, L5]
strength (verb: to gain strength) *convalēscō, -ere, -valuī, -valitus* [KL3, W9]

strengthen *confirmō* [KL3, W9]; *firmō* [KL3, W3]; *solidō* [KL2, W9]
stretch *tendō, -ere, tetendī, tentum* [KL2, L4]
strife *contentiō, -ōnis (f)* [KL3, W9]
strike *tangō, -ere, tetigī, tactum* [KL1, L27]; *pulsō* [K2L, W14]; **(through)** *percutiō, -ere, -cussī, -cussum* [KL1, W32; KL2, L3]
strike down *percutiō, -ere, -cussī, -cussum* [KL1, W32]
string *filum, -ī (n)* [KL1, W30]; *linea, -ae (f)* [KL3, W9]
strive *tendō, -ere, tetendī, tentum* [KL2, L4]
stroke (noun) *ictus, -ūs (m)* [KL3, W5]
strong *fortis, -e* [KL1, L19]
strongest *fortissimus, -a, -um* [KL1, W32]
student (female) *discipula, -ae (f)* & **(male)** *discipulus, -ī (m)* [KL1, L5]
stumbling block *scandalum, -ī (n)* [KL3, L12]
stunned (be) *stupeō, -ēre, -uī, ——* [KL3, W16]
subdue *domō, -āre, domuī, domitum* [KL1, L12]
substance *substantia, -ae (f)* [KL3, L13]
succeed *succēdō, -ere, -cessī, -cessum* [KL3, W2]
such (adj.) *iste, ista, istud* [KL1, L30]
such (of such a sort) (rel. adj.) *quālis* [KL3, L9]
such as (rel. adj.) *quālis* [KL3, L9]
such great *tantus, -a, -um* [KL3, L5]
such *tālis, -e* [KL3, L5]
sudden (adj.) *subitus, -a, -um* [KL3, W3]
suddenly *repentē* [KL1, L10]; *subitō/subitum* [KL3, L3]
suffer *expendō, -ere, -dī, -sum* [KL3, W6]; *patior, -ī, ——, passus sum* [KL2, L6]
suffering *miseria, -ae (f)* [KL3, W9]
suffice *sufficiō, -ere, -fēcī, -fectum* [KL2, W14]

sufficient(ly) *satis (adv. & indecl. adj./noun)* [KL1, L30]
suitable (verb: it is suitable) *decet, -ēre, ——, decuit (impers. + acc.)* [KL3, L1]
suitable (adj) *aptus, -a, -um* [KL3, W2]; *commodus, -a, -um* [KL3, W2]; *congruēns, -ntis* [KL3, W9]
sum(mary) *summa, -ae (f)* [KL2, W10]
summon *vocō (1)* [KL1, L1]
sun *sōl, sōlis (m)* [KL1, L12]
supply *cōpia, -ae (f)* [KL1, L15]
suppose *arbitror, -ārī, ——, -ātus sum* [KL3, L4]; *putō* [KL3, L3]; *reor, rērī, ——, ratus sum* [KL3, L16]
supine *resupīnus, -a, -um* [KL3, W7]
sure *certus, -a, -um* [KL3, L6]
surely *utique* [KL3, L12]
surely...not? *numquid* [KL2, L9]
surface (level surface) *aequor, -oris (n)* [KL3, L6]
surrender *trādō, -ere, -didī, -ditum* [KL1, W13; KL2, L4]
suspend *pendō, -ere, pependī, pensum* [KL3, L10]; *suspendō, -ere, -pendī, -pensum* [KL3, W5]
suspicious *suspīciōsus, -a, -um* [KL1, W21]
swamp *palus, palūdis (f)* [KL1, W13]
swear *iūrō* [KL2, L15]
sweet *dulcis, -e* [KL1, L19]
swift *celer, celeris, celere* [KL1, L19]
swim *nō (1)* [KL1, L14]
swimming pool *natātōria, -ae (f)* [KL2, W8]
sword *gladius, -ī (m)* [KL1, L4]; *ferrum, -ī (n)* [KL2, L15]
synagogue *synagōga, -ae (f)* [KL1, W26]

T

table *mensa, -ae (f)* [KL1, L31]
tail *cauda, -ae (f)* [KL1, W21]
take *accipiō, -ere, -cēpī, ceptum* [KL1, L31]; *capiō, -ere, cēpī, captum* [KL1, L31]

take away *removeō, -ēre, -mōvī, -mōtum* [KL1, L14]; *tollō, -ere, sustulī, sublātum* [KL1, W25; KL2, L13]

take an oath *iūrō* [KL2, L15]

take back/again *recipiō, -ere, -cēpī, -ceptum* [KL3, L11]; *referō, -ferre, -(t)tulī, -(l)lātum* [KL3, W9]

take for myself *adsūmō, -ere, -sumpsī, -sumptum* [KL1, W32]

take (up) *sumō, -ere, sūmpsī, sūmptum* [KL2, L10]; **(again)** *resūmō, -ere, -sūmpsī, -sūmptum* [KL3, W16]

tale *fābula, -ae (f)* [KL1, L2]

talk (noun) *sermō, -ōnis (m)* [KL2, L9]

tame *domō, -āre, domuī, domitum* [KL1, L12]

tax *tribūtum, -ī (n)* [KL1, W30]; *stīpendium, -iī (n)* [KL2, W15]

teach *doceō, -ēre, docuī, doctum* [KL1, L9]; *trādō, -ere, -didī, -ditum* [KL1, W13; KL2, L4]

teacher (female) *magistra, -ae (f)*/**(male)** *magister, -strī (m)* [KL1, L6]

teaching *doctrīna, -ae (f)* [KL3, L5]

tear (noun) *lacrima, -ae (f)* [KL3, L9]

tear (verb) *scindō, -ere, scidī, scissum* [KL3, L10]; *dīripiō, -ere, -ripuī, -reptum* [KL3, W1]; *dirumpō, -ere, -rūpī, -ruptum* [KL2, W14]

tease *lūdō, lūdere, lūsī, lūsum* [KL1, L26]

tell *narrō (1)* [KL1, L2]

temple *templum, -ī (n)* [KL1, W25; KL2, L10]

temptation *scandalum, -ī (n)* [KL3, L12]

ten *decem* [KL1, L21]

ten at a time *dēnī, -ae, -a* [KL3, W2]

tent *tabernāculum, -ī (n)* [KL1, W32]

tenth *decimus, -a, -um* [KL1, L23]

tepid *tepidus, -a, -um* [KL3, W16]

terrify *terreō, -ēre, -uī, -itum* [KL1, L9]

territory *prōvincia, -ae (f)* [KL3, W10]; *regiō, -ōnis (f)* [KL3, W2]

test *probō* [KL3, L14]

testify *testificor, -ārī, ——, -ātus sum* [KL3, W14]; *testor, -ārī, ——, -ātus sum* [KL3, W11]

testimony *testimōnium, -ī (n)* [KL2, L10]

text (noun) *lectiō, -ōnis (f)* [KL3, W9]

than *quam* [KL1, L28]

thank *grātiās agō (+ dat.)* [KL1, L27]

thanks *grātia, -ae (f)* [KL1, L27]

that (pron.) *quī*; **(conj.)** *quia* [KL1, L18]; *quoniam* [KL1, L26]; *ut (+ subj.)* [KL3, L5]

that (of yours) *iste, ista, istud* [KL1, L30]

that (adj./pron.) *ille, illa, illud* [KL1, L30]; *is, ea, id* [KL1, L17]

that (conj.) *quia* [KL1, L18]; *quod* [KL1, L10]

that not *nē* [KL3, L4]

their (own) *suus, -a, -um* [KL1, W31; KL3, L2]

themselves *suī* [KL3, L2]

then (therefore) *igitur* [KL2, L9]; *tunc* [KL2, L4]; *deinde* [KL1, L22]; *ergo (adv.)* [KL1, L18]; **(of time)** *ibī* [KL1, L5]; *ōlim* [KL1, L6]; *tum* [KL1, L15]

thence *illinc* [KL2, L11]; *inde*

there *ibī* [KL1, L5]; *illīc* [KL2, L11]

therefore *ergo (adv.)* [KL1, L18]; *itaque* [KL1, L2]; *ideo* [KL2, L14]; *igitur* [KL2, L9]; *īta* [KL2, L6]

thereupon *deinde* [KL1, L22]; *tum* [KL1, L15]; *tunc* [KL2, L4]

these *plural of hic, haec, hoc* [KL1, L30]

Theseus *Thēsēus, -eī (m)* [KL1, W30]

they *is, ea, id* [KL1, L9]

thick *crēber, -bra, -brum* [KL3, L2]

thin *gracilis, -e* [KL2, L5]; *rārus, -a, -um* [KL3, W2]; *tenuis, -e* [KL2, L11]

thing *rēs, reī (f)* [KL1, L28]

think *cōgitō (1)* [KL1, L6]; *arbitror, -ārī, ——, -ātus sum* [KL3, L4]; *putō* [KL3, L3]; *reor, rērī, ——, ratus sum* [KL3, L16]

think about *considerō* [KL2, W14]

third *tertius, -a, -um* [KL1, L23]

thirst (verb) *sitiō, -īre, -īvī, ——* [KL2, L12]

thirteen *tredecim* [KL1, L21]

thirteenth *tertius, -a, -um decimus, -a, -um* [KL1, L23]

this *hic, haec, hoc* [KL1, L30]; *is, ea, id* [KL1, L17]

thither *illūc* [KL2, L11]

those *plural of ille, illa, illud* [KL1, L30]

though *etsi* [KL3, W2]

thought *cōgitātiō, -tiōnis (f)* [KL3, L1]; *sententia, -ae (f)* [KL3, L9]

thousand *mīlle* [KL1, L21]

thousandth (one thousandth) *mīllēsimus, -a, -um* [KL1, L23]

thread *filum, -ī (n)* [KL1, W30]

threaten *comminor, -ārī, ——, -ātus sum* [KL3, W1]; *minor, -ārī, ——, -ātus sum* [KL2, W5]

three *trēs, tria* [KL1, L21]

three times *ter* [KL3, W5]

threshold *līmen, -minis (n)* [KL3, L3]

throat *faucēs, -ium (f, pl)* [KL3, W3]

throne *solium, -iī (n)* [KL3, W10]

throng *turba, -ae (f)* [KL1, L2]

through *per (+ acc.)* [KL1, L3]

throw *iaciō, -ere, iēcī, iactum* [KL1, L31]

throw down *dēiciō, -icere, -iēcī, -iectum* [KL1, W23]

throw (out) *ēiciō, -ere, -iēcī, -iectum* [KL2, L14]; **(to)** *adiciō, -ere, -iēcī, -iectum* [KL2, W14]; **(into/onto)** *iniciō, -ere, -iēcī, -iectum* [KL2, W15]; **(back)** *rēiciō, -ere, -iēcī, -iectum* [KL3, W7]; **(under)** *sūbiciō, -ere, -iēcī, -iectum* [KL3, W4]

thunder (noun) *tonitrus, -ūs (m)* [KL1, L25]

thunder (verb) *intonō, -āre, -uī/-āvī, ——* [KL3, W3]

thus *īta* [KL2, L6]; *sīc* [KL2, L4]

timber *māteria, -ae (f)* [KL3, W2]

tie *vinciō, -īre, vīnxī, vīnctum* [KL1, L30]

tie up *alligō* [KL3, W1]; *implicō* [KL3, W5]; *ligō* [KL3, W16]; **(back/up)** *religō* [KL3, W16]

tiger *tigris, tigridis (m/f)* [KL1, L12]

time *tempus, temporis (n)* [KL1, L13]

time of life *aetās, -tātis (f)* [KL2, L14]

times (the times) *saeculum, -ī (n)* [KL1, L6]

tip *summitās, -tātis (f)* [KL2, W10]

tired *fessus, -a, -um* [KL1, L20, KL3, W6]; *lassus, -a, -um* [KL3, W3]

tire out *dēfatīgō* [KL3, W2]; *fatigō* [KL2, W12]

Tmolus *Tmōlus, -ī (m)* [KL1, W28]

to *ad (+ acc.)* [KL1, L3]

to that place *illūc* [KL2, L11]

to the same place *eōdem* [KL3, L2]

to the same purpose *eōdem* [KL3, L2]

to this place *adhūc* [KL3, L12]; *hūc* [KL2, L11]

to *ut (+ subj.)* [KL3, L5]

to what/which place (?) *quō (?)* [KL2, L11]

today *hodiē* [KL1, L2]

together (all together) (adj.) *ūniversus, -a, -um* [KL3, L4]; **(adv.)** *simul* [KL2, L9]

together (prep.) *ūnā* [KL1, L29]

toil (noun) *labor, labōris (m)* [KL1, L28]

tomb *sepulcrum, -ī (n)* [KL2, L13]; *tumulus, -ī (m)* [KL2, W11]

tomorrow (adj.) *crastinus, -a, -um* [KL2, W14]; **(adv.)** *crās* [KL1, L6]

tomorrow (adv.) *crās* [KL1, L6]

tongue *lingua, -ae (f)* [KL1, L26]

too (also) *quoque* [KL1, L29]

too (much) *nimis* [KL3, L4]; *nimium* [KL2, W13]

too little *parum* [KL2, L7]

top *summa, -ae (f)* [KL2, W10]; *summitās, -tātis (f)* [KL2, W10]

topics [in a book] *loca (n, pl)* [KL2, L7]

torrent *torrens, -ntis (m)* [KL1, W32]

touch (noun) *tactus, -ūs (m)* [KL1, W28]

touch (verb) *tangō, -ere, tetigī, tactum* [KL1, L27]

toward *ad (+ acc.)* [KL1, L3]

tower *turris, turris (f)* [KL1, L18]

town *oppidum, -ī (n)* [KL1, L5]

track *vestīgium, -iī (n)* [KL2, W11]

tragedy *tragoedia, -ae (f)* [KL1, W4]

train *exerceō, -ēre, -uī, -itum* [KL1, L14]

trample *conculcō* [KL2, W14]

transfer *trānsferō, -ferre, -tūlī, -lātum* [KL3, L13]

transgress *peccō* [KL3, L11]

translate *trānsferō, -ferre, -tūlī, -lātum* [KL3, L13]

trap *fovea, -ae (f)* [KL3, W1]

traverse *mētior, -īrī, —, mēnsus sum* [KL2, L14]

treasure *thēsaurus, -ī (m)* [KL3, L11]

treaty *foedus, -deris (n)* [KL2, L12]

tree *arbor, arboris (f)*; *lignum, -ī (n)* [KL2, L13]; **(trunk)** *trabēs, -is (m)* [KL2, W14]; **(elm)** *abiēs, -etis (f)* [KL3, W2]; **(beach)** *fāgus, -ī (f)* [KL3, W2]; **(fig)** *fīcus, -ī (f)* [KL3, W8]

trek *iter, itineris (n)* [KL1, L13]

tremble *paveō, -ēre, pavī, —* [KL3, L15]; *tremō, -ere, -uī, —* [KL1, W25; KL3, W6]

trial *iūdicium, -ī (n)* [KL2, L9]

tribe *gens, -ntis (f)* [KL1, L31]

tribunal *tribūnal, -ālis (n)* [KL2, W15]

tribute *tribūtum, -ī (n)* [KL1, W30]

trick *lūdō, lūdere, lūsī, lūsum* [KL1, L26]

trickle *mānō* [KL3, W16]

triumph *triumphō* [KL3, W9]

troops *plural of cōpia, -ae (f)* [KL1, L15]

trouble (verb) *turbō* [KL2, W13]

troubled *sollicitus, -a, -um* [KL2, W14]

troy *Troia, -ae (f)* [KL2, W4]

true *vērus, -a, -um* [KL1, L22; KL2, W13]

truly *enim (postpositive conj.)* [KL1, L17]; *vērō* [KL2, L15]

trust (verb) *confīdō, -ere, —, confīsus sum (+ dat.) (semi-deponent)* [KL2, L6]

trust (noun) *fīdūcia, -ae (f)* [KL3, L7]

trustworthy *fīdus, -a, -um* [KL1, L7]

truth *vēritas, -tātis (f)* [KL1, L27]

try *cōnor, -ārī, —, cōnātus sum* [KL2, L6]; *probō* [KL3, L14]; *temptō* [KL1, W27; KL3, L7]

tub *lacus, -ūs (m)* [KL1, L27]

turban *mītra, -ae (f)* [KL1, W28]

turbulent *turbulentus, -a, -um* [KL3, W9]

turn (around) *vertō, -ere, vertī, versum* [KL1, L28; KL2, L11]; **(around/back)** *convertō, -ere, -vertī, -versum* [KL3, L9]; **(around/over)** *volvō, -ere, volvī, volūtum* [KL3, W1]; **(back)** *revertor, -vertī, —, reversus sum* [KL2, L6]

turning-post *mēta, -ae (f)* [KL1, W23]

turret *turris, turris (f)* [KL1, L18]

in turn (adv.) *deinceps* [KL3, W2]

twelfth *duodecimus, -a, -um* [KL1, L23]

twelve *duodecim* [KL1, L21]

twelve times *duodēnī, -ae, -a* [KL3, W2]

twentieth *vīcēsimus, -a, -um* [KL1, L23]

twenty *vīgintī* [KL1, L21]

twenty-first *vīcēsimus, -a, -um prīmus, -a, -um* [KL1, L23]

twenty-one *vīgintī ūnus, -a, -um (ūnus et vīgintī)* [KL1, L21]

twice *bis* [KL3, L6]

twin *geminus, -ī (m)* [KL1, L10]

two *duo, duae, duo* [KL1, L21]

twofold *bis* [KL3, L6]

U

ugliness *turpitūdō, -dinis (f)* [KL3, W9]

ugly *foedus, -a, -um* [KL1, L7]

Ulysses *Ulixēs, -is (m)* [KL2, W5]

unavoidable *necesse (n, indecl.)* [KL3, L1]

uncertain *incertus, -a, -um* [KL2, W11]

uncircumcised *incircumcisus, -a, -um* [KL1, W32]

uncle (father's brother) *patruus, -ī (m)* [KL1, L22]; **(mother's brother)** *avunculus, -ī (m)* [KL1, L22]

unclean *immundus, -a, -um* [KL3, L5]

unconquered *invīctus, -a, -um* [KL3, W13]

under *sub (+ acc.)* [KL1, L24]; *īnfrā* [KL3, W16]

under(neath) *sub (+ abl.)* [KL1, L14]

understand *intellegō, -ere, -lēxī, -lēctum* [KL3, L2]

understanding *sensus, -ūs (m)* [KL2, L15]

undertake *ingredior, -gredī, ——, -gressus sum* [KL2, L6]; *mōlior, -īrī, ——, mōlītus sum* [KL2, L6]

undertook *coepī, coepisse, ——, coeptum (defective)* [KL3, L1]

undeserved *inmeritus, -a, -um* [KL3, W16]

unexpectedly *subitō/subitum* [KL3, L3]

unfairness *inīquitās, -tātis (f)* [KL2, L10]

unfortunate *infēlix, (gen.) -līcis* [KL1, L19]

ungodliness *impietās, -tātis (f)* [KL3, W7]

unhappy *miser, -era, -erum* [KL1, L7]

unhurt *incolumis* [KL3, W2]; *intāctus, -a, -um* [KL2, W15]; *inviolātus, -a, -um* [KL3, W1]

unimportant *parvus, -a, -um* [KL1, L7]

uninjured *incolumis* [KL3, W2]; *intāctus, -a, -um* [KL2, W15]; *inviolātus, -a, -um* [KL3, W1]

unite *iungō, -ere, iūnxī, iūnctum* [KL1, L27]; *coniungō, -ere, -iūnxī, -iūnctum* [KL3, L9]

universe *mundus, -ī (m)* [KL1, L6]

unjust *iniūstus, -a, -um* [KL3, W16]

unless *nisi* [KL3, L11]

unlike *dissimilis, -e* [KL2, L5]

unlucky *infēlix, (gen.) -līcis* [KL1, L19]

unsure *incertus, -a, -um* [KL2, W11]

until now *adhūc* [KL3, L12]

until *antequam* [KL3, L15]; *dōnec* [KL3, W3]; *dum/dummodo* [KL2, L11]; *priusquam* [KL3, L15]; *quamdiu* [KL3, L9]; *quoad* [KL2, W15]

untouched *intāctus, -a, -um* [KL2, W15]; *integer, -tēgra, -tēgrum* [KL3, W2]

unveil *revēlō* [KL3, W9]

unwilling (am unwilling) *nōlō, nōlle, nōluī, ——* [KL2, L14]

unworthiness *indīgnitās, -tātis (f)* [KL2, W15]

up under *sub (+ acc.)* [KL1, L14]

upper arm *umerus, -ī (m)* [KL3, W3]

upright *iūstus, -a, -um* [KL1, L7; KL3, L7]

urn *urna, -ae (f)* [KL2, W11]

use *ūtor, ūtī, ——, ūsus sum (+ abl.)* [KL3, L2]

V

vacant *vacuus, -a, -um* [KL3, W4]

vain (in vain) *frustrā* [KL3, L3]

vale *vallēs, vallis (f)* [KL1, L18]

valley *vallēs, vallis (f)* [KL1, L18]

vast *ingēns, (gen.) -entis* [KL1, L19]; *vastus, -a, -um* [KL2, L6]

vehement *vehemens, -mentis* [KL2, W9]

veil *vēlāmen, -minis (n)* [KL2, W11]

venom *venēnum, -ī (n)* [KL1, L10; KL3, W6]

very (adv.) *māximē* [KL2, L7]; *valdē* [KL2, L10]; **(the very, adj.)** *ipse, ipsa, ipsum* [KL2, L3]

very much *magnoperē* [KL1, L29]

vessel *vās, vāsis (n)* [KL3, W1]

vex *vexō (1)* [KL1, L19]

vibrate *vibrō* [KL3, W6]

victor *victor, -toris (m)* [KL2, W13]

victory *victōria, -ae (f)* [KL1, L11]

view *cōnspectus, -ūs (m)* [KL2, L9]

vigorous *viridis, -e* [KL1, L17]

violate *violō* [KL3, W1]

violence *vīs, vīs (f)* [KL3, L5]

violent *vehemens, -mentis* [KL2, W9]

violet *hyacinthinus, -a, -um* [KL1, L17]; **(dark-violet)** *purpureus, -a, -um* [KL1, L17]

visible (am visible) *appareō, -ēre, -uī, -itum (+ dat.)* [KL3, L4]

voice *vōx, vōcis (f)* [KL1, L14]

void *vacuus, -a, -um* [KL3, W4]

vow *iūrō* [KL2, L15]

W

wage war *bellum gerō* [KL1, L28]

wailing *planctus, -ūs (m)* [KL3, W8]; *ululātus, -ūs (m)* [KL3, W10]

wait for *exspectō (1)* [KL1, L3]

walk *ambulō (1)* [KL1, L1]

wall *mūrus, -ī (m)* [KL2, L11]

walls (city walls) *moenia, -ium (n, pl)* [KL1, L18]

wander *errō (1)* [KL1, L14]

want instead *mālō, mālle, māluī, ——* [KL2, L14]

want more *mālō, mālle, māluī, ——* [KL2, L14]

want *volō/velle, voluī, ——, ——* [KL2, L14]

war *bellum, -ī (n)* [KL1, L15]

warm *caldus, -a, -um* [KL1, L7]; *tepidus, -a, -um* [KL3, W16]

warn *moneō, -ēre, -uī, -itum* [KL1, L9]; *admoneō, -ēre, -uī, -itum* [KL3, W9]; *praecipiō, -ere, -cēpī, -ceptum* [KL3, W5]

warrior *bellator, -toris (m)* [KL1, W32]

wash *lavō, -āre, lāvī, lōtum/lavātum* [KL1, W27; KL2, L11]

watch (noun) *custōs, -ōdis (m/f)* [KL3, L3]

watch (verb) *spectō (1)* [KL1, L1]; *custōdiō, -īre, -iī/-īvī, -ītum* [KL3, L3]; *observō* [KL3, W11]

watchman *custōs, -ōdis (m/f)* [KL3, L3]

water *aqua, -ae (f)* [KL1, L2]

wave *unda, -ae (f)* [KL1, L10]

way *via, -ae (f)* [KL1, L11]; *modus, -ī (m)* [KL3, L7]

we *nōs (pl.)* [KL1, L17]
weak *īnfīrmus, -a, -um* [KL3, W5]
weakness *īnfīrmitās, -tātis (f)* [KL3, W5]
wealth *dīvitiae, -ārum (f, pl)* [KL1, L2]
weapon *tēlum, -ī (n)* [KL3, L6]
weapons *arma, -ōrum (n, pl)* [KL1, W32; KL2, L3]
wear *induō, -ere, -duī, dūtum* [KL2, L14]
weary *fessus, -a, -um* [KL1, L20]
weather *tempestās, -tātis (f)* [KL1, L26]
weave *neō, nēre, nēvī, nētus* [KL2, W14]
wedding *nūptiālis, -e* [KL2, W2]
weep *fleō, -ēre, flēvī, flētum* [KL1, L14]
weeping *flētus, -ūs (m)* [KL3, W9]
weigh *pendō, -ere, pependī, pensum* [KL3, L10]
weight *onus, oneris (n)* [KL1, L13]; *gravitās, -tātis (f)* [KL3, W2]
well (adj.) *salvus, -a, -um* [KL1, L25]
well (adv.) *bene* [KL1, L1]
well (noun) *puteus, -ī (m)* [KL2, L12]
well (verb; be well) *salveō, -ēre, —, —* [KL1, L9]; *valeō, -ēre, valuī, valitūrum* [KL1, L9]
west (sunset) *vesper, vesperis (m)* [KL1, L14]
wet (sopping) *aquōsus, -a, -um* [KL1, W29]
what *quī, quae, quod* [KL2, L3]; **(what?)** *quis, quid* [KL2, L9]
what? *quid* [KL1, W19]
what kind of (interrog. adj.) *quālis* [KL3, L9]; **(what kind of?)** *quī? quae? quod?* [KL2, L9]
whatever *quīcumque, quaecumque, quodcumque* [KL2, L12]; *quisquis, quidquid (quicquid) (pron.)* [KL2, L12]
whatsoever *quīcumque, quaecumque, quodcumque* [KL2, L12]
when *cum; ut (+ indic.)* [KL3, L5]
when (?) *quandō* [KL1, L12]; *ubi* [KL1, L12]
whence (?) *unde* [KL2, L11]
where (?) *ubi* [KL1, L12]; *quō* [KL2, L11]

wherefore (?) *quārē* [KL3, L9]
whether *ūtrum* [KL2, L15]
whether...or *sīve/seū... sīve/seū* [KL1, L30]
which (of two)? *uter, utra (ūtra), utrum (ūtrum) (interrog.)* [KL2, L15]
which *quī, quae, quod* [KL2, L3]; **(which?)** *quī?, quae?, quod?* [KL2, L9]
whichever (of two) *uter, utra (ūtra), utrum (ūtrum) (interrog.)* [KL2, L15]
whichever *quīcumque, quaecumque, quodcumque* [KL2, L12]; *quisquis, quidquid (quicquid) (pron.)* [KL2, L12]
whichsoever *quīcumque, quaecumque, quodcumque* [KL2, L12]
while *cum* [KL3, L7]; *dum, dummodo* [KL2, L11]; *dōnec* [KL3, W3]
whither (?) *quō* [KL2, L11]
whirlwind *turbō* [KL2, W13]
whisper *susurrō (1)* [KL1, W28]
whistling *sībilus, -a, -um* [KL3, W6]
white (dead) *albus, -a, -um* [KL1, L17]; **(glittering)** *candidus, -a, -um* [KL1, L17]
who *quī, quae, quod* [KL3, L6]; **(who?)** *quis* [KL1, W31]
who (?) *quis* [KL1, W31]
whoever *quīcumque, quaecumque, quodcumque* [KL2, L12]; *quisquis, quidquid (quicquid) (pron.)* [KL2, L12]
whole *tōtus, -a, -um* [KL2, L3]; *ūniversus, -a, -um* [KL3, L4]
wholly *omnīnō* [KL3, L5]
whosoever *quīcumque, quaecumque, quodcumque* [KL2, L12]
why *cūr* [KL1, L2]; *quō (?)* [KL2, L11]; *quārē* [KL3, L9]
wicked *improbus, -a, -um* [KL1, L29]; *impius, -a, -um* [KL3, L1]; *malignus, -a, -um* [KL3, L13]
wickedness *malitia, -ae (f)* [KL2, L14]
wide *lātus, -a, -um* [KL1, L20]
widow *vidua, -ae (f)* [KL1, L22]
widowed *viduāta, -ae* [KL1, W19]

width *lātitūdō, -dinis (f)* [KL2, W9]
wife *coniūnx, -iugis (f)* [KL1, L22]; *uxor, -ōris (f)* [KL1, L30]
wild *ferus, -a, -um* [KL1, L7]
wilderness *dēserta, -ōrum (n, pl)* [KL3, L4]
will (noun) *voluntās, -tātis (f)* [KL3, L12]
will (verb) *volō/velle, voluī, —, —* [KL2, L14]
wind *ventus, -ī (m)* [KL1, W28; KL3, W16]; **(breath)** *anima, -ae (f)* [KL2, L4]
window *fenestra, -ae (f)* [KL1, L31]
wine *vīnum, -ī (n)* [KL1, L5]
wing *āla, -ae (f)* [KL1, L10]; *penna, -ae (f)* [KL3, W16]
winged *pennātus, -a, -um* [KL2, W6]; *volātilis, -e* [KL3, W4]
wisdom *cōnsilium, -iī (n)* [KL1, L30]; *sapientia, -ae (f)* [KL2, L10]
wise *doctus, -a, -um* [KL1, L13]; *sapiēns, -entis* [KL2, L4]
wish (noun) *voluntās, -tātis (f)* [KL3, L12]
wish (for) *cupiō, -ere, cupīvī, cupītum* [KL1, L31]; *volō/velle, voluī, —, —* [KL2, L14]
with *apud* [KL2, L4]; *cum* [KL3, L7]; *cum (+ abl.)* [KL1, L9]
withdraw *auferō mē* [KL3, L10]; *sēcēdō, -ere -cessī, -cessum* [KL3, W1]
withered *āridus, -a, -um* [KL1, L27]
within *intrā (prep. + acc.; adv.)* [KL2, L15]
without *sine (+ abl.)* [KL1, L9]
without (am without) *careō, -ēre, -uī, -itum (+ abl.)* [KL3, L6]
witness (noun) *testimōnium, -ī (n)* [KL2, L10]; *testis, -is (m)* [KL3, L5]
witness (verb) *testificor, -ārī, —, -ātus sum* [KL3, W14]; *testor, -ārī, —, -ātus sum* [KL3, W11]
woad *vitrum, -ī (n)* [KL2, W2]
woman *fēmina, -ae* [KL1, L2]; *mulier, mulieris (f)* [KL1, L22]; **(young woman)** *virgō, virginis (f)* [KL1, L12]

womb *uterus, -ī (m)* [KL2, W9]

wonder *prōdigium, -iī (n)* [KL3, W5]

wonderful *mīrus, -a, -um* [KL1, L7]; *mīrābilis, -e* [KL3, L3]

wood *līgnum, -ī (n)* [KL2, L13]

wooden *līgneus, -a, -um* [KL3, W6]

word *verbum, -ī* [KL1, L5]

work (noun) *labor, labōris (m)* [KL1, L12]; *opus, operis (n)* [KL2, L3]

work (verb) *labōrō (1)* [KL1, L22]; *operor, -ārī, ——, operātus sum* [KL2, L6]

worker *faber, -brī (m)* [KL3, W2]

world *mundus, -ī (m)* [KL1, L6]

worldly goods *substantia, -ae (f)* [KL3, L13]

worse (adj.) *pēior* [KL2, L5]

worse (adv.) *pēius* [KL2, L5]

worship *colō, -ere, coluī, cultum* [KL1, L29]; *adōrō* [KL2, W8]

worst (adj.) *pessimus, -a, -um* [KL2, L5]

worst (adv.) *pessimē* [KL2, L7]

worthless *vīlis, -e* [KL2, W15]

worthy (adj.) *dignus, -a, -um* [KL3, W5]

worthy (verb, am worthy of) *mereō, -ēre, -uī, -itum* [KL1, L23]

would that! *utinam* [KL3, L13]

wound (noun) *vulnus, vulneris (n)* [KL1, L13]; *plāga, -ae (f)* [KL3, L14]

wound (verb) *vulnerō (1)* [KL1, L1]; *laedō, -ere, laesī, laesus* [KL2, W6]

wrap (verb) *involvō, -ere, -volvī, -volutum* [KL2, W9]

wrathful *īrātus,-a, -um* [KL1, L15]

wreck *naufragium, -ī (n)* [KL1, W23]

wretched *miser, -era, -erum* [KL1, L7]

write *scrībō, -ere, scrīpsī, scriptum* [KL1, L26]

wrongly *male* [KL1, L1]

Y

year *annus, -ī (m)* [KL2, L7]

yes (expects a yes answer) *nōnne* [KL2, L7]

yes *vērō* [KL2, L15]

yesterday *herī* [KL1, L6]

yet *tamen* [KL1, L30]; *adhūc* [KL3, L12]; *at* [KL3, L1]

yield *cēdō, -ere, cessī, cessum* [KL1, L28]

yoke *iungō, -ere, iūnxī, iunctum* [KL1, L27]

you (sg.) *tū* [KL1, L17]; **(pl.)** *vōs* [KL1, L17]

young *viridis, -e* [KL1, L17]; *iuvenis, -e* [KL2, W2]

young child *īnfāns, -fantis (adj. & noun, m/f)* [KL1, W31; KL3, L12]

young man *adulescens, -entis (m)* [KL1, L30]

young woman *adulescens, -entis (f)* [KL1, L30]; *virgō, virginis (f)* [KL1, L12]

younger *minimus, -a, -um* [KL1, W31]

youngest *iuvenissimus, -a, -um* [KL1, W19]

your (sg.) *tuus, -a, -um* [KL1, L11]; **(pl.)** *vester, -stra, -strum* [KL1, L11]

yours (sg.) *tuus, -a, -um* [KL1, L11]; **(pl.)** *vester, -stra, -strum* [KL1, L11]

youth *adulescentia, -ae (f)* [KL1, W32]; *iuventūs, -tūtis (f)* [KL2, W15]

Z

zeal *zēlus, -ī (m)* [KL3, W7]

Appendix C
Latin-English Glossary

A

ā, ab, (+ abl.) *from, away from* [KL1, L3]

abeō, -īre, -iī, -itum *I go away, depart* [KL1, W32; KL2, L9]

abiēs, -etis (f) *fir (tree)* [KL3, W2]

absum, -esse, āfuī, āfutūrum *I am absent, am away (from)* [KL3, L3]

abyssus, -ī (f) *abyss, deep, infernal pit* [KL3, W9]

ac (atque) *and, and also* [KL1, L27]

accendō, -ere, -cēnsī, -cēnsum *I kindle, light, set on fire* [KL2, W15]

accidō, -ere, -cīdī, —— *I fall upon/out, happen, come to pass* [KL3, L10]

accingō, -ere, -cinxī, -cinctum *I gird on/about, equip, prepare* [KL2, W9]

accipiō, -ere, -cēpī, -ceptum *I accept, receive, take* [KL1, L31]

acclīnis, -e *leaning (on), inclined (to/toward)* [KL3, W7]

accūsō (1) *I accuse* [KL3, W1]

ācer, ācris, ācre *sharp, eager; fierce* [KL1, L20]

aciēs, -ēī (f) *sharp edge/point, sharpness (esp. of sight); battle line* [KL3, L14]

ad (+ acc.) *to, toward, at, near* [KL1, L3]

addūcō, -ere, -dūxī, -ductum *I lead to* [KL2, W8]

adeō, -īre, -iī, -itum *I go to(ward), approach* [KL2, L10]

adhūc *to this place, until now, still, yet* [KL3, L12]

adimpleō, -ēre, -ēvī, -ētum *I fill up, fulfill* [KL3, W1]

admoneō, -ēre, -uī, -itum *I admonish, warn, advise* [KL3, W9]

admonitiō, -ōnis (f) *admonition, reminding* [KL3, W9]

admonitor, -ōris (m) *admonisher, encourager* [KL3, W16]

adnūntiō (1) [**annūntiō, etc.**] *I announce, make known* [KL3, L7]

adiciō, -ere, -iēcī, -iectum *I throw to, add, increase* [KL2, W14]

adōrō (1) *I adore, worship* [KL2, W8]

adsūmō, -ere, -sumpsī, -sumptum *I take for myself* [KL1, W32]

adulēscēns, -entis (m/f) *young man/woman* [KL1, L30]

adulēscentia, -ae (f) *youth* [KL1, W32]

adventus, -ūs (m) *coming, arrival, advent* [KL3, L12]

adversus (+ acc.) *against* [KL3, W1]

advocātus, -ī (m) *advocate, legal assistant/counselor* [KL3, W11]

aedificium, -iī (n) *building, structure* [KL3, W2]

aedificō (1) *I build, make* [KL2, L4]

aeger, -gra, -grum *sick, diseased, ill* [KL3, W5]

Aegeus, -a, -um *Aegean* [KL1, W30]

Aegeus, -eī (m) *Aegeus* [KL1, W30]

aegis, -gidis (f) *an aegis* [KL2, W6]

aemulātiō, -ōnis (f) *envy, jealousy* [KL3, W7]

Aenēas, -ae (m) *Aeneas* [KL2, W13]

aēneus, -a, -um *(made of) bronze, copper* [KL2, W6]

aequor, -oris (n) *sea, level surface* [KL3, L6]

āēr, āēris (m) *air, atmosphere* [KL2, W12]

aes, aeris (n) *copper, bronze; money* [KL3, W2]

aestus, -ūs (m) *heat, fire, passion* [KL2, W9]

aetās, -tātis (f) *age, (time of) life* [KL2, L14]

aeternus, -a, -um *eternal* [KL1, L15]

afferō (adf-), -ferre (adf-), attulī (adt-), allātum (adl-) *I bring (to), carry (to)* [KL3, L5]

ager, agrī (m) *field* [KL1, L4]

aggredior, -ī, ——, -gressus sum *I approach, attack* [KL3, W7]

āgmen, -minis (n) *movement, course; army (on the march)* [KL3, L6]

agō, -ere, ēgī, actum *I do, act, drive* [KL1, L26]

agricola, -ae (m) *farmer* [KL1, L3]

āiō (defective) *I say, assert, affirm* [KL1, L14]

āla, -ae (f) *wing* [KL1, L10]

albus, -a, -um *(dead) white* [KL1, L17]

alchemia, -ae (f) *alchemy* [KL1, W27]

aliēnō (1) *I alienate, estrange* [KL2, W15]

aliēnus, -a, -um *of another, foreign, alien*

aliēnus, -ī (m) *stranger, foreigner* [KL2, L12]

aliquī, aliquae, aliquod (adj.) *some, any* [KL2, L12]

aliquis, aliquid (pron.) *someone, something, anyone, anything* [KL2, L12]

alius, alia, aliud *another, other* [KL1, W21; KL2, L4]

alligō (1) *I bind up, tie up* [KL3, W1]

alnus, -ī (f) *ship, alder (wood)* [KL1, L4]

alō, alere, aluī, altum/alitum *I nourish, feed, cherish* [KL3, W2]

altāre, -tāris (n) *altar, burnt offering (pl. forms often used with sg. meaning)* [KL2, L9]

alter, -era, -erum *the other (of two), second* [KL2, L4]

altus, -a, -um *high, lofty, deep* [KL1, L19]

amāritūdō, -dinis (f) *bitterness, sorrow, sadness* [KL3, W10]

amārus, -a, um *bitter* [KL3, W9]

ambulō (1) *I walk* [KL1, L1]

amīca, -ae (f) *(female) friend* [KL1, L15]

amīcus, -ī (m) *(male) friend* [KL1, L15]

amita, -ae (f) *aunt* [KL1, L22]

amō (1) *I love* [KL1, L1]

amor, amōris (m) *love* [KL1, L14]

amplector, amplectī, ——, amplexus sum *I embrace, hug* [KL2, W11]

āmittō, -ere, -misī, -missum *I send away, lose* [KL2, W6]

amplius *more, longer, further, besides* [KL3, L9]

animal, -ālis (n) *animal* [KL1, L18]

animus, -ī (m) *mind* [KL1, L29]

an *(introduces 2nd half of a question, often with ūtrum) or, or whether* [KL3, L9]

ancilla, -ae (f) *maidservant, female slave* [KL3, L10]

ancora, -ae (f) *anchor* [KL2, W12]

angelus, -ī (m) *angel, messenger* [KL3, W5]

angularis, -e *corner, placed at corners* [KL2, W9]

anguis, -is (m) *serpent, snake* [KL3, W5]

anima, -ae (f) *soul, spirit, life; wind, breath* [KL2, L4]

annus, -ī (m) *year* [KL2, L7]

ānser, -eris (m) *goose* [KL3, W2]

ante (+ acc.) *before* [KL1, L17]

antequam (conj.) *before, sooner than, until* [KL3, L15]

antīchristus, -ī (m) *antichrist, the Antichrist* [KL3, W12]

antīquus, -a, -um *ancient* [KL1, L7]

ānulus, -ī (m) *ring, signet ring* [KL3, W10]

aperiō, -īre, -uī, apertum *I open, expose* [KL1, L29]

Apollo, -inis (m) *Apollo (god of prophesy, music, archery, the sun, etc.)* [KL1, W20]

apostolus, -ī (m) *apostle* [KL1, L11]

appareō, -ēre, -uī, -itum (+ dat.) *I appear, am visible (impers. apparet, "it is evident/ apparent that")* [KL3, L4]

appellō (1) *I name, call* [KL1, L15]

appropinquō (1) *I approach, draw near* [KL1, L25]

aptus, -a, -um *suitable, suited, fitted* [KL3, W2]

apud (+ acc.) *among, at the house of, with* [KL2, L4]

aqua, -ae (f) *water* [KL1, L2]

aquōsus, -a, -um *sopping wet* [KL1, W29]

arbitror, -ārī, ——, -ātus sum *I judge, think, suppose* [KL3, L4]

arbor, arboris (f) *tree* [KL1, L20]

arca, -ae (f) *box, chest* [KL2, W6]

arcus, -ūs (m) *bow, arch, rainbow* [KL1, L27]

ardeō, ardēre, arsī, —— *I burn, blaze* [KL1, L20]

argenteus, -a, -um *silver(y)* [KL1, L17]

argentum, -ī (n) *silver, money* [KL1, L5]

arguō, -ere, arguī, argutus *I accuse* [KL2, W9]

Argus, -ī (m) *Argus, a hundred-eyed giant* [KL1, W21]

Ariadna, -ae (f) *Ariadne* [KL1, W30]

ārida, -ae (f) *dryness, dry place, dry land* [KL3, W1]

āridus, -a, -um *dry, withered* [KL1, L27]

ariēs, -ietis (m) *ram* [KL1, W32]

arma, -ōrum (n, pl) *arms, armor, weapons* [KL1, W32; KL2, L3]

arripiō, -ere, -ripuī, -reptum *I seize, snatch (up), lay hold of* [KL3, W9]

artus, -ūs (m) *joint, limb* [KL2, W6]

arundō, -inis (f) [= **harundō, -dinis**] *reed* [KL3, W1]

arvum, -ī (n) *(cultivated) field, region* [KL3, L15]

arx, arcis (f) *citadel, fort; hill* [KL2, L7]

ascendō, -ere, -scendī, -scensum *I go up, ascend, climb* [KL2, L9]

asinus, -ī (m) *donkey* [KL1, L19]

asper, -era, -erum *harsh, fierce* [KL2, W12]

at *yet, but* [KL3, L1]

āter, -tra, -trum *(dead) black, dark* [KL1, L17]

Athēnae, -ārum (f, pl) *Athens* [KL1, W30; KL2, L14]

Athēniensis, -is (m/f) *an Athenian* [KL1, W30]

atque (ac) *and, and also* [KL1, L27]

ātrium, -iī (n) *hall, court, entryway* [KL3, L10]

attendō, -ere, -ndī, -ntum *I turn toward, direct (the attention) toward* [KL3, W9]

audāx, -ācis *bold, courageous, daring* [KL2, W11]

audeō, -ēre, ——, ausus sum *I dare* [KL1, L11]

audiō, -īre, -īvī, -ītum *I hear, listen to* [KL1, L29]

auferō, -ferre, abstulī, ablatum (3rd conj. irreg.) *I carry away/off, remove;* **auferō mē** *I remove myself, withdraw* [KL1, W32; KL3, L10]

augeō, -ēre, auxī, auctum *I increase* [KL1, L19]

aula, -ae (f) *hall, inner/royal court* [KL1, W13; KL3, W10]

aura, -ae (f) *breeze, air, heaven* [KL3, L3]

auris, -is (f) *ear* [KL3, L4]

aureus, -a, -um *golden, gold* [KL1, L17]

aurīga, -ae (m/f) *charioteer, driver* [KL1, W23]

auris, -is (f) *ear* [KL1, W28]

aurum, -ī (n) *gold* [KL1, L5]

aut *or* [KL1, L1]

autem (postpositive conj.) *however, moreover* [KL1, L12]

auxilium, -ī (n) *help, aid* [KL1, L5]

avārus, -a, -um *greedy* [KL1, L7]

avēna, -ae (f) *pan pipe, shepherd's pipe* [KL1, W21]

avia, -ae (f) *grandmother* [KL1, L22]

avis, avis (f) *bird* [KL1, L18]

avunculus, -ī (m) *uncle (mother's brother)* [KL1, L22]

avus, -ī (m) *grandfather, ancestor* [KL1, L22]

B

Bacchus, -ī (m) *Bacchus, the god of wine* [KL1, W27]

baculum, -ī (n) *staff* [KL1, W32]

barbarus, -a, -um *foreign, strange, savage* [KL1, L31]

barbarus, -ī (m) *foreigner, barbarian* [KL1, L31]

basis, -is (f) *pedestal, base, foundation* [KL2, W9]

beātus, -a, -um *happy, blessed* [KL1, L7]

Beelzebul, -ulis (m) (sometimes indecl.) *Beelzebub* [KL3, W1]

bellator, -toris (m) *warrior* [KL1, W32]

bellum, -ī (n) *war* [KL1, L15]; **bellum gerō** *I wage war* [KL1, L28]

bēlua, -ae (f) *beast (esp. a ferocious or large one), monster* [KL3, L15]

bene *well* [KL1, L1]

benedīcō, -ere, -dīxī, -dictum (+ dat.) *I speak well, bless, praise* [KL3, L4]

bēstia, -ae (f) *beast* [KL1, L2]

Bethleem (indecl.) *Bethlehem* [KL1, W32]

Biblia Sacra, Bibliae Sacrae (f) *Holy Bible* [KL1, L11]

bibō, -ere, bibī, potum *I drink* [KL2, L10]

bis *twice, twofold* [KL3, L6]

blasphēmia, -ae (f) *blasphemy, slander* [KL3, W1]

bonus, -a, -um *good* [KL1, L7]

bōs, bovis (m/f) *cow, bull, ox* (pl.) *cattle* [KL1, L19]

bracchium, -ī (n) *arm* [KL1, W13; KL3, W3]

brevis, -e *short, small, brief* [KL1, L19]

breviter *shortly, for a short time* [KL3, W5]

C

cadaver, -veris (n) *dead body, carcass* [KL1, W32]

cadō, -ere, cecidī, cāsum *I fall, sink, drop* [KL1, L27]

caecus, -a, -um *blind* [KL1, L27]

caedō, -ere, cecīdī, caesum *I cut (down), kill* [KL2, L12]

caelum, -ī (n) *sky, heaven* [KL1, L5]

caeruleus, -a, -um *blue* [KL1, L17]

calamus, -ī (m) *reed, reed-pipe* [KL1, W28]

caldus, -a, -um *warm, hot, fiery* [KL1, L7]

calix, calicis (m) *goblet* [KL1, W13]

camēlus, -ī (m/f) *camel* [KL1, L4; KL2, W4]

candidus, -a, -um *(glittering) white* [KL1, L17]

canis, canis (m/f) *dog* [KL1, L18]

canticum, -ī (n) *song, solo*; Canticum Canticōrum, *Song of Songs* [KL3, L14]

cantitō (1) *I sing often, sing frequently* [this is called the frequentative form of cantō] [KL3, W9]

cantō (1) *I sing, play (music), predict* [KL1, L1]

canō, -ere, cecinī, cāntum *I sing, play, prophesy* [KL2, L10]

cantus, -ūs (m) *song, singing* [KL1, L25]

caper, -prī (m) *(billy) goat* [KL1, L4]

capillus, -ī (m) *hair* [KL2, W6]

capiō, -ere, cēpī, captum *I take, capture, seize* [KL1, L31]

capitulum, -ī (n) *chapter, section* [KL3, W9]

captō (1) *I hunt* [KL1, L10]

caput, -itis (n) *head* [KL1, L13]

carcer, -eris (m) *prison*; (generally in pl.) *starting gates (of a horse race)* [KL1, W23; KL3, L5]

cardō, -dinis (m) *hinge* [KL2, W11]

careō, -ēre, -uī, -itum (+ abl.) *I lack, am without* [KL3, L6]

cāritās, -tātis (f) *love, esteem* [KL3, L11]

carmen, -inis (n) *song, chant, poem, prophecy* [KL1, L13]

caro, carnis (f) *flesh, meat* [KL1, L31]

Carthāgo, -ginis (f) *Carthage (city in north Africa, now a suburb of Tunis, Tunisia)* [KL2, L14]

cārus, -a, -um *dear, beloved* [KL1, L13]

caseus, -ī (m) *cheese* [KL2, W4]

castellum, -ī (n) *castle* [KL1, L5]

castra, -ōrum (n, pl) *camp* [KL1, L15]

castus, -a, -um *pure, chaste* [KL3, W9]

cāsus, -ūs (m) *event, incident; misfortune, downfall* [KL1, L28]

cauda, -ae (f) *tail* [KL1, W21]

causa, -ae (f) *cause, reason*; **causā** (+ gen.) *on account of, for the sake of* [usually follows its gen. object] [KL2, L15]

cautēs, -is (f) *rough rock, crag* [KL3, W16]

caveō, -ēre, cāvī, cautum *I guard against, beware (of)* [KL1, L12]

caverna, -ae (f) *cavity, cavern* [KL2, W6]

cavus, -a, -um *hollow, empty* [KL3, W6]

cēdō, -ere, cessī, cessum *I go, move, yield* [KL1, L28]

celēbrō (1) *I celebrate* [KL3, W10]

celer, celeris, celere *swift, quick* [KL1, L19]

celō (1) *I hide* [KL1, W28]

cēna, -ae (f) *dinner, meal* [KL1, L20]

centaurus, -ī (m) *centaur* [KL1, L10]

centēsimus, -a, -um *one hundredth* [KL1, L23]

centum *one hundred* [KL1, L21]

Cerēs, -eris (f) *Ceres* [KL3, W3]

certāmen, -minis (n) *contest, race* [KL1, W23]

certātim *eagerly* [KL1, L20]

certus, -a, -um *certain, sure* [KL3, L6]

certe, *certainly* [KL3, L6]

cervīx, -vīcis (f) *neck* [KL3, W3]

cervus, -ī (m) *stag, deer* [KL1, L10]

cessō (1) *I cease from, stop* [KL3, W4]

cēterus, -a, -um *the other, the rest (usually used in pl.)* [KL2, L15]

cētus, -ī (m) *sea monster, kraken, whale* [KL1, L10; KL2, W7]

Christus, -ī (m) *Christ* [KL1, L4]

cibus, -ī (m) *food* [KL1, L4]

cinis, -neris (m) *ashes* [KL3, L10]

circā (adv. and prep. + acc.) *around, about* [KL2, L13]

circumvolō (1) *I fly around* [KL2, W12]

Circus Maximus, Circī Maximī (m) *the Circus Maximus, a famous racetrack at the foot of the Palatine Hill in Rome* [KL1, W23]

citara, -ae, (f) *harp* [KL2, W2]

cito *quickly, fast, speedily* [KL1, L27]

cīvis, -is (m/f) *citizen* [KL2, L7]

cīvitās, -tātis (f) *city, state, citizenship* [KL2, L7]

clādēs, -is (f) *destruction, ruin, loss* [KL2, W15]

clam *secretly* [KL1, L29]

clāmō (1) *I shout* [KL1, L1]

clāmor, -oris (m) *shout, cry* [KL1, W20; KL2, L13]

clārus, -a, -um *bright, clear* [KL3, W3]

classis, -is (f) *group, class, fleet (of ships)* [KL1, L30]

claudō, -ere, clausī, clausum *I close, shut (up)* [KL3, L15]

clēmentia, -ae (f) *mercy, clemency* [KL1, W21; KL3, W10]

clipeus (clypeus), -ī (m) *shield* [KL3, W3]

clypeum, -ī (n) *shield* [KL1, W32]

cōdex, -dicis (m) *book, writing* [KL3, W9]

coepī, coepisse, ——, coeptum (defective) *I began, undertook* [KL3, L1]

cōgitātiō, -tiōnis (f) *thought, opinion* [KL3, L1]

cōgitō (1) *I think* [KL1, L6]

cognōmen, -minis (n) *surname, family name, cognōmen* [KL2, W15]

cognoscō, -ere, -nōvī, -nitum *I learn, get to know;* pf. tense, *I know* [KL2, L10]

cōgō, -ere, -ēgī, -āctum *I drive together, force, compel* [KL1, L28]

cohors, -hortis (f) *cohort* [KL3, W2]

collis, collis (m) *hill* [KL3, L2]

collocō (1) *I place, set, arrange* [KL1, W21]

cōllum, -ī (n) *neck* [KL3, W6]

colō, -ere, coluī, cultum *I cultivate, inhabit, worship* [KL1, L29]

color, -ōris (m) *color* [KL2, W11]

coma, -ae *hair* [KL3, W3]

comedō, -ere, -ēdī, -ēsus *I eat up, consume* [KL3, W1]

comes, -mitis (m) *companion, comrade* [KL2, L13]

cōmessātio, -ōnis (f) *rioting, reveling* [KL3, W9]

comminor, -ārī, ——, -ātus sum *I threaten* [KL3, W1]

commodus, -a, -um *suitable, convenient* [KL3, W2]

commūnicō (1) *I share* [KL2, W6]

commūnis, -e *common* [KL3, W2]

complector, -plectī, ——, -plexus sum *I embrace, hug* [KL3, W3]

compleō, -ēre, -plēvī, -plētum *I fulfil, fill up* [KL2, W6]

concēdō, -ere, -cessī, -cessum *I grant, allow, concede* [KL3, W9]

concilium, -iī (n) *council, meeting* [KL3, L5]

conclūdō, -ere, -clūsī, -clūsum *I shut up, close* [KL2, W9]

conculcō (1) *I trample, tread underfoot* [KL2, W14]

concupiscentia, -ae (f) *longing, concupiscence, lust* [KL3, W9]

condiciō, -ōnis (f) *condition, demand, agreement* [KL2, W15]

confertus, -a, -um *crowded, thick, dense* [KL2, W15]

confīdō, -ere, ——, confīsus sum (+ dat.) (semi-deponent) *I trust, have confidence in* [KL2, W6]

confirmō (1) *I make firm, strengthen, confirm* [KL3, W9]

cōnfiteor, -ērī, ——, -fessus sum (+ dat./acc.) *I confess* [KL2, L6]

confundō, -ere, -fūdī, -fūsum *I pour together, confound, disturb* [KL3, L12]

congregō (1) *I collect (into a flock/herd), assemble* [KL2, L14]

congregātiō, -ōnis (f) *assembling, union* [KL3, W4]

congruēns, -ntis *suitable, appropriate* [KL3, W9]

coniungō, -ere, -iūnxī, -iūnctum *I join (together), unite* [KL3, L9]

coniunx, -iugis (m/f) *husband or wife* [KL1, L22]

cōnor, -ārī, ——, cōnātus sum *I try, attempt* [KL2, L6]

conquiēscō, -ere, -quiēvī, -quiētum *I fall silent, am still* [KL2, W9]

cōnsentiō, -īre, -sēnsī, -sēnsum (+ dat.) *I agree (with), consent (to)* [KL3, W5]

conservō (1) *I preserve, save* [KL3, W15]

considerō (1) *I inspect, examine, consider* [KL2, W14]

cōnsilium, -iī (n) *plan, counsel, advice; wisdom* [KL1, L30]

consistōrium, -iī (n) *assembly room, hall* [KL3, W10]

consōbrīna, -ae (f) *cousin (female, mother's side)* [KL1, L22]

consōbrīnus, -ī (m) *cousin (male, mother's side)* [KL1, L22]

cōnspectus, -ūs (m) *sight, view, appearance* [KL2, L9]

cōnspiciō, -ere, -spēxī, -spectum *I observe, perceive, gaze at* [KL3, W16]

cōnsternō (1) *I bring to confusion, terrify, dismay* [KL3, W7]

cōnstituō, -ere, -stituī, -stitūtum *I set up, establish, decide* [KL2, L15]

consūmō, -ere, -sūmpsī, -sūmptum *I consume, spend, invest* [KL3, L2]

contendō, -ere, -tendī, -tentum *I contend, strive with, stretch out* [KL2, W9]

contentiō, -ōnis (f) *contention, strife* [KL3, W9]

conticescō, -ere, -ticuī, —— *I become silent, fall silent* [KL3, W6]

continuō *immediately, at once* [KL2, L12]

continēns, -entis (f) *continent, mainland* [KL3, W2]

contrā (+ acc.) *against* [KL1, L11]

contrītiō, -ōnis (f) *contrition, grief* [KL3, W9]

contumēlia, -ae (f) *insult, reproach, abuse* [KL3, W5]

convalēscō, -ere, -valuī, -valitus *I grow strong, gain strength* [KL3, W7]

convertō, -ere, -vertī, -versum *I turn around/ back, change, convert* [KL3, L9]

convīvium, -iī (n) *banquet, social feast* [KL3, L10]

convocō (1) *I call together, assemble* [KL3, W5]

cōpia, -ae (f) *supply, plenty, abundance; (pl.) troops* [KL1, L15]

cor, cordis (n) *heart* [KL1, L13]

cōram (+ abl.) *in the presence of, before;* **(adv.)** *personally, openly* [KL1, L27]

cornū, -ūs (n) *horn* [KL1, L25]

corōna, -ae (f) *crown* [KL1, L2]

corpus, corporis (n) *body* [KL1, L13]

corripiō, -ere, -ripuī, -reptus *I seize/ snatch up, carry off* [KL3, W16]

coūtor, -ūtī, ——, —— (+ abl.) *I associate with, have dealings with* [KL3, W12]

crās *tomorrow* [KL1, L6]

crastinus, -a, -um *tomorrow's, next* [KL2, W14]

crēber, -bra, -brum *thick, frequent, numerous* [KL3, L2]

crēdō, -ere, -didī, -ditum *I believe* [KL1, L26]

cremō (1) *I burn, consume by fire* [KL1, L2]

creō (1) *I create* [KL1, L6]

crēscō, -ere, crēvī, crētum *I grow, increase* [KL2, L11]

Crēta, -ae (f) *Crete* [KL1, W30]

crīmen, -minis (n) *crime, fault, offence* [KL3, W1]

crūdēlis, -e *cruel, savage* [KL3, L10]

cruentō (1) *I stain with blood, make bloody* [KL2, W11]

cruentus, -a, -um *bloody* [KL2, W15]

crūs, crūris (n) *leg* [KL1, W19]

crustulum, -ī (n) *cookie, small cake* [KL1, L5]

crux, crucis (f) *cross* [KL1, L15]

cubīle, -is (n) *(marriage) bed; pl., fornication* [KL3, W9]

cubitum, -ī (n) *elbow; a cubit (distance from elbow to tip of middle finger; approx. 18 inches)* [KL2, L14]

cum (prep. + abl.) *with* [KL1, L9]; **(conj.)** *when, while, since, after, although* [KL3, L7]

cunctātiō, -ōnis (f) *delay, doubt, hesitation* [KL3, W9]

cunctor, -ārī, ——, -ātus sum *I delay, hesitate* [KL3, W7]

cunctus, -a, -um *all (of), every* [KL2, L9]

Cupīdō, -dinis (m) *Cupid (son of Venus and god of love)* [KL1, W20]

cupidus, -a, -um *eager, zealous* [KL3, W2]

cupiō, -ere, cupīvī, cupītum *I wish (for), desire, long (for)* [KL1, L31]

cūr *why?* [KL1, L2]

cūrō (1) *I care for, take care of, heal, cure* [KL1, L15]

curriculum, -ī (n) *lap (of a race), course* [KL1, W23]

currō, -ere, cūcurrī, cursum *I run* [KL1, L26]

custōdiō, -īre, -iī/-īvī, -ītum *I guard, watch, defend, keep* [KL3, L3]

custōs, -ōdis (m/f) *guard, watch(man), defender* [KL3, L3]

Cȳclōps, Cȳclōpis (m) *Cyclops* [KL2, W4]

D

Daedalus, -ī (m) *Daedalus (a skilled inventor and craftsman)* [KL1, W30]

daemonium, -iī (n) *demon, evil spirit* [KL3, L1]

Daphne, -ēs (f) *Daphne* [KL1, W20]

David (indecl.) *David* [KL1, W32]

dē (+ abl.) *from, down from, concerning* [KL1, L4]

dea, -ae (f) *goddess; dat. and abl. pl. usually* **deābus** [KL1, L6]

dēbeō, -ēre, -uī, -itum *I owe, ought* [KL1, L11]

decem *ten* [KL1, L21]

decet, -ēre, ——, decuit (impers. + acc.) *it is fitting, proper, suitable, right* [KL3, L1]

decimus, -a, -um *tenth* [KL1, L23]

dēclārō (1) *I declare, make clear, explain* [KL1, L10]

dēdicō (1) *I dedicate, consecrate* [KL3, W7]

dēfatīgō (1) *I tire (out), exhaust* [KL3, W2]

dēfendō, -ere, -fendī, -fēnsum *I defend* [KL1, L28]

dēiciō, -icere, -iēcī, -iectum *I throw down, cast down, hurl down* [KL1, W23]

APPENDIX C \\ LATIN-ENGLISH GLOSSARY

deinceps *successively, in turn* [KL3, W2]

deinde *from that place, then, thereupon, next* [KL1, L24]

dēleō, -ēre, -lēvī, -lētum *I destroy* [KL1, L9]

dēligō, -ere, lēgī, -lēctum *I pick, choose* [KL1, L28]

dēnī, -ae, -a *ten at a time, ten each* [KL3, W2]

dēnique *finally* [KL1, L10]

dēprecor, -ārī, ——, -ātus sum *I pray (for), intercede, beseech* [KL3, L10]

dēscendō, -ere, -scendī, -scensum *I come down, descend, fall (down)* [KL3, L7]

dēserta, -ōrum (n, pl) *desert places, wilderness* [KL3, L4]

dēsertus, -a, -um *deserted, solitary, forsaken* [KL3, L4]

dēsōlō (1) *I leave alone, forsake* [KL3, W7]

dēspiciō, -ere, -spexī, -spectum *I look down on, despise* [KL1, W32]

Deus, -ī (m) *God*; **deus, -ī (m)** *a god* [KL1, L4]

dexter, -tra, -trum (or -tera, -terum) *right(-handed); skilled, favorable* [KL1, L30]

diabolus, -ī (m) *devil* [KL3, L13]

diaeta, -ae (f) *cabin (of a ship)* [KL1, W18]

Diāna, -ae (f) *Diana (virgin goddess of the moon and hunting)* [KL1, W20]

dīcō, -ere, dīxī, dictum *I say, speak* [KL1, L26]

diciō, -ōnis (f) *authority, rule, sway* [KL3, W10]

diēs, diēī (m/f) *day, period of time* [KL1, L28]

differō, -ferre, distulī, dīlātum *I separate, differ* [KL3, W2]

difficilis, -e *difficult* [KL1, L20; KL2, L5]

dignus, -a, -um *worthy, deserving* [KL3, W5]

dīlēctus, -a, -um (adj.) *beloved* [KL1, L1]

dīligō, -ere, -lēxī, -lēctum *I choose out, love*

dīmidius, -a, -um *half (of)* [KL3, L10]

dīmittō, -ere, -mīsī, -missum *I send away, dismiss, forgive* [KL1, L30; KL2, W15]

dīripiō, -ere, -ripuī, -reptum *I tear apart, plunder* [KL3, W1]

dirumpō, -ere, -rūpī, -ruptum *I burst asunder, tear asunder* [KL2, W14]

discēdō, -ere, -cessī, -cessum *I separate, go away from* [KL3, W5]

discipula, -ae (f) *student (female), disciple* [KL1, L5]

discipulus, -ī (m) *student (male), apprentice, disciple* [KL1, L5]

discus, -ī (m) *discus* [KL2, W6]

dissecō (1) *I cut (to the heart)* [KL2, W5]

dissimilis, -e *dissimilar, unlike, different* [KL2, L5]

dissolvō, -ere, -solvī, -solūtum *I dissolve, destroy* [KL3, W5]

distō (1) *I stand apart, differ* [KL3, W9]

diū *for a long time* [KL1, L13]

dīversus, -a, -um *diverse, opposite* [KL3, W7]

dīvidō, -ere, -vīsī, -vīsum *I divide, separate* [KL2, W9]

dīvīnitus (adv.) *from heaven, by divine providence/will* [KL3, W9]

dīvīnus, -a, -um *divine* [KL3, W7]

dīvitiae, -ārum (f, pl) *riches, wealth* [KL1, L2]

dō, dare, dedī, datum *I give* [KL1, L1]

doceō, -ēre, docuī, doctum *I teach* [KL1, L9]

doctrīna, -ae (f) *teaching, instruction* [KL3, L5]

doctus, -a, -um *learned, wise, skilled* [KL1, L13]

dolor, -ōris (m) *pain, grief* [KL3, W3]

dolus, -ī (m) *deceit, fraud* [KL3, L6]

dominus, -ī (m) *lord, master* [KL1, L4]

dōmō, -āre, domuī, domitum *I tame, subdue* [KL1, L12]

domus, -ūs (f) *house, home* [KL1, L25]

dōnec *until; as long as, while* [KL3, W3]

dōnum, -ī (n) *gift* [KL1, L5]

dormiō, -īre, -īvī, -ītum *I sleep* [KL1, L29]

draco, dracōnis (m) *dragon* [KL1, L12]

dubitātiō, -ōnis (f) *doubt, uncertainty* [KL3, W9]

dubitō (1) *I doubt, am uncertain, question* [KL3, W7]

dubius, -a, -um *doubtful, dubious, uncertain* [KL3, W7]

dūcō, -ere, duxī, ductum *I lead, guide* [KL1, L26]

dulcis, -e *sweet* [KL1, L19]

dum/dummodo (conj.) *while, until; provided that, if only* [KL2, L11]

duo, duae, duo *two* [KL1, L21]

duodecim *twelve* [KL1, L21]

duodecimus, -a, -um *twelfth* [KL1, L23]

duodēnī, -ae, -a *twelve at a time, twelve each* [KL3, W2]

duodēvīcēsimus, -a, -um *eighteenth* [KL1, L23]

duodēvīgintī *eighteen* [KL1, L21]

dūrus, -a, -um *hard, rough, harsh* [KL3, W16]

dux, ducis (m) *leader, guide, general* [KL1, L14]

E

ē *see* **ex**

ēbrietās, -tātis (f) *drunkenness, carousing* [KL3, W9]

ēbrius, -a, -um *drunk, intoxicated* [KL1, W13; KL2, W4]

ecce *behold!* [KL1, L17]

ecclēsia, -ae (f) *church* [KL1, L11]

ēdictum, -ī (n) *edict, proclamation, command* [KL3, W10]

edō, -ere, ēdī, ēsum *I eat, devour* [KL3, L1]

ēdūcō, -ere, -dūxī, -ductum *I lead out/ forth, bring out* [KL3, L5]

efficiō, -ere, -fēcī, -fectum *I effect, cause, accomplish* [KL3, W10]

effugiō, -ere, -fūgī, -fugitum *I escape* [KL1, W10]

effundō, -ere, -fūdī, -fūsum *I pour out/ forth, shed* [KL3, L9]

ego (sg.) *I* [KL1, L17]

ēgredior, -gredī, ——, -gressus sum *I go out, march out* [KL2, L6]

ēgregius, -a, -um *outstanding, excellent* [KL1, L29]

ēheu (heu) *alas! oh! (expressing grief or pain)* [KL1, L22]

ēiciō, -ere, -iēcī, -iectum *I throw out, cast out, drive out* [KL2, L14]

ēlābor, -lābī, ——, -lapsus sum *I slip away, escape* [KL2, W6]

elephantus, -ī (m) *elephant* [KL1, L19]

ēligō, -ere, -lēgī, -lectum *I pick out, choose, elect* [KL3, L1]

emō, -ere, ēmī, ēmptum *I buy* [KL2, L10]

emundō, -āre, ——, -ātum *I cleanse, purify* [KL3, W11]

enigma, -matis (n) *riddle* [KL1, W19]

enim (postpositive conj.) *indeed, truly, certainly; for* [KL1, L17]

eō, -īre, iī (īvī), itum *I go* [KL1, L29]

eōdem (adv.) *in the same place, to the same place/purpose* [KL3, L2]

Ephratheus, -ī (m) *an Ephramite* [KL1, W32]

epulae, -ārum (f, pl) *feast* [KL1, L20]

eques, -quitis (m) *knight, horseman, cavalryman* [KL1, L20]

equitātus, -ūs (m) *cavalry* [KL3, W2]

equus, -ī (m) *horse* [KL1, L4]

ergō *therefore, then, consequently, accordingly* [KL1, L18]

ēripiō, -ere, -ripuī, -reptum *I snatch away/from, rescue* [KL2, L3]

errō (1) *I wander, err, am mistaken* [KL1, L14]

error, -ōris (m) *error, mistake* [KL3, W7]

esca, -ae (f) *food* [KL2, W14]

essedarius, -ī (m) *charioteer (fighter in a war-chariot, not just a driver); gladiator* [KL3, W2]

ēsuriō, -īre, -iī, -ītum *I hunger, desire food* [KL3, W1]

et *and, even, also;* et...et *both...and* [KL1, L1]

etiam *even, also, besides, still* [KL1, L22]

etsi *although, though* [KL3, W2]

eunūchus, -ī (m) *eunuch* [KL3, W10]

ēvādō, -ere, -vāsī, -vāsum *I go out/forth, escape* [KL3, W7]

ēvangelicus, -a, -um *evangelical, of the gospel* [KL3, W9]

ēvangelium, -ī (n) *good news, gospel* [KL1, L5]

ēvangelīzō (1) *I preach/proclaim (the Gospel)* [KL3, W5]

ēveniō, -īre, -vēnī, -ventum *I come to pass, happen* [KL3, W3]

ēvertō, -ere, -tī, -sum *I overturn, overthrow, destroy* [KL3, W7]

ex, ē (+ abl.) *out of, from* [KL1, L3]

exaltō (1) *I raise, exalt* [KL3, W5]

excelsus, -a, -um *high, lofty, noble* [KL2, L4]

excipiō, -ere, -cēpī, -ceptum *I take out, relieve* [KL3, W2]

excutiō, -ere, -cussī, -cussum *I shake out/off* [KL3, W3]

exemplar, -āris (n) *copy, example, exemplar* [KL3, W10]

exemplum, -ī (n) *example* [KL3, W7]

exeō, -īre, -iī (-īvī), -itum *I go out, go away* [KL2, L12]

exerceō, -ēre, -uī, -itum *I train, exercise* [KL1, L14]

exercitus, -ūs (m) *army* [KL1, L25]

exiguus, -a, -um *meager, scanty* [KL3, W2]

exitus, -ūs (m) *exit* [KL2, W13]

expendō, -ere, -dī, -sum *I pay for, suffer* [KL3, W6]

exprobrō (1) *I reproach* [KL1, W32]

exprōmō, -ere, -mpsī, -mptum *I take out, reveal, disclose* [KL2, W15]

expuō, -ere, -puī, -putum *I spit out* [KL2, W8]

exsanguis, -e *bloodless, pale* [KL3, W6]

exsilium, -iī (n) *exile, banishment* [KL3, W3]

exspectō (1) *I wait for, expect* [KL1, L3]

exstinguō, -ere, -stinxī, -stinctum *I put out, quench, exstinguish* [KL3, W1]

extendō, -ere, -tendī, -tensum *I stretch out, extend* [KL1, W26; KL3, W1]

extrā (adv.) *(on the) outside, besides, except;* (prep. + acc.) *outside (of), beyond* [KL3, L15]

exultō [exsultō] (1) *I leap up, exult, rejoice exceedingly* [KL3, W9]

F

Fabius, -ī (m) *Fabius* [KL1, W19]

faber, -brī (m) *worker, carpenter, smith* [KL3, W2]

fābula, -ae (f) *story, legend, tale* [KL1, L2]

faciēs, -ēī (f) *shape, form; face; character* [KL1, L28]

facile *easily* [KL2, L7]

facilis, -e *easy* [KL1, L20; KL2, L5]

faciō, -ere, fēcī, factum *I make, do (for present passive system, use* fīō*)* [KL1, L31]

fāgus, -ī (f) *beech (tree)* [KL3, W2]

falsus, -a, -um *false, deceitful* [KL2, W13]

fāma, -ae *rumor, report, reputation, fame* [KL1, W23; KL2, L13]

famēlicus, -a, -um *hungry* [KL1, L29]

familia, -ae *household, family* [KL1, L22]

fās (n, indecl.) *divine law;* (usu. transl. as adj.) *lawful, permitted, possible* [KL3, L2]

fātālis, -e *fatal, fated, deadly* [KL3, W6]

fatīgō (1) *I weary, tire* [KL2, W12]

fātum, -ī (n) *fate, prophecy, oracle* [KL1, L5; KL2, 13]

faucēs, -ium (f, pl) *throat, gullet* [KL3, W3]

fēlīciter in aeternum *happily ever after* [KL1, W6; KL2, W2]

fēlix, (gen.) -līcis *lucky, fortunate, happy* [KL1, L19]

fēmina, -ae (f) *woman* [KL1, L2]

fēmīnus, -a, -um *female* [KL3, W4]

fenestra, -ae (f) *window* [KL1, L31]

fēnum [faenum], -ī (n) *hay* [KL2, W14]

ferē *nearly, almost* [KL3, L3]

ferō, ferre, tulī, lātum (irreg. 3rd conj.) *I carry, bring (forth), bear* [KL1, W32; KL2, W11]

ferrum, -ī (n) *iron, sword* [KL2, L15]

ferus, -a, -um *fierce, wild* [KL1, L7]

fessus, -a, -um *tired, weary, exhausted* [KL1, L20; KL3, W6]

festīnō (1) *I hasten, hurry* [KL1, L9]

festūca, -ae (f) *straw* [KL2, W14]

fēstus, -a -um *festal, festive, joyful, merry* [KL3, W6]

fētus, -a, -um *pregnant, filled* [KL3, W6]

fīcus, -ī (f) *fig (tree)* [KL3, W8]

fidēlis, -e *faithful* [KL2, L4]

fidēs, -eī (f) *faith* [KL1, L28]

fīdūcia, -ae (f) *trust, faith, confidence* [KL3, L7]

fīdus, -a, -um *faithful, trustworthy* [KL1, L7]

fīlia, -ae (f) *daughter (dat. and abl. pl. often* **fīliābus***)* [KL1, L6]

fīliolus, -ī (m) *little son/child* [KL3, W10]

fīlius, -ī (m) *son* [KL1, L4]

fīlum, -ī (n) *thread, string* [KL1, W30]

findō, -ere, fidī, fissum *I split, part, cleave* [KL3, W16]

fīnis, -is (m) *end, boundary, limit* [KL1, W4]

fīō, fierī, ——, factus sum *I am made, am done, become, happen [used as present passive system of* **faciō***]* [KL1, L31]

firmāmentum, -ī (n) *support, prop; the firmament, the sky* [KL3, W4]

firmō (1) *I confirm, strengthen* [KL3, W3]

flēbilis, -e *tearful, lamentable* [KL3, W9]

fleō, -ēre, flēvī, flētum *I weep* [KL1, L14]

flētus, -ūs (m) *weeping, wailing* [KL3, W9]

flōreō, -ēre, -uī, —— *I flourish* [KL1, L17]

flōs, flōris (m) *flower* [KL1, L15]

flūmen, flūminis (n) *river* [KL1, L13]

foculus, -ī (m) *fire-pan, brazier* [KL2, W15]

fodiō, -ere, fōdī, fossum *I dig* [KL1, W28]

foedus, -a, -um *horrible, ugly* [KL1, L7]

foedus, -deris (n) *treaty, covenant, agreement* [KL2, L12]

folium *leaf* [KL1, W20]

fōns, fontis (m) *fountain, spring, source* [KL2, L11]

for, fārī, ——, fātus sum *I say, speak, prophesy* [KL3, L3]

forās *out(side), forth* [KL3, L6]

forma, -ae (f) *form, shape, appearance, beauty* [KL3, W16]

forsitan *perhaps, peradventure, maybe* [KL3, L13]

fortasse *perhaps* [KL1, L26]

forte *by chance, perhaps, perchance* [KL2, L3]

fortior, -tius (gen. fortioris) *braver* [KL1, W31]

fortis, -e *strong, brave* [KL1, L19]

fortissimus, -a, -um *bravest, strongest* [KL1, W32]

fortitūdō, -tudinis (f) *strength, bravery* [KL2, L12]

fovea, -ae (f) *pit, snare* [KL3, W1]

foveō, -ēre, fōvī, fōtum *I cherish, love, esteem* [KL1, L25]

fragor, -ōris (m) *a crashing, crash, noise, din* [KL3, W7]

frangō, -ere, frēgī, fractum *I break, smash, shatter* [KL1, L27]

frāter, frātris (m) *brother* [KL1, L12]

frōns, frondis (f) *foliage, garland, greenery* [KL3, W6]

frōns, -ontis (f) *forehead* [KL1, W32]

frūctus, -ūs (m) *fruit, profit* [KL1, L25]

frūmentum, -ī (n) *grain; (pl.) crops* [KL1, L15]

frustrā *in vain, in error* [KL3, L3]

fugiō, -ere, fūgī, fugitum *I flee, run away* [KL1, L31]

fulgeō, -ēre, fulsī, —— *I shine, glitter* [KL2, W13]

fulgur, -uris (n) *lightning* [KL1, W25]

fūmigō (1) *I smoke* [KL3, W1]

funda, -ae (f) *sling* [KL1, W32]

fundamentum, -ī (n) *foundation* [KL2, W9]

fundō, -ere, fūdī, fūsum *I pour (out), shed* [KL3, W3]

fundus, -ī (m) *farm, estate; foundation, lowest part* [KL3, W10]

fūnus, -neris (n) *funeral (rites)* [KL2, W13]

furō, -ere, -uī, —— *I rage, rave, am furious* [KL2, W13]

fūror, -ōris (m) *madness, fury, rage* [KL3, W6]

fūsus, -a, -um *spread out, scattered* [KL3, W6]

futūrus, -a, -um *future, about to be* [KL2, W10]

G

galea, -ae (f) *helmet* [KL2, W6]

Gallicus, -a, -um *Gallic, of/belonging to the Gauls* [KL3, W2]

gallīna, -ae (f) *hen* [KL3, W2]

gaudeō, -ēre, ——, gāvīsus sum *I rejoice* [KL1, L22]

gaudium, -ī (n) *joy, happiness* [KL1, L5]

gelidus, -a, -um *cold, icy* [KL1, L31]

gelū, -ūs (n) *frost, ice* [KL2, W9]

geminus, -ī (m) *twin* [KL1, L10]

gemitus, -ūs (m) *groan, complaint* [KL3, W6]

generātiō, -ōnis (f) *generation, begetting* [KL3, L7]

gens, -ntis (f) *clan, tribe, nation* [KL1, L31]

gentīlis, -is (m/f) *Gentile, pagan, heathen* [KL3, W7]

genu, -ūs (n) *knee* [KL1, L25]

genus, -neris (n) *birth, origin, race, kind* [KL2, L13]

germāna, -ae (f) *sister* [KL1, L4]

germānus, -ī (m) *brother* [KL1, L4]

germinō (1) *I sprout forth, bud, put forth* [KL3, W4]

gerō, -ere, gessī, gestum *I bear, carry on;* **bellum gerō** *I wage war* [KL1, L28]

gigās, gigantis (m) *giant* [KL1, L15]

gignō, -ere, genuī, genitum *I beget, create (in pass., I am born)* [KL2, L9]

gladius, -ī (m) *sword* [KL1, L4]

glōria, -ae (f) *fame, glory* [KL1, L15]

Gorgō, -onis (f) *a Gorgon* [KL2, W6]

grabātus, -ī (m) *pallet, mat, low couch* [KL3, W5]

gracilis, -e *slender, thin* [KL2, L5]

Graeae, -ārum (f, pl) *the Graeae (Gray Sisters)* [KL2, W6]

Graecus, -a, -um *Greek* [KL3, L6]

Graecus, -ī (m) (as noun) *a Greek* [KL3, L6]

grāmen, grāminis (n) *grass, greenery* [KL1, L13]

grandō, -dinis (f) *hail* [KL2, W9]

grātia, -ae (f) *grace, favor, kindness, thanks;* **grātiās agō (+ dat.)** *I give thanks, I thank* [KL1, L27]

grātus, -a, -um *grateful, pleasing* [KL1, L27]

gravis, -e *heavy, burdensome* [KL3, L6]

gravitās, -tātis (f) *weight, heaviness* [KL3, W2]

grex, gregis (m) *flock, herd* [KL1, L31]

gubernō (1) *I steer, direct, govern* [KL1, L25]

H

habēna, -ae (f) *rein, strap* [KL3, W8]

habeō, -ēre, -uī, -itum *I have, hold* [KL1, L9]

habitō (1) *I live, dwell, inhabit* [KL1, L3]

haereō, -ēre, haesī, haesum *I cling, stick* [KL3, W3]

hara, -ae (f) *pig-sty* [KL1, W25]

harēna, -ae (f) *sand, beach* [KL1, L3]

hasta, -ae (f) *spear* [KL1, L3]

haud *not at all, by no means* [KL3, L1]

hauriō, -īre, hausī, haustum *I draw up, draw out, drink up* [KL2, W12]

herī *yesterday* [KL1, L6]

Hesperidēs, -um (f, pl.) *the Hesperides* [KL2, W6]

heu (ēheu) *alas! oh! (expresses grief or pain)* [KL1, L22]

hic, haec, hoc *this, (pl.) these* [KL1, L30]

hīc *here, in this place* [KL2, L11]

hinc *from here, hence, from/on this side* [KL2, L11]

Hierusalem (indecl.) *Jerusalem*

hodiē *today* [KL1, L2]

homicīda, -ae (m/f) *murderer/murderess), homicide, manslayer* [KL3, L13]

homō, hominis (m) *man, human being* [KL1, L12]

hōra, -ae (f) *hour* [KL1, L31]

horrendus, -a, -um *dreadful, awful, fearful* [KL1, L13]

horreum, -ī (n) *barn, granary, storehouse* [KL2, W14]

hortus, -ī (m) *garden* [KL2, W6]

hospes, -pitis (m) *guest* [KL2, W6]

hostis, -is (m) *enemy (of the state)* [KL1, L18]

hūc *to this place, hither* [KL2, L11]

hūmānus, -a, -um *human, humane, cultured* [KL3, W2]

humilis, -e *humble, low(ly)* [KL2, L5]

humus, -ī (f) *ground, soil, earth* [KL2, L14]

hydria, -ae (f) *jug* [KL2, W12]

hyacinthinus, -a, -um *blue, purplish-blue, violet* [KL1, L17]

hydrus, -ī (m) *sea serpent* [KL1, W12]

hydrum, -ī (m) *sea serpent* [KL2, W4]

hypocrita, -ae (m) *hypocrite* [KL2, W14]

I

iaceō, -ēre, -uī, —— *I lie (flat), lie down* [KL1, L9]

iaciō, -ere, iēcī, iactum *I throw, cast, hurl* [KL1, L31]

iactūra, -ae (f) *a throwing (away/over)* [KL2, W7]

iam *now, already;* **nōn iam** *no longer* [KL1, L15]

ibī *there, at that place; then* [KL1, L5]

ictus, -ūs (m) *blow, stroke* [KL3, W5]

īdem, eadem, idem *the same* [KL3, L2]

ideo *therefore, for that reason* [KL2, L14]

īdōlum, -ī (n) *image, form, idol* [KL3, L7]

iēiūnium, -iī (n) *a fast, fasting, fast-day* [KL3, W10]

iēiūnō (1) *I fast, abstain from* [KL3, W10]

Iēsus, -ūs (m) *Jesus* [KL1, L25]

igitur *therefore, then* [KL2, L9]

ignis, ignis (m) *fire* [KL1, L18]

ignōrō (1) *I do not know, am ignorant of* [KL2, L15]

ille, illa, illud *that, (pl.) those; that famous* [KL1, L30]

illīc *there, in that place* [KL2, L11]

illinc *from there, thence, from/on that side* [KL2, L11]

illūc *to that place, thither* [KL2, L11]

illūminō (1) *I light up, give light, illuminate* [KL3, W4]

imāgō, -ginis (f) *image, likeness* [KL3, L4]

imber, -bris (m) *rain(storm), shower* [KL2, W9]

immānis, -e *enormous, monstrous, immense* [KL3, L7]

immemor, -oris *unmindful, heedless, not thinking* [KL2, W6]

immō *nay rather, on the contrary, no indeed* [KL3, W7]

immortālis, -e *immortal* [KL2, W6]

immundus, -a, -um [or **inmundus** etc.] *unclean, dirty, foul* [KL3, L5]

impediō, -īre, -īvī, -ītum *I hinder* [KL1, L29]

imperium, -iī (n) *command, authority, empire* [KL2, L13]

imperō (1) *I command, order* (alicuī aliquid) [KL3, L10]

impetus, -ūs (m) *attack, onset, impetus* [KL3, L9]

impietās, -tātis (f) *impiety, irreverence, ungodliness* [KL3, W7]

impius, -a, -um *irreverent, wicked, impious* [KL3, L1]

impleō, -ēre, -plēvī, -plētum *I fill up, satisfy, complete* [KL2, L7]

implicō (1) *I entwine, entangle* [KL3, W5]

impōnō, -ere, -posuī, -positum *I put on, establish* [KL2, W13]

importō (1) *I carry in, import* [KL3, W2]

impositiō, -ōnis (f) *a putting on, laying on* [KL3, W7]

improbus, -a, -um *wicked* [KL1, L29]

impudīcitia, -ae (f) *sexual immorality* [KL3, W9]

īmus, -a, -um *lowest, deepest* [KL2, L5]

in (+ acc.) *into, against;* **(+ abl.)** *in, on* [KL1, L3]

Īnachus, -ī (m) *Inachus (god of the Inachus River in Argos)* [KL1, W21]

inānis, -e *empty, void* [KL3, W4]

incarcerō (1) *I imprison, incarcerate* [KL2, W4]

incendō, -ere, -cendī, -censum *I kindle, set on fire* [KL2, W13]

incertus, -a, -um *uncertain, unsure* [KL2, W11]

incipiō, -ere, -cēpī, -ceptum *I begin, commence* [KL1, L31]

incircumcisus, -a, -um *uncircumcised* [KL1, W32]

inclūdō, -ere, -clūsī, -clūsum *I shut in/up, enclose* [KL3, W6]

incolō, -ere, -coluī, -cultum *I dwell in, inhabit, cultivate* [KL3, L2]

incolumis, -e *safe, unhurt, uninjured* [KL3, W2]

inde *from there, thence* [KL2, L10]

indicō (1) *I declare, show, make known* [KL3, L11]

indigeō, -ēre, -diguī, —— (+ gen./abl.) *I need, require, lack* [KL2, W14]

indīgnitās, -tātis (f) *unworthiness, indignity* [KL2, W15]

induō, -ere, -duī, -dūtum *I put on, clothe, wear* [KL2, L14]

ineō, -īre, -iī (-īvī), -ītum *I go in(to), enter, begin* [KL3, L4]

īnfāns, -fantis (adj. & noun, m/f) *baby, infant* [KL1, W31; KL3, L12]

īnfēlix, (gen.) -līcis *unlucky, unfortunate, miserable* [KL1, L19]

īnfēnsus, -a, -um *enraged, hostile* [KL2, W15]

īnferior, -ius *lower* [KL2, L5]

īnferō, -ferre, intulī, illātum (+ dat. or + ad/ in + acc.) *I bring in, carry in* [KL3, L2]

īnferus, -a, -um *below* [KL2, L5]

inficiō, -ere, -fēcī, -fectum *I put/dip in, dye* [KL3, W2]

infīgo, -ere, -fixī, -fixum *I fix in, fasten in* [KL1, W32]

īnfimus, -a, -um *lowest, deepest* [KL2, L5]

infīnītus, -a, -um *boundless, infinite* [KL3, W2]

īnfīrmitās, -tātis (f) *infirmity, sickness, weakness* [KL3, W5]

īnfīrmus, -a, -um *feeble, weak, infirm* [KL3, W5]

īnfrā (adv. and prep. + acc.) *below, under* [KL3, W16]

infundō, -ere, -fūdī, -fūsum (+ dat.) *I pour in(to)* [KL3, W9]

ingēns, (gen.) -entis *huge, vast, enormous* [KL1, L19]

ingredior, -gredī, ——, -gressus sum *I go in, advance, undertake* [KL2, L6]

iniciō, -ere, -iēcī, -iectum *I throw in/on, put in/on, cast in/on* [KL2, W15]

inimīcus, -ī (m) *(personal) enemy* [KL1, L10]

inīquitās, -tātis (f) *injustice, unfairness, iniquity* [KL2, L10]

initium, -iī (n) *beginning, commencement, entrance* [KL3, L7]

iniūstus, -a, -um *unjust, unreasonable* [KL3, W16]

inmeritus [imm-], -a, -um *undeserved, undeserving, innocent* [KL3, W16]

innoxius, -a, -um *harmless* [KL3, W3]

innumerus, -a, -um *innumerable, countless* [KL3, W16]

inperitus, -a, -um *unskilled, inexperienced, ignorant* [KL2, W9]

īnsānia, -ae (f) *insanity, madness* [KL3, W6]

īnsānus, -a, -um *insane, mad* [KL3, W3]

īnscius, -a, -um *not knowing, ignorant* [KL3, W16]

īnsidiae, -ārum (f, pl) *ambush, plot* [KL2, L15]

īnsōmnium, -iī (n) *dream* [KL2, W13]

īnsonō, -āre, -uī, -ītum *I resound, echo* [KL2, W6]

īnsula, -ae (f) *island* [KL1, L3]

īnstar (indecl) *likeness, appearance, worth* [KL2, W13]

īnstō, -āre, -stitī, -stātum *I press on, urge forward* [KL2, W6]

intāctus, -a, -um *untouched, uninjured* [KL2, W15]

integer, -tēgra, -tēgrum *whole, fresh, untouched* [KL3, W2]

intellegō, -ere, -lēxī, -lēctum *I understand, perceive* [KL3, L2]

inter (+ acc.) *between, among* [KL1, L19]

intereā *in the meantime, meanwhile* [KL2, L12]

interficiō, -ere, -fēcī, -fectum *I kill, slay, destroy* [KL1, L31]

interim *meanwhile, in the meantime* [KL1, L9]

interior, -ius (gen. -teriōris) *inner, interior* [KL3, W2]

interrogō (1) *I ask, interrogate* [KL2, W8]

intervāllum, -ī (n) *interval, distance [of space or time]* [KL3, W2]

intonō, -āre, -uī/-āvī, —— *I thunder, make a noise* [KL3, W3]

intrā (prep. + acc.; adv.) *within, inside, inwardly* [KL2, L15]

intrō (1) *I enter* [KL1, L9]

inveniō, -īre, -vēnī, -ventum *I come upon, find* [KL1, L29]

invicem *reciprocally (i.e., "[to] one another")* [KL1, W26]; *in turn, by turns; one another, each other* [KL2, L12]

invīctus, -a, -um *unconquered, invincible* [KL3, W13]

invideō, -ēre, -vīdī, -vīsum *I envy* [KL1, W29]

invidus, -a, -um *envious, unfavorable (to)* [KL2, W11]

inviolātus, -a, -um *unharmed, unhurt* [KL3, W1]

involvō, -ere, -volvī, -volutum *I wrap (in)* [KL2, W9]

Īō, -ōnis (f) *Io (a beautiful nymph and daughter of Inachus)* [KL1, W21]

ipse, ipsa, ipsum *himself, herself, itself; the very* [KL2, L3]

īra, -ae (f) *anger* [KL1, L2]

īrāscor, -scī, ——, īrātus sum *I am angry, am in a rage* [KL3, W9]

īrātus, -a, -um *angry, wrathful* [KL1, L15]

is, ea, id *he, she, it, they; this, that* [KL1, L17]

Isai (indecl.) *Jesse* [KL1, W32]

Israhel (indecl.) or Israhel, -is *Israel* [KL1, W32; KL2, W3]

Israhelita, -ae (m) *Israelite* [KL1, W32]

iste, ista, istud *that (of yours); such (sometimes used with tone of contempt)* [KL1, L30]

īta *so, thus, therefore* [KL2, L6]

Ītalia, -ae (f) *Italy* [KL1, W8; KL2, W5]

itaque *and ēo, therefore* [KL1, L2]

iter, itineris (n) *journey, road, route, trek* [KL1, L13]

iterum *again, a second time* [KL1, L25]

iubeō, -ēre, iussī, iussum *I order, command* [KL3, L2]

Iudaeus, -a, -um *Jewish* [KL2, W3]

iūdex, -dicis (m) *judge* [KL1, W28; KL3, L1]

iūdicium, -ī (n) *judgment, decision, trial* [KL2, L9]

iūdicō (1) *I judge, decide* [KL2, L14]

Iūlia, -ae (f) *Iulia or Julia* [KL1, W11]

Iūlius, -iī (m) *Iulius or Julius* [KL1, W19]

iūmentum, -ī (n) *beast (of burden)* [KL3, W4]

iungō, -ere, iūnxī, iunctum *I join, unite, yoke* [KL1, L27]

Iūnia, -ae (f) *Iunia or Junia* [KL1, W11]

Iūno, -ōnis (f) *Juno (queen of the gods and wife of Jupiter)* [KL1, W21; KL3, W3]

Iuppiter, Iovis (dat. Iovī, acc. Iovem, abl. Iove) (m) *Jupiter/Jove (king of the gods)* [KL1, W21; KL2, W6]

iūrō (1) *I swear, vow, take an oath* (**iūs iūrandum** [*or as one word*, **iūsiūrandum**] *an oath*) [KL2, L15]

iūs, iūris (n) *justice, right, duty* [KL2, L15]

iūstitia, -ae (f) *justice, righteousness* [KL3, L12]

iūstus, -a, -um *just, right, fair, righteous* [KL1, L7; KL3, L7]

iuvenis, -e *young* [KL2, W2]

iuvenissimus, -a, -um *youngest* [KL1, W19]

iuventūs, -tūtis (f) *youth* [KL2, W15]

iuvō, -āre, iūvī, iūtum *I help* [KL1, L22]

iūxta (adv. & prep. + acc.) *near (to), close to/by* [KL1, L28]

L

lābor, -ī, ——, lapsus sum *I slip, fall, glide* [KL2, L6]

labor, labōris (m) *work, toil, labor, hardship* [KL1, L12]

labōrō (1) *I work* [KL1, L22]

lābrum, -ī (n) *lip* [KL3, W2]

labyrinthus, -ī (m) *labyrinth, maze* [KL1, W30]

lac, lactis (n) *milk* [KL1, L13]

lacrima, -ae (f) *tear* [KL3, L9]

lacus, -ūs (m) *lake, tub, hollow* [KL1, L27]

laedō, -ere, laesī, laesus *I wound, offend* [KL3, W6]

laetitia, -ae (f) *joy, gladness* [KL3, L7]

laetus, -a, -um *happy, joyful, glad* [KL1, L7]

lambō, -ere, lambī, lambitum *I lick (up), touch* [KL3, W3]

lapis, -idis (m) *stone* [KL1, W27; KL2, L14]

lassus, -a, -um *tired, weary, faint* [KL3, W3]

Latīnus, -a, -um *Latin, of Latium* [KL2, W13]

lātitūdō, -dinis (f) *width, extent, latitude* [KL2, W9]

lātus, -a, -um *wide, broad* [KL1, L20]

latus, -eris (n) *side, flank* [KL3, L6]

laudō (1) *I praise* [KL1, L1]

laurus, -ī (m) *laurel-tree* [KL1, W20]

laus, laudis (f) *praise* [KL1, L15]

lavō, -āre, lāvī, lōtum/lavātum *I wash, bathe* [KL1, W27; KL2, L11]

lea, -ae (f) *lioness* [KL2, W11]

lectiō, -ōnis (f) *a reading, text* [KL3, W9]

lectulus, -ī (m) *bed, small couch* [KL3, W5]

lēgātus, -ī (m) *ambassador, envoy, lieutenant* [KL2, L15]

legiō, -ōnis (f) *legion* [KL3, W2]

legō, -ere, lēgī, lectum *I read, choose* [KL1, L28]

leō, leōnis (m) *lion* [KL1, L12]

lepus, -oris (m) *hare* [KL3, W2]

levis, -e *light* [KL2, W6]

leviter *softly, lightly* [KL2, W6]

levō (1) *I lift up, raise* [KL3, W1]

lēx, lēgis (f) *law, covenant* [KL2, L10]

liber, librī (m) *book* [KL1, L11]

līberī, -ōrum (m, pl) *children* [KL1, L10]

līberō (1) *I set free* [KL1, L1]

licet, licuit, - (impers. + dat./acc.) *it is permitted/lawful/allowed* [KL1, W26; KL3, L1]

līgneus, -a, -um *wooden* [KL3, W6]

lignum, -ī (n) *wood, tree* [KL2, L13]

ligō (1) *I bind (up/together), tie* [KL3, W16]

līlium, -iī (n) *lily* [KL3, W13]

līmen, -minis (n) *threshold, doorway, house* [KL3, L3]

limpidissimus, -a, -um *very bright, very clear* [KL1, W32]

linea, -ae (f) *line, string* [KL3, W9]

lingua, -ae (f) *language, tongue* [KL1, L26]

līnum, -ī (n) *flax* [KL3, W1]

līquidus, -a, -um *liquid, flowing, pure* [KL3, W16]

littera, -ae (f) *letter of the alphabet; (pl) letter, epistle* [KL1, L26]

lītus, lītoris (n) *shore, shoreline* [KL1, L13]

locus, -ī (m) *place;* **loca, -ōrum (n, pl)** *places [geographic]* [KL2, L7]; **locī, -ōrum (m, pl)** *places, passages, topics [in a book]* [KL2, L7]

longē *a long way off, far off* [KL3, L3]

longinquus, -a, -um *distant, far away* [KL1, L7]

longus, -a, -um *long* [KL1, L20]

loquor, -quī, ——, locūtus sum *I say, speak* [KL2, L6]

lūceō, lūcēre, lūxī, —— *I shine, am bright* [KL1, L11]

lūctus, -ūs (m) *grief, sorrow, mourning* [KL3, W13]

lūdō, lūdere, lūsī, lūsum *I play, tease, trick* [KL1, L26]

lumbus, -ī (m) *loin* [KL2, W9]

lūmen, -minis (n) *light, lamp* [KL3, L11]

lūmināre, -āris (n) *light(-giver), heavenly body, luminary* [KL3, W4]

lūna, -ae (f) *moon* [KL1, L2]

lutum, -ī (n) *mud, clay* [KL3, W8]

lux, lūcis (f) *light* [KL1, L12]

lyra, -ae (f) *lyre* [KL1, W28]

M

māchina, -ae (f) *machine, device, (military) engine* [KL3, W6]

magis *more, rather* [KL2, L7]

magicus, -a, -um *magic, magical* [KL2, W2]

magister, -strī (m) *teacher (male)* [KL1, L6]

magistra, -ae (f) *teacher (female)* [KL1, L6]

magistrātus, -ūs (m) *magistrate* [KL3, W5]

magnanimus, -a, -um *brave, bold, noble* [KL1, W9]

magnoperē *greatly, very much* [KL1, L29]

magnus, -a, -um *large, big, great* [KL1, L7]

māior, māius (gen. māioris) *greater, older* [KL1, W31; KL2, L5]

male *badly, ill, wrongly* [KL1, L1]

maledīcō, -ere, -dīxī, -dictum (+ dat.) *I speak ill, curse, slander* [KL1, W30; KL3, L4]

malignus, -a, -um *evil, wicked, malicious, malignant* [KL3, L13]

malitia, -ae (f) *malice, wickedness* [KL2, L14]

malus, -a, -um *bad, evil* [KL1, L7]

mālō, mālle, māluī, —— *I prefer, want more/ instead* [KL2, L14]

mandātum, -ī (n) *command(ment), order* [KL2, L10]

mandō (1) *I order, command; commit, entrust* (alicuī aliquid) [KL3, L10]

mandūcō (1) *I chew, eat* [KL1, L6]

māne *in the morning, early* [KL1, W19; KL2, L6]

maneō, -ēre, mansī, mansum *I remain* [KL1, L10]

manifestō (1) *I reveal, make clear, manifest* [KL2, W8]

manifestus, -a, -um *manifest, evident* [KL3, W1]

mānō (1) *I flow, trickle, drop* [KL3, W16]

manus, -ūs (f) *hand* [KL1, L25]

mappa, -ae (f) *starting flag (lit., "napkin")* [KL1, W23]

mare, maris (n) *sea* [KL1, L18]

maritimus, -a, -um *of/belonging to the sea* [KL3, W2]

marmoreus, -a, -um *(made of) marble, marble-like* [KL3, W16]

Mars, Martis (m) *Mars* [KL2, W13]

masculus, -a, -um *male* [KL3, W4]

māter, mātris (f) *mother* [KL1, L12]

māteria, -ae (f) *material, timber* [KL3, W2]

māternus, -a, -um *of/belonging to a mother, maternal* [KLS, W16]

mātrimōnium -ī (n) *marriage* [KL1, L20]

mātūtīnus, -a, -um *of the (early) morning, early* [KL3, W9]

māximē *most, especially, very* [KL2, L7]

māximus, -a, -um *biggest, greatest* [KL1, W31; KL2, L5]

mediōcris, -e *ordinary* [KL1, L19]

mediterrāneus, -a, um *inland* [KL3, W2]

medius, -a, -um *middle (of), midst (of)* [KL1, L26]

melior, -ius *better* [KL1, W28; KL2, L5]

melius *better* [KL2, L7]

memor, -oris *mindful, remembering* [KL3, L9]

memoria, -ae (f) *memory, remembrance* [KL3, L2]

mendācium, -iī (n) *lie, falsehood, counterfeit* [KL3, L6]

mendāx, -dacis (m/f) *liar* [KL3, L6]

mendicō (1) *I beg (for)* [KL2, W8]

mendicus, -ī (m) *beggar* [KL2, W8]

mensa, -ae (f) *table* [KL1, L31]

mensis, -is (m) *month* [KL3, L10]

mēnsūra, -ae (f) *measurement, measure* [KL2, L14]

mentior, -īrī, ——, -ītus sum *I lie, deceive, say falsely* [KL3, L6]

Mercurius, -ī (m) *Mercury (the messenger god)* [KL1, W21; KL2, W6]

mereō, -ēre, -uī, -itum *I deserve, earn, am worthy of* [KL1, L15; KL3, W6]

merīdiēs, -ēī (m) *noon* [KL1, L28]

Messīā(s), -ae (m) *Messiah, Anointed One* [KL2, W12]

-met (intensifying suffix on personal pronouns) *-self* [KL3, L7]

mēta, -ae (f) *turning-post, goal* [KL1, W23]

mētior, -īrī, ——, mēnsus sum *I measure, traverse* [KL2, L14]

metō, -ere, messuī, messum *I reap, harvest* [KL2, W14]

metuō, -ere, -uī, -ūtum *I fear, am afraid of, revere* [KL3, L15]

metus, -ūs (m) *fear, dread* [KL1, L26]

meus, -a, -um *my, mine* [KL1, L11]

micō, -āre, -uī, —— *I glitter, flash* [KL3, W3]

Midās, -ae (m) *Midas (king of Phrygia)* [KL1, W27]

mīles, mīlitis (m) *soldier* [KL1, L12]

mille *one thousand* [KL1, L21]

mīllēsimus, -a, -um *one thousandth* [KL1, L23]

Minerva, -ae (f) *Minerva* [KL3, W6]

minimē *least, not at all* [KL2, L7]

minimus, -a, -um *least, younger* [KL1, W31; KL2, L5]

minister, -strī (m) *attendant, servant, minister* [KL3, L10]

minor, -ārī, ——, -ātus sum *I threaten, menace* [KL2, W5]

minor, minus *smaller* [KL2, L5]

Mīnōs, -ōnis (m) *Minos* [KL1, W30]

Mīnōtaurus, -ī (m) *the Minotaur* [KL1, W30]

minus *less* [KL2, L7]

minūtātim *gradually, bit by bit* [KL1, L20]

mīrābilis, -e *marvelous, wonderful* [KL3, L3]

mīror, -ārī, ——, mīrātus sum *I marvel at, am amazed at, admire* [KL2, L6]

mīrus, -a, -um *strange, wonderful* [KL1, L7]

miser, -era, -erum *unhappy, wretched, miserable* [KL1, L7]

misereor, -ērī, ——, misertus sum (+ gen.) *I pity, have mercy on* [KL2, L6]

miseria, -ae (f) *misery, distress, suffering* [KL3, W9]

misericordia, -ae (f) *mercy, pity* [KL2, L10]

mītigō (1) *I calm, soothe, pacify* [KL3, W7]

mītra, -ae (f) *turban* [KL1, W28]

mittō, -ere, mīsī, missum *I send, let go* [KL1, L26]

modicus, -a, -um *moderate, ordinary, little* [KL2, L14]

modus, -ī (m) *measure, way, manner, sort* [KL3, L7]

modo *only, just, merely, now, but* [KL1, L27]

moenia, -ium (n, pl) *fortifications, city walls* [KL1, L18]

mōlior, -īrī, ——, mōlītus sum *I labor, build, undertake* [KL2, L6]

monachus, -ī (m) *monk* [KL3, W7]

monastērium, -iī (n) *monastery* [KL3, W7]

moneō, -ēre, -uī, -itum *I warn* [KL1, L9]

mōns, montis *mountain* [KL1, L18]

mōnstrum, -ī (n) *monster* [KL1, W30]; *omen, portent* [KL3, W3]

monumentum, -ī (n) *monument, memorial* [KL2, W11]

mordeō, -ēre, momordī, morsum *I bite, sting* [KL1, L9]

morior, morī, ——, mortuus sum *I die* [KL2, L6]

mors, mortis (f) *death* [KL1, L18]

mortālis, -e *mortal* [KL2, W6]

mortuus, -a, -um *dead* [KL2, L3]

mōrus, -ī (f) *mulberry tree* [KL2, W11]

mōs, mōris (m) *manner, custom; (pl.) character, morals* [KL2, L13]

moveō, -ēre, mōvī, mōtum *I move* [KL1, L14]

mox *soon* [KL1, L15]

mulier, mulieris (f) *woman* [KL1, L22]

multiplicō (1) *I multiply, increase* [KL3, W20]

multitūdō, -tudinis (f) *multitude, crowd* [KL2, L12]

multum *much* [KL2, L7]

multus, -a, -um *much, many* [KL1, L7]

mundō (1) *I clean, cleanse* [KL3, L5]

mundus, -a, -um *clean, neat, elegant* [KL3, L5]

mundus, -ī (m) *world, universe* [KL1, L6]

mūnītiō, -ōnis (f) *fortification, bulwark* [KL3, W2]

mūnus, -neris (n) *office, duty, gift* [KL2, L15]

mūrus, -ī (m) *wall* [KL2, L11]

musicus, -ī (m) *musician* [KL1, W28]

mūtō (1) *I change* [KL1, L20]

mūtus, -a, -um *mute* [KL3, W1]

N

nam *for; certainly* [KL1, W32; KL2, L9]

narrō (1) *I tell, relate, recount* [KL1, L2]

nāscor, -scī, ——, nātus sum *I am born, am begotten, arise* [KL2, L12]

natātōria, -ae (f) *pool, place for swimming* [KL2, W8]

nātīvitās, -tātis (f) *birth, nativity* [KL2, W8]

naufragium, -ī (n) *wreck, crash (lit., shipwreck)* [KL1, W23]

nauta, -ae (m) *sailor* [KL1, L3]

nāvicula, -ae (f) *boat* [KL1, W31]

nāvigō (1) *I sail* [KL1, L4]

nāvis, -is (f) *ship* [KL1, L18]

-ne *interrogative enclitic indicating a simple yes/no question* [KL2, L7]

nē (adv.) *not, no* [KL3, L4]

nē (conj.) *that not, lest* [KL3, L4]

nec (neque) *and not, nor;* **nec...nec** *neither....nor* [KL1, L14]

necesse (n, indecl.) *necessary, unavoidable;* **necesse est (impers. + dat./acc.)** *it is necessary* [KL3, L1]

necō (1) *I kill, slay* [KL1, L1]

nefās (n, indecl.) *sin, crime; (when transl. as adj.) forbidden* [KL3, L2]

negō (1) *I say no, deny (often used instead of* nōn dīcō*)* [KL3, L3]

negōtium, -iī (n) *business, occupation* [KL3, W9]

nēmō, neminis (m/f) *no one, nobody* [KL2, L4]

neō, nēre, nēvī, nētus *I spin, weave* [KL2, W14]

nepōs, -pōtis (m/f) *descendant, grandson/ granddaughter, nephew/ niece* [KL2, L13]

Neptūnus, -ī (m) *Neptune* [KL2, W7]

nequaquam *by no means, not at all* [KL2, W8]

neque (nec) *and not, nor;* **nec...nec** *neither....nor* [KL1, L14]

nesciō, -īre, -īvī, -ītum *I do not know, am ignorant (of)* [KL1, L30; KL3, L3]

neuter, -tra, -trum *neither* [KL2, L15]

nex, necis (f) *(violent) death, slaughter, murder* [KL3, W10]

niger, -gra, -grum *(shining) black, dark-colored* [KL1, L17]

nihil (n. indecl.) *nothing;*

nihil (adv.) *not at all* [KL1, L6]

nimis (adv.) *too (much), excessively* [KL3, L4]

nimium *too much, too, excessively* [KL2, W13]

nisi *if not, unless, except* [KL3, L11]

nix, nivis (f) *snow* [KL2, L9]

nō (1) *I swim* [KL1, L14]

nōbilis, -e *noble, famous* [KL2, W15]

nocēns, -ntis *harmful, injurious* [KL2, W11]

nōlō, nōlle, nōluī, —— *I do not wish, do not want, am unwilling* [KL2, L14]

nōmen, nōminis (n) *name* [KL1, L13]

nōminō (1) *I name, give a name to, call* [KL3, W13]

nōn *not* [KL1, L1]

nōndum (adv.) *not yet* [KL3, L7]

nōnne *interrogative adverb expecting a yes answer* [KL2, L7]

nōnus, -a, -um *ninth* [KL1, L23]

nōs (pl.) *we* [KL1, L17]

nōscō, -ere, nōvī, nōtum *I learn, get to know; pf. tense, I know* [KL2, L9]

noster, -stra, -strum *our, ours* [KL1, L11]

novem *nine* [KL1, L21]

noverca, -ae (f) *step-mother* [KL1, W22]

novus, -a, -um *new* [KL1, L26]

nox, noctis (f) *night* [KL1, L18]

nūbes, nūbis (f) *cloud, gloom* [KL1, L18]

nūbō, -ere, nūpsī, nūptum *I marry, am married to (of a bride)* [KL3, W2]

nūdus, -a, -um *naked, bare, exposed* [KL3, W7]

nūllus, -a, -um *no, none, not any* [KL2, L4]

num *interrogative adverb expecting a no answer* [KL2, L7]

nūmen, -minis (n) *divinity, god, divine will* [KL2, L7]

numerus, -ī (m) *number* [KL3, L2]

nummus, -ī (m) *coin* [KL1, W22]

numquam *never* [KL1, L5]

numquid (emphatic form of num) *interrogative adv. expecting a no answer (can be translated "surely...not? is it really possible that...?" etc.)* [KL2, L9]

nunc *now* [KL1, L1]

nuntiō (1) *I announce, declare* [KL1, L14]

nuntius, -ī (m) *messenger* [KL2, L12]

nūptiālis, -e, *of a wedding, wedding (adj.), nuptial* [KL2, W2]

nūtō (1) *I nod, shake, sway to and fro* [KL3, W7]

nympha, -ae (f) *nymph* [KL1, W20; KL2, W6]

O

ob (+ acc.) *on account of, for; in front of* [KL2, L3]

obcaecō (1) *I (make) blind, darken, conceal* [KL3, W12]

oblīvīscor, -vīscī, ——, oblītus sum (+ gen.) *I forget* [KL2, L7]

oboediō [obediō], -īre, -īvī, -ītum (+ dat.?) *I obey, serve, heed* [KL3, W5]

obsecrō (1) *I beseech, beg, implore;* [tē/vōs] obsecrō *please, pray* [KL3, L13]

observō (1) *I observe, watch, keep, guard* [KL3, W11]

obsideō, -ēre, -sēdī, -sessum *I besiege, remain near* [KL1, L10]

obsidiō, -ōnis (f) *siege, blockade* [KL2, W15]

obsistō, -ere, -stitī, -stitum *I oppose, withstand, resist* [KL3, W7]

obstō, -stāre, -stitī, -stātūrum (+ dat.) *I stand in the way, hinder, obstruct* [KL2, W11]

obumbrō (1) *I overshadow, cover, cast a shadow (on)* [KL3, W4]

obviam (adv.) *in the way, against* [KL3, W7]

occāsiō, -ōnis (f) *occasion, opportunity* [KL3, W10]

occīdō, -ere, -cīdī, -cīsum *I kill, cut down, slay* [KL1, L30]

occultō (1) *I hide, conceal* [KL1, L22]

occupō (1) *I seize* [KL1, L6]

Ōceanus, -ī (m) *ocean, [the deity] Ocean* [KL3, W6]

ōceanus, -ī (m) *ocean* [KL1, L4]

octāvus, -a, -um *eighth* [KL1, L23]

octō *eight* [KL1, L21]

oculus, -ī (m) *eye* [KL2, L3]

ōdī, ōdisse, [fut. prt.] ōsūrum [defective] *I hate, dislike* [KL3, L6]

odium, -iī (n) *hatred, disgust* [KL3, L4]

offerō, offerre, obtulī, oblātum *I offer, bring/ carry to* [KL2, L11]

oleum, -ī (n) *oil, olive oil* [KL3, L14]

ōlim *once upon a time, formerly, then* [KL1, L6]

omnīnō *altogether, wholly, at all* [KL3, L5]

omnipotēns, -tentis *omnipotent, all-powerful, almighty* [KL3, W2]

omnis, -e *every, all* [KL1, L19]

onus, oneris (n) *burden, load, weight* [KL1, L13; KL3, L3]

operor, -ārī, —, operātus sum *I work, labor, am busy* [KL2, L6]

oportet, -ēre, -tuit, -tuitum (impers. + acc.) *it is proper, necessary* [KL3, L1]

oppidum, -ī (n) *town* [KL1, L5]

oppugnō (1) *I attack* [KL1, L4]

optimē *best* [KL2, L7]

optimus, -a, -um *best* [KL2, L5]

optio, optiōnis (f) *choice* [KL1, W12]

opus, operis (n) *work, deed* [KL2, L3]

ōra, -ae (f) *shore* [KL1, L13]

ōrāculum, -ī (n) *oracle, prophecy* [KL1, W31; KL2, W6]

orba, -ae (f) *orphan (female)* [KL1, L22]

orbus, -a, -um *deprived of parents or children, bereft* [KL1, L22]

orbus, -ī (m) *orphan (male)* [KL1, L22]

ōrdō, -dinis (m) *line, row, order* [KL2, L15]

orior, -īrī, —, ortus sum *I (a)rise, am born/created* [KL2, L6]

ornātus, -ūs (m) *preparation, furnishing, adornment, ornament* [KL3, W6]

ōrō (1) *I pray, speak (takes double acc.)* [KL1, L6]

ōs, ōris (n) *mouth* [KL1, L13]

os, ossis (n) *bone* [KL3, L15]

ōsculum, -ī (n) *a kiss* [KL2, W11]

ostendō, -ere, -dī, -sum/tum *I show, point out, declare* [KL3, L5]

ōstium, -iī (n) *door, gate, entrance* [KL2, L4]

Oswaldus, -ī (m) *Oswald* [KL1, W19]

ovis, ovis (f) *sheep* [KL2, L3]

P

Pactōlus, -ī (m) *Pactolus (a river in Lydia in Asia Minor)* [KL1, W27]

paene (adv.) *almost* [KL1, L19]

paenitentia, -ae (f) *repentance, penitence* [KL3, W5]

pactus, -a, -um *agreed upon, covenanted, appointed* [KL2, L13]

palleō, -ēre, -uī, —— *I am/grow pale* [KL3, W7]

pallium, -ī (n) *cloak, cover(ing)* [KL3, W7]

Pallas, -adis (f) *(Pallas) Athena* [KL3, W6]

palma, -ae (f) *hand* [KL1, W14]

palus, palūdis (f) *swamp* [KL1, W13]

Pān, Pānos (acc. Pāna) (m) *Pan (god of woods, shepherds, and flocks)* [KL1, W28]

pānis, -is (m) *bread* [KL1, L29]

parcō, -ere, pepercī, parsūrum (+ dat.) *I spare* [KL2, L13]

parēns, -ntis (m/f) *parent, father, mother* [KL1, W11; KL2, W8]

pariō, -ere, peperī, par(i)tum *I bring forth, give birth to, beget* [KL3, L13]

pariter *equally* [KL3, L1]

parō (1) *I prepare* [KL1, L14]

pars, partis (f) *part; side, direction* [KL2, L3]

parum *(too) little, not enough* [KL2, L7]

parvus, -a, -um *little, small, unimportant* [KL1, L7]

pascō, -ere, pāvī, pastum *I feed, pasture* [KL1, W32; KL2, W14]

passim *everywhere, far and wide* [KL2, L13]

pastor, pastōris (m) *shepherd* [KL1, L20]

pastorālis, -e *of/belonging to a shepherd, pastoral* [KL1, W32]

pater, patris (m) *father* [KL1, L12]

patior, -ī, —, passus sum *I suffer, endure* [KL2, L6]

patria, -ae (f) *native land* [KL1, L3]

pātrō (1) *I bring to pass, accomplish* [KL3, W4]

patruēlis, -is (m/f) *cousin (on the father's side)* [KL1, L22]

patruus, -ī (m) *uncle (father's brother)* [KL1, L22]

paucī, -ae, -a (pl) *few* [KL1, L7]

paulātim *little by little, gradually* [KL3, W7]

pauper, -eris *poor* [KL3, L9]

paveō, -ēre, pavī, —— *I dread, fear, tremble* [KL3, L15]

pāvo, -ōnis (m) *peacock* [KL1, W21]

pāx, pācis (f) *peace* [KL1, L15]

peccātor, -ōris (m) *sinner* [KL3, L5]

peccātrix, -trīcis (f) *sinner* [KL3, L5]

peccātum, -ī (n) *sin, fault, offense* [KL3, L11]

peccō (1) *I sin, offend, transgress* [KL3, L11]
pecūnia, -ae (f) *money* [KL1, L3]
pecus, -coris (n) *cattle, herd* [KL3, L2]
pēior, pēius *worse* [KL2, L5]
pēius (adv.) *worse* [KL2, L7]
pellis, -is (f) *skin, hide* [KL3, W2]
penātēs, -ium (m, pl) *the Penates* [KL3, W3]
pendō, -ere, pependī, pensum *I weigh, suspend, ponder* [KL3, L10]
penna, -ae (f) *feather*; in pl., *wing(s)* [KL3, W16]
pennātus, -a, um *winged* [KL2, W6]
per (+ acc.) *through* [KL1, L3]
pēra, -ae (f) *bag, satchel* [KL1, W32]
percutiō, -ere, -cussī, -cussum *I strike down/through, cut down, beat, pierce* [KL1, W32; KL2, L3]
perdō, -ere, perdidī, perditum *I destroy, ruin, lose* [KL1, L27]
perficiō, -ere, -fēci, -fectum *I complete, finish* [KL1, W23; KL3, L14]
perfundō, -ere, -fūdī, -fūsus *I pour over, drench* [KL3, W6]
perīculum, -ī (n) *danger* [KL1, L5]
permaneō, -ēre, -mansī, -mansum *I remain, continue, abide (in)* [KL3, L7]
permittō, -ere, -mīsī, -missum *I permit, allow* [KL1, W30]
perpetuō, *forever* [KL2, W2]
persequor, -sequī, ——, -secutus sum (deponent) *I pursue (with hostile intent), hunt down* [KL1, W32; KL2, W6]
perspiciō, -ere, -spēxī, -spectum *I perceive, ascertain* [KL3, W2]
persuādeō, -ere, -suāsī, -suāsum (+ dat.) *I persuade* [KL1, W15; KL3, L10]
pertūsus, -a, -um *leaky* [KL1, W29]
perveniō, -īre, -vēnī, -ventum *I arrive, come through to, reach* [KL2, L11]
pēs, pedis (m) *foot* [KL3, W3]
pessimē *worst* [KL2, L7]

pessimus, -a, -um *worst* [KL2, L5]
petītiō, -ōnis (f) *petition, request* [KL3, W16]
petō, -ere, -īvī, -ītum *I shoot* [KL1, W20]; *I seek, ask (for); attack* [KL2, L12]
Pharisaeus, -ī (m) *Pharisee* [KL2, W3]
Philistheus, -ī (m) *Philistine* [KL1, W32]
phoenīx, -nīcis (m) *phoenix* [KL3, W3]
Phrygia, -ae (f) *Phrygia (a land in Asia Minor)* [KL1, W27]
pietās, -tātis (f) *duty, piety, loyalty* [KL2, W13]
pila, -ae (f) *ball* [KL1, W30]
pinguis, -e *fat* [KL1, W25]
pīnus, -ī (f) *pine (tree), fir (tree)* [KL3, W7]
pīrāta, -ae (m) *pirate* [KL1, L2]
piscātor, -ōris (m) *fisherman* [KL3, W6]
piscis, -is (m) *fish* [KL1, L19]
piscor, -ārī, ——, -ātus sum (deponent) *I fish* [KL1, W29]
placeō, -ēre, -cuī, -citum *I please, am pleasing (often impers.* placet/placuit *[+ dat.]; rarely, a first conjugation verb)* [KL3, L1]
placidus, -a, -um *calm, quiet* [KL1, W29]
placitum, -ī (n) *principle, agreement* [KL3, W9]
placitus, -a, -um *pleasing, agreeable* [KL3, W12]
plāga, -ae (f) *a blow, wound; plague, destruction* [KL3, L14]
planctus, -ūs (m) *lamentation, wailing* [KL3, W8]
platēa, -ae (f) *street, broad way* [KL3, L1]
plēnus, -a, -um *full, plump, abundant* [KL2, L4]
plērumquē (adv.) *generally, for the most part* [KL3, W7]
plumbeus, -a, -um *leaden, of lead* [KL1, W20]
plumbum, -ī (n) *lead* [KL3, W2]
plūrimum *most* [KL2, L7]

plūrimus, -a, -um *most* [KL2, L5]
——, plūs *more* [KL2, L5]
Plūto, -tōnis (m) *Pluto* [KL2, W6]
pluvia, -ae (f) *rain* [KL2, L9]
poena, -ae (f) *penalty, punishment*; **poenās dō** *I pay the penalty* [KL1, L27]
poēta, -ae (m) *poet* [KL1, L2]
polliceor, -ērī, ——, pollicitus sum *I promise, offer, declare* [KL3, L7]
Polyphēmus, -ī (m) *Polyphemus* [KL2, W4]
pōmum, -ī (n) *fruit, apple* [KL3, W11]
pōmifer, -era, -erum *fruit-bearing* [KL3, W6]
pōnō, -ere, posuī, positum *I put, place* [KL1, L26]
pōns, pontis (m) *bridge* [KL1, W19]
populus, -ī (m) *people, nation* [KL1, L11]
porcus, -ī (m) *pig* [KL1, L10]
porta, -ae (f) *door, gate* [KL1, L31]
porticus, -ūs (f) *portico, porch, colonnade* [KL3, W5]
portō (1) *I carry* [KL1, L4]
postquam *after* [KL2, L10]
postulō (1) *I ask, demand, desire (aliquid ab/ de aliquō; aliquem aliquid)* [KL3, L10]
portus, -ūs (m) *harbor, port* [KL1, L25]
poscō, -ere, pōposcī, —— *I request, ask earnestly* [KL3, W12]
possum, posse, potuī, —— *I am able, can* [KL1, L11]
post (+ acc.) *after, behind* [KL1, L17]
postea *afterwards* [KL1, L28]
postnatus, -ī (m) *oldest [son]* [KL1, W19]
postquam (conj.) *after* [KL1, W15]
potēns, (gen.) -entis *powerful* [KL1, L19]
potius (adv.) *more, rather* [KL3, L7]
pōtō, -āre, -āvī, pōtātum or pōtum *I drink, drink heavily* [KL1, L6]
prae (adv. & prep. + abl.) *below* [KL2, L5]
praebeō, -ēre, -uī, -itum *I give, show, expose* [KL3, W7]

praecīdō, -ere, -cīdī, -cīsum *I cut off, lop* [KL1, W32; KL2, W6]

praecipiō, -ere, -cēpī, -ceptum *I anticipate, warn, command* [KL3, W5]

praeda, -ae (f) *spoil, booty, plunder* [KL2, L15]

praedicō (1) *I proclaim, preach, declare* [KL3, W7]

praedīcō, -ere, -dīxī, -dictum *I predict, prophesy* [KL1, W31]

praeferō, -ferre, -tulī, -lātum *I seek after, prefer* [KL2, W11]

praemium, -ī (n) *reward* [KL1, W27]

praeter (prep. + acc.) *beside, beyond, past* [KL2, L13]

prātum, -ī (n) *meadow, plain* [KL2, W15]

premō, -ere, pressī, pressum *I press, crush, overpower* [KL2, L10]

pretiōsus, -a, -um *expensive* [KL2, W2]

prīmum/prīmō *(at) first* [KL2, L7]

prīmus, -a, -um *first* [KL1, L23]

prīnceps, -cipis (m) *leader, chief, prince* [KL2, L3]

prīncipium, -iī (n) *beginning, origin* [KL3, L4]

prior, prius *former, before* [KL2, L5]

priusquam (conj.) *before, sooner, rather, until* [KL3, L15]

prō (+ abl.) *before, in front of; for (the sake of), instead of* [KL1, L18]

probō (1) *I try, examine, test, prove, approve (of)* [KL3, L14]

procul *at/from a distance, (a)far* [KL2, L11]

prōdeō, -īre, -iī, -itum *I go/come forth* [KL3, L12]

prōdigium, -iī (n) *prophetic sign, wonder, portent* [KL3, W5]

prōdūcō, -ere, -dūxī, -ductum *I lead forth, bring forth, produce* [KL3, W4]

proelium, -ī (n) *battle* [KL1, L15]

proficīscor, -ficīscī, ——, -fectus sum *I start, set out* [KL2, L7]

profundum, -ī (n) *depth, chasm* [KL3, W9]

prōmittō, -ere, -mīsī, -missum *I send forth, let grow* [KL3, W2]

prope (adv./prep. + acc.) *near, next to* [KL1, L19]

properō (1) *I hurry, rush* [KL1, L20]

prophēta, -ae (m) *prophet, soothsayer* [KL3, L4]

propior, -ius *nearer* [KL2, L5]

propinquō (1) (+ dat./acc.) *I approach, come near* [KL2, W3]

propitiātiō, -ōnis (f) *propitiation, atonement* [KL2, W11]

prōpositiō, -tiōnis (f) *a setting forth, proposition, resolution* [KL3, W1]

propter (+ acc.) *because of, on account of, near* [KL1, L25]

proptereā *therefore* [KL2, L10]

prōra, -ae (f) *prow* [KL2, W13]

prōrumpō, -ere, -rūpī, -ruptum *I break forth, burst forth* [KL2, W9]

prōvidentia, -ae (f) *providence, provision, forethought* [KL2, W9]

prōvincia, -ae (f) *province, territory* [KL3, W10]

prōvocō (1) *to challenge* [KL1, W32]

proximus, -a, -um *next, nearest* [KL2, L5]

puella, -ae (f) *girl* [KL1, L3]

puer, puerī (m) *boy* [KL1, L5]

pugna, -ae (f) *fight, battle* [KL2, W9]

pugnō (1) *I fight* [KL1, L1]

pulcher, -chra, -chrum *beautiful, handsome* [KL1, L7]

pulsō (1) *I strike, knock* [K2L, W14]

purpureus, -a, -um *purple; dark-red, dark-violet, dark-brown* [KL1, L17]

puteus, -ī (m) *a well, pit* [KL2, L12]

putō (1) *I consider, think, suppose* [KL3, L3]

pseudoprophēta, -ae (m) *false prophet* [KL3, W14]

pyra, -ae (f) *funeral pyre* [KL1, W8]

Q

quadrīgae, -ārum (f, pl) *four-horse chariot* [KL1, W23]

quaerō, -ere, quaesīvī, quaesītum (-situm) *I ask, seek, inquire* [KL2, L3]

quālis (interrog. adj.) *of what sort, what kind of*; **(rel. adj.)** *of such a sort, such as, as* [KL3, L9]

quam *as, than, how* [KL1, L28]

quamdiu *how long?; as long as, until* [KL3, L9]

quandō *when (?), ever; since, because* [KL1, L12]

quantō (adv.) *(by) how much* [KL2, W14]

quantus, -a, -um *how much, how many, how great* [KL2, W13]

quārē *by what means? how? why? wherefore (?)* [KL3, L9]

quārtus, -a, -um decimus, -a, -um *fourteenth* [KL1, L23]

quārtus, -a, -um *fourth* [KL1, L23]

quasi *as if, just as; almost, nearly, about* [KL3, L11]

quassō (1) *I shake violently, batter* [KL3, W1]

quatiō, -ere, quassī, quassus *I shake, brandish* [KL3, W5]

quater (adv.) *four times* [KL3, W6]

quattuor *four* [KL1, L21]

quattuordecim *fourteen* [KL1, L21]

-que, (enclitic) *and* [KL1, L10]

quemadmodum (adv.) *how, in what manner* [KL3, L9]

quī, quae, quod *who, what, which, that* [KL2, L3]

quī? quae? quod? (interrog. adj.) *what (kind of)? which?* [KL2, L9]

quia (conj.) *because, since, that* [KL1, L18]

quīcumque, quaecumque, quodcumque *whoever, whichever, whatever; whosoever, etc.* [KL2, L12]

APPENDIX C \\ LATIN-ENGLISH GLOSSARY

quid *what?* [KL1, W19]

quīdam, quaedam, quiddam (pron.) *a certain one/thing; someone, something* [KL2, L12]

quīdam, quaedam, quoddam (adj.) *a certain; some* [KL2, L12]

quidem *indeed, certainly, even* [KL2, L3]

quiēscō, -ere, quiēvī, quiētum *I rest, keep quiet* [KL3, W7]

quīndecim *fifteen* [KL1, L21]

quīngentēsimus, -a, -um *five hundredth* [KL1, L23]

quīngentī *five hundred* [KL1, L21]

quīnquāgēsimus, -a, -um *fiftieth* [KL1, L23]

quīnquāgintā *fifty* [KL1, L21]

quīnque *five* [KL1, L21]

quīntus, -a, -um decimus, -a, -um *fifteenth* [KL1, L23]

quīntus, -a, -um *fifth* [KL1, L23]

quis *who?* [KL1, W31]

quis, quid (interrog. pron.) *who? what?; why?* [KL2, L9]

quisquam, quidquam/quicquam *anyone, anything, someone, something* [KL3, L1]

quisque, quaeque, quidque (pron.) and quodque (adj.) *each (one), every(one)* [KL3, L2]

quisquis, quidquid (quicquid) (pron.) *whoever, whichever, whatever* [KL2, L12]

quō *in/to what place (?), in/to which place (?), whither (?), where (?); why; in order that* [KL2, L11]

quoad *until* [KL2, W15]

quod *because, that* [KL1, L10]

quōmodo *how, in what way* [KL1, L25]

quondam *ever, once, formerly* [KL2, L13]

quoniam *because, since* [KL1, L26]

quoque *also, too* [KL1, L29]

R

rādō, -ere, rāsī, rāsum *I shave* [KL3, W2]

rapiō, -ere, rapuī, raptum *I snatch, seize, carry (off)* [KL1, L31]

raptus, -ūs (m) *kidnapping, abduction* [KL1, W31]

rārus, -a, -um *thin, scattered* [KL3, W2]

recēns, -centis *fresh, recent* [KL2, W11]

recipiō, -ere, -cēpī, -ceptum *I take back/again, receive* [KL3, L11]

redeō, -īre, -iī, -itum *I go back, come back, return* [KL3, L2]

referō, -ferre, -(t)tulī, -(l)lātum *I bring/take back, apply* [KL3, W9]

reficiō, -ere, -fēcī, -fectum *I repair, remake* [KL1, W29; KL3, W2]

rēgālis, -e *royal, regal, kingly* [KL3, W10]

rēgia, -ae (f) *palace* [KL1, L2]

rēgīna, -ae (f) *queen* [KL1, L2]

regiō, -ōnis (f) *boundary, territory, region* [KL3, W2]

regnō (1) *I rule, govern, reign* [KL1, L6]

regnum, -ī (n) *kingdom* [KL1, L5]

regō, -ere, rexī, rectum *I rule* [KL1, L26]

regredior, -gredī, ——, -gressus sum *I go back, return* [KL3, L10]

rēgula, -ae (f) *rule, example, pattern* [KL3, W9]

rēiciō, -ere, -iēcī, -iectum *I throw back, fling back* [KL3, W7]

religiō, -ōnis (f) *religion, reverence* [KL3, W7]

religō (1) *I bind (back/up), fetter* [KL3, W16]

reliquus, -a, -um *remaining, rest (of)* [KL2, L6]

relinquō, -ere, -līquī, -lictum *I abandon, leave behind* [KL1, L28]

remissiō, -ōnis (f) *remission, forgiveness* [KL3, W5]

remittō, -ere, -mīsī, -missum *I send back, remove, forgive* [KL3, L11]

removeō, -ēre, -mōvī, -mōtum *I remove, take away* [KL1, L14]

rēmus, -ī (m) *oar* [KL2, W5]

reor, rērī, ——, ratus sum *I think, suppose, imagine* [KL3, W16]

repellō, -ere, reppulī, repulsum *I drive back, push back, repel* [KL3, W2]

repentē *suddenly* [KL1, L10]

repetō, -ere, -īvī/-iī, -ītum *I repeat, seek again* [KL3, W9]

rēpleō, -ēre, -plēvī, -plētum *I fill (up), fill again, complete* [KL3, L5]

reprehendō, -ere, -hendī, -hensum *I hold back, rebuke, censure, find fault with* [KL3, W13]

reprimō, -ere, -pressī, -pressum *I hold/keep back, restrain* [KL3, W9]

reprōmissiō, -ōnis (f) *(formal) promise, guarantee, counter-promise* [KL3, W12]

reptilis, -e *creeping, reptile* [KL3, W4]

reptō (1) *I crawl, creep* [KL1, L14]

requiēscō, -ere, -quiēvī, -quiētum *I rest* [KL3, L4]

rēs, reī (f) *thing* [KL1, L28]

resistō, -ere, -stitī, —— *I stand back/still, halt* [KL3, L2]

rēspiciō, -ere, -spēxī, -spectum *I look back, regard* [KL2, L14]

respondeō, -ēre, -spondī, -sponsum *I answer, respond* [KL1, L9]

rēstinguō, -ere, -stinxī, -stinctum *I put out, exstinguish* [KL3, W3]

restituō, -ere, -stituī, -stitutus *I restore, revive* [KL3, W1]

resūmō, -ere, -sūmpsī, -sūmptum *I resume, take up again, take back* [KL3, W16]

resupīnus, -a, -um *backwards, lying on one's back, supine* [KL3, W7]

resurgō, -ere, -surrēxī, -surrēctum *I rise again* [KL1, L29]

retrō *back(ward), behind* [KL1, W23; KL3, W3]

revēlō (1) *I unveil, reveal, disclose* [KL3, W9]

revertor, -vertī, ——, reversus sum *I turn back, return, go back (not always deponent)* [KL2, L6]

revocō (1) *I call back, call again* [KL3, W2]

rēx, rēgis (m) *king* [KL1, L12]

rīdeō, -ēre, rīsī, rīsum *I laugh, smile* [KL1, L9]

rīma, -ae (f) *crack, fissure* [KL2, W11]

rogō (1) *I ask (takes double acc. or phrase with dē)* [KL1, L6]

Rōma, -ae (f) *Rome (capital city of ancient and modern Italy)* [KL2, L14]

Rōmānus, -a, -um *Roman;* **(subst.)** *a Roman* [KL2, L15]

rōs, rōris (m) *dew* [KL2, W9]

ruber, -bra, -brum *red, ruddy* [KL1, L17]

rūfus, -a, -um *red, ruddy* [KL1, W32]

rumpō, -ere, rūpī, ruptum *I burst, break* [KL2, L12]

ruō, -ere, ruī, rutum [but ruitūrus] *I fall down (violently), rush (down), hurl down* [KL3, L4]

rursum/rursus *back(wards), again* [KL3, L3]

rūs, rūris (n) *country, farm* [KL2, L14]

rusticus, -a, -um *of the county, rustic, rural;* **(as noun)** *a countryman, rustic, peasant* [KL3, W7]

S

sabbata, -ōrum (n, pl) *Sabbath* [KL1, W26]

sabbatum, -ī (n) *the Sabbath (often plural with singular meaning)* [KL3, L1]

saccus, -ī (m) *sack, bag* [KL2, W6]

sacer, -cra, -crum *holy, sacred* [KL2, L3]

sacerdōs, -dōtis (m) *priest* [KL2, L3]

sacrificium, -iī (n) *sacrifice, offering* [KL2, L4]

saeculum, -ī (n) *generation; the spirit of the age, times* [KL1, L6]

saepe *often* [KL1, L6]

saevus, -a, -um *savage, cruel, fierce* [KL2, W11]

sagitta, -ae (f) *arrow* [KL1, L3]

saliō, -īre, -uī, saltum *I jump, leap, spring* [KL1, W29; KL2, W12]

saltem *at least, anyhow* [KL3, W5]

salum, -ī (n) *the (salt) sea* [KL3, W6]

salūs, -ūtis (f) *salvation, deliverance, health, safety* [KL3, L7]

salvātor, -ōris (m) *savior, redeemer* [KL3, L5]

salveō, -ēre, ——, —— *I am well;* **salvē(te)**, *Good day! Be well!* [KL1, L9]

salvus, -a, -um *safe, saved, well, sound* [KL1, L25]

sanctificō (1) *I make holy, sanctify* [KL3, L4]

sanctus, -a, -um *holy, sacred, consecrated* [KL1, L25]

sanguis, -guinis (m) *blood* [KL2, L3]

sānus, -a, -um *healthy* [KL3, W1]

sapiēns, -entis *wise* [KL2, L4]

sapientia, -ae (f) *wisdom* [KL2, L10]

Satanās, -ae (m) *Satan* [KL3, W1]

satis (adv. & indecl. adj./noun) *enough, sufficient(ly)* [KL1, L30]

satrapa, -ae (m) *satrap, governor* [KL3, W10]

Saul (indecl.) *Saul* [KL1, W32]

saxum, -ī (n) *rock* [KL1, L29]

scandalum, -ī (n) *stumbling block, temptation, cause of offense* [KL3, L12]

scelus, -leris (n) *crime, sin* [KL3, L6]

schisma, -matis (n) *schism, division* [KL2, W8]

scīlicet *of course, naturally, it is clear* [KL3, L6]

scindō, -ere, scidī, scissum *I cut, tear, rend* [KL3, L10]

sciō, -īre, sciī (scīvī), scītum *I know* [KL1, L29]

scopulus, -ī (m) *cliff* [KL1, W30]

scrība, -ae (m) *scribe, clerk, secretary* [KL3, L10]

scrībō, -ere, scripsī, scriptum *I write* [KL1, L26]

scūtum, -ī (m) *shield* [KL1, L10]

sē (acc. reflexive pronoun) *himself, herself, itself* [KL1, W8]

sēcēdō, -ere -cessī, -cessum *I withdraw, go apart* [KL3, W1]

sēcrētum, -ī (n) *secret* [KL3, W28]

secundum (adv. & prep. + acc.) *after; according to* [KL1, L28]

secundus, -a, -um *second* [KL1, L23]

sed *but* [KL1, L1]

sēdecim *sixteen* [KL1, L21]

sedeō, -ēre, sēdī, sessum *I sit* [KL1, L9]

sēdūcō, -ere, -dūxī, -ductum *I lead aside/astray, seduce, deceive* [KL3, W11]

sella, -ae (f) *seat, chair* [KL1, L31]

sēmen, -minis (n) *seed, offspring, origin* [KL3, W4]

semper *always* [KL1, L5]

senātus, -ūs (m) *senate* [KL3, W15]

senex, senis (m) *old man* [KL1, L14]

senior, -ōris (adj.) *older, elder;* **(as noun)**, *an elder* [KL3, L5]

sensus, -ūs (m) *sense, feeling, understanding* [KL2, L15]

sententia, -ae (f) *thought, opinion, sentence* [KL3, L9]

sentiō, -īre, sēnsī, sēnsum *I feel, realize, perceive* [KL3, L3]

sepeliō, -īre, -īvī, sepultus *I bury* [KL3, W5]

sepulcrum (sepulchrum), -ī (n) *grave, tomb* [KL2, L13]

septem *seven* [KL1, L21]

septendecim *seventeen* [KL1, L21]

septimus, -a, -um decimus, -a, -um *seventeenth* [KL1, L23]

septimus, -a, -um *seventh* [KL1, L23]

sequor, sequī, —, secūtus sum (deponent) *I follow* [KL1, W30; KL2, L6]

sermō, -ōnis (m) *speech, talk, conversation* [KL2, L9]

serō, -ere, sēvī, satum *I sow, plant* [KL2, W11]

sērō, sērius, sērissimē (adv.) *late* [KL2, L11]

serpēns, -pentis (m/f) *serpent, snake* [KL2, W2]

serva, -ae (f) *female slave, servant* [KL1, L4]

serviō, -īre, -īvī, -ītum (+ dat.) *I serve, am a slave to* [KL2, L10]

servō (1) *I save* [KL1, L6]

servus, -ī (m) *male slave, servant* [KL1, L4]

seū (sīve) *or;* **seū…seū** *whether…or* [KL1, L30]

sex *six* [KL1, L21]

sextus, -a, -um decimus, -a, -um *sixteenth* [KL1, L23]

sextus, -a, -um *sixth* [KL1, L23]

sī (conj.) *if* [KL1, L18]

sībilus, -a, -um *hissing, whistling* [KL3, W6]

Sibylla, -ae (f) *the Sibyl* [KL2, W13]

sīca, -ae (f) *dagger* [KL1, L3]

sīc *so, thus* [KL2, L4]

Sicilia, -ae (f) *Sicily* [KL2, W5]

sīcut *as, just as, like* [KL1, L20]

sīdus, sīderis (n) *constellation, star, heavenly body* [KL3, L15]

sīgnō (1) *I mark out, point out* [KL3, W3]

sīgnum, -ī (n) *sign, signal, miracle* [KL3, L4]

silentium, -iī (n) *silence, stillness* [KL3, W9]

Sīlēnus, -ī (m) *Silenus (pudgy old fellow [usually drunk], former tutor and longtime companion of Bacchus)* [KL1, W27]

sileō, -ēre, -uī, —— *I am silent, keep silent* [KL3, W10]

silva, -ae (f) *forest* [KL1, L3]

similis, -e *similar, like* [KL2, L5]

similitūdō, -dinis (f) *likeness, resemblance* [KL3, W4]

simul *together, at the same time;* **simul atque/ac** *as soon as* [KL2, L9]

simulacrum, -ī (n) *statue, likeness, image, idol* [KL1, W25; KL3, L6]

sine (+ abl.) *without* [KL1, L9]

singulī, -ae, -a *one at a time, single, separate* [KL2, L13]

sinister, -stra, -strum *left(-handed); inauspicious* [KL1, L30]

sinō, -ere, sīvī, situs *I let, allow* [KL2, W13]

sitiō, -īre, -īvī, —— *I thirst (for), am thirsty* [KL2, W12]

sive *whether* [KL3, W1]

sīve (seū) *or;* **sīve…sīve** *whether…or* [KL1, L30]

societās, -tātis (f) *society, fellowship, community* [KL3, W11]

socius, -iī (m) *ally, companion* [KL2, L13]

sōl, sōlis (m) *sun* [KL1, L12]

solea, -ae (f) *sandal* [KL2, W6]

soleō, -ēre, ——, solitus sum (semi-deponent) *I am accustomed (to), am in the habit of* [KL3, L9]

solidō (1) *I make firm, strengthen* [KL2, W9]

sōlitūdō, -dinis (f) *solitude, loneliness* [KL3, W9]

solium, -iī (n) *throne, seat* [KL3, W10]

sollicitus, -a, -um *anxious, troubled* [KL2, W14]

sōlum (adv.) *only, alone, merely* [KL3, L7]

sōlus, -a, -um *only, single* [KL1, W12; KL2, L4]

solvō, -ere, solvī, solūtum *I loose, set free, pay* [KL2, L10]

somniō (1) *I dream* [KL1, W18]

somnus, -ī (n) *sleep* [KL2, W13]

sonitus, -ūs (m) *noise, sound* [KL3, W3]

sopor, -ōris (m) *(deep) sleep* [KL3, W6]

soror, sorōris (f) *sister* [KL1, L12]

sors, -rtis (f) *lot, oracle, chance, destiny* [KL3, L6]

spargō, -ere, sparsī, sparsum *I scatter, sprinkle* [KL2, W9]

speciēs, -ēī (f) *appearance, likeness, species* [KL3, W4]

spectō (1) *I look at, watch* [KL1, L1]

spēlunca, -ae (f) *cave* [KL1, L3]

spērō (1) *I hope, expect* [KL3, L1]

spēs, speī (f) *hope* [KL1, L28]

spīca, -ae (f) *point, head (of grain), ear (of corn)* [KL3, W1]

spīna, -ae (f) *barrier (lit., "spine," the wall dividing a race course in half lengthwise)* [KL1, W23]

spīra, -ae (f) *coil, fold* [KL3, W6]

spīrō (1) *I breathe, blow* [KL2, W3]

spīritus, -ūs (m) *spirit, breath* [KL1, L25]

spūmō (1) *I foam, froth, spray* [KL3, W6]

spurius, -a, -um *spurious* [KL1, W32]

squāmeus, -a, -um *scaly* [KL3, W6]

statim *immediately* [KL1, L13]

statuō, -ere, -uī, -ūtum *I cause to stand, set (up), place* [KL2, W7]

stella, -ae (f) *star* [KL1, L11]

sternō, -ere, strāvī, strātum *I spread (out), scatter, extend* [KL2, L13]

stīpendium, -iī (n) *pay, stipend, tax* [KL2, W15]

stō, stāre, stetī, statum *I stand* [KL1, L1]

strātum, -ī (n) *covering, blanket* [KL3, W10]

stringō, -ere, strinxī, strictum *I draw (out), pull* [KL3, W7]

stultitia, -ae (f) *foolishness, folly* [KL1, W27]

stultus, -a, -um *foolish* [KL1, L7]

stupeō, -ēre, -uī, —— *I am stunned, am astonished, am stupefied* [KL3, W16]

stupor, -ōris (m) *amazement, astonishment* [KL1, W28]

suādeō, -ēre, suāsī, suāsum *I persuade, exhort* [KL3, W13]

sub (+ acc.) *under, up under, close to;* **(+ abl.)** *below, under(neath), at the foot of* [KL1, L14]

subdūcō, -ere, -dūxī, -ductum *I draw up, haul up* [KL2, W2]

sūbiciō, -ere, -iēcī, -iectum *I throw/place under, subdue* [KL3, W4]

subitō/subitum *suddenly, unexpectedly, immediately* [KL3, L3]

subitus, -a, -um *sudden, unexpected* [KL3, W3]

substantia, -ae (f) *substance, essence; property, fortune, worldly goods* [KL3, L13]

subsistō, -ere, -stitī, —— *I halt, stand still, pause* [KL3, W6]

subvertō, -ere, -vertī, -versus *I overturn, overthrow, ruin* [KL3, W7]

succēdō, -ere, -cessī, -cessum *I succeed, replace* [KL3, W2]

sufficiō, -ere, -fēcī, -fectum *I am sufficient, suffice* [KL2, W14]

——, suī *(3rd person reflexive pron.)* *himself, herself, itself, themselves* [KL3, L2]

sum, esse, fuī, futūrum *I am* [KL1, L3]

summa, -ae (f) *top, main point, sum(mary)* [KL2, W10]

summitās, -tātis (f) *top, tip, summit, height* [KL2, W10]

summus, -a, -um *highest, greatest* [KL2, L5]

sūmō, -ere, sūmpsī, sūmptum *I take (up), assume* [KL2, L10]

super (+ acc. /+ abl.) *over, above, beyond* [KL1, L26]

superbia, -ae (f) *pride, arrogance* [KL3, L12]

superbus, -a, -um *proud, haughty* [KL1, W18; KL2, L4]

superior, -ius *higher* [KL2, L5]

superō (1) *I conquer, defeat* [KL1, L2]

superus, -a, -um *above, high* [KL2, L5]

suprā (adv. & prep. + acc.) *above, over* [KL1, L14]

suprēmus, -a, -um *highest, greatest* [KL2, L5]

surgō, -ere, surrēxī, surrēctum *I (a)rise* [KL1, L28]

suscitō (1) *I raise up [from the dead], awaken, stir up* [KL3, W5]

suspendō, -ere, -pendī, -pensum *I hang (up), suspend* [KL3, W5]

suspīciōsus, -a, -um *suspicious* [KL1, W21]

susurrō (1) *I whisper* [KL1, W28]

suum negōtium agō *(idiom) I mind my own business* [KL1, W29]

suus, -a, -um *(3rd person reflexive possessive adj.) his (own), her (own), its (own)* [KL1, W31; KL3, L2]

synagōga, -ae (f) *synagogue* [KL1, W26]

T

tabernāculum, -ī (n) *tent* [KL1, W32]

taceō, -ēre, -uī, -itum *I am silent* [KL1, W26]

tactus, -ūs (m) *touch* [KL1, W28]

tālāria, -ium (n, pl) *winged sandals/shoes; ankles* [KL3, W16]

tālis, -e *such* [KL3, L5]

tam *so, so much;* **tam...quam** *so...as* [KL3, L5]

tamen *yet, nevertheless, still* [KL1, L30]

tandem (adv.) *finally, at last* [KL3, L15]

tangō, -ere, tetigī, tactum *I touch, strike* [KL1, L27]

tantum (adv.) *only, merely, but; so, so much/ greatly* [KL3, L14]

tantus, -a, -um *so/such great, of such size* [KL3, L5]

taurus, -ī (m) *bull* [KL3, W6]

tellūs, tellūris (f) *the earth, ground, land* [KL1, L14]

tēlum, -ī (n) *weapon* [KL3, L6]

temere *rashly, at random, by chance* [KL3, W15]

tempestās, -tātis (f) *weather, storm* [KL1, L26]

templum, -ī (n) *temple, shrine* [KL1, W25; KL2, L10]

temptō (1) *I attempt, try, handle* [KL1, W27; KL3, L7]

tempus, temporis (n) *time* [KL1, L13]

tendō, -ere, tetendī, tentum *I stretch; hasten, strive; aim* [KL2, L4]

tenēbrae, -ārum (f, pl) *darkness, gloomy place, shadows* [KL1, L11]

tenebrōsus, -a, -um *gloomy, dark* [KL2, W15]

teneō, -ēre, tenuī, tentum *I hold, possess* [KL1, L9]

tenuis, -e *thin, slender* [KL2, L11]

tepidus, -a, -um *warm, tepid* [KL3, W16]

ter *three times, thrice* [KL3, W5]

tergum, -ī (n) *back, rear* [KL3, L6]

terminus, -ī (m) *limit, bound(ary), end* [KL3, L15]

terra, -ae (f) *earth, land* [KL1, L4]

terreō, -ēre, -uī, -itum *I frighten, terrify* [KL1, L9]

tertius, -a, -um decimus, -a, -um *thirteenth* [KL1, L23]

tertius, -a, -um *third* [KL1, L23]

testificor, -ārī, ——, -ātus sum *I testify, bear witness* [KL3, W14]

testimōnium, -ī (n) *testimony, evidence, witness* [KL2, L10]

testis, -is (m) *witness* [KL3, L5]

testor, -ārī, ——, -ātus sum *I testify, bear witness* [KL3, W11]

thēsaurus, -ī (m) *treasure, hoard* [KL3, L11]

Thēseūs, -eī (m) *Theseus* [KL1, W30]

tigris, tigridis (m/f) *tiger* [KL1, L12]

timeō, -ēre, -uī, —— *I fear* [KL1, L9]

timor, -ōris (m) *fear* [KL3, L14]

Tmōlus, -ī (m) *Tmolus (a god and a mountain in Lydia)* [KL1, W28]

tollō, -ere, sustulī, sublātum *I lift up, raise up; take away, destroy* [KL1, W25; KL2, L13]

tonitrus, -ūs (m) *thunder* [KL1, L25]

tonsor, -ōris (m) *barber* [KL1, W28]

torrens, -ntis (m) *a torrent, stream* [KL1, W32]

torreō, -ēre, torruī, tostum *I burn, parch, dry up* [KL1, L17]

tot (indecl. adj.) *so many, so great a number* [KL3, L9]

tōtus, -a, -um *all, every, whole* [KL2, L3]

trabēs, -is (m) *tree trunk, beam* [KL2, W14]

trādō, -ere, -didī, -ditum *I hand over, surrender; hand down, teach* [KL1, W13; KL2, L4]

tragoedia, -ae (f) *tragedy* [KL1, W4]

trahō, -ere, trāxī, trāctum *I draw, drag* [KL1, L30]

tranquillus, -a, -um *quiet, calm* [KL3, W9]

trāns (+ acc.) *across* [KL1, L11]

trānseō, -īre, -iī, -itum *I go across/over, cross (over), pass (by/over)* [KL2, L15]

trānsferō, -ferre, -tulī, -lātum *I carry/bear/bring across/over, transfer, translate* [KL3, L13]

tredecim *thirteen* [KL1, L21]

tremō, -ere, -uī, —— *I tremble, quake* [KL1, W25; KL3, W6]

trēs, tria *three* [KL1, L21]

tribūnal, -ālis (n) *judgment seat, tribunal* [KL2, W15]

tribūtum, -ī (n) *tribute, tax* [KL1, W30]

trīstis, -e *sad, gloomy, dismal* [KL1, L20; KL2, L3]

triumphō (1) *I triumph, exult, rejoice exceedingly* [KL3, W9]

Troia, -ae (f) *Troy* [KL2, W4]

Trōiānus, -a, -um *Trojan, of Troy* [KL2, W5]

tū (sg.) *you* [KL1, L17]

tum *then, at that time; next, thereupon* [KL1, L15]

tumulus, -ī (m) *tomb, grave mound* [KL2, W11]

tunc *then, thereupon, at that time* [KL2, L4]

turba, -ae (f) *crowd, mob, throng* [KL1, L2]

turbō (1) *I disturb, trouble* [KL2, W13]

turbō, -binis (m) *whirlwind* [KL2, W9]

turbulentus, -a, -um *restless, stormy, turbulent* [KL3, W9]

turpitūdō, -dinis (f) *ugliness, shame, dishonor* [KL3, W9]

turris, turris (f) *tower, turret* [KL1, L18]

tūtus, -a, -um *safe, secure* [KL3, L7]

tuus, -a, -um *your (sg), yours* [KL1, L11]

U

ūber, -eris *rich, fruitful, abundant* [KL2, W11]

ubi *where (?), when* [KL1, L12]

ubīque *everywhere* [KL1, W29]

Ulixēs, -is (m) *Ulysses (Odysseus)* [KL2, W5]

ūllus, -a, -um *any; anyone, anything* [KL1, W27; KL2, L4]

ulterior, -ius *farther* [KL2, L5]

ultimus, -a, -um *farthest* [KL2, L5]

ultrā (adv.) *beyond, farther* [KL2, L5]

ululātus, -ūs (m) *howling, shrieking, wailing [of mourning]* [KL3, W10]

ululō (1) *I howl, scream* [KL1, L6]

umbra, -ae (f) *shadow, shade, ghost* [KL3, L3]

umerus, -ī (m) *shoulder, upper arm* [KL3, W3]

umquam (adv.) *ever, at any time* [KL3, L14]

ūnā *together, in one* [KL1, L29]

ūnctiō, -ōnis (f) *anointing, ointment* [KL3, W12]

uncus, -a, -um *hooked, curved* [KL3, W16]

unda, -ae (f) *wave* [KL1, L10]

unde *from where (?), whence (?)* [KL2, L11]

ūndecim *eleven* [KL1, L21]

ūndecimus, -a, -um *eleventh* [KL1, L23]

ūndēvīcēsimus, -a, -um *nineteenth* [KL1, L23]

ūndēvīgintī *nineteen* [KL1, L21]

undique *on/from all sides, from every direction* [KL1, L30; KL2, L15]

ūnicus, -a, -um *one, only, sole* [KL1, W22]

unigenitus, -a, -um *only-begotten, only* [KL2, W3]

ūniversus, -a, -um *all together, whole, entire* [KL3, L4]

ūnus, -a, -um *one* [KL1, L21]

urbānus, -a, -um *polite* [KL1, W29]

urbs, urbis (f) *city* [KL1, L18]

urna, -ae (f) *urn* [KL2, W11]

ursus, -ī (m) *bear* [KL1, W32]

usquam *anywhere, at/in any place* [KL3, L9]

usque (adv.) *continuously, constantly;* **(prep. + acc.)** *all the way up to, as far as* [KL3, L4]

ut (conj. + indic.) *as, when, how;* **(+ subj.)** *(so) that, in order that/to, to* [KL3, L5]

uter, utra (ūtra), utrum (ūtrum) (interrog.) *which (of two)?;* **(relat.)** *whichever (of two), the one which;* **(indef.)** *either, one (of two)* [KL2, L15]

uterus, -ī (m) *womb, belly* [KL2, W9]

utinam *would/oh that! if only! I wish that!* [KL3, L13]

utique *certainly, surely* [KL3, L12]

ūtor, ūtī, ——, ūsus sum (+ abl.) *I use, enjoy* [KL3, L2]

ūtrum (adv.) *whether (translated by tone of voice in direct questions)* [KL3, L9]

uxor, -ōris (f) *wife* [KL1, L30]

V

vacuus, -a, -um *empty, vacant, void* [KL3, W4]

vādō, -ere, vāsī, —— *I go, proceed* [KL2, L9]

valde *very, exceedingly* [KL2, L10]

valeō, -ēre, -uī, -itum *I am well/strong;* **valē(te)** *Goodbye! Be well!* [KL1, L9]

valles, vallis (f) *valley, vale* [KL1, L18]

vās, vāsis; pl. vāsa, -ōrum (n) *vessel, equipment* [KL3, W1]

vastō (1) *I devastate, lay waste* [KL1, L14]

vastus, -a, -um *vast, enormous, desolate* [KL2, L6]

vātēs, -is (m/f) *prophet/prophetess* [KL1, W31]

vehemens, -mentis *violent, vehement* [KL2, W9]

vehō, -ere, vexī, vectum *I carry, ride, convey* [KL1, L27]

vel *or, or rather* [KL2, L9]

vēlāmen, -minis (n) *veil, covering* [KL2, W11]

vellō, -ere, vulsī/vellī, vulsum *I pluck, pull* [KL3, W1]

vēlum, -ī (n) *sail* [KL1, W30]

vendō, -ere, -didī, -ditum *I sell* [KL3, W9]

venēnum, -ī (n) *venom, poison* [KL1, L10; KL3, W6]

venia, -ae (f) *mercy, pardon, forgiveness* [KL3, W12]

veniō, -īre, vēnī, ventum *I come* [KL1, L29]

ventus, -ī (m) *wind* [KL1, W28; KL3, W16]

verbum, -ī (n) *word* [KL1, L5]

vereor, -ērī, ——, veritus sum *I respect, reverence, fear* [KL2, L6]

vēritas, -tātis (f) *truth* [KL1, L27]

vērō *truly, certainly [can also be used to say "yes"]* [KL2, L15]

versus, -ūs (m) *row, line (of poetry), furrow* [KL1, L27]

vertō, -ere, vertī, versum *I turn, change* [KL1, L28; KL2, L11]

vērumtamen *however, nevertheless* [KL3, L13]

vērus, -a, -um *true* [KL1, L22; KL2, W13]

vesper, vesperis (m) *evening, evening star, west* [KL1, L14]

vester, -stra, -strum *your (pl), yours (pl)* [KL1, L11]

vestīgium, -iī (n) *footstep, footprint, track* [KL2, W11]

vestīmentum, -ī (n) *clothing, garment* [KL2, L14]

vestis, vestis (f) *clothing, garment* [KL1, L18]

vetō, -āre, vetuī, vetitum *I forbid, prevent* [KL3, W11]

vetus, (gen.) -teris *old* [KL1, L30]

vexō (1) *I vex, ravage, annoy* [KL1, L19]

via, -ae (f) *road, way* [KL1, L11]

vibrō (1) *I vibrate, flicker* [KL3, W6]

vīcēsimus, -a, -um prīmus, -a, -um *twenty-first* [KL1, L23]

vīcēsimus, -a, -um *twentieth* [KL1, L23]

vīcīnus, -a, -um *neighbor(ing), near(by)* [KL3, L9]

victor, -toris (m) *victor, conqueror* [KL2, W13]

victōria, -ae (f) *victory* [KL1, L11]

videō, -ēre, vīdī, visum *I see* [KL1, L9]

vidua, -ae (f) *widow* [KL1, L22]

viduō (1) *I deprive of* (**viduāta, -ae** *widowed*) [KL1, W19]

vīgintī *twenty* [KL1, L21]

vīgintī ūnus, -a, -um (ūnus et vīgintī) *twenty-one* [KL1, L21]

vīlis, -e *cheap, worthless* [KL2, W15]

villa, -ae (f) *farmhouse, country house* [KL1, L2]

vinciō, -īre, vinxī, vinctum *I bind, tie* [KL1, L30]

vincō, -ere, vīcī, victum *I defeat, conquer* [KL1, L26]

vīnum, -ī (n) *wine* [KL1, L5]

violō (1) *I violate, profane, dishonor* [KL3, W1]

vir, virī (m) *man* [KL1, L4]

virga, -ae (f) *branch, rod, staff* [KL3, L10]

virgō, virginis (f) *maiden, young woman* [KL1, L12]

viridis, -e *green; fresh, young, vigorous* [KL1, L17]

virtūs, virtūtis (f) *manliness, courage, strength* [KL1, L12]

vīs, vīs (f) *strength, force, power, violence* [KL3, L5]

vīscus, -eris (n) *internal organs, entrails, inward parts; (metaphorically) heart* [KL3, L13]

vīta, -ae *life* [KL1, L11]

vītō (1) *I avoid, shun* [KL1, L30]

vitrum, -ī (n) *woad* [KL2, W2]

vīvō, -ere, vīxī, victum *I live* [KL1, L27]

vīvus, -a, -um *living* [KL1, L20]

vix *scarcely, hardly* [KL3, L3]

vocō (1) *I call, summon, invite* [KL1, L1]

volātilis, -e *flying, winged* [KL3, W4]

volō (1) *I fly* [KL1, L10]

volō/velle, voluī, ——, —— *I wish, want, will* [KL2, L14]

voluntās, -tātis (f) *will, wish, desire* [KL3, L12]

voluptās, -tātis (f) *pleasure, enjoyment* [KL3, W2]

volvō, -ere, volvī, volūtum *I roll, turn around/over* [KL3, W1]

vōs (pl.) *you* [KL1, L17]

vox, vōcis (f) *voice* [KL1, L14]

vulnerō (1) *I wound* [KL1, L1]

vulnus, vulneris (n) *wound* [KL1, L13]

vultus, -ūs (m) *face, expression* [KL1, L25]

Z

zēlus, -ī (m) *zeal, jealousy* [KL3, W7]

APPENDIX D
Sources and Helps

Bennett, Charles E. *New Latin Grammar*. Wauconda, IL: Bolchazy-Carducci Publishers, 1998. A good resource for your grammar questions.

Biblia Sacra Vulgata. Stuttgart, Germany: Deutsche Bibelgesellschaft, 1994. If you have extra time, read a bit from the Vulgate every day to improve your Latin skills.

Davis, William Stearns. *A Day in Old Rome*. New York: Biblo and Tannen, 1962.

Gildersleeve, B. L. and Lodge, G. *Gildersleeve's Latin Grammar*. Mundelein, IL: Bolchazy-Carducci Publishers, 2012. This is another helpful and very thorough Latin grammar. It is organized a little differently than Bennett's *New Latin Grammar* and *Allen and Greenough's*, which can be helpful for looking at grammar concepts in a new way.

Glare, P. G. W. *The Oxford Latin Dictionary*. Oxford: Oxford University Press, 1983. The *OLD* is of course "the" standard for all Latin dictionaries, although occasionally I have found nuggets in *Lewis and Short* that were not in the *OLD*.

Greenough, J. B., et al., ed. *Allen and Greenough's New Latin Grammar*. Newburyport, MA: Focus Publishing, R. Pullins & Company, 2001. A fantastic resource; I referred to it frequently regarding grammar concepts of all kinds.

Jenney, Charles Jr., et al. *Jenney's First Year Latin*. Newton, MA: Allyn and Bacon, 1987. I consulted this text for the order of teaching various grammatical concepts. I studied Latin from it back in my junior high days, and have always been fond of it (although it is a little too addicted to Caesar for my liking). Although short on explanations, it contains plenty of exercises and translations to practice each concept.

LaFleur, Richard A. *Love and Transformation: An Ovid Reader*. Glenview, IL: Scott Foresman-Addison Wesley, 1999. I referred to this Latin text (in addition to online texts) for some of the myths in the Latin to English translations.

The Latin Library: http://www.thelatinlibrary.com/. This website has numerous Latin texts and I used it for some of the Latin to English passages.

Latin Vulgate: http://www.latinvulgate.com/. This website is helpful because it has side-by-side translations from the Vulgate. Although most of us are familiar with Biblical texts and stories, sometimes the Vulgate has completely different wording than what we are used to.

Lee, A. G., ed. *Ovid: Metamorphoses, Book I*. Wauconda, IL: Bolchazy-Carducci Publishers, 1988. I also referred to this book (in addition to online texts) for some of the myths in the Latin to English translations.

Lewis, Charlton T. and Short, Charles. *A Latin Dictionary.* Oxford, United Kingdom: Oxford University Press, 1958. Lewis and Short's dictionary is a standard resource and has helpful examples and commentary on many entries. You can also access it online at http://www.perseus.tufts.edu/hopper/text?doc=Perseus%3atext%3a1999.04.0059.

Martin, Charles, trans. *Ovid: Metamorphoses.* New York: W. W. Norton & Company, 2004. I consulted this English translation as well as Latin texts for some of the myths found in the Latin to English translations.

Mountford, J. F., ed. *Bradley's Arnold Latin Prose Composition.* Wauconda, IL: Bolchazy-Carducci Publishers, 2006. This book is great for practicing English-to-Latin composition, especially when using advanced grammar concepts.

Simpson, D. P. *Cassell's New Latin Dictionary.* New York: Funk & Wagnall's, 1959. I picked this up at a used bookstore (always check out the language section for Latin books!), and it has an especially helpful English to Latin section.

Smith, William and Hall, Theophilus D. *A Copious and Critical English-Latin Dictionary.* Nashville, TN: Wimbledon Publishing Company Ltd., 2000. This is a very thorough English-to-Latin dictionary, besides having a fabulous title.

Stelten, Leo F. *Dictionary of Ecclesiastical Latin.* Peabody, MA: Hendrickson Publishers, 1995. I consulted this dictionary for the translations adapted from the Vulgate, since some dictionaries don't include ecclesiastical words.

Wheelock, Frederic M.; revised by Richard A. LaFleur. *Wheelock's Latin*, 6th ed. rev. New York: HarperCollins Publishers, 2005. I have taught out of this book for several years and referred to it for some grammar matters as well as researching in what order grammatical concepts were presented. It is a good standard text and resource, but not the best for someone trying to teach himself Latin.

Whitaker, William. "Words." http://www.archives.nd.edu/cgi-bin/words.exe. This website (from which you can also download a program) has Latin to English and English to Latin search engines. You can type in any form of a Latin word and it will parse it for you and give you the meaning—pretty handy! All students seem to know about this, so it's best to face it head on. I told my students they were welcome to use it, but that they not become dependent upon it (and of course they shouldn't use it to "cheat" on parsing exercises). It's best to use it when you are stumped by a particular form and need to look it up. The English to Latin search can be very helpful when writing stories or sentences.

Vulgate Frequency: http://www.intratext.com/IXT/LAT0001/_FF1.HTM. This website tells you which words appear the most often in various Latin texts. Since I'm especially fond of the Vulgate and Vergil, I consulted this site to see which words from those sources needed to be incorporated into the vocabulary lists.

Appendix E
Verb Formation Chart

Which principal part is used for which tense, voice, and mood? Keep this handout all year, and fill it in as you learn the various verb forms. The principal parts of *necō* (I kill) are provided as an example.

	FIRST	SECOND	THIRD	FOURTH
	necō	necāre	necāvī	necātum
DEFINITION/ FUNCTION				
INDICATIVE				
IMPERATIVE				
INFINITIVE				
SUBJUNCTIVE				
PARTICIPLE				

[This page intentionally left blank]

www.ingramcontent.com/pod-product-compliance
Lightning Source LLC
Chambersburg PA
CBHW080222170426
43192CB00015B/2722